Building Coalitions, Making Policy

Building Coalitions, Making Policy

The Politics of the
Clinton, Bush, and Obama Presidencies

Edited by

Martin A. Levin, Daniel DiSalvo,
and Martin M. Shapiro

The Johns Hopkins University Press
Baltimore

© 2012 The Johns Hopkins University Press
All rights reserved. Published 2012
Printed in the United States of America on acid-free paper
9 8 7 6 5 4 3 2 1

The Johns Hopkins University Press
2715 North Charles Street
Baltimore, Maryland 21218-4363
www.press.jhu.edu

Library of Congress Cataloging-in-Publication Data

Building coalitions, making policy : the politics of the Clinton,
Bush, and Obama presidencies / edited by Martin A. Levin,
Daniel DiSalvo, and Martin M. Shapiro.
    p. cm.
  Includes bibliographical references and index.
  ISBN-13: 978-1-4214-0508-7 (hbk. : alk. paper)
  ISBN-10: 1-4214-0508-3 (hbk. : alk. paper)
  ISBN-13: 978-1-4214-0509-4 (pbk. : alk. paper)
  ISBN-10: 1-4214-0509-1 (pbk. : alk. paper)
  ISBN-13: 978-1-4214-0595-7 (electronic)
  ISBN-10: 1-4214-0595-4 (electronic)
    1. Political planning—United States.   2. Decision making—
United States.   3. Electoral coalitions—United States.
4. United States—Politics and government—1993–2001.
5. United States—Politics and government—2001–2009.
6. United States—Politics and government—2009–   I. Levin,
Martin A.   II. DiSalvo, Daniel.   III. Shapiro, Martin M.
  JK468.P64B85 2012
  973.93—dc23   2011037771

A catalog record for this book is available from the British
Library.

*Special discounts are available for bulk purchases of this book. For
more information, please contact Special Sales at 410-516-6936 or
specialsales@press.jhu.edu.*

The Johns Hopkins University Press uses environmentally
friendly book materials, including recycled text paper that is
composed of at least 30 percent post-consumer waste, whenever
possible.

Contents

Acknowledgments   *vii*

Introduction. Getting Past No: Building Coalitions and Making
Policy from Clinton to Bush to Obama   1
Martin A. Levin, Daniel DiSalvo, and David Emer

1   The Electoral Connection and the Dissonant Game of
    Coalition Building in an Era of Partisan Policymaking   17
    Martin A. Levin and Daniel DiSalvo

2   Why LBJ Is Smiling: The Bush Administration, "Compassionate
    Conservatism," and No Child Left Behind   43
    Frederick M. Hess

3   Splitting the Coalition: The Political Perils and Opportunities
    of Immigration Reform   75
    Daniel J. Tichenor

4   Embracing the Third Rail? Social Security Politics from
    Clinton to Obama   119
    R. Kent Weaver

5   The Bush Administration and the Politics of Medicare Reform   150
    Jonathan Oberlander

6   A Solution for All Seasons: The Politics of Tax Reduction in the
    Bush Administration   181
    Tim Conlan and Paul Posner

7   The Bush Administration and the Uses of Judicial Politics   215
    Thomas F. Burke and Nancy Scherer

8   A Feint to the Center, a Move Backward: Bush's Clear Skies
     Initiative and the Politics of Policymaking   247
     David Emer

9   National Security, the Electoral Connection, and Policy Choice   275
     James M. Lindsay

10   The Dynamics of Presidential Policy Choice and Promotion   308
     Daniel J. Galvin

11   Touching the Bases: Parties and Policymaking in the
     Twenty-First Century   332
     Daniel DiSalvo

12   Bush's "Our Crowd"   363
     Martin M. Shapiro

13   Politics, Elections, and Policymaking   369
     David Mayhew

     List of Contributors   *391*
     Index   *395*

Acknowledgments

The myth of the lone scholar is just that—a myth. Following Plato, we believe that it is impossible to do anything without friends. Research and writing, like most pursuits, are best done in community.

The editors of this book and the earlier four in this series created an interactive conversation from which we all have learned much. Their creative feedback through the long process of preliminary seminars, drafts, conference papers, and then draft chapters produced an illuminating dialogue that broadened our thinking. It transformed a collection of individual works by many authors into a book with coherent themes, arguments, and conclusions. We are grateful to these three dozen plus authors for making these rich products and stimulating journeys. Special thanks to Eugene Bardach, Tom Burke, Robert Kagan, and Peter Schuck.

We were fortunate to have Jeb Barnes involved in this project from the outset, and his individual and synoptic contributions at the book conference were particularly helpful. At that time he had completed a final draft of an outstanding chapter entitled "Tort Reform Legislation during the Bush Administration." But, as they euphemistically say in the political news, "scheduling conflicts" (with another publisher) prevented his chapter from appearing in this book, much to our regret. We look forward to connecting with him again soon.

At Brandeis, Steve Burg and Bernie Yack gave great personal and intellectual backup for the Gordon Center and the Gordon Foundation. We had the fine administrative assistance of the Gordon Center's energetic staff: Brian Asquith, Nicole Ancheta, Nickolaus Anzalone, and Rosanne Colocouris.

We appreciate the Johns Hopkins University Press's intelligent, well-managed editorial process in the persons of the late Henry Tom, Linda Forlifer, and the staff of the marketing department. We thank especially Suzanne Flinchbaugh, who was an ideal editor—smart, clever, and wise—and was always adding value to our work. Jeremy Horsefield was a fine copy editor—thoughtful, tough, and temperate.

Eve Lesses again contributed practical ideas and powerful pushes for this project and for several others going on at the same time, as she has done so ably for all our books, and we are grateful.

The trustees of the Gordon Foundation—John Adelsdorf, Sanford Bank, Robert Green, and especially their chair, David Silberberg—have our appreciation for their gracious and enduring support and intellectual interest for this project, our earlier books, and other endeavors of the Gordon Center.

As in several of our earlier books, we were most fortunate to stand on the shoulders of both David Mayhew's pioneering scholarship and his incisive personal contributions during the project's entire development.

An old friend and long-time collaborator in many of the series' other books, Marc Landy, was not directly involved in this project. But, as always, he gave us astute advice as this project advanced. Like Peter Schuck, he made major contributions to our early book conference.

David Emer, a new colleague, wrote and cowrote two important chapters and provided strong and creative ideas, as well as thoughtful brakes, for the book's synoptic chapters and its architecture.

Warm thanks for her thoughtful substantive suggestions and level-headed support go to Deyonne Bryant, the smartest political scientist on the block with a PhD in English.

Building Coalitions, Making Policy

Getting Past No

Building Coalitions and Making Policy from Clinton to Bush to Obama

Martin A. Levin, Daniel DiSalvo, and David Emer

This book focuses on getting past no through an examination of successful and failed attempts to build coalitions—that critical connection between politics and policymaking. Indeed, the number of points where someone can say no to a new policy initiative famously characterizes the American policy-making process. Getting past no requires building coalitions—intraparty coalitions to keep those on your side from saying no and interparty coalitions to get key people on the other side to say yes.

In the 1990s, close elections, thin congressional margins, and ultimately divided government brought forth from Clinton Democrats a coalition-crafting strategy of trying to both maintain the support of the party's base and increase the support of voters ranging from the political center through to new constituencies that might expand the party coalition. Clinton's "third way" approach produced such "balanced" moderate policies as welfare reform and deficit reduction. This, in part, is the story of *Seeking the Center: Politics and*

Policymaking at the New Century (Georgetown University Press), the second book in our New Politics of Policymaking series.

The current volume carries this story onward into the George W. Bush administration and the early Obama years, with analyses of a range of policies—tax cuts, Social Security privatization, Medicare prescription drug reform, education reform, immigration, environmental policy, judicial politics, and national security policy.

Standing on the shoulders of a giant, this book also incorporates David Mayhew's pioneering 1974 tale of seeking to win elections, *Congress: The Electoral Connection*. In that era of weak parties, Mayhew focused on individual members of Congress and their efforts at making electoral connections. In today's era of stronger parties, we analyze politics from the perspective of how *parties* seek to win elections.

In addition to carrying forward these threads from our *Seeking the Center* and from Mayhew's *The Electoral Connection*, we bring them together: this book is about how the president and congressional party leaders tried to build winning party coalitions in today's era of stronger parties and how this electoral strategy shaped policy choice during George W. Bush's presidency, with comparative perspectives from the Clinton administration. Success at this game requires navigating the tensions between their base and the political center to try to maintain the election support of both. As Mayhew suggests in chapter 13, this balancing process was "a complex, tension-ridden, inside-outside strategy."

The essays in this volume discuss the contemporary politics of policymaking in general and building party coalitions in particular. We are constructing a general model of coalition building. This is the first book to analyze this structural imperative of leaders navigating the center and base of their party and to apply this analysis to a range of policy areas.

The political and policy issues of how leaders manage these tensions and demands go beyond the first decade of the twenty-first century, the period from which we draw most of our data. President Obama was directly confronted by the issue of managing his base and the center in his efforts to get his ambitious agenda passed. He began by trying, in fits and starts, to draw in moderates of his party and the Republicans, while holding on to support from his Democratic liberal base.

We use the analyses and conclusions of this book to connect with and illuminate our understanding of the Obama administration's first two years.

In the final sections of each policy-specific chapter, we examine Obama's policymaking for that area. We begin this analysis and integration of the Obama administration's politics of policymaking with broad analyses and overviews in this introductory chapter's final section, "Once and Future Coalition Building for Policymaking." There we integrate our discussion of coalition building in all three administrations—Clinton's, Bush's, *and* Obama's—with concrete examples from the Obama years: We analyze how the politics of coalition building shaped the politics of policymaking of the Obama administration, across a range of issues, from the economic stimulus package to financial reform, immigration, and his environmental-energy proposals. We especially focus on Obama's health care coalition politics.

Two types of coalition building and their dilemmas and difficulties are analyzed here for the Bush and Clinton administrations and then applied to the Obama administration as well. One is interparty coalition building; the other is intraparty. There are tensions and dilemmas in trying to carry them out.

Interparty coalition building takes place between different parties. It is an effort at bipartisanship—bringing two (or more) parties closer together for making policy. But it is in tension with intraparty coalition building. The latter is a necessary first step for winning elections—gaining and maintaining power. Intraparty coalition building involves balancing the party's base and median voters. The tensions and dilemmas intrinsic to these two types of coalition building, which so dominated the Clinton and Bush administrations, have also continued to dominate the politics of policymaking in the early years of the Obama administration. The same tensions also came to frustrate the House Republican leadership after they won the 2010 midyear election.

These tensions so characteristic to coalition building are intrinsic to our political system because, as Samuel Lubell famously argued in his "Sun and Moon theory of parties," our parties—like our Sun—are always in the process of coming apart. (Normatively, one might say that our parties are always in *danger* of coming apart.) The intrinsic nature of these tensions is therefore endemic and frequent.

The nature and frequency of these tensions are perhaps best indicated by their most extreme manifestation—they frequently lead to significant and influential third-party presidential candidates.[1] Third parties are much more common in American politics than usually acknowledged by the narrow conventional trope that "we have a two party system—period!" We do indeed have a two-party system, but there are significant third-party presidential candidates with some frequency—in about a third of the presidential elections from 1900 through 2000. For starters, we just note the most recent instances of these influential third-party candidates—Perot received 19 and 9 percent of the vote in 1992 and 1996, respectively. Perot both probably altered the 1992 outcome and prodded the Democrats to shift toward the center. Nader received 3 percent of the vote in the 2000 split decision election in which the Electoral College was decided by a recount of a very close vote in Florida. In 2010, the Tea Party faction won eighty seats in the House as part of the Republican victory. In 2012, the Tea Party faction promises to be a significant force in shaping the Republican presidential nomination, as well as again being influential in congressional elections.[2]

All this shows the depth and frequency of significant tensions and dilemmas in coalition building. If presidents and party leaders pay insufficient attention to their base because they are seeking to build an interparty coalition by appealing to centrists, they may weaken their intraparty coalition by alienating its least centrist participants.

From Clinton to Bush

This volume analyzes the politics of policymaking in the period since the writing of *Seeking the Center: Politics and Policymaking at the New Century* in 2000. Like the four previous books in our New Politics of Policymaking series (from various publishers), it is a book about the determinants of public policy. Our analyses describe what happened in national policymaking in the George W. Bush administration and the Obama administration's early years and then explain why it happened by examining the political dynamics of what government does. This is the realm of that crucial, though rarely considered, connection between politics and policymaking. Thus, our series and this book in particular restore the politics of policymaking to the forefront of the political science agenda.

Tracking the political dynamics of government activity is indeed what most people think political science is all about, but increasingly, the discipline of political science has become devoted to abstract theorizing and formalisms of various sorts. The public policy schools bring the study of government down to earth. But their goal is problem solving and efficiency, not political analysis. For the most part, they try to fix the leaks in the plumbing rather than understand the political basis of policy developments.

Seeking the Center described an unusual pattern of political party interaction in the 1990s: frequent alternation in power among evenly divided parties. We also observed in *Seeking the Center* that "one of the most anomalous aspects of that decade [was] the lack of a serious foreign policy crisis." But we added that this anomaly "may not continue. . . . Indeed much of the current political and policy consensus, with its odd mix of surliness and resistance to change, *may only be an economic recession or a foreign policy disaster away from dissolving*" (emphasis added).

This book follows more recent developments in the politics of policy, drawing significant parallels and defining discontinuities. If the elections of the 1990s were competitive and close, the first decade of the new century began with an even closer election in 2000 for both the presidency and the Senate. The decade also started with another parallel to the 1990s, but one that would not last—a relative calm in the foreign policy arena.

The 2000 presidential election was more than close—it was a "split decision." Bush won the constitutionally determinative Electoral College while losing the popular vote. So the Republicans had reason to be politically anxious in January 2001 as they looked ahead to the next election—the 2002 off-year election. In the first off-year election, the party in the White House typically loses seats. Then in April 2001, just after the Republican-controlled Congress passed large tax cuts, the party lost its razor-thin control of the Senate with the defection of Vermont's Jeffords to the Democratic caucus. This was only the second time in the nation's history that such a change in party control occurred between congressional elections.

The concern of the Bush administration about winning the forthcoming elections—especially in 2002—was significant. And we analyze how this concern played out in policymaking as well as in politics: it greatly shaped their policy choices.

As soon as the Bush administration took office in January 2001, it acted as if it had its mind on getting elected again—in 2002 and 2004. As noted, the 2002 off-year election was particularly worrisome. But even as early as the 2000 campaign Bush tried to balance satisfying the Republican's base voters and attracting the electorate's median voters as the way to win office. The campaign's theme of "compassionate conservatism" sought to reach beyond the base of the party's Reagan conservatism. In particular, during the campaign Bush proposed a moderate education reform—No Child Left Behind—which Hess shows was the Republicans' attempt to target moderate voters whom they had lost to Clinton in 1996. Hess suggests that if Clinton's welfare reform bill could be viewed as "Reagan's last policy," then No Child Left Behind was "Clinton's last policy," both in substance and in its reaching out toward the center.

But the decisive early months of Bush's first year were marked by even more vigorous efforts to satisfy the party's base, especially their core supporters in business. Major tax cuts were the prime products for these supporters. Yet, as Conlan and Posner indicate, even in tax policy, the administration maintained the pursuit of their Downsian strategy of also trying to satisfy median voters with some calculated sweeteners.

This electoral focus is not surprising in the American system of government. But what was different, at least in degree, in the decades at both sides of the new century was the extent of *policy targeting*, by which we mean the targeting of specific policies to specific voting groups. This shaping of policy choice by electoral strategy is what this book is about.

Our analysis of this policy targeting is best summed up in Mayhew's conclusion: "In one respect, possibly no president in American history has surpassed George W. Bush. Especially in his first term, Bush stood out as an eyes-open promoter of a policy menu targeting, on the one hand, 'the party base' but also, on the other hand, the 'center' or 'the median voter' or voters who might 'expand the party coalition.' . . . [It] was a judicious inside-outside mix."

Bush's pursuit of policy and office alternated, as DiSalvo concludes, between "seeking the center and satisfying the base": No Child Left Behind, Medicare prescription drug reform, and expansionary immigration bills aimed at constituencies beyond the Republicans' traditional base. The Medicare drug reform was targeted at increasing seniors' support for Bush. But, as Oberlander shows, it also was favored by the insurance and drug industries. The two immigration proposals were framed for Hispanic voters as expansionary. But as Tichenor indicates, they also included elements for border hawks and business. By contrast, as Conlan, DiSalvo, and Burke all show, tax cuts, an energy program, bankruptcy legislation, and federal judicial appointments were aimed at the business and social conservatives' core of the Republican base.

This balancing strategy proved to be a complex and tension-ridden one. Indeed, often this dissonant process is unsuccessful in terms of both policy and politics. No legislation may get enacted. This failure can lead to electoral connection failures to satisfy both the party's base voters and the median voters. Tichenor shows that these are the outcomes of Bush's unsuccessful efforts to use the crafting of expansionary immigration legislation to expand and solidify the party's coalition.

These balancing difficulties, and the political precariousness for Bush of the first eight months of 2001, meant that the 9/11 attacks later that year were fortuitous for the administration. Now it could frame the political agenda to take advantage of the conventional voter wisdom that the Republicans are strong and the Democrats weak on national security. The party was to a significant extent relieved of the need to balance dissonant elements of its coalition. Bush had a set of issues that would attract base voters and median voters at the same time.

As Lindsay shows, the Bush administration framed every election campaign after 9/11 (2002, 2004, and 2006) around its aggressive positions on national security issues—from the Afghan and Iraq Wars to the Patriot Act. In turn, it won two major victories in 2002 and 2004. The historically unusual 2002 congressional victory indicated the breadth of support that the national security issue could develop *outside* the party's base. This victory, but even more so that of 2004, seems to have emboldened the Bush administration's foreign and even domestic policy positions. The Bush administration concluded that it had earned the political and policy capital to spend on ambitious domestic policymaking. As Weaver suggests, the Social Security privatization plan is a striking product of this calculus.

This political and policy bubble of national security was pierced from mid-2005 through 2006 with the souring of the Iraq War and the Hurricane Katrina debacle. The Republicans in turn lost the 2006 congressional election and the 2008 presidential election, with local and national candidates in both openly distancing themselves from President Bush and his policies.

Ultimately, this book is principally concerned with a pattern of policy decision making determined by the goal of holding the party base but also winning middle voters by targeting policy proposals attractive to particular constituencies such as Hispanics, seniors, or those especially concerned with education. This is the pattern of the earliest months of the Bush administration and most of the later domestic initiatives. But it was significantly interrupted by 9/11 and the Iraq and Afghan Wars, which allowed the administration to depend far less on the delicate task of knitting together base and center.

From Bush to Obama

The dilemmas and difficulties of interparty and intraparty coalition building, analyzed here for the Bush and Clinton administrations, apply to the Obama administration as well. For Obama, these dilemmas arose across a range of issues: the economic stimulus package, health care reform, financial regulatory reform, immigration, the environment, and taxing and spending policies. For the Obama administration's signature issue—health care reform—the politics of coalition building were particularly crucial.

Obama first tried interparty—bipartisan—coalition building. But it was interparty coalition building of a particular sort. In Mayhew's felicitous phrase, it was a "partisan project." In such projects the opposition party opposed in principle initially, or provided some lukewarm backers, or soon came to oppose.

For the "partisan project" of health care reform, Obama sought only a handful of Republicans in the Senate. For six months, they were wooed by congressional Democrats. Initially, a broad coalition appeared unnecessary because of the sixty Democratic Senate seats, but five of the most conservative Democratic senators were not reliable votes and were demanding significant sweeteners (and ultimately politically embarrassing ones when they were acceded to) to support the bill. Oberlander suggests that perhaps the administration was only seeking the appearance of bipartisanship as a cover to get the support of one or two of these conservative Democratic senators.

The Obama administration here, in effect, was seeking to build a coalition to pass health care reform that reprised the one that Oberlander described when the Bush Republicans were enacting Medicare prescription drug reform: overwhelming support from the president's own party, with only small backing from the opposition to give the reform a bipartisan imprimatur. At times the Democrats seemed ready to settle for one Republican—Maine senator Olympia Snowe.

Ultimately, even this single Republican vote was unattainable. After this interparty failure, the Obama administration attempted to build an intraparty coalition. It tried to build a coalition between the liberal Democratic base and more median voters in the party, along with some independents and moderate Republicans. But bridging the gap between the liberal and the moderate elements of his own party proved to be at least as difficult, if not more so, for Obama than building a bipartisan coalition. And the Obama

White House was acutely aware of the dilemmas of coalition building. Some there, like Chief of Staff Rahm Emmanuel, privately counseled a more moderate approach than was initially proposed by the president.

Mayhew describes these dilemmas: "The party's activist base was insistent: enact [broad] health care or else, at whatever cost." On the other hand, congressional and White House centrists and pragmatists "aimed at the median voter: Even if the reform appeared questionable [to these voters] while being enacted, its actual benefits, the hope was, would win friends by the time of the 2010 or at least the 2012 election," a hope that did not pan out. These dilemmas played out in the legislative history. First, the focus was on the Senate bill that needed all sixty Democratic votes because of a promised Republican filibuster. By reaching out to more moderate Democratic senators, the administration alienated many liberal party members in the House. In particular, the "public option" was scrapped to win over moderate Democrats, first in the Senate and then in the House, a move that ultimately resulted in the loss of some liberal base support in the House.

During the long search for the sixtieth vote—no Republican would join them—the Democrats lost their sixty-vote majority in the Senate when Republican Scott Brown won a special election to replace the late Ted Kennedy. Overcoming the filibuster now seemed impossible. The Democrats then turned to the process of budgetary reconciliation, which only requires a fifty-one-vote majority.

Large numbers of the more liberal members of the House Democratic caucus were unhappy with many of the changes made to pass the Senate bill, while many Democratic House moderates thought the bill too liberal. These tensions in the House Democratic coalition in part were a product of increased diversity in the House Democratic caucus after an unusual number and range of Democrats were elected in 2006. At first—and for almost the next six weeks—it became more difficult to get the more liberal members of the Democratic coalition to agree to the new bill. And each new adjustment to the bill to recruit their support tended to alienate the moderate element of the Democratic coalition, a group of about thirty-five members, almost all anticipating difficult reelection contests in mostly marginal and highly competitive districts. Further complicating efforts to get both segments of the diverse Democratic House coalition to support the bill was the legislation's abortion elements. Compromises on these abortion-related elements tended to risk alienating members on both sides of that issue.

In March, after a month of moderately successful balancing of these two wings of the Democratic House coalition, the Obama administration's bill passed the House by using a reconciliation procedure that accepted the Senate bill and thus did not require a resubmission of the bill to the Senate.

These problems that the Obama administration faced in both types of coalition building for health care reform correspond with the dilemmas and difficulties of coalition building encountered by the Bush and Clinton administrations.

And while Obama's chief goal for coalition building—health care reform—was accomplished, this victory may have yielded a short-term net loss in voter support for the Democratic Party by alienating both some of its liberal base and its centrists and alienating even more independents. This is precisely what Tichenor describes in our immigration reform chapter as happening to Bush when he tried to build coalitions around his ultimately unsuccessful expansionary immigration bills in 2003 and 2005. He was trying to appeal to Hispanic voters, but both failed to win them over and also lost support among conservative immigration security hawks.

The Republicans and Coalition Building: "Just Say No"

During the Obama administration the Republican congressional leadership has acted as if it fully understood the major themes of this book—the centrality, difficulties, and dilemmas of coalition building in this era's policymaking process. A major aim of the Republicans since Obama took office has been first to prevent interparty coalition building and then to make intraparty coalition building within the Democratic Party more difficult. They have done so by persuading almost all Republicans in both houses to "say no" to almost all pieces of Obama's reform legislation, notably health care and cap and trade environmental reform. The Republican leadership has also sought to expand the range of the filibuster process beyond its traditional target of civil rights to extend to cover almost any piece of reform legislation. The Republicans' extreme emphasis on using a litmus test for almost any spending legislation of whether it contributes to increasing the deficit is also designed to make coalition building more difficult. This litmus test is aimed at splitting off the support of both fiscally moderate median voters and conservative Democrats from any Obama coalition.

Party Bases and Competitive Elections

Efforts at building party coalitions will continue in the future, of course, despite these dilemmas and difficulties. These efforts have confronted escalating problems during the last three presidencies, and this too is likely to continue in the future. Obama's continuing problems with these types of coalition building, like George W. Bush's before him, seem to spring primarily from a number of changes in the past two decades. Both parties have become more internally homogeneous. Thus, beginning with President Clinton, interparty coalition building has become much more difficult. In particular, it became much harder to craft "strange bedfellow's" coalitions such as Southern Democrats aligning with Republicans or Liberal Republicans aligning with Northern Democrats.

Intraparty coalition building also became more difficult as a result of this increased internal party homogeneity—a homogeneity built in dominance by those moving toward the extreme rather than the centrist ends of the two parties. These moves away from the center are reflected in increased party primary challenges, especially from both parties' bases. For example, in the spring of 2010, Charlie Crist in Florida, John McCain in Arizona, Michael Castle in Delaware, and Lisa Murkowski in Alaska all faced strong challenges in the Republican senatorial primary from elements in their party's rightist base. In 2006, the same phenomenon occurred, but spurred by elements of the left of the Democratic Party base, which launched a successful primary challenge to Senator Lieberman in the Connecticut primary. Lieberman managed to win the seat as an independent. However, though he then caucused with the Democrats in the Senate most of the time, his departure from the state party ultimately weakened that Democratic caucus and the party nationally.

In the future, all these changes will most likely mean that there will be more party primary challenges. Primaries are a particularly good arena for the base to launch successful challenges because their typically low voter turnout favors the more intensely motivated base. In turn, these primary challenges from a party's base further increase internal party homogeneity. This book provides notable examples, such as immigration and health care, in which the Bush and Obama administrations faced policy difficulties with their party bases.

Moves of both parties away from the center also help to explain another striking pattern that this volume shows. Since 1992 neither party has been able to remain dominant for an extended period, as was the usual pattern in American politics from 1860 to 1992. Failure to maintain unified party control over the presidency and both houses for extended time periods obviously complicates the politics of coalition building and policymaking more generally. Contrary to the claims by the justly esteemed Paul Pierson and Jacob Hacker and others that the American political system is "off-center," the essays in this book suggest that this unusual pattern of frequent alternation in power among evenly divided parties is very likely to continue in the twenty-first century.

Once and Future Coalition Building for Policymaking

"Capping the reach of this volume is the explosive midterm election of November 2010." This is David Mayhew's description of the Republicans' big victory in the House in that election and their significant gains in the Senate.

The 2010 election is a striking case of the connection between the process of coalition balancing and its shaping of both political and policy consequences. It seems to be a reprise of the two dynamics that we find throughout the analyses of this book's cases. First, parties and candidates get punished at the polls if they move too far from the median voters. This is a pattern we have seen increasingly since 1992—both over time and across parties. Second, coalition building is characterized by difficult dilemmas and tough trade-offs that often have significant negative political and policy consequences.

In the 2010 midterm election the Democrats seem to have been in part punished at the polls for being too far away from the median voter, as were the Clinton Democrats in 1994 and the Bush Republicans in 2006. (The election of 2002 seems to have been different because of some "halo effect" of 9/11 for the Bush Republicans, which contributed to an almost historic gain rather than loss in seats.) The 2010 election indicates another connection between the Bush and Obama administrations. In 2006, the voters punished the Republicans under Bush for their policies on the Iraq War, a partial privatizing of Social Security, and what Mayhew describes as a "stream of lesser domestic issues." And then in 2010, as Mayhew goes on to note, this voter disaffection was "matched" for the Democrats under Obama for the weak economy—the Great Recession—and their stimulus spending packages, health care reform, and cap and trade energy reform; the "voter verdict was deadly both times." In 2008, Obama had won independents by 8 percent, but in 2010 Democrats lost them by 19 percent.

The process that produced Obama's health care reform law (especially in the House) is a striking instance of the negative potential of coalition building. Mayhew describes the push and pull between the Democrats' liberal base in the House and its moderate–conservative center, which produced this historic legislation, as "a strained and curious exercise in coalition building. Neither the [party's] base nor the center ended up pleased. For much of the party's liberal base, the reform as enacted fell considerably short. For the median voter of 2010, the measure seemed to approach root canal territory—a costly, invasive, and gratuitous liberal enterprise."

No doubt it was a strained process in that it did not produce the intended outcome of increasing political support in general and support for Obama's health care reform bill in particular. But we differ with Mayhew that this was a "curious exercise in coalition building." Rather, we suggest that such dissatisfactions with the coalition building process's policy result seem to be the predictable product of the nature of this enterprise in our political system. In our large, diverse polity (with parties to match), coalition building is inherently and endemically fraught with risky dilemmas—risky to each contending element of the coalition. Thus, not infrequently, even when there are policy successes, there may be political costs to the very party with the policy success. We saw this pattern in the 2010 midterm election: the Democrats' striking victory in health care ironically seems to have yielded significant political costs and may have contributed measurably to the party's loss of the House. As the Bush immigration legislative failure shows, even failed coalition building may contribute to electoral failure.

In our fragmented and pluralistic political system, so much balancing of interests and compromising is necessary to get past no that the outcomes are frequently neither pure nor ideal from most players' perspectives. Indeed, at the outset of his concluding chapter, Mayhew himself characterizes the process as usually dissonant and sometimes even discordant and contradictory.

One additional point about the political consequences of Obama's health care reform legislation should be made: the very weak economy—the Great Recession—in 2010 may have had a contributing effect in shaping the ultimate political consequences of health care reform, as well as its coalition building consequences. The polls in the fall of 2010 showed that a majority of voters favored almost all the individual items in this legislation, but they disapproved of the legislation as a whole. Perhaps this reflected the voters' growing anxiety about the weak economy. In turn, they may have projected this anxiety and negativity onto the health care reform—the most salient issue of the day other than the economy. This explanation seems persuasive because both parties (the Republicans from a negative perspective and the Democrats from a positive one) cued voters to focus on health care as the central issue of the time and the best way to evaluate the Obama administration.

We have noted that divided government presents particular challenges to the employment of coalition strategies to achieve policy goals. The causal dynamics behind the productive lame-duck session of December 2010 yield significant insights into twenty-first-century coalition building processes in general and how they are evolving for the Obama administration. The following significant legislation passed in the session: First, there was the package, described in the conclusion to Conlan and Posner's chapter, of the Republican-backed temporary extension of the Bush-era tax cuts (including for those with incomes over $250,000). The Democratic half of the bargain was extended unemployment benefits to the long-term unemployed plus various stimulus measures, including a significant payroll tax cut. Second, there was the repeal of the "Don't Ask Don't Tell" policy, and third was the passage of the new START Treaty described in the conclusion to Lindsay's chapter.

Mayhew describes the lame-duck session as coming "to *feel* like an exercise, perhaps a rehearsal" for productive divided party control. But in the end, he concludes that "it was not exactly that." There does not seem to be a high probability that the coalition building dynamics that produced the legislative successes in the lame-duck session of 2010 will become a model for the future. Subsequently, the Republicans gained full control of the House. Second, the issues facing new Congresses may well be of broader range than the legislative agenda of the lame duck.

Nevertheless, the lame duck's coalition dynamics do give some sense of future productive possibilities. Indeed, during the lame-duck session, the coalitional dynamic between the Democratic president and the Republicans in the House (still in minority status) seems to have changed simply *in anticipation* of future shift in party alignments in the House. Specifically, the politics of policymaking during the lame-duck session shifted from a focus on the intraparty coalition building process that produced Obama's health care reform to one of interparty coalition building, such as the package of paired tax cuts and the extension of unemployment benefits to the long-term unemployed that gained Republican votes at the cost of losing votes from the House Democratic base.

In the passage of this package, Obama shifted from the deference that he had shown House liberals during the regular session—especially in trying to get his health care reform passed—to one of making a deal with House Republicans. This was strikingly similar to the way Bill Clinton passed welfare reform in 1995 after the Republicans took over the House in 1994: he had most Republicans voting for it in the House and only a third of the Democrats, and it passed. In short, in the 2010 lame-duck session, both parties' leaders (with both sets of followers in only partial agreement) pulled off a package of policies that were both balanced and centrist.

Obama moved even further in this centrist direction after the package passed. Not only did he drop his deference to the House Democrats, but he publically criticized some of them for their purism and impracticality in being willing to forego the other tax cuts in order to stop the cut for those with incomes over $250,000. He noted that these are the same people who were willing to forego all the elements of what he called a fine broad health care reform act just because it didn't include the public option. This was a critique he never made of them *before* the 2010 election—that is, before he began to face the prospect of working with a Republican majority in the House.

We see playing out in the Obama years the basic tensions and dilemmas between base and center wings of each of the two parties and various mix-and-match coalition strategies for dealing with those tensions and dilemmas. For example, when the Obama administration made interparty coalition-fostering moves, they came at a cost to intraparty coalition potential. This happened with the successful tax cut—the extension of the Bush-era tax cuts, including for those with incomes over $250,000—during the 2010 lame-duck session. Despite these tensions and dilemmas, this game will undoubtedly go on, and shifting patterns of election outcomes and unified versus divided government are likely to elicit many and various balances of intra- and interparty coalition building.

NOTES

1. By significant and influential third party presidential candidates we mean candidates that receive approximately 10% of the popular vote and/or alter the outcome of the election or—perhaps most significantly—cause one or both of the parties to shift their major positions in search of the voters that this third party is luring away.

2. There are many other instances of significant third parties in the last one hundred years or so. Eight of the twenty-five presidential elections—close to a third—from 1900 through 2000 meet our criteria for having significant and influential third party presidential candidates. To note just the major ones, in 1948 third (Dixiecrats) and fourth (Progressive) parties split off from both wings of the Democrats and won large numbers of votes and states. In 1912 the Progressives with Theodore Roosevelt split the Republican vote so much that a Democrat won a major upset. George Wallace carried five southern states in 1968. Before an assassin's bullet halted his 1972 race, Wallace had pushed the Republicans toward a southern-oriented strategy that has lasted into the twenty-first century. In the 1924 election the Progressive Party candidate received over 17% of the vote.

CHAPTER ONE

The Electoral Connection and the Dissonant Game of Coalition Building in an Era of Partisan Policymaking

Martin A. Levin and Daniel DiSalvo

Literary critics often ask two questions: First, what happens in the story? Second, and more significantly, what is the story about? As to the first, this volume examines policymaking across a broad range of policies during George W. Bush's administration, with comparative perspectives from Clinton's and Obama's. Individual chapters include analyses of the Bush tax cuts, efforts to privatize Social Security, Medicare prescription drug reform, education reform, immigration policy, environmental policy, judicial nominations, and the development of national security policy. These specific chapters are bookended by three broader chapters—one on the development of the political parties from a historical perspective, another on the presidency in the context of the electoral connection and policy choice, and the third on overall workings of American governmental institutions in this same context.

What happens in this story is that we analyze how presidents and congressional party leaders try to build party coalitions. Both major political parties need to secure the support of middle-of-the road "swing voters" because their choices on Election Day help determine who wins. Both parties also need to energize a set of constituencies with deep partisan commitments for electoral mobilization, which includes financial contributions and campaign volunteers. However, the policy preferences and political understandings of these two groups often diverge substantially.

Presidents and congressional party leaders thus face dilemmas in crafting their agendas and determining priorities. They try to shore up their parties' electoral prospects by choosing to push certain policy initiatives in a certain order. These policy agendas are the map they use to navigate between their base, the political center, and new constituencies.

We are, therefore, interested in how the policy choices of party leaders are tied to their desire to win elections. This book argues that one of the main factors shaping policy choices is the electoral connection: how presidents, Congress, and parties try to win elections by their choices of what legislation to push.

Individual chapters in this volume focus on how in making policy choices policymakers either try to maintain the support of the party's base, appeal to median voters, or increase their support among new constituencies who might expand the party coalition.

Balancing between Base and Median Voters: "A Difficult, Dissonant Game"

The concepts "center" and "base" are so often used colloquially that they can easily lead the reader astray. It is therefore important to specify these categories with as much precision as possible. In this book, the political "center" can refer to two different groups in society. Usually, it designates "median voters" in presidential elections—a key barometer for party leaders. A move to the center is thus a policy initiative that appeals to median voters in the electorate at large. In today's party system those who identify themselves as liberals in opinion surveys vote for Democrats and those who identify as conservatives vote for Republicans.[1] In between is a slice of self-described "moderates" or "independents" that have swung back and forth between the parties from one election to another. This group is difficult to describe demographically. With many significant qualifications, these centrist voters tend to include, among others, white working-class men and women, those who live in suburbia, and those who live away from the coasts in the Rust Belt and the Great Lakes regions. Some Latino voters also fall into the political center because their party loyalties are yet to be fixed and because they are open to Republican appeals turning on family and religion but attracted to Democrats' economic message.

The category "center" can also point to the median preferences of voters on particular policy dimensions. The median voter on tax or immigration policy specifically can be distinguished from both the median voter in the general electorate and the preferences of a party's base. Therefore, policymakers must seek to do three things simultaneously: (1) discover the median voter's preference on a given policy issue, (2) frame the issue to speak to that preference, and (3) ensure that that framing does not position the party too far from the presidential election median voter. Policymakers are deeply concerned with ensuring that the way they frame an issue does not adversely position them vis-à-vis centrist voters in the general electorate. This is a tricky process indeed.

On the other hand, the party "base" refers to four overlapping groups to the right or left of the median voter in presidential elections: liberal or conservative identifiers, primary election voters, organized interests allied to the party, or the median member of congressional parties' caucus. The notion of a party's base points to each party's core constituencies. For Republicans this tends to include, for example, small business owners, religious conservatives, and older, small-town voters. For Democrats it tends to include, for example, well-educated liberals, members of public sector unions, black Americans, and younger voters who are clustered largely in the big cities, along the coasts, and in university towns. Both parties' bases are also tied in with an array of interest groups and think tanks detailed in later chapters. More specifically, the base of each party indicates those individuals and groups that are more active in the political process in support of candidates and policies. The positions of the base are often in tension with the preferences of median voters generally and on specific issues in particular. It is these tensions that are the stuff of coalition building. Dealing with these tensions is the difficult game described by Mayhew in his chapter.

Anthony Downs famously and persuasively argued that, in a two-party system such as ours, parties have a powerful incentive to seek the political center to capture median voters.[2] However, this incentive is constrained by the fact that if the parties do not—in both campaigning and governing—do enough to cater to their base voters on their side of the median, electoral support and participation may drop off. Furthermore, parties must always be alert for constituencies that have yet to be mobilized into the political system or whose loyalty to the other party is weak, leaving them open to new appeals. According to David Mayhew, the effort by party leaders to balance base, median, and target voters to win elections is "a difficult, dissonant game" (chap. 13). Indeed, "balancing" is a euphemism for the more problematic task of trying to please all three groups. But trying to appease them all, at least up to a point, is necessary for a successful electoral strategy.

The connection between policy choice and electoral strategy thus raises a number of important questions. How do presidents and party leaders fashion an agenda that maintains or expands the appeal of their party with key constituencies and potential voters? When do presidents and parties take risks on behalf of their base or in trying to expand their coalition? What are the conditions under which presidents and congressional party leaders will take risks to press certain policy initiatives? Do important voting blocs respond to appeals made by enacting or attempting to enact public policies designed to please them? Each of the chapters in this volume takes up some or all of these questions.

In navigating between the political center and their base, party leaders are also confronted with the fact that they rarely, if ever, work on blank slates. Rather, the policy status quo imposes itself. Many interest groups are attached to particular policies and have powerful incentives to protect the status quo.[3] In many cases, a balance of power persists that makes change very difficult to achieve.[4] For instance, new constituencies aren't big enough to offset the losses to a party's coalition that would make reform possible. Therefore, path dependence theorists emphasize how policymakers' choices are constricted by the situation they inherit.[5] Yet other policies are sustained by weak coalitions or experience crises that make reform possible. Since major legislation usually is a significant departure from the status quo, it produces contentious politics and new configurations of groups. Some of the policies treated here appear highly path dependent, others less so. Each chapter investigates the complex and sometimes downright messy legislative processes that pit a new course of action against the policy status quo, which can either set policy on a new path or preserve the old one. Indeed, we have already examined such complex and messy legislative struggles in some detail in the introduction's analysis of Obama's ultimately successfully passed health care reform legislation and the 2010 lame-duck session's grand bargain package of extension of Bush-era tax cuts (including for those with incomes over $250,000) for the

Republicans and three significant and expensive stimulus policies for the Democrats. And one of this volume's central themes is under what conditions policy innovation triumphs or is defeated.

The Context for Policy Choice
Programmatic Parties

This book seeks to understand the dynamics of policy choice. The politics of policymaking in the new century is shaped by the context in which these choices are made. The context for policy choice has become an intense competition between our more programmatic political parties. It is also a time when the impact of large events, including wars and economic crises, has shaped the issues that make it onto the national agenda and upon which party leaders must make balancing decisions.

Taking our bearings from Mayhew's seminal work, *Congress: The Electoral Connection*, we can take the measure of the changes in the American political system over the past thirty years. In 1974, Mayhew significantly placed on the last page of his book his concern that "in the long run congressional survival may require institutional maintenance arrangements more sophisticated than the ones that have sufficed in the past. It may be necessary to build in selective incentives to reward members who take an interest in *programmatic impact*" (emphasis added).[6] But was this type of change possible in Mayhew's view? And how great a change did he think this would be? Based on his understanding of the fundamental characteristics of the American political system, Mayhew's judgment in 1974 was not optimistic. After suggesting that Congress's survival probably depended on such changes, he added, "[But] to do so would be to violate the canons of American legislative politics as we have come to know them."

Mayhew's focus was on the individual member of Congress because the early 1970s was a time when parties were at their nadir and were weak factors in shaping the behavior of legislators. Individual members had to fend for themselves, especially in getting elected. As one member at the time put it, "If we depended on the party organization to get elected, none of us would be here" (26–27). Since 1974, Mayhew's concerned conclusion apparently was neither much noted nor long remembered. Mayhew himself did not even allude to it in the second edition of the book on its twenty-fifth anniversary (1999). This is despite the fact that by 1999 much had changed with respect to the extent of programmatic orientation of Congress and our political institutions generally.

At the start of the twenty-first century, parties are stronger. So this volume shifts the level of analysis from that focus on the individual member operating independently of the party to an analysis of the party itself, insofar as it has become stronger vis-à-vis members. Indeed, the chapters in this book suggest that starting in the mid-1990s parties became more programmatic, more nationalized, and ultimately more cohesive and coherent. In turn, congressional parties have become more disciplined, cohesive, and coherent. As Thomas Mann and Norman Ornstein have recently argued, "there is a 'new Congress' and an 'old Congress.' . . . The 'old' Congress was a decentralized, committee and subcommittee based institution. Today, it is increasingly a centralized one where *party trumps committee.*"[7]

As Daniel DiSalvo details in his chapter, at least three things account for this change. One is the regional realignments of the Northeast and South. The parties have become more internally coherent as their electoral bases have shifted. Specifically, the decline of liberal Republicans in the Northeast and conservative Democrats in the South has reshuffled the two parties. The Republican Party has become more conservative and the Democratic Party more liberal on nearly all policy issues. All this is well reflected in Levendusky's felicitous title noted above—*The Partisan Sort: How Liberals Became Democrats and Republicans Became Conservatives.*

One result of these changes is a tendency toward some "polarization," where neither party has a wing that overlaps the center. Party unity scores in Congress—the frequency with which members of the same party vote together—have increased dramatically in the past decade. In 2007–8, the Democratic caucus in the House of Representatives voted as a block 92 percent of the time and Senate Democrats voted together 87 percent of the time. House Democrats' party unity score was the highest since *Congressional Quarterly* began tracking this indicator in 1952.

Another cause is the empowerment of the congressional party leadership through the employment of new procedural tools and fundraising techniques. This is a major increase in congressional "select incentives." It has produced a pattern of members becoming congressional leaders in part based on their ability to raise and then spread among members campaign money. The rise of leadership political action committees (PACs) has increased the control of senior members and the leadership over rank-and-file members. Congressional leaders in turn are strengthened by subsequent patterns of members being taxed by their party for campaign money redistributed to their colleagues. This internal flow of money makes each member more dependent on leadership and party money—much of it raised in Washington rather than in states and districts—than in the past. "Contrary to the view that a members' only goal is their own reelection," DiSalvo writes, "today they are increasingly concerned with the fate of their comrades. . . . The power to deliver major campaign monies has handed the leadership a powerful control instrument." In addition, the Hill committees' power makes winning their support and the resources they provide almost necessary conditions to be elected.

Finally, presidents have increasingly resorted to ideological and programmatic agendas as the blueprints for governing. Modern presidents have sought to remake their parties in their own administration's programmatic image. The link (or lack thereof) between policy choice and electoral outcomes is illustrated by the ambitious policy agendas crafted by the Clinton, Bush, and Obama administrations. All sought far-reaching changes in public policy. All hoped that such changes could win their party solid majorities in the future. Bill Clinton came into office in 1993 pronouncing himself a "new kind of Democrat" and seeking to move the Democratic Party toward the political center. Based on analyses of the Democratic Leadership Council, his hope was to sustain long-term Democratic majorities. To satisfy liberals and solidify middle-class support for the Democratic Party, he undertook a major health care policy initiative. This was a traditionally liberal package that, had it passed, would have greatly expanded government role in the health care sector. On the other hand, Clinton promoted a number of "centrist" policies to weaken notions that the Democratic Party was big spending, beholden to unions, unconcerned with government inefficiency, and insufficiently supportive of the American work ethic.[8] These included deficit reduction, NAFTA ratification, "reinventing government," and welfare reform.

George W. Bush arrived in the White House in 2001 with a short but ambitious agenda. "The forty-third president," George C. Edwards has written, "more than most of his predecessors over the previous half century, explicitly focused on developing and implementing a strategy for governing."[9] Dubbed "compassionate conservatism" during the campaign, Bush tried to combine traditional conservative principles such as individual responsibility, free enterprise, and low taxes with an acceptance that government had a positive role to play in bettering citizens' lives. He sought to use tax cuts to retain support of the business community for Republicans, increases in educational accountability as a way to attract both middle-class and minority support, a prescription drug benefit for the elderly to win over senior citizens, immigration reform (including a substantial amnesty) to draw Latinos into the GOP, and partial Social Security privatization as a way to attract young voters suspicious of the program's financial prospects.

For most of Obama's first two years in office, he sought to position himself halfway between centrist reformism and traditional liberalism. Predictably this dissatisfied both the base and median elements of his party. Indeed, as we explained in the introduction, "in our large, diverse polity (with parties to match), coalition building is inherently and endemically fraught with risky dilemmas—risky to each contending element of the coalition. . . . [For] our fragmented and pluralistic political system, so much balancing of interests and compromising is necessary to get past no that the outcomes are frequently neither pure nor ideal from most players' perspectives."

Thus, Obama's first initiative, the roughly $787 billion stimulus bill, sought to split the difference between the party's factions. Predictably, independents and conservatives thought it was too large a government handout, and liberals believed that an even larger package was necessary to restart the economy. Similarly, on Obama's signature policy, health care reform, the administration's approach struck independents as overreach and simultaneously disappointed liberals because it didn't include the public option.

But following the Democrats' loss of the House in the 2010 midterm election, Obama took a different approach. In the lame-duck session that followed this defeat, Obama shifted from a focus on the intraparty coalition-building process that produced his health care reform to one of interparty coalition building. This produced a package extending Bush-era tax cuts (including for those with incomes over $250,000) for the Republicans and with three significant and expensive stimulus policies for the Democrats. It was a package of policies that was both balanced politically and centrist in policy substance.

The Republicans ended, at least temporarily, their "just say no" refrain that they had almost universally followed for the previous two years. They were willing to participate in the deal that produced this package in order to get their part of it—the extension of the Bush tax cuts for those with incomes of over $250,000. In a moment we will explain the Republicans' apparent flexibility and pragmatism as part of their larger pattern of focusing on satisfying the core of their base—business.

As the contrast between Mayhew's concerned conclusions at a time of weaker parties in 1974 and our political intuitions at the turn of the new century indicates, these shifts in a more programmatic direction are quite significant. As DiSalvo puts it in his chapter, "Today, the parties are more national, more programmatic, and more closely divided than at any time in the modern period. Intense party competition for control of government has produced a new set of incentives and constraints that powerfully shape government policymaking. Despite many obstacles, *parties have made governance and electoral strategy once again a collective affair*" (emphasis added).

The War on Terrorism

In addition to the increased programmatic orientation of our parties at the new century, the context for policy choice in this period was shaped significantly by the impact of the terrorist attacks on the World Trade Center and the Pentagon on September 11, 2001. The attacks brought national security to the top of the national agenda for the first time since the end of the Cold War. The September 11 attacks set the Bush administration on a new and unforeseen course. Less than a month after the attacks, the United States invaded Afghanistan to destroy cells of terrorist activity within that country and to overthrow the fanatical Taliban regime. Bush's response to 9/11 temporarily changed perceptions of him as a partisan president who arrived in the White House after a hotly contested election into a forceful leader. Before the attacks, Bush had been a more polarizing figure than Clinton; after them, his approval rating stood at 60 percent. Amidst this flurry of activity, the administration also began to plan the invasion of Iraq.

The 9/11 crisis also raised significant policymaking choices domestically. The Bush administration quickly found itself in a pitched battle over whether to create a new cabinet-level department of homeland security—a step the administration at first opposed and then embraced. Simultaneously, the terrorist attacks yielded *potential* political advantage to the Republican Party. The change in the political context engendered by the attacks shifted public attention away from a host of prior problems: Bush was under fire for "defunding" the federal government and weakening Social Security financing as a result of his first tax cut. Unemployment was also rising, and fears that the country was entering a recession were growing.

This political precariousness for Bush in the first eight months of 2001 meant that the 9/11 attacks later that year were fortuitous for the administration. As we noted in the introduction, Lindsay shows that the Bush administration framed every election campaign after 9/11 (2002, 2004, and 2006) around its aggressive positions on national security issues—from the Afghan and Iraq Wars to the Patriot Act. This provided the Bush administration with a set of issues that could attract base voters and median voters at the same time. Thus, it relieved them of the need to balance these dissonant elements of their coalition.

In turn, the Bush administration won two major victories in 2002 and 2004. The historically unusual 2002 congressional victory indicated the breadth of support that the national security issue could develop *outside* the party's base. This victory, but even more so that of 2004, seems to have emboldened the Bush administration's foreign and even domestic policy positions.

However, as noted in the introduction, with the souring of the Iraq War (2005) and the Hurricane Katrina debacle (2006), this political and policy bubble of national security was pierced. The Republicans in turn lost the 2006 congressional election and the 2008 presidential election.

Policy Choices in Context: The Bush Administration

George W. Bush assumed the presidency after one of the closest elections in American history. Bush lost the popular vote to Al Gore by a half-million votes and barely eked out a victory in the Electoral College thanks to the Supreme Court's decision in *Bush v. Gore*, which settled the voting controversies in the state of Florida. The election results (in which Republicans also lost seats in both houses of Congress) meant that Bush could not claim a mandate of any kind. Many in the Washington press corps and the Democratic Party adopted the view that the circumstances of Bush's election would force him to govern in a bipartisan fashion. With very slim majorities in both houses of Congress, Bush spurned the conventional Beltway wisdom and decided to forge ahead. As Vice President Cheney put it, "We had an agenda, we ran on the agenda, we won the election—full steam ahead."[10]

We now turn to analysis of how the Bush administration pursued the policy areas covered by this book's specific policy chapters. Perhaps the best background and context for analyzing how the Bush administration pursued the specific elements of its agenda is to get a sense of the administration's focus on the core of its base—*business*.

These chapters tell a story of an administration keenly sensitive to the preferences of median voters during this era of highly competitive elections and frequent alternations in power. But at the same time, the administration never forgot the business base. And within this core target their ultimate focus was on the energy sector of business, from which (not accidentally) the president and vice president (the latter in his most immediately preceding position) came. Many policies developed by the Bush administration, as they reached for median voters and new constituencies, provided for consumer beneficiaries. But as they reached for median voters while holding on to base voters, the administration was almost equally focused on providing for the providers, which in most instances were large businesses. By contrast, the beneficiaries were largely unorganized consumers.

This overriding concern for these providers seems to have been in the spirit of the classic movie depiction of the political boss who famously explains to a newcomer the way development works in the new West: "You gotta realize that dams are built more to hold concrete than to hold water."

The Bush administration did not quite turn things entirely on their head as in the movie tale. But they seemed to almost turn them "sideways"—giving almost equal focus to providers as to beneficiaries. We will see this played out in four major policy areas.

First, the passage of Medicare Part D expanded Medicare by adding a new benefit—prescription drug coverage. This was designed to appeal to Medicare beneficiaries and those nearing this age—both of which tended to be closer to the Democrats than to the Republicans. But as well as providing a new benefit for the consumer beneficiaries in Medicare, Oberlander shows that the Part D reform also provided for the providers.

The benefit was contracted for and delivered by private insurance companies. The drugs themselves were provided by private drug companies without the requirement typical in government-supported programs of purchasing according to prices negotiated within government-imposed price controls.

Second, following their 2004 presidential election victory the Bush administration boldly proposed partial privatization of Social Security. This would always be appealing to the market-oriented elements of the Republicans' conservative base, but it also targeted a potential new constituency—younger voters. The electoral strategic thinking was to target younger voters because they tend to lean Democratic. But according to polls at the time, these younger voters were losing faith that the Social Security system would be sufficiently strong when they retired. So the Republicans hypothesized that this constituency might find their advocacy of partial privatization an appealing policy position.

But the details of the policymaking were developed, as was so often the case in the Bush administration, with an eye toward the business core of their base: privatization was designed to appeal directly to the financial services industry. Thus, it was more attractive to business than the earlier traditional conservative approach to Social Security—say, of the younger Ronald Regan—which was to advocate abolishing it. This approach advocated both privatizing it and then providing for the providers.

Third, the Bush administration's perhaps most pro-business policymaking came in the environmental area—the Clear Skies air pollution initiative. It was a combination of probably the most targeted policymaking by Bush and the most striking instance of the administration's pattern of policymaking by indirection and inertia, so well captured by the felicitous title of Emer's chapter—"Feign to the Center, Move Backward: Bush's Clear Skies Initiative and the Politics of Policymaking."

Emer analyzes all this indirection, inertia, policy targeting, and feigning with the following explanatory framework. The Bush administration took three contingent approaches: First, the administration tried a legislative route that would achieve their goals and the goals of business by enacting the Clear Skies legislative proposal. Ostensibly the initiative was designed to appeal to median voters by increasing air pollution standards, but in fact objective sources show that this legislation would have permanently set back air pollution policy by eliminating many Clean Air Act programs and would likely delay the rate of air pollution reductions.

Second, in lieu of legislative success, the Bush administration sought these business-satisfying goals of decreasing and delaying air pollution reductions through the implementation of administrative rules. The Clean Air Act would not have been altered as fundamentally as under the Clear Skies legislative initiative, but these administrative rule changes would have slowed down air pollution reductions for the time being.

The third contingency ultimately was achieved in fact—the delay of any new pollution standards. The Bush administration failed to enact the legislative proposal and was blocked by the courts in enacting most of the administrative changes. But this last contingency—the delay of expanded implementation of the Clean Air Act through the entire time Bush was in office—was a valuable result for the business base. As environmental consultant Michael Bradley explained, "The Bush administration bought the coal industry a pass for eight years. It was worth millions and millions."

The fourth case of the Republican's primary priority being satisfying their business base was their approach, during the 2010 lame-duck session, to the major interparty debate about the extension of the Bush-era tax cuts—especially for those with incomes over $250,000. The Republicans were willing to sacrifice one of their highest policy priorites—deficit reduction—in order to satisfy the goals of business on this tax cut issue.

The Republicans' highest single policy priority during Obama's first two years—designed to appeal to median *and* base voters—was reducing spending in the face of a large and growing budget deficit (a deficit ironically created initially by George W. Bush's spending and tax cuts). But in order to achieve the policy so strongly sought by business—extension of Bush-era tax cuts for those with incomes over $250,000—the House Republican leadership and a large proportion of the party's House members were willing to agree to a tax cut package bargain with Obama that added greatly to the deficit. In addition to the original quid pro quo that Obama sought in exchange for *all* these Bush-era tax cuts—extension of long-term unemployement benefits—Obama also added to the package two major policies that did in fact further contribute significantly to the deficit: a major set of additional lesser stimulus policies and a reduction in the payroll tax for two years.

The total Obama side of the package was such a major addition to the deficit that a small but not insignificant number of House Republicans broke with their leadership and voted against the total package despite its inclusion of the tax cut for the wealthiest. Indeed, Conlan and Posner call it a "surprisingly large $858 billion package." But the Republican leadership and the bulk of their party members in the House persisted to put through this business-satisfying tax cut and the expensive package that Obama demanded in return, even though both elements of the package would contribute so much to the deficit.

With this background and context in mind, let us now turn to more full analyses of the particular policy areas.

Tax Cuts, Business, and the Median Voter

Upon arriving in the White House, the Bush administration sought immediately to act on one of the central issues on which it campaigned: the largest tax cut in American history. The eleven-year, $1.35 trillion tax cut bill that was passed right out of the gates was very close to the president's initial proposal, cutting income taxes across the board, removing 40 million people from paying any income tax at all, and deeply cutting the top rates for the wealthiest Americans. The political aims of the tax cuts were to shore up support in the Republican base within the business community, especially small business, which was the driving force behind the legislation. As Conlan and Posner put it in their chapter, "Key elements of President Bush's 2001 tax legislation were chosen purposefully for their strong appeal to core Republican constituencies, including the sizable reduction of top marginal rates and the phaseout of the estate tax." The White House was thus well aware that tax cuts unified and energized Republicans. The president and his advisors also knew that liberal Democrats would oppose their package but that many independents and some conservative Democrats would support or at least tolerate it.

The tax package was not widely understood by the majority of voters. Although voters had a hard time distinguishing between Bush's and Gore's tax plans during the 2000 campaign, there was, according to polls, considerable support among voters for tax cuts. Polls also showed that tax cuts had much greater salience among Republicans than Democrats. Even for those citizens paying a modicum of attention, the administration's rationale for the tax cut changed drastically over time. It went from "returning the anticipated surplus in 2000 and early 2001 to citizens, to providing countercyclical economic stimulus in 2001 and 2002, to promoting investment and long-term economic growth, to reducing progressivity and 'double taxation' in the tax code." Nonetheless, there had been broad support in the electorate for tax cuts, and both Bush and Gore had campaigned on the issue in 2000. Hence, under the guise of a centrist initiative, the administration could use its strategic advantages to push a policy much closer to the preferences of its party base.

A highly partisan process in the House and an unevenly bipartisan approach in the Senate characterized the legislative politics of tax cuts in 2001. The administration was willing to rely on its side for political support, eschew bipartisanship, and induce significant polarization to ram through a policy closest to its preferences. Given the 50-50 balance of powers in the Senate, with Vice President Cheney as the tie breaker, the administration made its tax cuts part of the budget reconciliation process, so that they could avoid filibusters and only need to assemble a simple majority. Even that proved daunting and required much arm-twisting. Similarly hard-driving legislative politics prevailed in the 2003 round of tax cuts as well. Republican ideological agreement on taxes, especially the House Conference, made it easy for them to shift policy to the right and forego compromise with the Democrats. In the end, a united, albeit slim, majority prevailed and the president was able to claim credit for dramatically lowering taxes. Not only did passing the big tax cut chime with the policy preferences of the GOP base, but it also had the advantage of setting the terms of policy debate down the line. By severely limiting government revenue, it would restrain Democrats' ability to use the budget surplus for expanded social spending.

Reaching Beyond the Base: No Child Left Behind

In the 2000 presidential campaign, Bush responded to Downsian incentives by adopting education reform as his signature centrist initiative. With tax cuts targeted at the base but with sufficient cover given public ignorance of the proposals details, Bush and his team could highlight education as an appeal to median voters. Indeed, the campaign's theme of "compassionate conservatism" sought to reach beyond the base of the party's Reagan conservatism. Frederick Hess shows that education reform was the Republicans' attempt to try to win back moderate voters they had lost to Clinton in 1996, according to their data. This proposal came to be known as the No Child Left Behind (NCLB) program. Hess describes how the Bush administration "aggressively courted the center" on this issue. NCLB's politics and its policy substance were moderate and even Clintonian. Indeed, as Hess notes, NCLB was based on a plan from Clinton's Department of Education. (The term "no child left behind" itself was coined by the Democrat stalwart Marian Wright Edelman of the Children's Defense Fund.) Indeed, Hess suggests that if welfare reform could be viewed as "Reagan's last policy," then NCLB was "Clinton's last policy."

The Bush administration had at least three objectives in pushing for the passage of NCLB. One was to inoculate the Republican Party from Democratic criticism by taking a significant wedge issue off the table. Republican strategists were deeply concerned about the GOP's weakness on the education issue in the wake of the 1996 elections, when polls showed that it had damaged Kansas senator Bob Dole's presidential bid. However, the party's base was not keen on greater federal involvement in what it considered a local issue. Indeed, it had only been seven years since the congressional Republicans' policy manifesto, the Contract with America, had called for the abolition of the federal Department of Education. Another objective was to weaken an important part of the Democratic Party's base: teachers' unions. The vouchers, accountability, and testing measures the administration proposed put the unions on the defensive in the short term and had the potential to undercut union power in the long run. The third objective was to appeal to target constituencies of African Americans and Latinos whose children were often in some of the nation's worst performing schools.

Consequently, the president partnered with the "Liberal Lion," Massachusetts senator Ted Kennedy, to pass NCLB over the opposition of nearly a third of the House Republican Conference. As Hess demonstrates, the Bush administration was willing to deeply offend conservatives to achieve education reform. Indeed, according to Hess, "the administration embraced a moralistic conception of accountability, race-conscious policy, and energetic federal intervention rather than the limited, incentive-based, deregulatory model of policy that had emerged from decades of conservative critiques of Great Society designs." The implementation of the law also elicited howls of protest from liberals and their media allies. The criticism effectively nullified any political advantages Bush or Republicans might have hoped to gain.

Expansion Causes Division: The Case of Immigration Reform

A Republican president had not advocated expansionary immigration policy in one hundred years (although they had signed expansionary bills coming out of Democratic Congresses in 1986 and 1990). The Bush administration broke from this pattern with expansionary immigration proposals both in 2003 and again in 2006. Their political target in these bills was to increase the party's support among the traditionally Democratic-oriented Hispanics, whom Bush had successfully courted while governor of Texas.

President Bush first proposed a major overhaul of the system in January of 2004, bringing immigration reform to the top of the domestic agenda.[11] Prior to the president's speech, however, vast divisions between the Right and the Left made the issue untouchable. Bush's proposal aimed to cut through the stalemate by staking out a centrist position that drew on proposals from both liberals and conservatives.[12] The objective of the administration's immigration reform was twofold. On the one hand, Bush sought to target Latinos—a voting bloc that is growing—many of whom remain loosely tied to the Democratic Party. On the other, the aim was to assist businesses that rely on immigrant labor but want to avoid running afoul of the law.

In 2005, a bipartisan bill written by Senators Ted Kennedy (D-MA) and John McCain (R-AZ), which reflected the president's proposals, passed in the Senate. But the measure sparked vigorous opposition from within the president's own party as conservative House Republicans derided the measure as providing "amnesty" to those in the country illegally. The standoff between the House and Senate led to the passage, just before the 2006 elections, of the Secure Borders Act. But this hardly constituted comprehensive reform.[13] After Democrats won control of both houses of Congress in 2006, however, many predicted that the president and the "new majority" could find grounds to cooperate on immigration policy, as Democrats' preferences were thought to be closer to those of the president. A bipartisan coalition in support of reform seemed to be in the offing, but in June 2007, after much maneuvering, a reform bill failed to pass the Senate. This effectively ended the administration's drive for comprehensive immigration reform.

Bush was successful neither in passing his immigration reform proposals nor in significantly increasing Hispanic voters' support. Hispanic voters' support for Republicans did go up in 2004 to a modest degree, but it plummeted in 2006 and 2008. Moreover, on balance these proposals were a net loss for the party's coalition building because they deeply offended the party's base, which has a significant component of anti-immigration elements. One of the principle supporters of reform, John McCain, almost saw his hopes of winning the GOP's presidential nomination dashed in the fall of 2007, as conservatives lined up against him. He was then forced to adopt a tougher line that prioritized border security. Ultimately, neither President Bush nor Senator McCain received any credit among Latinos for their troubles. According to exit polls, in 2008, Latinos voted two-to-one in favor of Obama. In sum, the president's immigration policy proposals failed to yield a major legislative breakthrough or a successful electoral connection for the party.

Growing the Welfare State and New Opportunities for Patients and Providers: Prescription Drugs for Seniors

In the shadow of war, the Bush administration boldly pushed ahead with the largest expansion of the welfare state since the Great Society: the addition of a prescription drug benefit to the Medicare program. A costly program that many conservatives were skeptical of, if not downright opposed to, barely squeaked through Congress. One objective of the legislation was to score points for the Bush administration's "compassionate conservative" theme. The Medicare Modernization Act of 2003 created a new government role in enhancing the accessibility of prescription drugs for senior citizens.

Senior citizens were the target constituency that Republicans hoped to appeal to by passing the program. Bush and his Republican congressional allies also sought to inoculate their party from Democratic attacks by blunting the perception that they were rabidly hostile to the welfare state. Republicans sought to show they were capable of taking on health care, a policy area normally dominated by the Democrats. This was especially important given the high rates of voting participation among seniors. Republicans could ill afford to lose a large percentage of seniors on Election Day. By providing an expansive benefit that was important to seniors, Republicans hoped they could shore up support among them.

Nonetheless, in enacting Medicare Part D, the Republicans did not ignore their conservative base. The details of the measure provided enormous benefits for drug manufacturers and insurance companies. These elements of the business community could go along with the assurance that government's role would not crowd them out of their market position but actually enhance it. Indeed, as Oberlander argues, business and insurance groups, along with their Republican legislative allies, saw the possibility that programmatic details would force the privatization of many aspects of the Medicare program down the road.

In the end, however, the Medicare Modernization Act turned out to be too "centrist" for many conservatives, who criticized the program's costs and the principle of government intervention in this area. The Bush administration thus suffered a falloff in support from its base. Many speculated that hostility to such a large spending initiative led conservative activists and donors to sit on their hands in the 2006 and 2008 elections to register their disapproval.

New Opportunities for Wall Street and New Risks for Beneficiaries: Social Security Privatization

In the wake of a slim but solid victory in the 2004 election, President Bush launched a major campaign for reform of Social Security. Conservatives have never much liked the keystone of the American welfare state. Ronald Reagan was twice burned by publicly criticizing the program (once on the campaign trail and later in office). Despite Social Security's reputation as the third rail of American politics, the Bush administration boldly set out to partially privatize the program. Such an effort satiated the ideological proclivities of market-oriented conservatives. The reforms were also designed to appeal to certain elements of the financial services industry. Yet the target constituency that really interested Republican strategists was younger voters. Younger voters lean Democratic but, according to polls, had lost faith that the Social Security system would be there when they retired. Therefore, loosening their partisan attachments could bear fruits down the line for the GOP.

Nonetheless, President Bush's most extensive and vigorous effort to persuade the public to support his position ended in failure. Not only was the public unresponsive, but the more the president talked, the less the public supported his ideas. The administration's congressional allies quickly dropped consideration of the president's proposals. Interestingly, Republican strategists realized even before they launched their public relations efforts that there was little slack in public opinion on the Social Security issue. Therefore, they concentrated their efforts primarily on energizing their partisan base rather than trying to alter the preferences of median voters of target constituencies. After beginning with bipartisan hopes, the administration ended up preaching to the converted.

Clear Skies: Feigning to the Center, Moving Backward

David Emer's chapter delves into the politics of the Bush administration's approach to clean air policy. The politics and policy of clean air are dominated by the Clean Air Act of 1970, which set the goal of clean air for every American. Under this law, the Environmental Protection Agency (EPA) determines which pollutants degrade air quality and sets national standards to protect air quality.

Politically, air pollution is the subject of intense battles between the energy industry and environmental groups. The Bush administration waded into the debate with its "Clear Skies" program. The Clear Skies legislative proposal consisted of new "market-based" cap and trade programs to regulate sulfur dioxide, nitrogen oxides, and mercury that would replace "command-and-control" environmental permitting programs, among other programs. The substance of Clear Skies benefited the GOP base in the business community, especially the energy sector, because, on balance, according to the Congressional Research Service and National Academies of Science, it would have weakened the Clean Air Act. At the same time, in order to make the policy appeal to moderates, the administration cast Clear Skies as environmental policy reform. However, the bill lacked any new programs for regulating carbon dioxide, one of the supposed causes of global warming and the most recognizable pollutant to the public. And the two main thrusts of the program, an easing of the permitting provisions and the administration's approach to mercury, proved highly controversial. Finally, passing such a bill would have eliminated many Clean Air Act programs and would have slowed the reduction of pollutants in the air.

Consequently, the administration's proposal—which was considered twice by Congress—was roundly condemned by environmentalists without finding a coalition that could support it. On the heels of legislative defeat, the administration tried to implement much of the policy through rulemaking at the EPA. The courts struck down most of the rules on the grounds that they were not consistent with the Clean Air Act, the statute under which they were issued. Emer's chapter shows that the ultimate outcome for the administration was stalemate on both the legislative and administrative fronts.

Yet stalemate does not mean that there were no policy effects. To the Democrats, stalemate was a poor result because they wanted an expanded clean air policy that would include carbon dioxide regulation. To the Republican business base, though, delay was a reasonable alternative to a faithfully implemented Clean Air Act and a far better alternative to expansionary legislation that included global warming pollutants. On air pollution policy, the Bush administration "feigned to the center" to appeal to moderates, but its actions resulted in a policy that benefited the business base.

The Politics of the Law: Tort Reform and Judicial Appointments

Legal issues also provided the Bush administration an opening to pursue policies balancing the center and the base. The critique of plaintiff lawyers and "runaway litigation" as a cause of the nation's economic ills is a Republican theme with a long history. In both of his terms, President Bush called for "tort reform"—that is, legal changes to reduce the size and frequency of personal injury damage claims, mostly against businesses, insurers, and professionals. According to critics, the current system of torts is a haphazard and inefficient means to regulate business. If tort reform as envisaged by Republicans ever passed, it would have the added advantage of undermining plaintiff lawyers' profits, a group that contributes vast sums of money to the Democratic Party. The administration was well aware that tort reform could assist their base allies in business and weaken their Democratic rivals.

However, the Senate proved to be a burial ground for the president's proposals. The House passed bills capping damages in medical malpractice lawsuits but could not overcome the threat of a filibuster in the Senate. In 2005, however, with Republicans having expanded their majority in the Senate, they were able to attract enough Democratic votes to enact the "Class Action Fairness Act." The principle aspect of this law was to move some class action lawsuits from state to federal court. Some see the latter as more favorable to business.

The White House was more successful in using legal controversies to appeal to social conservatives in the party's base. Judicial appointment policy and the rhetoric surrounding it provided the means. The administration used and benefited the Federalist Society, a conservative legal group, by awarding its members a welter of appointments to federal judgeships. Indeed, both of Bush's Supreme Court nominees that won Senate confirmation were Federalist Society members. This strategy, as Tom Burke shows in his chapter, satisfied a key element of the conservative intelligentsia and offered a number of opportunities for rhetorical appeals to rank-and-file traditionalists.

Putting It All Together: The Political Context

The range and direction of the initiatives in the Bush years were often contradictory in their political and policy thrusts. To help make sense of the diverse objectives of the administration's initiatives, this volume offers a series of chapters on the larger dynamics at work in the American political system. These chapters examine the broader political context through the lenses of parties, presidents, and political history.

DiSalvo's chapter details how over the last thirty years the parties have evolved into centralized, ideological, and polarized entities. He analyzes the factional origins of contemporary ideological divisions, how competition has spurred party organization, and the unification and nationalization of campaign strategies. The result is a treatment of how recent party development has shaped the policymaking context of the new century, which spotlights the link between party change and policy outputs.

Daniel Galvin's chapter examines the institution of the presidency in this new partisan context and what incentives and constraints operate on the occupant of the Oval Office. He explores the conditions under which presidents are likely to pursue what sorts of policy. He looks beyond presidents' personal proclivities to the political situation in which presidential decisions are made. The political situation is defined by the strength or weakness of the president's party in electoral competition at any given time and the structural features of the public policy under consideration. By looking across these political situations using the cases at hand, Galvin finds that we see more regularity in presidential policy choice and agenda priorities than we do simply by looking at a president's personal characteristics.

Finally, Mayhew's conclusion provides a wide-ranging overview that puts the last two decades in historical perspective. He shows how the politics of the policies treated in this volume invite a reconsideration of Anthony Downs's classic argument about the role of the median voter in democratic electoral and policy processes. He claims that Downs properly understood holds that "a major party in a two-party system always needs to pursue a complex, tension-ridden, inside-outside strategy that appeases the median voter but also, given the existence of a dominant ideological dimension, caters to the range of voters all the way to the left or right extreme on its own side of the median." Mayhew then follows through with this characterization to show how many of the policy areas treated here follow elements of this logic. He does this by taking into account a variety of policy types, past and present, as well as a number of policymaking styles. His chapter is, not surprisingly, full of rich insights that embroider existing theoretical reflection on the American political system.

Conclusion

The chapters in this volume show that crafting a party coalition is difficult for several reasons. First, there is the Downsian quality of the American two-party system. In that system, party leaders confront a persistent dilemma between attempting to satisfy their base and appealing to the median voter or new constituencies. Powerful incentives push and pull them in different directions. Indeed, parties must appeal to each of these groups pretty much all of the time. One faction or the other will ultimately find reasons to be dissatisfied with the party's leadership, opening the door to the other party's seeking to capitalize on the disaffection of the base or the alienation of median voters. Often both are dissatisfied, as the introduction describes in relation to both Obama's health care reform and Bush's immigration legislation.

Dissatisfactions with the coalition-building process's policy result seem to be the predictable product of the nature of this enterprise in our large diverse polity—with parties to match. As we suggested in the introduction, it is a process inherently fraught with dilemmas for each contending element of the coalition. Even when there are policy successes, ironically there may be political costs to the winning party as we saw with Obama's health care reform. And, as we saw with Bush's defeated immigration legislation, even failed coalition building may contribute to electoral difficulties.

Second, it is difficult to maintain the support of party activists and median voters simultaneously because they are really different animals. A party's base tends to be more made up of elites—issue activists, intellectuals, lawyers, business people, and so on. These people tend to pay more attention to politics, think more about public policy's long-term implications, and have well-thought-out ideas about what government should do. On the other hand, the median voters tend not to pay as much attention to politics, focus more on public policy's short-term implications, and do not have as clear preferences on many important governmental decisions. The base and the median are so different that party leaders must really do different things to win them over. For the base, it is more about satisfying and solidifying people who are already part of a party coalition and are likely to remain so for the foreseeable future. For the median voters, it is about drawing in people whose preferences are less fixed and are more likely to bounce back and forth between the parties over the course of a few election cycles. One of the consequences of the movement of this substantial and perhaps growing part of the electorate is the frequent alternation in power among evenly divided parties that we have seen in the past two decades and that we detail below.

Third, party majorities are also constantly undercut by the institutional order, especially the fact of separate institutions sharing overlapping powers. These separations and power sharing create presidential and congressional wings of the parties. The tension between these wings of the party was evident during the Clinton and Bush years, and it has continued under Obama. Congressional Democrats disagreed sharply with the Clinton administration (which was itself divided) over welfare reform. Likewise, congressional Republicans essentially defeated Bush's immigration and Social Security policy initiatives. On the other hand, presidents can successfully resist initiatives stemming from their own party's congressional caucus's independence and even its rebellions. Clinton ultimately passed his welfare reform despite the defection of the majority of House Democrats. Similarly, during the 2010 lame-duck session, in the face of opposition from many liberal House Democrats, Obama passed the package that extended the Bush-era tax cuts (including those for incomes over $250,000) and, in return, garnered three major stimulus items for the Democrats. This paralleled Obama's earlier successful effort to remove from his health care reform package the jewel in these House liberals' crown—the public option. These institutional differences, stemming in large part from the different electoral coalitions upon which congressmen and presidents rely, mean that driving forward a programmatic agenda is always going to be fraught with difficulty and the potential for defection.

All these factors together also help explain why neither party has been able to gain the upper hand for very long since 1992. A pattern of periods of extended dominance by one party existed in American politics for over one hundred and thirty years: the Republicans from 1860 to 1932, the Democrats from 1933 to 1968, the Republicans from 1969 to 1992. But in the past two decades, there has been frequent alternation in power among evenly divided parties: the Democrats won in 1992, the Republicans in 1994, and the Democrats again in 1996 and 1998 (they gained seats in the House in both those years, as well as winning the presidency in 1996 and later getting fifty-five votes in the Senate against Clinton's impeachment). The Republicans won the presidency in 2000 (though in a close election, which really was a "split decision"), but the Senate was literally a "draw" and then went Democratic again in April 2001 with the Jeffords defection from the Republicans. The Republicans won in 2002 (historically a very unusual midterm victory for the party in the White House) and 2004, the Democrats in 2006 and 2008, and the Republicans in 2010.

This alternation in election victories has made it harder to maintain unified party control over the presidency and both Houses for extended time periods. This alternation and its contribution to divided government have moderated policymaking because they have prevented one party from dominating not only the electoral arena but also the policymaking agenda for any extended period. Indeed, as we showed in detail in the introduction, from Clinton to Bush to Obama, immoderation in policymaking was consistently punished at the polls. All these consequences—especially the electoral punishing of policy immoderation—indicate a very different pattern than the claims by the justly esteemed Paul Pierson and Jacob Hacker and others that the American political system is "off-center." Indeed, the chapters in this book suggest why this unusual pattern of frequent alternation in power among evenly divided parties is continuing in the twenty-first century. The results of the 2010 midterm election, which erased the Democrats' gains of 2006 and 2008 and handed control of the House to the Republicans, confirm this pattern.

NOTES

1. Matthew Levendusky, *The Partisan Sort: How Liberals Became Democrats and Republicans Became Conservatives* (Chicago: University of Chicago Press, 2009).

2. Anthony Downs, *An Economic Theory of Democracy* (New York: Harper & Row, 1957).

3. Jacob Hacker, *The Divided Welfare State: The Battle over Public and Private Social Benefits in the United States* (New York: Cambridge University Press, 2002), 28–70.

4. Frank R. Baumgartner and Bryan D. Jones, *Agendas and Instability in American Politics* (Chicago: University of Chicago Press, 1993).

5. Paul Pierson, "Increasing Returns, Path Dependence, and the Study of Politics," *American Political Science Review* 94, no. 2 (2000): 251–67. See also Pierson, *Politics in Time: History, Institutions, and Social Analysis* (Princeton, NJ: Princeton University Press, 2004).

6. David R. Mayhew, *Congress: The Electoral Connection* (New Haven, CT: Yale University Press, 1975).

7. Thomas Mann and Norman Ornstein, *The Broken Branch: How Congress Is Failing America and How to Get It Back on Track* (New York: Oxford University Press, 2006).

8. Elizabeth Drew, *On the Edge: The Clinton Presidency* (New York: Simon & Schuster, 1994); Steven M. Gillon, *The Pact: Bill Clinton, Newt Gingrich, and the Rivalry That Defined a Generation* (New York: Oxford University Press, 2008).

9. George C. Edwards III, *The Strategic President: Persuasion and Opportunity in Presidential Leadership* (Princeton, NJ: Princeton University Press, 2009), 166.

10. Cheney cited in Bob Woodward, *Plan of Attack* (New York: Simon & Schuster, 2004), 28.

11. George W. Bush, "Remarks by the President on Immigration Policy," White House Press Office (Washington, DC, January 7, 2004).

12. This discussion draws on Daniel DiSalvo, "Four Traps," *American Interest* (March/April 2009).

13. David Stout, "Bush, Signing Bill for Boarder Fence, Urges Wider Overhaul," *New York Times*, October 27, 2006.

CHAPTER TWO

Why LBJ Is Smiling

The Bush Administration, "Compassionate Conservatism," and No Child Left Behind

Frederick M. Hess

Our formula is as simple as it is sweeping: the federal government has no constitutional authority to be involved in school curricula or to control jobs in the work place. That is why we will abolish the Department of Education [and] end federal meddling in our schools. . . . We therefore call for prompt repeal of the Goals 2000 program and the School-To-Work Act of 1994, which put new federal controls, as well as unfunded mandates, on the States.

—1996 REPUBLICAN PARTY PLATFORM

U.S. Secretary of Education Margaret Spellings today honored President Lyndon Baines Johnson in a ceremony officially renaming the U.S. Department of Education building at 400 Maryland Avenue, S.W. in Washington, D.C. as the Lyndon Baines Johnson Department of Education Building. "President Johnson worked tirelessly to provide an equal education to all children," Secretary Spellings said.

—U.S. DEPARTMENT OF EDUCATION PRESS RELEASE, SEPTEMBER 17, 2007

While it was oft depicted by academics and pundits as ideologically conservative, the Bush administration was a far more complex animal. Symbolic was the administration's support for renaming the U.S. Department of Education after Lyndon B. Johnson, architect of the Great Society. Indeed, its signature domestic policy victory—the passage of the 2001 No Child Left Behind Act (NCLB)—dramatically expanded the federal role in schooling and traded conventional conservative themes for those borrowed from the civil rights community.

In the 2000 presidential campaign, candidate Bush aggressively courted the center on schooling. Drawing on his six years as governor of Texas, where he had earned national recognition as a champion of the state's accountability system, Bush used education reform to reassure moderates that the GOP could govern "compassionately," woo key liberal constituencies like Latinos and African Americans, and fracture the Democratic coalition by weakening the teachers' unions.

Bush criticized "the soft bigotry of low expectations" and denounced policies that had "left behind" millions of African American and Latino children, emphasizing the language of civil rights and social justice. Bush speechwriter Michael Gerson would later explain the decision to reject "leave us alone" conservatism for a more expansive vision, arguing, "Only this kind of early ideological shock treatment could shift a durable Republican image of heartlessness."[1]

Bush's aspirational stance proved to be good politics, allowing him to promise dramatic action while remaining vague about costs and consequences. However, in a lesson that would have been familiar to an earlier generation of Great Society Democrats who watched public sentiment sour on their grand designs, the complex reality of NCLB proved less appealing than had its promise. The assault on the racial "achievement gap" earned plaudits and won a clutch of key allies in the civil rights community, but ultimately at the cost of alienating suburban parents worried that the emphasis on simple metrics and basic skills was harming their children and their schools.

The Bush diagnosis held the nation's schools to be plagued by mediocrity, low expectations, and insufficient attention to the basics. Its solution was to remake the culture of schooling through the kind of blunt force trauma that would come from holding schools accountable for boosting performance and closing achievement gaps in the "3 R's." Given this objective, politics and policy were closely intertwined. Testing and accountability would push educators and state and local officials to focus on basic skills and on marginalized students.

Those who pushed back would be met with the challenge, "Whose child would you leave behind?"—a rejoinder intended to slam the door on the status quo. For the White House and its progressive allies, the operative concern was less the coherence of program design or alignment of incentives than creating a sense of urgency and driving cultural transformation by reshaping state and local politics. The law was more a vote of confidence in the power of statutory intent than a sound framework for accountability or deregulation.

NCLB's soaring goals, emphasis on racial "achievement gaps," and call for expanded federal leadership read like the Elementary and Secondary Education Act (ESEA) that President Lyndon Johnson would have yearned for in 1965 or the ESEA reauthorization that President Bill Clinton would have preferred in 1994. Most notably, NCLB required each state to define "proficiency" in reading and math, ensure that a minimum percentage of students at each school were proficient, and increase those targets over time so as to ensure 100 percent proficiency by 2014.

Given that no responsible observer imagined it feasible that any state would achieve that goal—not if "proficiency" was to have any meaning—the provision made clear that NCLB was in many ways a civil rights manifesto dressed in the guise of pragmatic school reform. Indeed, at a 2007 National Association for the Advancement of Colored People (NAACP) conference, Education Secretary Margaret Spellings would declare, "The No Child Left Behind Act . . . is not just an education law. It's a civil rights law."[2]

The audacious goal provided a useful point of agreement for Bush and his progressive allies, but at the cost of abandoning the careful attention to metrics, incentives, and targets that had characterized more than a decade of centrist and conservative efforts to promote accountability and "reinvent government." NCLB represented a sharp departure from contemporary conservatism's familiar concerns with unintended consequences, federalism, and the limited capacities of government.

At the very moment of what was popularly regarded as a conservative "victory" on education, it can seem remarkable that the administration embraced a moralistic conception of accountability, race-conscious policy, and energetic federal intervention rather than the limited, incentive-based, deregulatory model of policy that had emerged from decades of conservative critiques of Great Society designs. Yet, given the exigencies of governing coalitions and Bush's desire to pass NCLB with substantial bipartisan support, this development may be less surprising than it might seem. The aftermath has illustrated the mixed fruits of this victory, with leading Republicans gripped by buyer's remorse, discontent brewing within traditional GOP strongholds, and voters reverting to a historic preference for Democrats on education.

A Quick Overview of No Child Left Behind

In 2001, the thirty-six-year-old Elementary and Secondary Education Act was reauthorized as the No Child Left Behind Act. The major federal legislation governing K–12 schooling, ESEA had historically been an assemblage of categorical grants and funding formulas with no mechanism for assessing student outcomes. The signature innovation of NCLB was the requirement that states use standardized assessments to hold schools accountable for student performance in reading and math. NCLB did not dictate what state standards should entail, what state tests should assess, or how state tests ought to be scored. Specifically, it required schools to test students every year in grades 3 through 8 and once in grades 10 through 12.

Schools and districts were to be held accountable not just for overall student performance on state standards but also for the performance of individual subgroups defined by ethnicity and race, income, special needs, and English proficiency. Schools or districts in which any subgroup failed to perform adequately would be deemed as failing to make "adequate yearly progress" (AYP), with remedies spelled out for those earning that designation in consecutive years. Remedies would include nods to familiar GOP proposals for school vouchers and "school choice" and also the possibility that persistently low-performing schools could be reopened as charter schools or contracted out. The law's other major new innovation was a "highly qualified teacher" provision that called for states to ensure that all teachers in "core" subjects met certain state-determined criteria.

Presidential Politics and Education: From the Elementary and Secondary Education Act to No Child Left Behind

The federal government first addressed K–12 education systematically in 1965, when, as a pillar of his efforts to build a "Great Society," President Lyndon Johnson won passage of the ESEA. Despite Johnson's success, education remained peripheral to national debates until President Jimmy Carter succeeded in creating a federal Department of Education in 1979.

That act drew notice in 1980 when Ronald Reagan mounted a fierce attack on bloated, intrusive government. The 1980 Republican platform called for "deregulation by the federal government of public education and . . . the elimination of the federal Department of Education" and charged that Democratic education policy had yielded "huge new bureaucracies to misspend our taxes."

Reagan's victories in 1980 and 1984 spurred new backlash among the Left. In the late 1980s, a group of Democratic Southern governors and moderates responded to the Reaganite challenge by forming the centrist Democratic Leadership Council. Favoring a message of limited government, public investment, and fiscal prudence, these New Democratic leaders—including Arkansas governor Bill Clinton—regarded education and welfare as areas of pressing interest.

By 1988, polls reported that education had become a significant national issue for the first time. Vice President George H. W. Bush promised during his presidential campaign to be "the education president." Echoing a theme championed by Reagan, and especially former Reagan secretary of education William Bennett, Bush discussed the importance of states establishing rigorous standards and the need to ensure that students mastered those standards.

In 1988, Republicans also began to embrace school choice more aggressively. Proponents argued that school vouchers could unleash competition and permit students to escape failing schools, constituting a reform strategy consistent with GOP principles that could appeal to African Americans and Latinos—all without requiring new dollars, new bureaucracies, or an expanded federal role. These efforts, however, would bear little political fruit. While polling found that choice enjoyed support among African Americans and urban residents, that support, for a variety of reasons, did not translate into votes for Republicans.

Meanwhile, the New Democrats pioneered a rhetoric that reframed education and infrastructure as sensible investments in a postindustrial economy. The 1992 Democratic Party platform called for government to cease "throwing money at obsolete programs" and to hold schools accountable for "high standards of educational achievement."

In 1992, Arkansas governor Bill Clinton used New Democratic themes to unseat President George H. W. Bush. Republicans responded by promoting school choice and insisting, as in the 1992 GOP platform, that "the critical public mission in education is to set tough, clear standards of achievement and ensure that those who educate our children are accountable for meeting them." While Republicans sought to hold the education establishment's feet to the fire, they resisted calls for such activity to be pursued at the federal level.

Table 2.1   What is the nation's most important problem (1960–2000)?

Year	Candidates	Issue rated most important by voters	Relative ranking of education	Standardized rank of education
1960	Kennedy-Nixon	Foreign relations	14th of 20 issues	Lower 33%
1964	Johnson-Goldwater	Civil rights	24th of 24 issues	Last
1968	Humphrey-Nixon	Vietnam	17th of 17 issues	Last
1972	McGovern-Nixon	Vietnam	26th of 26 issues	Last
1976	Carter-Ford	Inflation	Not listed among 27 issues	Last
1980	Carter-Reagan	Inflation	23rd of 41 issues	Middle 33%
1984	Mondale-Reagan	Recession	17th of 51 issues	Upper 33%
1988	Dukakis-Bush	Drugs	8th of 26 issues	Upper 33%
1992	Clinton-Bush	Economy	5th of 24 issues	Upper 33%
1996	Clinton-Dole	Crime	6th of 52 issues	Upper 33%
2000	Gore-Bush	Education	1st of 11 issues	First
2004	Kerry-Bush	War/Iraq	7th of 43 issues	Upper 33%

Source: Roper Center at University of Connecticut, Public Opinion Online.

In 1994, Republicans made historic midterm gains. In its "Contract with America," the new Republican majority committed to roll back the federal government and abolish several cabinet agencies, including the Department of Education. This push encountered broad opposition, however, with 80 percent of voters rejecting proposals to eliminate the department.[3]

In 1996, Republicans nominated Senate Majority Leader Bob Dole for president. Dole's primary educational plank was a firm embrace of school choice. The effort fell flat. Clinton enjoyed a 64 percent to 31 percent advantage when the public was asked to choose between the candidates on education.[4] Some accounts gave Clinton an even larger margin—CNN exit polling, for instance, showed a staggering 78 percent to 16 percent edge.[5] For Republicans, this deficit loomed especially large because education, once deemed an afterthought at the federal level, had become a consistently top-tier issue in the 1990s (see table 2.1).

Education and the 2000 Election

In 2000, the Republicans nominated Texas governor George W. Bush. Bush espoused a "compassionate conservatism," his vision of which was spelled out most clearly in his July 22, 1999, "duty of hope" speech. While proclaiming that his would "not be the failed compassion of towering, distant bureaucracies," Bush criticized conservatives who doubted that the federal government could help solve social problems. Rejecting Ronald Reagan's famed formulation that "government is the problem," Bush dismissed as "a destructive mindset . . . [the] idea that if government would only get out of our way, all our problems would be solved."[6]

Key to Bush's compassionate conservatism was his pledge that "no child would be left behind." As governor, Bush had championed Texas's accountability plan as an engine of opportunity for the disadvantaged. His embrace of the state's nationally heralded model, with its emphasis on standards, testing, and accountability, positioned Bush to advocate school choice and to criticize the public school establishment without appearing hostile to teachers or public schooling.

Prodded by polls reporting that voters saw education as the most pressing issue for a prosperous and peaceful nation, both Bush and Democratic nominee Al Gore promised aggressive action.[7] Bush touted Texas's standards-based accountability program, leavened with charter schools and school choice. Gore sounded similar notes, declaring, "Every state and every school district should be required to identify failing schools, and work to turn them around—with strict accountability for results, and strong incentives for success. And if these failing schools don't improve quickly, they should be shut down fairly and fast."[8] Their similar stances reflected agreement that school improvement required states to set explicit academic standards, ensure that students and schools met those standards, and intervene in schools that failed to meet them.

In addressing school choice and accountability, Bush inverted the now familiar Republican formula—giving pride of place to standards, testing, and accountability rather than to choice. This tactic proved effective, as polling suggested that voters were more disposed to believe that Republicans could deliver effective accountability than in the promise of vouchers.

As Clinton had previously, Gore called for more spending and used that charge to challenge his opponent's commitment to schooling. However, Bush's bona fides permitted him to effectively respond that compassion

Table 2.2 Public attitudes toward the major-party candidates
on education, 1984–2000

Year	Democrat	Republican	Advantage for Democrat
1984	42% (Mondale)	39% (Reagan)	+3
1988	51% (Dukakis)	34% (Bush)	+17
1992	47% (Clinton)	24% (Bush)	+23
1996	64% (Clinton)	31% (Dole)	+33
2000	44% (Gore)	42% (Bush)	+2
2004	50% (Kerry)	41% (Bush)	+9

Source: Roper Center at University of Connecticut, Public Opinion Online.

should be measured by results, not dollars, and to depict Gore as a captive of the public school establishment. In 2000, exit polls showed Bush erasing the enormous lead that Clinton had enjoyed over Dole on education, running even with Gore on the issue that voters termed the most important in a photo finish election (see table 2.2).

Some conservatives worried about the price of "compassionate conservatism" and its implications for new federal activity. In *Feds in the Classroom*, Cato Institute analyst Neal McCluskey argued that "Bush was . . . abandoning the wing of his party that still pined for abolition of the Department of Education and a return to state and local control of education. Indeed, at the 2000 Republican Convention Bush succeeded in excluding a plank from the platform calling for abolition of the department and claimed when he introduced his blueprint that 'change will not come by disdaining or dismantling the federal role in education.' "[9]

The No Child Left Behind Act

On January 8, 2002, President Bush signed NCLB into law. Surrounded by smiling members of the Democratic and Republican leadership, he declared, "As of this hour, America's schools will be on a new path of reform, and a new path of results."[10]

Enacted less than four months after the September 11, 2001, terrorist attacks, NCLB's passage in many ways marked the high-water mark of post-9/11 bipartisan comity. After a spring and summer spent wrestling over thorny technical disputes regarding programs and requirements, the key figures quickly resolved the final points of dispute and reached a compromise that flew through both houses of Congress with large, bipartisan majorities. The vote was 87–10 in the Senate and 381–41 in the House of Representatives.

Bush's leadership largely squelched concerns about "big government" among conservatives who had helped to sink the Clinton administration's less ambitious 1999 proposal. Eager to support a Republican president after eight years under a Democratic White House, conservatives who had backed the 1994 pledge to abolish the Department of Education swallowed their doubts and backed NCLB—allowing Bush to win landmark legislation that would have likely floundered in a GOP-controlled Congress had it been pushed by a Democratic president.

Representative John Boehner, Republican from Ohio and chair of the House Committee on Education and the Workforce, termed the law his "proudest achievement" in his years on Capitol Hill. Ted Kennedy, senator from Massachusetts and the ranking Democrat on the Senate Health, Education, Labor, and Pensions Committee, proclaimed, "This is a defining issue about the . . . future of democracy, the future of liberty, and the future of the United States. . . . No piece of legislation will have a greater impact or influence on that."[11]

The Elementary and Secondary Education Act

Formally, NCLB was the seventh reauthorization of ESEA, first enacted in 1965. The original ESEA included five titles. Of these, the most significant was Title I, which provided federal aid for disadvantaged children. Like all legislation, ESEA had to be reauthorized at regular intervals. Reauthorizations in the 1970s and 1980s added new provisions and tinkered with formulas but did not revisit ESEA's fundamental design.

From its inception, there were concerns that schools were not accountable for student learning under ESEA. In securing the passage of the bill, U.S. commissioner of education Francis Keppel addressed Democratic senator Robert Kennedy's desire for evidence that new dollars would make a difference in the education of poor and minority children. While Keppel promised that ESEA would be carefully evaluated, it was not until the 1990s that policymakers proposed holding schools and districts responsible for the achievement of Title I students.[12]

The first attempt to reshape ESEA occurred in 1994, when President Bill Clinton pursued a reauthorization that built on previous reform efforts. He successfully proposed a companion bill to the 1994 ESEA. Under the new ESEA and companion "Goals 2000," states were required to establish academic standards in each grade and create tests to assess performance. Tests were to be administered at least three times between grades 3 and 12.

The U.S. Department of Education's ability to enforce the provisions was limited, however, by compromises, particularly those demanded by congressional Republicans fearful of federal overreach. Given weak federal enforcement, most states failed to act. In 2002, two years after the target date for full compliance, just sixteen states had fully complied with the 1994 law.

In 1999, ESEA was again due for reauthorization. The Clinton administration forwarded a proposal that built on the 1994 law, requiring states to regularly test all students and envisioning a bigger federal role in ensuring compliance. Republicans countered with a plan called the Academic Achievement for All Act ("Straight A's"), which proposed to provide states with flexibility in return for results-based accountability. Democratic senators Evan Bayh and Joe Lieberman offered a centrist alternative, "Three R's," which proposed a less radical kind of accountability-for-flexibility swap. The proposals went nowhere.

The Bush Administration and No Child Left Behind

In 2001, within days of taking office, Bush sent a legislative blueprint to Capitol Hill that drew heavily on his Texas experience. The slender twenty-six-page document entitled "No Child Left Behind" rested on four principles. It sought to "increase accountability for student performance," "focus on what works," "reduce bureaucracy and increase flexibility," and "empower parents."[13] In the first weeks of the new administration, as Bush promised to reach across the aisle, the proposal was seized by receptive Democrats seeking common ground. Bush's proposal particularly earned a favorable reaction from several New Democrats who noted that key elements were similar to those in their proposal for the 1999 reauthorization.

Bush suggested a simple bargain: the federal government would demand more accountability for achievement while providing schools and states more flexibility and funding. The White House proposal called for annual testing of all students in grades 3 through 8, with student performance publicly reported and broken out by race and class. Schools that failed to demonstrate acceptable performance for two straight years would be subjected to corrective action. If schools failed to perform adequately for three straight years, disadvantaged students could use Title I funds to attend any high-performing public or private school of their choice—essentially transforming federal aid into a voucher. States were also to be granted more flexibility. For instance, they were offered new leeway in spending federal dollars for teacher quality, with aid targeted to states that embraced reforms like merit-based pay. The document also proposed a federally funded "Reading First" initia tive and emphasized improved math and science instruction, English fluency for "Limited English Proficient" students, parental options, and school safety.[14]

This vision had much in common with Clinton's 1994 and 1999 proposals. One congressional aide who had worked in Clinton's Department of Education said, "The Bush administration took the Clinton administration's ideas and ran with them."[15] Tom Payzant, who served in Clinton's Department of Education, observed, "NCLB is consistent with the 1994 reauthorization, but there's a level of prescription with respect to implementation that [Democrats] would have been soundly criticized for."[16] Republican representative Bob Schaffer of Colorado would later note, "[NCLB] was not a unique idea by candidate George Bush . . . it was attempted during the Clinton Administration, too. The difference is this: When President Clinton was in the White House . . . not only did [Republicans] kill the bills . . . we boasted . . . we had avoided this train wreck of consolidating education authority in Washington."[17]

Meanwhile, despite concerns about Bush's proposal, conservatives generally held their fire. While Republicans had called for abolishing the U.S. Department of Education as recently as the 1996 party platform, no vocal criticism of the Bush plan emerged from the Right.

In January 2001, ten senators reintroduced the New Democrats' 2000 proposal the same day that Bush unveiled his NCLB blueprint. In February 2001, Senator Dianne Feinstein sent Bush a letter reporting that many New Democrats shared the White House's emphasis on student results, local flexibility, parental choice and charter schooling, and reduced regulation and bureaucracy.[18]

From the outset, the Bush administration also sought support from more liberal members of Congress. The New Democrats were themselves leery of seeming too out of step with the party's liberal wing. Accordingly, both Bush and the New Democrats actively courted two key liberals—Massachusetts senator Edward Kennedy and California representative George Miller, the ranking Democrats on the education committees. Miller and Kennedy, long-time champions of federal educational efforts, would play an outsized role in shaping the final legislation.

Crafting a Bipartisan Bill

The price of broad congressional support was a radical overhaul of the original White House proposal. The final, elephantine compromise melded Bush's blueprint to a host of equity-oriented provisions, while sharply curbing proposals for school choice and state flexibility. Although NCLB came to be seen as a "Bush" law—in no small part because the White House spent the next several years touting it while Democrats backpedaled—the final bill's 681 pages were filled with a tangled assemblage of White House proposals, New Democratic ideas, and provisions championed by Kennedy and Miller.

At the same time, the White House skirmished with and occasionally appeased die-hard conservatives. Republican representative Bob Schaffer's proposal to "prohibit the Department of Education from dictating or controlling state education curricula" was adopted by a simple voice vote. A leading skeptic of NCLB, the Colorado representative worked with other conservative backbenchers to insist on language limiting efforts to extend the federal government's reach. Consequently, NCLB's expansive ambitions and language were more aspirational than explicit, a state of affairs that would greatly complicate life for the Department of Education when it came to implementation. For instance, the law's complicated "remedy cascade" was to be administered by states and school districts and involved hardly any measures that would directly impact the livelihood of individual educators or school officials.

Appeasing Republican backbenchers without alienating its Democratic allies was important for a White House confronting fierce opposition from the public education establishment, the National Education Association, and progressives skeptical of additional testing. Anti-testing crusader and popular author Alfie Kohn argued in January 2001, just days after the initial White House plan was unveiled, "The people who understand how kids learn are appalled at this. This is horrendous, simplistic, test-driven reform."[19] In the House, Democrat Betty McCollum of Minnesota offered an amendment that sought to remove all language stipulating standardized testing in grades 3 through 8 and replacing it with a "Sense of Congress" resolution encouraging districts to adopt testing. The voice vote on the amendment was close, but, per an agreement with George Miller, McCollum never called for a roll call vote.[20]

A useful rallying point for the White House and its allies was the decision to require that every school would have 100 percent of tested students proficient in reading and math by 2014 (twelve years after the law took effect). This audacious goal provided civil rights groups with a statutory lever with which they might shame local authorities and pry loose new resources in the courts, progressives with a bold commitment to the disadvantaged, and the administration with evidence of its compassion and an inspiring goal that could help to shift school cultures.

The final bill's most significant provisions dealt with testing, accountability, and teacher quality. Building on Bush's initial blueprint, the testing and accountability provisions were draped in ambiguity in an attempt to avoid anything that smacked of a national curriculum or national tests. In the end, federal funding was conditioned on states adopting standards, regular tests, and a system for identifying and addressing schools deemed as failing to make AYP, but the law carefully specified that the feds would not mandate particular standards, tests, targets, or definitions of AYP.

NCLB marked both a revolution and a continued evolution in federal education policy. On the one hand, the law merged two decades of reform efforts, but, as Chester Finn and this author observed in *The Public Interest*, "In other respects, it has no precedent: it creates stern federal directives regarding test use and consequences; puts federal bureaucrats in charge of approving state standards and accountability plans; sets a single nationwide timetable for boosting achievement; and prescribes specific remedies for underperforming schools."[21]

Some on the left viewed the final bill as a massive progressive triumph. Indeed, Robert Gordon, an education advisor to Democratic presidential nominee John Kerry during the 2004 election, would attack the Democratic critics of NCLB for betraying liberal values. Writing in the *New Republic*, Gordon explained, "Progressives are misled by the logic of their own Bush-hatred: Bush is for NCLB, so NCLB must be bad. Never mind that President Clinton embraced accountability before President Bush." He elaborated, "At its heart, [NCLB] is the sort of law liberals once dreamed about. In the 1970s, liberal litigators fell one vote short of a Supreme Court decision requiring evenhanded education funding. NCLB doesn't guarantee funding, but it goes one step further by demanding educational results. . . . The law requires a form of affirmative action: States must show that minority and poor students are achieving proficiency like everyone else, or else provide remedies targeted to the schools those students attend."[22]

School Choice

Perhaps nowhere was conservative displeasure with NCLB greater than when it came to school choice and vouchers. Bush's original blueprint called for increased school choice, including funds to "assist charter schools with start-up costs, facilities, and other needs associated with creating high-quality schools."[23] It also proposed funding for vouchers, stating, "If the school fails to make adequate yearly progress after three years, disadvantaged students within the school may use Title I funds to transfer to a higher performing public or private school, or receive supplemental education services from a provider of choice."[24] While school choice and vouchers in particular were ostensibly Bush priorities, the administration determined early on—in spring 2001—that it lacked the votes for school vouchers and would not let such proposals be a deal breaker.[25]

While NCLB was under consideration in the House, three members of the GOP leadership—Dick Armey, John Boehner, and Tom DeLay—offered an amendment to reinsert the voucher provision, emphasizing that it was a part of the "President's original plan."[26] Democratic representative Dale Kildee of Michigan opposed the amendment, stating, "In committee, all private school voucher provisions were removed from the bill with bipartisan support. I believe that the passage of this amendment does jeopardize the many months of bipartisan work that have gone into producing this legislation."[27] Democratic representative David Wu of Oregon declared that the amendment's passage would fracture the bill's fragile bipartisan coalition, saying, "It is a make-or-break amendment as to whether we are going to have a truly bipartisan bill." The Armey-Boehner-DeLay Amendment was eventually defeated 155–273.[28]

Whether this result represented a strategic decision or merely a lack of votes is an open question. Then undersecretary of education Eugene Hickock would later explain that the president did not want to "sacrifice accountability on the altar of school choice."[29] The administration's chief NCLB negotiator, Texas attorney Sandy Kress, disputed that account, declaring, "We fought for [vouchers] and found insufficient support for it or anything like it to pass. . . . We never compromised on choice. There were votes on a variety of choice proposals. Other than public-school choice and supplemental services, they all went down by significant margins."[30]

Under the final legislation, the only explicit school choice option that remained was the provision that students attending a Title I school that failed to make AYP for two consecutive years would have the option of transferring to an "adequately" performing public school.

The Highly Qualified Teacher Provision

When it came to the law's groundbreaking "highly qualified teacher" provision, Bush's original blueprint contemplated nothing like the provision that emerged. Bush had proposed combining eighty-seven federal teacher training programs into "performance-based grants to states and localities" in order to give states and localities more flexibility and to promote innovative programs like merit pay.[31]

To help win bipartisan backing, however, House education chair John Boehner gave George Miller the lead in drafting the teacher quality provision. Miller, a veteran with a long-standing interest in teacher quality, crafted prescriptive requirements intended to increase the number of licensed teachers in schools serving poor communities. Miller called for requiring new and veteran teachers to hold a college degree and full state certification and to demonstrate subject content mastery via majoring in the subject or passing a test. Miller's proposal stood in stark contrast to the results-in-return-for-flexibility approach favored by Bush and the New Democrats.

Miller's stance represented a frontal rejection of the conservative argument that schools of education and teaching licensure were part of the problem. Conservative scholars argued that there was little evidence that certification vouchsafed teacher quality or that required preparation improved teacher effectiveness and there was reason to fear that these requirements deterred potentially promising candidates. During the year preceding the enactment of NCLB, Rod Paige, Bush's first-term secretary of education, called for loosening licensure regulations and endorsed alternative licensure programs.

The administration ultimately accepted Miller's proposal—taking solace in the stipulation that teachers would be required to demonstrate content knowledge, a provision they hoped would also discipline schools of education. During negotiations, however, Ted Kennedy, a long-standing ally of teachers' unions, eroded the significance of the content knowledge requirement by crafting an exception for veteran teachers termed a "high objective uniform state standard of evaluation" (HOUSSE). HOUSSE allowed veteran teachers to demonstrate subject matter competence without having to pass a test. Critics decried the measure as a sop to the teachers' unions, with Stanford University professor Terry Moe asserting, "The HOUSSE provisions create a loophole big enough to drive three million veteran teachers through."[32]

As on so many counts, the administration accepted the Miller-Kennedy language as the price of success—but political officials at the Department of Education would later struggle to interpret the language in a way that protected nontraditional teacher recruitment programs like Teach for America.

Flexibility

Both the Bush administration's early blueprint for NCLB and the reform proposals floated by the New Democrats included plans to reduce paperwork and provide flexibility by consolidating small programs into broad funding streams. NCLB did promote simplification in a few areas, giving states and districts limited freedom to reallocate federal aid and creating a flexibility demonstration project, but even these measures ultimately reflected a compromise.

In general, conservatives deemed NCLB a disappointment when it came to offering schools, districts, and states more flexibility and reducing paperwork. Prior to Bush's election, most conservatives supported the extremely aggressive 1999 Straight A's bill, which would have given any state or district broad flexibility to use funds from fourteen different programs in exchange for meeting certain student achievement goals. One proposed amendment along the lines of "Straight A's," offered by Republican representative Jim De-Mint of South Carolina, was withdrawn at Bush's request.[33] Instead, a compromise negotiated by Republican representative Peter Hoekstra of Michigan with Ted Kennedy made it into the final bill as the tiny Straight A's demonstration program.[34]

Conservative Disenchantment

Cheered as a reassuring example of post-9/11 unity, the compromise-laden bill enjoyed lukewarm support among the small government conservatives who had resisted Clinton's efforts. Nonetheless, Republicans held their noses and supported the new president. House Republican minority whip Roy Blunt explained, "I always had misgivings. But I did vote for it on the basis that maybe he was right and this was his big domestic initiative and let's give him a chance."[35] Representative Michael Castle of Delaware, an influential Republican on education, would later observe, "If a president's sailing along at 80 percent approval rating, members are going to be very reluctant to say no. People were willing to give the president the benefit of the doubt."[36] As political scientist Andrew Rudalevige remarked shortly after the law's passage, "Many lawmakers wanted the president to succeed (especially on a campaign priority) more than they needed to be faithful to past positions."[37]

Former Republican representative Bob Schaffer of Colorado has been one of the most explicit critics of NCLB, suggesting that it foreshadowed a broader retreat from principle. In a 2007 speech, he declared, "I think people believed that they needed to give the President a win. . . . In some ways, it foretold what was going to happen on some other issues, including spending. The Congress rolled over for this White House and, I think, moved away from some of our principles."[38]

Perhaps the most revealing insight into how Bush changed education politics was that no conservative of any note challenged the administration's support for an accountability system that explicitly categorized students by race. Amidst ongoing challenges to affirmative action in state law and higher education, a federal measure requiring states to identify every student by race and then report test scores—and impose sanctions—on that basis marked a radical departure. It might have been expected to provoke a firestorm. Instead, even prominent champions of color-blind policies remained silent.

The Implementation of No Child Left Behind

Implementing NCLB proved a staggering challenge. Monitoring state accountability systems, ensuring fidelity to the NCLB remedies, and overseeing implementation relating to matters such as "scientifically based research" would prove incompatible with machinery first employed by ESEA in 1965 to funnel dollars to states, districts, and schools. The expectation that states would devise standards, seize low-performing districts, and monitor the quality of supplemental service providers, or that districts could restructure troubled schools, proved to sorely overestimate both capacity and will.[39] In practice, the Department of Education had to rely on moral suasion and political allies to push states and districts along.

Moreover, in crafting NCLB, the administration and its allies had found common ground in part by embracing unassailable sentiments like "universal proficiency." The result was a popular bill that promised 100 percent proficiency, offered impressive-sounding remedies for low-performing schools, guaranteed that every class would be taught by a "highly qualified teacher," and insisted that federal dollars would be spent in accord with "scientifically based research." The problem was ambiguity as to what these terms meant, yielding immense confusion about how these provisions should be implemented and giving little attention to possible unanticipated consequences. The requirement that states set steadily increasing proficiency targets, coupled with an ability to manipulate the proficiency bar, had the perverse effect of rewarding states that set a low bar. In an ironic twist, fifty states setting divergent standards under the nominally uniform framework of NCLB fueled calls for national standards—a decade after Hill Republicans had fought to squelch the Clinton administration's proposed voluntary national standards.

Two former Republican secretaries of education would argue in the *Washington Post* that the politically expedient compromise had proven unworkable. They wrote, "Out of respect for federalism and mistrust of Washington, much of the GOP has expected individual states to set their own academic standards and devise their own tests and accountability systems. That was the approach of the No Child Left Behind Act—which moved as boldly as it could while still achieving bipartisan support. It sounds good, but it is working badly."[40]

Weak sanctions and uncertain interventions further undermined the notion that NCLB was harnessing incentives or market pressures. In schools subject to NCLB-mandated public school choice, for instance, there were no adverse effects for any educator. The only consequence for schools or districts was the requirement that they might have to spend some Title I dollars providing student transportation. The supplemental services provision might require a small portion of district Title I money to flow to private providers, but as of 2007 there was no evidence that this spending had cost a single educator a job or pay raise—and most of the outlays, even by for-profit providers, were flowing back to local teachers teaching after hours for these firms.[41]

Effective behavior-changing regimes are rooted in realistic expectations. That pragmatism leads self-interested workers to take goals seriously. When goals are patently unreachable, as is the case for many schools and districts, the logic of accountability changes in important ways. If employees know they are unlikely to reach their objective, their primary motivation is merely to avoid trouble when they fail. Since unrealistic goals make failure inevitable, they have the perverse effect of focusing employees on compliance rather than on the ostensible goals.

Keeping the States in Line

One awkward question posed by NCLB was how the administration would respond to states that pushed back against new requirements in the name of states' rights. The White House faced a thorny choice: acquiescing and allowing states to undercut the reach of NCLB or challenging those states willing to forfeit federal dollars by opting out of NCLB. The administration aggressively chose to rein states in.

This was consistent with the strategy of wielding the law as a cudgel with which to change the culture of public schools. Refusing to tolerate any substantial criticism of the law, the administration tended to freeze out those officials, analysts, and educators it regarded as critics. In 2006, Secretary of Education Margaret Spellings famously told reporters, "I like to talk about No Child Left Behind as Ivory soap. It's 99.9 percent pure. There's not much needed in the way of changes."[42] Doubling down on that party line, Deputy Secretary Ray Simon echoed the once popular Bush administration mantra on Iraq, telling the *Washington Post*, "We need to stay the course. The mission is do-able, and we don't need to back off that right now."[43]

By 2004, more than a dozen states had expressed interest in throwing off the mandates embodied in the ambitious law. In Virginia, the Republican-controlled House of Delegates voted 98–1 to condemn NCLB for "represent[ing] the most sweeping intrusions into state and local control of education in the history of the United States."[44]

In 2005, with reliably Republican Utah on the verge of opting out of NCLB, the U.S. Department of Education responded by mounting a full-scale assault.[45] The department leadership implied that the anti-NCLB leaders were insufficiently concerned about the plight of minority children. The Education Department issued a release that declared, "States across the nation who have embraced *No Child Left Behind* have shown progress: student achievement is rising and the achievement gap is closing. The same could be true in Utah, whose achievement gap between Hispanics and their peers is the third largest in the nation and has not improved significantly in over a decade."[46]

In its response to Utah, the administration lined up with the influential, progressive education advocacy group the Education Trust (a spin-off from the left-leaning bastion the Children's Defense Fund). The Education Trust charged in the Utah case that although achievement among minority students was lagging that of white students in the state, "some lawmakers and educators in Utah are expending enormous energy to fend off . . . the federal law that aims to raise overall achievement and close gaps between groups."[47] Similar language was used by the administration and its allies to answer Connecticut's objections to NCLB.[48]

The Politics of Spending

The administration found itself, out of necessity or conviction, bragging about its largesse when it came to K–12 education. Despite criticism from Democrats, funding for education increased more dramatically under President Bush than it had under President Clinton. In Bush's first term, between 2001 and 2004, federal education appropriations nearly doubled, from $29.4 billion to $55.7 billion. It was not until after Republicans lost Congress in 2006 that the president would seek to make a virtue of budgetary discipline.

As former Department of Education staffer Lawrence Uzzell wryly wrote in critiquing NCLB, "Especially striking is the boast that Bush has increased federal spending on education faster than any president since Lyndon Johnson. That is a reversal as profound as the Clinton administration's welfare reform in 1996; in both cases the party in power accepted ideas long associated with its opponents. The Republican reversal is the more stunning of the two because . . . as recently as 1996, the party's platform pledged to abolish the U.S. Department of Education."[49]

Just as Democrats have long had trouble getting credit for tax cuts, the Bush administration had trouble scoring political points or winning Democratic plaudits even for its relatively lavish spending. Miller and Kennedy, Bush's erstwhile partners, were particularly critical. Miller said, "The Bush administration and congressional Republicans have retreated from the level of funding promised."[50] Kennedy argued in a *Washington Post* op-ed, "The federal government has failed to provide the resources that states and school districts need. . . . Assessment and accountability without the funding needed to implement change is a recipe for failure."[51]

The New Politics of Education

Where Republicans had once enjoyed success blaming the problematic consequences of popular Great Society initiatives on fuzzy thinking and undisciplined spending, now Democrats could reciprocate by critiquing the Bush administration for incompetent implementation and inadequate funding (justly or not). Whereas programs like Model Cities and Aid to Families with Dependent Children had once provided conservatives with flesh-and-blood examples of incompetence and perverse incentives—enabling them to embrace a "safety net" in principle while decrying Democratic legislation—so NCLB now permitted Democrats to critique troubling examples of testing while voicing support for the principle of accountability.

Key members of the Bush team had always recognized that implementation would depend in critical ways on the inclination of educators to "do the right thing." As the administration's chief NCLB negotiator Sandy Kress recalled in 2007, "Curricula only narrow when poor teachers and/or administrators allow that to happen. It's pathetic. Poor practitioners do this and then blame it on NCLB. Ridiculous. . . . That some engage in goofy practice should never be the basis for policy."[52] Ultimately, though, the law offered few tools, and the Department of Education had few ideas beyond moral suasion with which to ensure that educators did not respond to NCLB by embracing "goofy" practices.

By 2007, the administration faced a full-fledged backlash from Republicans on Capitol Hill, in a clash that looked much like the intraparty fight over immigration reform. "Small government conservatives" accused the White House of abandoning conservative principles in the service of grandiose ambition and flawed political strategy, while Bush championed his compassionate vision and attacked his opponents for small-mindedness, bigotry, and a lack of vision. By summer 2007, five Republican senators and more than fifty House members were calling for a repeal of NCLB.

NCLB was due for reauthorization in 2007. A weakened administration, despite fervent efforts, could not reach a deal with Kennedy and Miller, now chairing the respective education committees in a Democratic Congress. This reflected both disagreements among NCLB's authors on needed revisions and Miller and Kennedy's increasing distance from the post-2006 Democratic majority—which felt far less investment in NCLB than did they.

The American public has a pragmatic but precarious view of educational accountability—one that worked for Bush when he spoke abstractly of the "soft bigotry of low expectations" in 2000, but which has since fed discontent with NCLB. Americans express a strong affection for accountability in principle but have much more mixed opinions of it when it affects real schools and students, especially those in their community. Attitudes toward NCLB have grown more skeptical over time. In 2003, 18 percent of respondents were positive about NCLB, and 13 percent were negative.[53] By 2008, opinion was split, with 32 percent favorable and 33 percent unfavorable. Public skepticism forced federal officials to engage in a delicate dance to retain public support. In fact, in 2008, Gallup reported that if "large numbers of public schools fail" to make the NCLB requirements, 42 percent of respondents would regard that as evidence of school failure while almost as many, 38 percent, would see it as evidence that the law was flawed.[54]

While opposition to NCLB proved a reliable applause line for Democratic presidential nominees in 2004 and 2008, no major Democratic candidate suggested abandoning testing and accountability. In 2008, Democratic presidential nominee Barack Obama called for more funding and major revisions while vaguely endorsing standards, testing, and accountability. Obama's opponent, Republican presidential nominee John McCain, voiced similarly vague support for accountability and the principles of NCLB. Despite concerns and criticism, the tenets of NCLB appear likely to shape the contours of federal education policy for years to come.

Conclusion

Just as some have described welfare reform as Ronald Reagan's greatest domestic accomplishment, so might NCLB be aptly termed Bill Clinton's crowning achievement. Just as welfare reform required time to mature and a Democratic president to win crucial Democratic votes and validate the emergence of a new consensus, so did New Democratic efforts to establish federal leadership on educational accountability require a Republican president to broaden the coalition and quiet conservative concerns about federal overreach. The irony is that NCLB leavened the New Democratic push for accountability with Great Society–style ambition and race-conscious rhetoric and machinery, while lacking the attention to program design that characterized Clinton-era efforts to reform welfare and "reinvent government." The resulting regime relied more on moral exhortation than on more calculated goals, metrics, or incentives.

Whatever one makes of the Bush record when it came to tax cutting, foreign affairs, or judicial appointments, it is difficult to argue that the administration championed conservative principles when it came to domestic programs or fiscal discipline. In K–12 schooling, the Bush White House involved Washington in defining teacher quality, embraced an accountability system that labels children by race, made closing racial achievement gaps in basic skills the central tenet of school reform, and turned bragging about increased education spending into a bipartisan sport. In so doing, it established expansive precedents for future Democratic administrations and created commitments that will be difficult for the GOP to unwind.

In fact, on questions like education and immigration, the administration adopted the rhetoric and tactics that conservatives traditionally associate with periods of unified Democratic control. This showed up in the administration's preference for grand, aspirational policies, willingness to condone large budgetary commitments, and tendency to depict opponents—particularly those on its right—as mean-spirited or racially insensitive. The Bush experience raises the question as to whether some of these behaviors typically disparaged by conservatives as "liberal" are instead merely the tools of majoritarian governance—employed to prod reluctant legislators and voters to support ambitious bills whose tangled provisions might otherwise attract skepticism.

Given the degree to which it sought to accommodate Democratic concerns and forge a bipartisan bill, why did Bush receive so little credit from the Left and why did Democrats later walk away from the bill? At least four explanations apply. First, growing polarization over the war in Iraq colored popular perception of Bush and led many on the left and right to react based on passion rather than the particulars of policy. Elected officials are consistently forced to decide between pragmatic governance and the demands of party loyalty—and that tension may become all-consuming under a president as polarizing as Bush. Second, Democrats wanted NCLB funded at rates that exceeded even the substantial increases the administration proposed. Third, the National Education Association (NEA), the larger and more influential of the nation's two major teachers' unions, was dead set against NCLB's key accountability, testing, and remedy provisions. While some "reform" Democrats stood with the administration, many others were inclined to line up with the NEA's 2.5 million members—meaning that the law's bipartisan basis was always more fragile than it may have appeared. Finally, the American public consistently embraces accountability in the abstract but expresses concerns about how it works in practice—and the Democrats, as the opposition party, were naturally inclined to cater to those sentiments.[55]

When NCLB was enacted, in the months after 9/11, Bush enjoyed extraordinary public approval ratings of 90 percent or more. Bush's declining support later allowed Democrats to walk away from the law's unpopular details while blaming any concerns on insufficient funding and the administration's botched implementation. As George Miller, by then chair of the House education committee, opined in 2006, "I would give [NCLB] an 'A'" for "trying to develop a system to make sure that each and every child is proficient," but "an 'F' for funding" and a "'C' for implementation."[56] Senator Kennedy declared in 2007 that NCLB "has become a symbol of controversial, flawed and failed policy."[57]

Meanwhile, White House efforts did not yield the anticipated political rewards. In 2008, the annual Gallup poll of education found that voters thought Democrats cared more about education than Republicans by 44 to 27 percent.[58] Michael Petrilli, a former Bush Department of Education official, opined in 2008, "President Bush set out to improve America's public schools—and to ensure that his Republican Party got credit for it. According to the public at least, he failed on both counts."[59] The largest problem for Republicans was anger among suburban voters who thought that NCLB's focus on poor and minority children was narrowing curricula, shifting attention from advanced programs, and leading schools to shortchange proficient students.

For all its reversals, the administration could claim notable advances. NCLB yielded immense transparency, focused unprecedented attention on achievement, offered political cover to superintendents eager to challenge the status quo, and did reshuffle the national politics of schooling. Influential civil rights groups, most notably the Citizens Commission for Civil Rights and the Education Trust, became stalwart administration allies. Abandoning an earlier era's focus on desegregation and court-ordered remedies, they embraced NCLB as a way to force districts to focus on educating poor and minority students. In this fight, progressives allied with business groups like the U.S. Chamber of Commerce and the Business Roundtable that regarded NCLB as a critical win in addressing the quality of the workforce. These developments marked a historic break between key civil rights advocates and once-staunch allies in the teachers' unions.

The shape of Bush's education legacy will ultimately hinge on which proves more lasting: the cultural transformation that the administration sought, or the disenchantment, implementation headaches, and unanticipated consequences that accompanied it. The Bush administration launched a new era in K–12 schooling, one marked by the emergence of a "reform" wing willing to battle the teachers' unions inside the Democratic Party, educators focused on the racial achievement gap, and china-rattling superintendents in cities from New York to Washington, D.C., to New Orleans. Whether that new era will deliver the political or educational returns that Bush once envisioned will only become clear on his successor's watch.

The Early Obama Years

In 2008, Barack Obama ran a presidential campaign that extolled the importance of reforming and investing in education, energy, and health care in order to create a sustainable, globally competitive economy. When it came to education, he was particularly forceful—talking more bluntly about the need to improve schools and to boost teacher quality than did any previous Democratic candidate for president. In a September campaign appearance in Dayton, Ohio, Obama said, "We need a new vision for a 21st century education, one where we aren't just supporting existing schools, but spurring innovation; where we're not just investing more money, but demanding more reform; where parents take responsibility for their children's success; where our schools and government are accountable for results; where we're recruiting, retaining, and rewarding an army of new teachers, and students are excited to learn because they're attending schools of the future."[60]

This tone helped reassure independents that Obama was a forward-thinking reformer and not merely a tax-and-spend liberal. Whereas Bush used education to reassure moderates that he really was compassionate, Obama used talk of merit pay and charter schooling to reassure independents that he would not be a tool of labor but instead would pursue transformative programs.

This pitch met with popular appeal. When respondents were asked whom they would vote for if the election were solely about how to strengthen public schools, Obama led his 2009 general election opponent John McCain by 46 percent to 29 percent. People also found Obama much more likely than McCain—59 percent to 18 percent—to close the achievement gap between white and minority students. Obama even outpolled McCain on the classically Republican question of promoting parental choice, with respondents having more faith in Obama on that score by a margin of 43 percent to 32 percent.[61]

In January 2009, Barack Obama took office as the forty-fourth president. With the nation in economic distress, he immediately pushed for an enormous "stimulus" package that he said would help minimize the fallout and spur recovery. Republicans objected that the $787 billion bill that emerged from Congress was a pork-laden liberal wish list, all paid for with borrowed dollars. In conjunction with conservative critiques of Obama's efforts on health care, his calls for cap and trade legislation, his push for new financial regulations, his continuation of President Bush's Troubled Asset Relief Program, and his moves to bail out big banks, General Motors, and troubled borrowers, the vision of Obama as a popular post-partisan figure morphed into public concerns that government was out of control. His approval rating among independents plummeted from 62 percent when he took office to 44 percent by mid-November 2009, while the percentage of people who felt that the government was "doing too much" grew from 47 percent in March 2009 to 57 percent in August 2009.[62]

In response, the White House placed enormous weight on its efforts to use education as a way to reassure independents and suburban voters that Obama could be an aggressive force for reform who was willing to challenge the unions. In this, the administration was aided by the efforts of popular secretary of education Arne Duncan. Duncan, the former superintendent of Chicago Public Schools, was enthusiastically received on both sides of the aisle. In his Senate confirmation hearings, Republican senator Lamar Alexander, education secretary under President George H. W. Bush, told Duncan that "among several distinguished Cabinet appointments . . . I think you're best."[63]

The stimulus included more than $100 billion for education. Most of those dollars were distributed via familiar funding formulas, but the administration also convinced the Democratic Congress to tuck in $5 billion to fund two federal school reform programs: Race to the Top (RTT) and Investing in Innovation (i3). The administration used these competitive grant programs to signal that the American Recovery and Reinvestment Act (ARRA) was about reform as well as recovery. "This competition," Obama said of RTT, "will not be based on politics, ideology, or the preferences of a particular interest group. Instead, it will be based on a simple principle—whether a state is ready to do what works. . . . Not every state will win and not every school district will be happy with the results. But America's children, America's economy, and America itself will be better for it."[64] Arne Duncan praised the program as "a once-in-a-lifetime opportunity for the federal government to create incentives for far-reaching improvement in our nation's schools."[65]

The programs were novel. Both were vaguely defined in the ARRA legislation, leaving enormous room for Duncan's Department of Education to shape them as they saw fit. ARRA provided $4.35 billion for the RTT program, which would award funds to states that pursued four priorities: adopting internationally benchmarked standards; recruiting, developing, rewarding, and retaining effective teachers and principals; building data systems; and turning around the lowest-performing schools. The i3 program provided $650 million to support promising innovations. Both programs were unlike anything the department had previously done, in ambition and scale. By summer 2009, RTT—under the leadership of former NewSchools Venture Fund executive Joanne Weiss—had been shaped into an expansive competition that required interested states to pen sprawling plans that addressed nineteen programmatic elements. The applications, written with the aid of big-dollar consultants, stretched to many hundreds of pages—offering grand promises along with "assurances" of support from many school districts and teachers' union locals. The i3 program took shape a little more slowly, ultimately entailing three categories of competition—"Scale-up" grants for proven ventures with the potential to reach hundreds of thousands of students, "Validation" grants for promising programs ready to expand their evidence base, and "Development" grants for high-potential practices. Out of the nearly two thousand districts and nonprofits that applied for the grants, forty-nine were selected as grant recipients, with well-known ventures including the KIPP Academies and TFA claiming "Scale-up" grants of about $50 million.

RTT and i3 enjoyed raucous cheers from both sides of the aisle. Joe Williams, executive director of Democrats for Education Reform, said his group liked "the way the administration is using Race to the Top to send a message about its priorities" and the way the competition's "gotten states to take a close look at their laws and practices."[66] Even as President Obama was battered by Republicans for the stimulus and for his proposed health care reform, he was getting kudos for his education proposals from prominent conservative voices like the *Wall Street Journal*'s editorial page and *New York Times* columnist David Brooks. In March of 2009, the *Journal* ran an editorial asserting that Obama's initial education address "had him siding, in the main, with school reformers," while Brooks called for policymakers on the left and right to "push hard to fulfill the Obama administration's education reforms [which] encourage charter school innovation, improve teacher quality, support community colleges and simplify finances for college students and war veterans."[67]

The challenge was negotiating a tenuous peace with the teachers' unions, which regarded administration support for charter schooling, merit pay, and removing ineffective educators as an attack. The administration sought to negotiate that tension by emphasizing that the bulk of the $100 billion in ARRA was to support state and local government and to preserve jobs and by aggressively pushing for a successful $10 billion "Edujobs" bill in August 2010 that provided additional funds to preserve jobs and compensation for teachers. Both Obama and Duncan also worked hard to favor language that would signal their reform-mindedness without unduly offending the unions and took care to manage their relationship with union leaders.

At least through the grim midterm 2010 elections, Obama could count his educational efforts as a substantial success—with the president using the issue to burnish his credentials as an independent-minded reformer, even as he successfully pushed more than $100 billion in new federal funding out to states and districts. Whether Obama is able to credibly continue that stance, promoting education reform from Washington while simultaneously working to placate the unions with promises of new funds, is an open question in a more fiscally constrained environment.

NOTES

1. Michael Gerson, "The Audacity of Cynicism," *Washington Post*, July 2, 2008, A15.

2. At the NAACP's Seventh Biennial Daisy Bates Education Summit in Little Rock, Spellings said, "We honor the actions of the Little Rock Nine by fighting for the new civil right of a quality education for all. The *No Child Left Behind Act* is up for renewal in Congress this year. I believe it is not just an education law, it's a civil rights law." U.S. Department of Education, "Press Release: Secretary Spellings Delivers Keynote

Address at NAACP 7th Biennial Daisy Bates Education Summit," May 19, 2007, www .ed.gov/news/pressreleases/2007/05/05192007.html.

3. Roper Center for Public Opinion Research, *Public Opinion Online*, March 1995, accession no. 0232151, question no. 16, and June 1995, accession no. 0237493, question no. 24.

4. Frederick M. Hess and Patrick J. McGuinn, "Seeking the Mantle of Opportunity: Presidential Politics and the Educational Metaphor," *Education Policy* 16, no. 1 (2002): 85.

5. CNN, "Presidential Election Exit Poll Results," November 6, 1996, www.cnn .com/ALLPOLITICS/1996/elections/natl.exit.poll/index2.html.

6. George W. Bush, "The Duty of Hope," speech delivered on July 22, 1999, in Indianapolis, Indiana, www.cpjustice.org/stories/storyreader$383.

7. Frank Newport, "Economy, Education, Health, Crime and Morality Most on Americans' Minds This Election Year," *Gallup News Service*, June 22, 2000, available at www.gallup.com/poll/2797/Economy-Education-Health-Crime-Morality-Most-Americans-Mind.aspx; The Harris Poll, "Democrats Increase Lead over Republicans in Race for Congress," July 20, 2006, www.harrisi.net/harris_poll/printerfriend/index.asp ?PID=683.

8. Dave Boyer, "Bush Campaign Says It's in the Bag; Top Strategist Sees 320 Votes," *Washington Times*, November 6, 2000, A1.

9. Neal P. McCluskey, *Feds in the Classroom: How Big Government Corrupts, Cripples, and Compromises American Education* (Lanham, MD: Rowman & Littlefield, 2007), 84.

10. Office of the White House Press Secretary, "Press Release: President Signs Landmark Education Bill," January 8, 2002, www.whitehouse.gov/news/releases/2002/01 /20020108-1.html.

11. As quoted in Andrew Rudalevige, "No Child Left Behind: Forging a Congressional Compromise," in *No Child Left Behind? The Politics and Practice of School Accountability*, ed. Paul E. Peterson and Martin R. West (Washington, DC: Brookings Institution Press, 2003), 24.

12. Diane Ravitch, "A Historical Perspective on a Historic Piece of Legislation," in *Within Our Reach: How America Can Educate Every Child*, ed. John Chubb (New York: Rowman & Littlefield, 2005), 35–51.

13. President George W. Bush, "No Child Left Behind," a White House blueprint report submitted to the Speaker of the U.S. House of Representatives and the President of the U.S. Senate on January 23, 2001, www.whitehouse.gov/news/reports/no-child -left-behind.pdf.

14. Bush, "No Child Left Behind."

15. Siobhan Gorman, "Bipartisan Schoolmates," *Education Next* 2, no. 2 (2002): 36–43.

16. Julia Hanna, "The Elementary and Secondary Education Act: 40 Years Later," *Ed. Magazine*, June 1, 2005, www.gse.harvard.edu/news/2005/0819_esea.html.

17. Robert Schaffer and Peter Hoekstra, "Educational Freedom in the Wake of No Child Left Behind," *Heritage Lectures*, no. 1016 (April 25, 2007), 4.

18. Gorman, "Bipartisan Schoolmates."

19. Michelle Melendez and Martha Deller, "Bush Education Plan Gets Mixed Response," *Fort Worth Star-Telegram*, January 28, 2001, 1.

20. David Nather, "Compromises in ESEA Bills May Imperil Republican Strategy," *CQ Weekly* 59, no. 18 (May 5, 2001): 1009–11.

21. Chester E. Finn Jr. and Frederick M. Hess, "On Leaving No Child Behind," *Public Interest* 157 (Fall 2004): 38–39.

22. Robert Gordon, "Class Struggle," *New Republic* 232, no. 21/22 (June 6, 2005): 24–27.

23. Bush, "No Child Left Behind," 18.

24. Ibid., 9.

25. "Confessions of a 'No Child Left Behind' Supporter: An Interview with Sandy Kress," *Education Next* 7, no. 2 (Spring 2007): 30–37.

26. "Proceedings and Debates of the 107th Congress, First Session," *U.S. Congressional Record* 147, no. 72 (May 23, 2001): H2590.

27. Ibid., H2590.

28. Ibid., H2595.

29. As quoted in Rudalevige, "No Child Left Behind," 40.

30. "Confessions of a 'No Child Left Behind' Supporter."

31. Bush, "No Child Left Behind," 12.

32. Terry Moe, "The Qualified Teacher Charade," *Hoover Daily Report*, October 13, 2004, www.hoover.org/pubaffairs/dailyreport/archive/2827866.html.

33. "Proceedings and Debates of the 107th Congress, First Session," H2606.

34. David Nather, "As Education Bills Head for Floor Votes, Big Ideological Tests Loom in House," *CQ Weekly* 59, no. 20 (May 2001): 1157–58.

35. Peter Baker, "An Unlikely Partnership Left Behind," *Washington Post*, November 5, 2007, A01.

36. Ibid.

37. Rudalevige, "No Child Left Behind," 42.

38. Schaffer and Hoekstra, "Educational Freedom in the Wake of No Child Left Behind," 6.

39. Frederick M. Hess and Chester E. Finn Jr., "Conclusion," in *No Remedy Left Behind: Lessons from a Half-Decade of NCLB*, ed. Frederick M. Hess and Chester E. Finn Jr. (Washington, DC: AEI Press, 2007), 309–29.

40. William J. Bennett and Rod Paige, "Why We Need a National School Test," *Washington Post*, September 21, 2006, A25.

41. Ibid.

42. Lois Romano, "Tweaking of 'No Child' Seen," *Washington Post*, August 31, 2006, A04.

43. Amit Paley, "'No Child' Target Is Called Out of Reach; Goal of 100% Proficiency Debated as Congress Weighs Renewal," *Washington Post*, March 14, 2007, A1.

44. Lorraine M. McDonnell, "No Child Left Behind and the Federal Role in Education: Evolution or Revolution?" *Peabody Journal of Education* 80, no. 2 (2005): 19–38.

45. Associated Press, "Utah Snubs Federal 'No Child Left Behind,'" May 2, 2005, www.msnbc.msn.com/id/7713931/.

46. U.S. Department of Education, "Press Release: Statement by Secretary Spellings on Recent Legislative Action in Utah," April 20, 2005, www.ed.gov/news/pressreleases/2005/04/04202005a.html.

47. Education Trust, "Education Trust Statement: Utah Must Confront Inequities in Public Education," March 1, 2005, www.edtrust.org/dc/press-room/press-release/education-trust-statement-utah-must-confront-inequities-in-public-educat.

48. Margaret Spellings, "Testing Serves Students," *Hartford Courant*, March 20, 2005, A6.

49. Lawrence A. Uzzell, "No Child Left Behind: The Dangers of Centralized Education Policy," *Cato Institute Policy Analysis*, no. 544 (May 31, 2005), 2.

50. George Miller, "How to Leave No Child Behind," *Washington Post*, September 25, 2003, A32.

51. Edward M. Kennedy, "No Retreat on School Reform," *Washington Post*, March 26, 2007, A15.

52. "Confessions of a 'No Child Left Behind' Supporter."

53. Lowell C. Rose and Alec M. Gallup, "The 35th Annual Phi Delta Kappa/Gallup Poll of the Public's Attitudes toward the Public Schools," *Phi Delta Kappan* 85, no. 1 (September 2003): 45.

54. William J. Bushaw and Alec M. Gallup, "The 40th Annual Phi Delta Kappa/Gallup Poll of the Public's Attitudes toward the Public Schools," *Phi Delta Kappan* 90, no. 1 (September 2008): 19.

55. Frederick M. Hess, "Refining or Retreating? High-Stakes Accountability in the States," in *No Child Left Behind? The Politics and Practice of School Accountability*, ed. Paul E. Peterson and Martin R. West (Washington, D.C.: Brookings Institution Press, 2003), 55–79.

56. Business Roundtable Speech Transcript, "The Fourth Annual No Child Left Behind Forum: Assessing Progress, Addressing Problems, Advancing Performance," September 20, 2006, www.businessroundtable.org/newsroom/document.aspx?qs=5976BF807822B0F1ADD408422FB51711FCF53CE.

57. Baker, "An Unlikely Partnership Left Behind."

58. Bushaw and Gallup, "40th Annual Phi Delta Kappa/Gallup Poll," 10.

59. Michael Petrilli, "New Education Next Survey: The Nation's Sour Mood Bleeds into Education," weblog, *Flypaper*, August 12, 2008, Thomas B. Fordham Institute, www.educationgadfly.net/flypaper/2008/08/new-education-next-survey-the-nations-sour-mood-bleeds-into-education/.

60. Barack Obama, "A 21st Century Education" (remarks at campaign event in Dayton, OH, September 9, 2008), http://my.barackobama.com/page/community/post/amandascott/gG5pB4.

61. Amy Hetzner, "Poll Shows Obama Leads McCain on Education Issues," *Milwaukee Journal Sentinel*, August 21, 2008, www.jsonline.com/news/education/32603544.html.

62. Polling data compiled by Gallup, Inc. Approval rating numbers available at www.gallup.com/poll/124922/Presidential-Approval-Center.aspx. "View of Government" polling data available at www.gallup.com/poll/27286/Government.aspx.

63. Maria Glod, "Education Nominee Is Warmly Received in Senate," *Washington Post*, January 14, 2009, www.washingtonpost.com/wp-dyn/content/article/2009/01/13/AR2009011301651.html.

64. U.S. Department of Education, "President Obama, U.S. Secretary of Education Announce National Competition to Advance School Reform," July 24, 2009,

www.whitehouse.gov/the-press-office/president-obama-us-secretary-education-dun can-announce-national-competition-advance.

65. Arne Duncan, "The Race to the Top Begins" (remarks announcing the Race to the Top Competition, July 24, 2009), www.ed.gov/news/speeches/race-top-begins.

66. Sam Dillon, "Dangling Money, Obama Pushes Education Shift," *New York Times*, August 16, 2009, www.dfer.org/2009/08/dangling_money.php#more.

67. Editorial, "Obama's Education Opening," *Wall Street Journal*, March 14, 2009, http://online.wsj.com/article/SB123698751663025791.html; David Brooks, "An Innovation Agenda," *New York Times*, December 7, 2009, www.nytimes.com/2009/12/08 /opinion/08brooks.html.

CHAPTER THREE

Splitting the Coalition
The Political Perils and Opportunities of Immigration Reform

Daniel J. Tichenor

Immigration reform has long presented a political minefield for American policymakers, periodically inspiring fierce battles within even the most unified party coalitions. To be more precise, this has proven especially true of contemporary efforts to address illegal immigration and the presence of millions of undocumented immigrants living and working in the United States. Legal immigration reform in recent times certainly has spurred debate, but it also has attracted broad cross-party majorities by allowing for distributive politics and few up-front costs in an era of budget austerity.[1] By contrast, reforms targeting illegal immigration have sparked redistributive conflicts,[2] raised unpopular policy alternatives opposed by powerful organized interests and mass publics, highlighted chronic government inefficacy at the border, and been enacted only by very narrow bipartisan majorities willing to stomach difficult compromises.[3] Little wonder that most modern presidents and congressional party leaders over time have approached the issue warily or pursued evasive tactics.

Presidents Bill Clinton and George W. Bush both confronted demands for comprehensive immigration reform to fix a system considered "broken" by ordinary citizens, state and local officials, pressure groups, and congressional activists. Their strategies for dealing with this contentious and nettlesome issue, however, were markedly different. Consistent with other chapters in this volume, three key objectives inform my analysis of recent immigration reform politics in the pages that follow. The first is to explain how the Clinton and Bush administrations formulated strategic responses to the tough choices posed by illegal immigration, and why the Bush White House advanced initiatives where its predecessor did not. The second is to account for why significant reforms governing immigrants passed in 1996 in the form they did, and why the Bush proposals and competing plans were decisive failures during his two terms in office. The final objective is to take stock of what these presidential strategies toward immigration reform have wrought in terms of coalition building, management, or decline.[4]

This chapter begins by explaining why the competing ideas and interests associated with immigration reform defy the familiar partisan and ideological divides of American politics, regularly split partisan bases, and require strange bedfellow coalitions for initiatives to gain enactment. The second section discusses why illegal immigration poses particularly daunting political challenges for presidents and congressional leaders as they try to guard or expand their partisan bases: the mobilization of rival interest groups and ordinary citizens that make even basic problem definition arduous, past implementation problems, the necessity of painful compromise and unpalatable grand bargains, and the inadequacy of present policy prescriptions. The remaining sections analyze the strategic choices of the Clinton and Bush administrations on immigration policy, the radically different outcomes they yielded, and their consequences for the expansion, maintenance, or decline of their party coalitions. Let us now turn to the competing ideas and interests that immigration reform routinely has inspired, yielding fractious politics that require incongruous political alliances and unappealing policy bargains to resolve.

Rival Ideas and Interests: Disorienting Conflicts and Strange Bedfellow Coalitions

Immigration is a potent cross-cutting issue in American national politics, one that defies the standard liberal-conservative divide and often polarizes major party coalitions. Whereas ideational frameworks may help clarify the policy choices and rationales of partisan and ideological camps in other venues (such as the efficiency of markets, deregulation, family values, national sovereignty and cultural protectionism on the right or cultural pluralism, equal rights, economic security, and work standards on the left), they often clash and frustrate action in immigration policymaking. This is hardly new: Americans have been arguing and taking stands on immigration since the earliest days of the republic. It was an issue that exercised Franklin, Jefferson, Hamilton, Madison, and Wilson, not to mention the Anti-Federalists. Over time, we can identify four rather durable ideological traditions that have found expression in national debates and political struggles over immigration. Consider two dimensions: the first focuses on immigration numbers and divides those who support expansive immigration opportunities and robust numbers from those who favor substantial restrictions on alien admissions; the second concentrates on the rights of noncitizens residing in the United States and distinguishes those who endorse the provision of a broad set of civil, political, and social rights (as defined by T. H. Marshall) to newcomers from those who advocate strict limitations on the rights accorded to noncitizens.[5] These two dimensions of immigration policy reveal tensions between cosmopolitans and economic protectionists on the left and between pro-business expansionists and cultural protectionists and border hawks on the right.

Liberal cosmopolitans embrace the universality of the American experiment, professing deep faith in the social, economic, cultural, and political benefits of diverse mass immigration. Whether Jane Addams in the Progressive Era or Senator Edward Kennedy in recent times, they have supported expansive admissions policies for family reunification, refugee relief, and other legal preference categories, as well as a broad set of legal protections and entitlements for noncitizens. A rich variety of organizations have favored expansionist policy goals over time, including the German American Alliance, the American Jewish Committee, the Japanese American Citizenship League, the National Council of La Raza, the National Immigration Forum, and numerous other ethnic, religious, and humanitarian groups. Organized labor has emerged as critical to this camp in recent years, with the American Federation of Labor and Congress of Industrial Organizations (AFL-CIO) and Change to Win championing immigrants who represent a pivotal target of current unionizing efforts.

By contrast, economic protectionists oppose porous borders and soaring immigration on the grounds that they imperil the material security of the nation's working class and its least advantaged citizens. More than a century ago, Frederick Douglass favored limits on immigration, lamenting that "every hour sees the black man elbowed out of employment by some newly arrived immigrant."[6] He also defended broad rights for Chinese and other workers already in the United States. A later generation of labor leaders such as Samuel Gompers of the American Federation of Labor favored sweeping immigration restrictions because they believed that immigrants undercut the wages, working conditions, and job security of American workers.[7] The labor movement traditionally has been the most visible left-wing constituency advancing restrictive policies. Although leading national labor unions and federations today have shifted to the pro-immigration column, Building and Trades unions as well as many rank-and-file workers have remained protectionist in orientation.[8] Likewise, former congresswoman Barbara Jordan, who chaired the Commission on Immigration Reform during the Clinton years, made it clear that she supported reduced immigration to provide economic opportunity for disadvantaged citizens but also equal benefits for those already here.[9] Today prominent organizations like the National Urban League have produced fissures within the civil rights coalition by demanding that citizens "be given the first right" to jobs routinely given to temporary and immigrant workers.[10] A final sign that the Democratic base and its congressional caucus are far from unified on immigration reform can be found in the tendency of many moderate Democrats in Congress from swing states and districts to distance themselves from expansive proposals.

Free-market and pro-business conservatives tend to support large-scale immigration to meet the labor needs of business interests and to promote national prosperity. During the Gilded Age, capitalists such as Andrew Carnegie described the flow of tractable immigrant workers into the country as a "golden stream."[11] Contemporary business leaders and conservative politicians from Ronald Reagan to John McCain draw the same conclusion, arguing that the nation's economy benefits from foreign workers willing to do jobs and accept wages that U.S. citizens would not. These pro-immigration conservatives are particularly supportive of newcomers who are economically self-sufficient and do not require government assistance, an orientation captured well by the rallying cry of lawmakers like Spencer Abraham and Dick Armey in the 1990s: "Immigration yes, welfare no!" Powerful business interests such as the American Farm Bureau Federation, the U.S. Chamber of Commerce, Microsoft, service industries, and numerous other immigrant employers have defended imported labor as essential to U.S. competitiveness in a global economy. The value of immigrant labor to the national economy is a familiar refrain of the editorial pages of the *Wall Street Journal* and conservative think tanks like the Cato and Manhattan Institutes.

Finally, cultural protectionists and border hawks advocate stringent border control, tough limits on alien rights, and reductions in immigrant admissions. Historically, immigration activists of this ideological tradition have worried about significant shifts in the ethnic, racial, or religious composition of immigration. As Harvard president A. Lawrence Lowell, a supporter of the Immigration Restriction League (IRL), argued during the Progressive Era, "the need for homogeneity in a democracy" justifies policies "resisting the influx of great numbers of a greatly different race."[12] Today many, although not all, border hawks are haunted by cultural anxieties over what Patrick Buchanan dubs as a "Third World invasion" of unprecedented Latino and Asian immigrants: "The children born in 2006 will witness in their lifetimes the death of the West."[13] One consistent position of restriction-minded conservatives after the terrorist attacks of September 11, 2001, is that porous borders and mass immigration pose significant security risks. "The consequences of uncontrolled immigration are far more serious than our leaders want us to believe," declared Representative Tom Tancredo (R-CO), leader of the restrictionist Congressional Immigration Reform Caucus. "The safety of Americans and the security of our way of life are on the line." The restrictionist agenda has been advanced at the grassroots by causes such as California's Save Our State campaign and the Minutemen movement, while organizations such as the Federation for American Immigration Reform (FAIR) have demanded restrictive legislation for decades.

These distinctive ideological traditions remind us that American political debate over immigrant admissions and rights reflects a depth and texture that eludes those who try to define a clear "conservative" or "liberal" position on immigration reform. Equally significant, none of these immigration activists have secured nonincremental policy change independently. Over time, major policy innovation almost invariably has required the building of incongruous left-right alliances. These strange bedfellow coalitions sometimes produce large bipartisan majorities in favor of legislation, especially when dealing with legal immigration, in which opportunities for credit claiming can abound. Such was the case when the Immigration Act of 1990 cheerfully unified pro-immigration Democrats and Republicans behind a 40 percent increase in annual visa allocations benefiting both family-based and employment-based admissions.[14] Yet nonincremental initiatives addressing illegal immigration yield very different politics, in which painful choices, shrill conflicts, and blame-avoidance strategies abound.[15]

Painful Policy: The Inherited Challenges of Illegal Immigration

A daunting set of constraints and barriers litter the path to comprehensive reform on illegal immigration and the presence of 8–12 million undocumented aliens in the United States. The rival ideologies and interests of various constituencies mobilized on this issue make problem definition and legislative majorities elusive. Another formidable challenge is that policymakers are well aware that major reform in this area entails difficult negotiations that produce unpalatable compromise packages. Moreover, past implementation failures and policy inertia generally have an expansive effect with regard to illegal immigration, compounding over time the problems associated with porous borders. The federal government's failure to control the borders in either the distant or recent past also has bred widespread cynicism and mistrust about the capacity and will of the national state to enforce its immigration laws. Finally, the most prominent policy prescriptions on the table today appear inadequate to meet the problem. Let us briefly consider each of these impediments in turn.

Political Cacophony: Elusive Problem Definition and Congressional Majorities

The rival commitments of ideology and interest unleashed by illegal immigration make basic problem definition a tall order for policymakers. Indeed, recent immigration reform efforts captured profoundly different assumptions and conceptions of what the problem is, or, for some, whether a problem even exists. Moreover, powerful organized interests and competing constituencies regularly mobilize and clash over immigration reform. The resulting battles not only pit interest groups and constituencies allied with the Republican Party against those allied with the Democratic Party, but they also divide organized interests within these partisan coalitions and sometimes even among those associated with the same interest or constituency, such as internal fights on this issue within the labor movement or among environmental and population control groups.

For cosmopolitans, or pro-immigration liberals, the problem is not *the presence* of millions of undocumented aliens in the United States but rather *their status* as vulnerable, second-class persons. The chief imperative for these activists is to make the estimated 10–15 million unauthorized migrants living in the country eligible for legal membership. "What we want . . . is a pathway to their legalization," Representative Luis Gutierrez (D-IL) explains, "so that they can come out of the shadows of darkness, of discrimination, of bigotry, of exploitation, and join us fully."[16] Since powerful democracies such as the United States profit from the economic exploitation of unauthorized immigrants, progressives such as Marc Rosenblum of the Migration Policy Institute argue that "all American employers, consumers, and lawmakers—all of us—share the 'blame' for undocumented migration."[17] Legalization or "earned citizenship" initiatives draw strong support today from Latino organizations, the leading federations of organized labor, and various civil rights and ethnic groups.

Economic protectionists have been particularly hostile toward illegal immigration, which they view as enhancing the wealth of corporate and professional America with little concern of the consequences for blue-collar workers or the unemployed. As much as Cesar Chavez complained bitterly in the late 1960s that undocumented Mexicans were being recruited to undermine his efforts to organize legal farm workers, Carol Swain recently pointed to the deleterious "impact that high levels of illegal immigration [are] having in the communities when it comes to jobs, when it comes to education, when it comes to health care."[18] CNN's Lou Dobbs regularly sounds similar themes, claiming that illegal immigration has "a calamitous effect on working citizens and their families" and "that the industries in which illegal aliens are employed in the greatest percentages also are suffering the largest wage declines."[19] Economic protectionists endorse employer sanctions against unscrupulous employers who knowingly hire undocumented aliens, and they vehemently oppose guest worker programs that they associate with a captive workforce subject to exploitation, abuse, and permanent marginalization. These views resonate among many rank-and-file members of labor unions and the constituencies of moderate Democrats in Congress.

For pro-immigration conservatives devoted to free markets and business growth, the chief problem is that existing federal policies fail to address "the reality," as President Bush put it, "that there are many people on the other side of our border who will do anything to come to America to work." In short, the U.S. economy has grown dependent on this supply of cheap, unskilled labor.[20] The solution for this camp lies in regularizing employers' access to this vital foreign labor; if the back door is to be closed, then this labor supply must be secured through temporary worker programs and an expansion of employment-based legal immigration. Powerful business groups in this camp also oppose employer sanctions as an unwelcome and unfair regulatory burden placed on American businesses large and small.

Border hawks today see the illegal immigration problem as nothing short of an unprecedented breakdown of American sovereignty, one that compromises national security, the rule of law, job opportunities for citizens, public education, and social services.[21] Mobilized by conservative talk radio, columnists, and television commentators, many Main Street Republicans are outraged that the nation's fundamental interest in border control and law enforcement has been trumped by the power of immigrant labor, rights, and votes. Amnesty or legalization proposals inspire hostile resistance from this camp as unethical rewards to those who break the rules and as stimulants to new waves of undocumented immigrants anticipating similar treatment. Likewise, temporary worker programs are scorned by these activists because many guest workers historically have remained illegally and because they contest the notion that only foreign workers will do certain menial jobs. Border hawks believe that enforcement must come first. They favor a strengthened Border Patrol and tougher security measures along the nation's borders, as well as crackdowns on unauthorized immigrants and their employers within U.S. territory. They endorse a strategy of attrition in which targeted deportation efforts, workplace enforcement, and denial of social services and other public benefits would persuade many unauthorized migrants to return home.

It is hard to imagine more widely divergent definitions of a public policy problem, or, concomitantly, more disparate blueprints for reform. Building majority support for legislation involving tough choices is always challenging, but it is especially so amid ideological disorientation and intraparty warfare. Clashing interests and ideals have meant that when policy initiatives are designed to meet the demands of one important constituency, they invariably incur the wrath of others. The diverse responses of states and localities to immigration enforcement and immigrant policy, as subnational governments enter the void when Washington fails to act, further cloud the picture.[22]

The Long Way Home: Prolonged Negotiation and Unpalatable Compromise

National policymakers are well aware of the tortured path that earlier reformers traversed to secure comprehensive legislation on illegal immigration. False starts, painful negotiations, and unappealing compromises are par for the course, at least for the past quarter century. For much of the 1970s, liberal House Democrat Peter Rodino (D-NJ) waged a quixotic campaign for employer sanctions legislation to discourage unauthorized entries.[23] This effort to punish employers who knowingly hired undocumented aliens was strongly advocated by the AFL-CIO and labor unions. But organized agricultural interests initially succeeded in stalling Rodino's legislation in the Senate, where conservative Democrat James Eastland (D-MS) refused to allow the Judiciary Committee he chaired to take action.[24] When Rodino again pressed the initiative later in the decade, new resistance emerged in both the House and Senate from liberal Democrats who warned that the measure would lead to job discrimination against Latinos, Asians, and anyone who looked or sounded foreign. Most Latino organizations and civil rights groups were now lined up in opposition to employer sanctions.[25]

Despite warnings from congressional Democrats like Rodino and Kennedy that illegal immigration had become a political buzz saw, the Carter administration wasted little time in proposing a comprehensive plan in 1977 for addressing the problem. The reform package included stiff civil and criminal penalties for employers who engaged in a "pattern or practice" of hiring undocumented aliens; use of the Social Security card as an identification document for verifying employee eligibility; enhanced Border Patrol forces at the Mexican border; and an amnesty program that would confer legal resident alien status on all aliens living in the country before 1970.[26] The White House proposal galvanized opposition from growers and other free-market expansionists as unfair to employers; from the National Council of La Raza (NCLR), Mexican-American Legal Defense and Education Fund (MALDEF), and various cosmopolitans as detrimental to civil rights; and from law-and-order conservatives and classic restrictionists as rewarding lawbreakers with amnesty.[27] The Carter proposal languished.

During the next decade, the bipartisan team of Republican senator Alan Simpson (R-WY) and Democratic congressman Romano Mazzoli (D-KY) took the lead in pressing for immigration reform. Early in 1982, the pair introduced omnibus legislation on illegal and legal immigration. The measure met fierce resistance from a broad coalition of business interests (the U.S. Chamber of Commerce, National Association of Manufacturers, agribusinesses, the Business Roundtable), ethnic and civil rights groups such as NCLR and MALDEF, the American Civil Liberties Union (ACLU), religious lobbies, and a new immigrant rights organization, the National Immigration Forum. Left-right opposition to the Simpson-Mazzoli initiative was reflected in the resistance of both the Reagan administration, which saw employer sanctions and national identification cards working at cross-purposes with its regulatory relief agenda, and House Democrats led by the Hispanic and Black Caucuses, which raised familiar concerns about discriminatory impacts of sanctions and other provisions. Simpson and Mazzoli got nowhere for five years before eleventh-hour deal making produced the compromise Immigration Reform and Control Act of 1986 (IRCA). Gridlock was overcome by a compromise package of watered-down employer sanctions provisions, legalization for undocumented aliens living in the country since 1982, and a new Seasonal Agricultural Worker program to appease grower interests. Final vote tallies were tight, and major components of the "grand bargain" were almost undone during bruising amendment battles on the floor. This history of painful negotiations and compromises has only intensified national policymakers' dread of the illegal immigration problem.

Implementation Failures and Inertia: Fostering Cynicism and Illegal Expansion

The capacity and will of the national state to enforce its immigration laws have long been beleaguered in the United States by a tradition of inadequate resources, erratic enforcement, and poor oversight. Nearly all advanced industrial democracies have struggled to control their borders, and scholars such as Mae Ngai remind us that the presence of undocumented immigrants is inevitable.[28] Yet the recognition that governments cannot eliminate illegal immigration does not mean that they are incapable of exercising a measure of control over their borders. Moreover, early policy choices (and silences) by wealthy democracies are significant because they can nurture and entrench the forces that spur large-scale illegal immigration. Indeed, policy inertia often has had the effect of expanding unauthorized flows. Equally important, past implementation failures have bred deep mistrust or cynicism among ordinary citizens and enforcement-minded lawmakers that the federal government will control its borders. This skepticism is a major impediment to immigration reform today.

A contemporary illustration of lax enforcement can be seen in the implementation of the IRCA's employer sanctions provisions. As stated above, the absence of a reliable identification system for verifying employee eligibility made it relatively easy for undocumented aliens to evade detection at the workplace. Soon after passage of the IRCA, an underground industry of fraudulent documents flourished in both Mexico and the United States, enabling unauthorized migrants to obtain work with ease. But if the legislative design of employer sanctions discouraged their efficacy, the Reagan administration was less than zealous in their enforcement. The Immigration and Nationalization Service (INS) tended to enforce employer sanctions with considerable forbearance toward offenders. Alan Nelson, the INS commissioner under Reagan, was urged to pursue a policy of "least employer resistance" by stressing business education over penalties.[29] The IRCA authorized a 70 percent increase in the INS budget, with an annual $100 million targeted for employer sanctions enforcement. Tellingly, $34 million was spent on enforcing sanctions in FY 1987, $59 million in 1988, and below $30 million annually in ensuing years.[30]

From his perch on the Senate immigration subcommittee, Senator Simpson pressed the Reagan and Bush administrations to take a harder line on employer sanctions. Yet despite his clout as Republican minority whip, Simpson made little headway during either Republican presidency. "Even when we direct the Administration to do such things as 'study' the employer sanctions verification system and develop a more secure system, if necessary, we get no action," he lamented.[31] Few of Simpson's congressional colleagues shared his alarm over the inefficacy or uneven enforcement of employer sanctions. In fact, the most vigorous oversight of sanctions focused on whether they should be repealed because they unfavorably burdened small businesses (led by Orrin Hatch) or because they engendered increased job discrimination against legal aliens or citizens who look or sound foreign (led by Edward Kennedy). Few conservative politicians of the 1980s, most of whom embraced "regulatory relief" and free markets, or their liberal counterparts, dedicated to universal rights and inclusion, worried about the efficacy of employer sanctions.

IRCA's implementation failures helped fuel the dramatic expansion of illegal immigration in recent decades, yielding an undocumented population in the United States that estimates suggest is three to four times larger than it was in the early 1980s. They also have raised profound doubts among activists, policymakers, and citizens that the federal government either can or would adequately control its borders. The resulting cynicism poses substantial hurdles to reform.

Bad Options: Inadequate or Unappealing Policy Solutions

A final source of pain for political leaders tackling illegal immigration is that many of the most prominent policy prescriptions on the table today appear inadequate, too costly, unpopular, or likely to have unintended consequences. A few examples from recent immigration reform are illustrative. Amnesty or legalization programs are designed to adjust the status of undocumented immigrants living and working in the country for a given duration of time, but they may serve as a magnet for new unauthorized entries by migrants hoping for similar treatment in the future. Efforts to make past "amnesty" programs into "earned citizenship" (through payment of fines, back taxes, and "touchback" provisions requiring immigrants to return to their home countries) face potentially large numbers of undocumented immigrants refusing to participate. As a result, many of these unauthorized residents, perhaps millions, would remain "illegal." Likewise, the adoption of new guest worker programs to meet business demands and to regularize the flow of foreign workers overlooks the fact that similar programs in the past were accompanied by unauthorized flows and that many temporary workers chose to remain illegally.[32]

Enforcement proposals feature their own share of unanticipated woes. Creating strict, militarized control over the 2,000-mile U.S.-Mexico border will not come cheap in terms of constructing border fences, surveillance technology, or personnel. Adequate enforcement will slow the movement of tourists and commercial goods, and it will reinforce the incentives for those who entered without inspection (EWIs) to avoid returning home and thereby risk not getting back in.[33] The notion of mass deportation campaigns or systematic internal enforcement draws little support in opinion polls, would require major new budget commitments, and could involve significant incursions upon the civil liberties of legal immigrants and citizens. Along similar lines, effective employer sanctions would entail new mechanisms for verifying employee eligibility that will produce sacrifices in privacy as well as higher costs for businesses and consumers alike. Whereas legal immigration reform recently has included something to please almost everyone mobilized on the issue, comprehensive initiatives on illegal immigration promise plenty of bitter pills to go around.

Ceding the Initiative: Clinton, Immigration Reform, and Cautious Opportunism

Given all of these profound challenges, it is little wonder that most presidents and congressional leaders have sought to avoid politically exhausting struggles over illegal immigration, especially highly public ones. That is, most have approached immigration politics with a healthy dose of caution, if not aversion. Given its propensity to upend stable alliances and produce strange bedfellows, immigration reform has struck most presidents and congressional leaders as a potent threat to their party coalitions. Indeed, most have viewed choices in the policy realm with an eye for *guarding*, rather than building, their party coalitions. With these political perils in mind, most modern presidents have taken a measured approach while Congress routinely takes the lead on major immigration reform. The Clinton years are no exception to this norm. As we shall see, Clinton pursued a cautious, reactive strategy toward immigration reform, one in which he was able to turn congressional Republican initiative on the issue into Democratic political gains.

Early on, the Clinton administration demonstrated little or no interest in placing immigration reform high on its domestic agenda. Yet it could not afford to appear inattentive on an issue that was so salient to important constituencies. Beyond the Washington Beltway, FAIR and other restrictionist groups were busy building grassroots opposition to immigration in key receiving states such as California, Texas, and Florida.[34] California was of special concern to Clinton, who carried the state and its fifty-two electoral votes in 1992 with 46 percent of the vote and who worried about replicating the feat in 1996. California's growing restiveness about unprecedented numbers of legal and illegal immigrants settling in the state was unmistakable. Meanwhile Latino, Asian, and other ethnic organizations called on the White House to denounce restrictive policy proposals.

Clinton responded to these cross pressures by acknowledging that porous borders were a problem, but also by drawing sharp distinctions between legal immigrants who "play by the rules" and undocumented ones who do not. "The solution to the problem of illegal immigration is not simply to close our borders," he told reporters in August 2003. "The solution is to welcome legal immigrants and legal legitimate refugees and to turn away those who do not obey our laws. We must say no to illegal immigration so we can continue to say yes to legal immigration."[35] Since the 1990 Immigration Act created an immigration commission to study the impact of policy innovation, Clinton had a ready explanation for why he should not take action. His only significant policy decision during his first years in office was to name Barbara Jordan, a respected former congresswoman and African American leader who took moderate positions on immigration, as chair of the commission. Vowing to wait for the Jordan commission to issue recommendations, Clinton did not have to address immigration reform until 1995.

While Clinton avoided the issue, restriction-minded activists in California formed a new organization called Save Our State (SOS). Its central purpose was to promote Proposition 187 to deny illegal aliens and their children welfare benefits, nonemergency health care, and public education. As one SOS leader explained, "It made sense to target the most objectionable recipients first— illegals. Then we could put the issue of too much legal immigration on the table."[36] California governor Pete Wilson (R) threw his support behind Proposition 187 during his 1994 reelection campaign, calling for wholesale restrictions on immigrant access to public benefits. Struggling to survive a serious statewide economic slump and related budget shortages, Wilson decried what he claimed was a $4.8 billion expenditure the previous year for health, welfare, education, and criminal justice costs of legal and illegal immigrants. Ethnic, religious, and educational organizations in the state vigorously opposed Proposition 187, and they drew on prominent Democrats such as Jesse Jackson and Republicans such as William Bennett and Jack Kemp to denounce the measure. But Wilson's staunch backing of Proposition 187 made it a partisan issue, especially when the state GOP added its endorsement.[37]

Popular support for restricting immigration also seemed to intensify across the country by 1994. Immigration restriction not only gained in popularity in 1994 (roughly 65% favored major reductions in legal admissions), but its salience for the general public also appeared to surge.[38] When ordinary citizens were asked which issues mattered most to them in the 1994 election, 20 percent placed illegal immigration at the top of their lists; the most common answers were crime at 33 percent and welfare reform at 28 percent.[39] Another poll conducted just before the election found that 72 percent of respondents saw mass immigration as a "critical threat" to the "vital interests of the United States."[40] Jack Citrin and his colleagues found that voters were increasingly connecting immigration to negative economic experiences and economic uncertainty in the two elections after 1992.[41] Events such as the 1994 bombing of the World Trade Center in New York City by Islamic terrorists, who had gained entry into the country with relative ease, heightened public anxieties over international migration.

When the dust settled on a contentious California race in November, Wilson won reelection and Proposition 187 carried the state with 59 percent of the vote. As restrictionists in various southern and western states prepared to replicate the substance and success of Proposition 187, the measure was immediately enjoined by a federal court that held that its denial of public education to the children of undocumented aliens was unconstitutional. If judicial intervention blunted popular assaults on immigrant rights at the state level, a dramatic changing of the guard in Congress seemed to offer new opportunities for restrictionist policy innovations supported by large majorities of the public. For the first time since 1952, the Republican Party gained control of both houses of Congress. Alan Simpson assumed leadership of the Senate Immigration Subcommittee, while Representative Lamar Smith (R-TX) became immigration subcommittee chair on the House side. Both of these lawmakers envisioned a fresh round of restrictive immigration reform to limit legal admissions, to make immigrants ineligible for welfare benefits, and to finally curb illegal immigration. In the House, a considerable number of Republican members were eager to support tighter controls over illegal flows and cuts in legal immigrant admissions and welfare rights. The Republican delegations of California and Texas were particularly dogged in urging Speaker Newt Gingrich (R-GA) to facilitate restrictive reform.

These Republican lawmakers, mobilized by the success of Proposition 187 and opinion poll trends, became convinced that immigration restriction could be used effectively as a "wedge" issue to win crucial blue-collar Democratic votes (especially in key battleground states like California and Florida).[42] Gingrich responded to intraparty pressures by creating a special task force on immigration reform chaired by Edward Gallegly (R-CA), known for his hard line on illegal immigration and legal immigrant welfare eligibility. Senate Majority Leader Robert Dole (R-KS) joined many fellow partisans in supporting immigration curbs, appearing on television to decry the unfair immigration costs imposed on California, Florida, and Texas and to denounce policymakers "not willing to protect our borders."[43] Immigration defenders poised themselves for a formidable restrictionist assault.

The Jordan Commission's 1994 report on illegal immigration focused on making employer sanctions more effective through the creation of a computerized registry for verifying worker eligibility using data provided by the INS

and Social Security Administration.[44] It issued a new report on legal immigration one year later that endorsed large-scale admissions but called for modest
cuts in annual visa numbers and the elimination of the fifth preference for
extended family members of U.S. citizens.[45] Yet the commission report was
adamant that immigrants should have access to welfare and other public benefits. Polls in 1995 indicated that the public supported the commission's recommendations. At the same time, Smith, Simpson, and the Republican-led
Congress clearly were ready to advance comprehensive reform addressing legal
and illegal immigration and noncitizen access to welfare benefits. Against this
backdrop, the Clinton administration praised the nation's immigrant traditions while endorsing the recommendations of the Jordan Commission. It also
took a hard line on mass asylum, clarifying that Cuban and Haitian boat people intercepted at sea would not be allowed to enter the United States; this
marked a significant break from three decades of treating all Cuban escapees as
refugees.[46]

While Smith and Simpson eagerly pressed their sweeping immigration initiatives, conservatives were hardly of one mind on the issue. Many continued
to positively associate robust immigration with business demands for cheap
and skilled foreign labor, entrepreneurial newcomers, and refugee relief for
those fleeing communist regimes. Others argued that any reform that provided fewer visas for reuniting families was anathema to a conservative pro-
family agenda.[47] Dick Armey (R-TX) was one of several prominent figures of
the House Republican leadership team who vigorously defended expansive
legal immigration. Tellingly, the Gallegly task force established by Gingrich
skirted legal immigration conflicts by confining its recommendations to illegal
flows and public benefits for immigrants. The panel endorsed increased Border
Patrol resources, pilot programs for verifying worker eligibility, tougher sanctions for using fake documents or knowingly hiring undocumented aliens,
and expedited procedures for removing aliens (including asylum seekers) who
entered the country without authorization. Hoping to draw from the success of
Proposition 187, the task force also called for denying educational benefits to
the children of undocumented aliens.

Lamar Smith had a far more ambitious restrictionist agenda in mind when
the Republican 104th Congress convened in 1995, and his immigration subcommittee wasted little time in holding hearings and drafting reform legislation. But as he devised a blueprint for restricting legal immigration and tough-
ening enforcement against illegal immigration, the American Immigration

Lawyers Association and immigration defenders such as Rick Swartz, founder of the National Immigration Forum, worked to rebuild an incongruous coalition of business, ethnic, religious, labor, libertarian, and civil rights groups that had fueled the 1990 act's expansions in family- and employment-based visas. John Juddis dubbed this revived coalition of odd bedfellows the "huddled elites."[48] Of these coalition members, Republican politicians were particularly uneasy about various businesses that relied on skilled and unskilled immigrant labor. As Microsoft lobbyists chastised restrictionists for missing "the point that to succeed in foreign markets, you need foreign personnel," the National Association of Manufacturers warned that "this country is not producing the workers we need to be globally competitive." Employers of unskilled workers also made their presence felt on Capitol Hill. During a meeting with lobbyists for the National Restaurant Association, an organization whose large membership relied heavily on unskilled alien workers, Gingrich offered assurances that he had no intention of cutting their supply to immigrant labor.[49] Occupational visas were emerging as a "third rail" for Republican lawmakers.

Smith's immigration reform bill, as reported by the full House Judiciary Committee, reflected these interest group pressures. The initiative included provisions for reducing legal immigration, constricting immigrant access to public benefits, strengthening enforcement against illegal immigration at the border and at the workplace, expediting the deportation of criminal aliens, limiting the adjudication of asylum claims, and extending refugee relief to those escaping regimes with coercive population control policies. In terms of legal admissions, Smith's bill called for three preference categories: family-based, employment-based, and humanitarian. Family-based entries were reduced from 480,000 to 330,000 annually by eliminating preferences for siblings and adult children.[50]

The full committee markup of Smith's bill revealed important political alignments. Not surprisingly, a clear partisan divide emerged in this committee on provisions that threatened the substantive and procedural rights of legal aliens, such as expedited deportations and limiting access to social welfare programs. Yet there was broad consensus across party lines on efforts to strengthen enforcement against illegal immigration, as well as some indication that more than a few Republicans were uncomfortable with Smith's plans to shrink legal admissions. Fearful that employer groups and free-market Republicans would oppose his bill, Smith cut a deal with business lobbyists before the Judiciary Committee vote that left employment-based visas untouched in exchange for their support.[51] Even when Smith took occupational visas out of the mix, Republicans quarreled amongst themselves over family preferences.

On the Senate side, Simpson and his immigration subcommittee drafted legislation with provisions on illegal immigration enforcement and limits on alien eligibility for public benefits that closely resembled the House bill. It also included new limits on legal admissions; but unlike Smith's plan, its restrictions took their heaviest toll on employment-based immigration. The Simpson bill proposed reducing occupational visas from 140,000 to 90,000 annually and assessing a fee of $10,000 on employers for each skilled immigrant worker they hired; family-based immigration was reduced by 30,000 annually. In addition, Simpson called for restrictions on the asylum process and a firm cap of 50,000 annual refugee admissions. But the refugee cap never survived subcommittee markup, as every senator but Simpson backed a Kennedy amendment striking it. While business groups such as Microsoft, the U.S. Chamber of Commerce, and the National Association of Manufacturers brokered a deal with Smith in the House, they joined with ethnic, religious, and immigrant rights groups of the Left in their efforts to defeat legal immigration reform in the Senate. As in 1990, a potent left-right alliance of organized interests championed expansive legal immigrant admissions. Amid fierce lobbying, the full Senate Judiciary Committee voted to split legal and illegal immigration reform by a 12–6 margin. The "split-the-bill" amendment was deftly shepherded by Michigan Republican Spencer Abraham; six of ten Republicans deserted Simpson to pass the amendment.

These committee patterns reflected broader political trends in Washington. As GOP leaders recognized, pro-immigration and restrictionist conservatives were most unified behind proposals to scale back alien rights to various social welfare benefits and procedural due process claims. Whereas the Republicans' 1994 Contract with America said nothing about restricting immigration, it offered clear plans to deny Medicaid, Supplemental Security Income (SSI), Aid to Families with Dependent Children, and Food Stamps to legal immigrants. Some Republican lawmakers such as Senator Nancy Kassebaum (R-KS) opposed these efforts, but they were outliers on the alien rights issue.[52] Pro-business and free-market defenders of immigration in the Reagan mold celebrated newcomers who were hardworking and economically self-sufficient, not those who relied on the government for income support. As

Gingrich proclaimed on the House floor, "Come to America for opportunity. Do not come to America to live off the law-abiding American taxpayer."[53] "Immigration yes, welfare no" was the slogan that caught fire among pro-immigration conservatives on Capitol Hill. The failure of many legal aliens to naturalize also struck various conservatives as disloyal and unpatriotic. "If they don't want to pledge their allegiance to the United States," Representative Gallegly averred, "they shouldn't be eligible for food stamps."[54] By contrast, liberal Democrats defended the rights of aliens to receive public benefits.

In keeping with their fealty to civil rights, most Democratic politicians opposed both Proposition 187 and Gallegly's efforts to legislate the denial of educational benefits and birthright citizenship to the children of undocumented aliens. But fighting illegal immigration had become a valence issue that attracted strong bipartisan support, one that Gingrich and the Republican 104th Congress failed to translate into a partisan triumph. Not to be outflanked on illegal immigration, the Clinton White House repeatedly denounced illegal immigration and issued an executive order early in 1996 that denied federal contracts to businesses who knowingly hired undocumented aliens.[55]

The decoupling of legal and illegal immigration reform was a major victory for the left-right coalition of pro-immigration groups determined to protect expansive family and occupational admissions. As organized interests mobilized effectively against the legal reform plans of the Smith and Simpson bills, the Clinton White House shifted in 1995 away from its earlier position in favor of the Jordan Commission's call for modest visa reductions and flatly disavowed any restrictions on legal admissions. Many prominent Republicans proved equally unwilling to reduce legal admissions, as William Kristol, Jack Kemp, William Bennett, and other prominent conservatives argued that immigration restriction contradicted the GOP's celebration of global markets, individual opportunity, and families. Even the Christian Coalition mobilized against legal immigration reform because "scaling back the ability of Americans to be reunited with their families will not improve national security, and could severely damage the American family."[56]

In the wake of the pro-immigration coalition's victory in the Senate Judiciary Committee markup, the battle over legal immigration restriction shifted to the House floor in March 1996. There, Howard Berman (D-CA) and two pro-immigration conservatives, Sam Brownbeck (R-KS) and Dick Chrysler (R-MI), offered an amendment to gut the Smith bill's legal immigration reduction provisions. High-tech companies hired Republican insider Grover Norquist to lobby against legal immigration reform. In a chamber defined by partisan estrangement, the amendment was carried by a cross-party majority. By contrast, a Gallegly amendment to deny public education to undocumented children carried with a party-line vote. Clinton responded by publicly assailing the Gallegly proposal as mean-spirited and said it would justify a presidential veto.[57]

The final version of the Smith bill, now largely an enforcement measure targeting undocumented aliens, visa violators, and criminal aliens, passed by a lopsided 333–87 vote. On April 15, Simpson's illegal immigration reform initiative reached the Senate floor. In a last-ditch effort to achieve restrictions in legal admissions, Simpson offered an amendment that would impose a temporary five-year reduction in family-based immigration. By focusing on family admissions, he hoped to gain support from business groups and Republican colleagues who opposed his original plan. The effort proved quixotic, as forty Republicans and forty Democrats defeated the amendment. Simpson's illegal immigration bill ultimately passed 97–3. The Illegal Immigration Reform and Immigrant Responsibility Act (IIRIRA) made its way to conference committee.

The final version of IIRIRA enhanced the federal government's ability to guard national borders, tightened asylum procedures, limited immigrant access to public benefits, required U.S. financial sponsors for newcomers, and established stringent provisions for criminal and undocumented aliens. Under a firm threat of presidential veto, the Gallegly amendment modeled after Proposition 187 was struck in conference negotiations. But in the heat of a national presidential campaign, legislation primarily designed to get tough on illegal immigration was hard to resist for politicians of either party. IIRIRA passed easily in both houses and was signed into law the last week of September. Although anything but expansive, this new enforcement law disappointed restrictionists who wanted reductions in legal immigration. "Your hopes of reining in uncontrolled immigration were dashed," FAIR told supporters. "In the end, Congress sold out to the special interests."[58]

Welfare reform was a product of party competition in a presidential election year that had important consequences for immigrants. The Personal Responsibility and Work Opportunity Act of 1996 (PRWOA) barred noncitizens from a broad set of federal benefits programs. President Clinton told the press that he was offended by the legislation's harshness toward legal immigrants, but that he chose to sign the reform package because of his devotion to fundamentally restructure the larger welfare system. Together, the immigration and welfare reform laws marked a retrenchment of the legal protections and social entitlements that legal and undocumented aliens could claim. It was a triumph for pro-business and free-market conservatives, who allied with pro-immigration liberals to sustain robust legal admissions and with anti-immigrant conservatives to trim the substantive and procedural rights of noncitizens. The outcomes of 1996 suggested that large-scale immigration would flow into the United States uninterrupted for the foreseeable future, and that those who arrived would enjoy fewer membership rights until they acquired citizenship.

In 1995, several prominent Republican congressional leaders expressed optimism behind closed doors that the immigration issue would help them shore up additional working-class votes.[59] At the start of the 1996 election, Pete Wilson made immigration control a signature feature of his short-lived presidential campaign; Pat Buchanan assailed Third World immigration as a source of economic and cultural insecurity at home; and Bob Dole, the eventual Republican standard bearer, associated himself with the stringent immigration enforcement measures then working their way through Congress.[60] The 1996 Republican platform pledged support for national legislation barring children of undocumented aliens from public schools. In the later stages of the election, however, Dole and other Republican candidates took heed of new reports that immigrants and kindred ethnic groups had become energized by anti-immigration politics. But it was too late for backpedaling.

The results of the 1996 election left little doubt about two crucial developments: immigrants constituted the nation's fastest-growing voting bloc, and Democrats were the immediate beneficiaries of their emergent electoral clout. Naturalization rates soared after 1995, as record numbers of aliens became citizens. More than 1 million people naturalized in 1996 alone. At the same time as unprecedented numbers of immigrants petitioned for naturalization in the mid-1990s, Clinton instructed the INS to implement the so-called Citizenship USA initiative. In the words of the agency, the initiative "was designed to streamline the naturalization process and greatly increase naturalizations during 1996." Voter registrations among Latinos grew by 1.3 million, or 28.7 percent, between 1992 and 1996; the percentage of Latinos on the voter rolls rose from 59 percent of those eligible in 1992 to 65 percent in 1996. Bill Clinton's cautious opportunism paid electoral dividends in his reelection bid. He drew 72 percent of the Latino vote in 1996 (up from 60% in 1992). Asian voters, a smaller yet important swing bloc, increased their support for the Democratic ticket in the same years from 29 to 43 percent.[61] Dole registered an all-time GOP low of 21 percent of the Latino vote in 1996, and he became the first Republican presidential candidate to lose Florida since Gerald Ford in 1980.

Political leaders have strong incentives to try to broaden their electoral coalitions, and they may try to widen their partisan base by advancing policy initiatives designed to win over promising new constituencies. These efforts rarely succeed. Ironically, Clinton expanded his party's appeal among immigrant voters and kindred ethnic groups by going slow on immigration reform and by opportunistically reacting to aggressive leadership on the issue by congressional Republicans. Clinton entered office as ambivalent on immigration policy and willing to preside over modest restrictions, but he left it as the perceived great defender of new immigrants from intolerant xenophobes.

From Widening to Exploding the Base: Bush and Immigration Reform

Between 1990 and 2000 in sheer numbers, more immigrants arrived in the United States than during any previous period in American history. In this decade alone, the immigrant population in the United States grew by roughly 1 million persons per year, rising from 19.8 million to 31.1 million. Immigration reform was not among the ten items that Gingrich and House Republicans promised to address in the first one hundred days of the 104th Congress. Yet Gingrich and many of his lieutenants calculated that making immigrants ineligible for welfare, new crackdowns on illegal immigration, and the Gallegly amendment would pay electoral dividends among agitated native-born voters in states from California to Florida, especially working-class Americans. Dole accepted the same bet in his presidential bid. These efforts unquestionably failed to widen the Republican base among working-class and native-born voters and cost them dearly among naturalized voters and kindred Latino and Asian constituencies who associated the GOP with measures—from Proposition 187 to PRWOA—that they saw as draconian and anti-immigrant.

By the 2000 election, Republican national and state organizations drew up plans to attract new Asian and Latino voters. They were emboldened by party strategists who warned that "if we're only getting 25 percent of the Hispanic vote, you wait three, four presidential elections, and we'll be out of business." Then Texas governor George W. Bush was hailed by many party leaders as the ideal candidate to court new immigrant voters in 2000, and he reminded Latinos throughout the campaign that early on he had "rejected the spirit of Prop 187," opposed "English-only" proposals, and refused "to bash immigrants" when it was popular. Vice President Al Gore in turn reminded Latino and Asian constituencies that Republicans led the way in stripping welfare benefits and other rights for noncitizens and assured them that Democrats would continue to defend expansive legal immigration. Yet Bush dramatically outspent Democrats in his appeal to Latino voters in 2000, devoting millions of campaign dollars to Spanish-language advertising and direct-mail appeals. He also gave television interviews in Spanish and had his bilingual nephew George P. Bush stump for him extensively among Latino constituencies.[62] Bush's "compassionate conservatism" on immigration policy and his direct campaigning had clear electoral ramifications. An estimated 7.8 million Latino voters, or 6 percent of all voters (up from 4% in 1996), cast ballots in the 2000 election. Gore maintained the Democrats' traditional edge in Latino voting, but Bush gained an estimated 34 percent among Latinos—thirteen points higher than Dole's 1996 total and only three points off the previous GOP record of 37 percent attained by Ronald Reagan in the 1984 election.[63] The Bush team clearly was focused on adding more Latinos, the fastest-growing sector of the electorate and a crucial swing constituency in battleground states, to the GOP base.

Expanding its electoral coalition was certainly not the only factor that informed the Bush administration's decision to take the initiative on controversial immigration reform soon after taking office. Bush personally believed that his plan was a sound policy solution to a bedeviling problem. Indeed, the president regularly explained that as a Texan he particularly understood the need to streamline and expand the legal inflow of low-wage workers from abroad.[64] "If somebody is willing to do jobs others in America aren't willing to do," he told reporters after nine months in office, "we ought to welcome that person to the country, and we ought to make that a legal part of the economy."[65] Bush said that his Texas roots also convinced him that Mexican and other undocumented immigrants in the country should be given an opportunity to stay in this country, frequently telling audiences that "compassion" and "family values don't stop at the Rio Grande."[66] Moreover, Bush's immigration initiatives clearly benefited and appealed to the business community that was squarely rooted in his coalition. Various employers of low-wage, low-skill work-ers readily supported the president's proposals, from Fortune 500 companies to smaller agribusinesses, builders, restaurant owners, and other service com-panies. Finally, Bush's decision to pursue a contentious immigration initiative also reflected steady political demands for border control while public opinion was uneven on specific proposals (such as the legalization of undocumented immigrants) and seemingly open to presidential influence.[67]

Bush and Mexican president Vincente Fox took office within a few months of each other, and they soon began bilateral talks about a new temporary worker program and ways to legalize several million undocumented Mexi-cans living in the United States. Bush's first foreign trip was to Fox's ranch in February 2001, and he was eager to work out a bilateral agreement that helped the business community, won him points with Latino voters, and burnished foreign policy skills. Fox and Bush portrayed themselves as "common-sense ranchers" who wanted to make the flow of persons across their shared border "safe, orderly, and legal." For several months after this first meeting, the Bush administration worked on blueprints for both a large new temporary worker program and the legalization of undocumented Mexican immigrants who worked and paid taxes in the United States. In August of 2001, new polling found that 59 percent of Americans favored reductions in legal immigration but 62 percent also endorsed legalizing a significant number of taxpaying undocumented aliens.[68] During a September 6, 2001, visit to Washington, Fox called for a joint agreement on a guest worker program and legalization "by the end of the year," and Bush replied that he intended to "accommodate my friend" and hailed Mexico as the United States' most important ally.[69] But discussions ended abruptly after the terrorist attacks five days later.

In the wake of the 9/11 attacks and its transformation of the immigration policy environment, the Bush administration felt it had little choice but to set aside comprehensive reform. Border hawks such as Representative Tan-credo made headlines in December 2001 by underscoring how porous bor-ders presented an appalling national security problem. Organized interests favoring immigration restriction and strict border control ran ads around the country blaming lax immigration policies for the September 11 terrorist at-tacks. Plans for a guest worker program and legalization fell off the agenda. Instead, large bipartisan majorities in Congress agreed in 2002 to abolish the INS in favor of a new Immigration and Customs Enforcement agency (ICE) housed in the freshly created Department of Homeland Security. Bush officials pointed out that noncitizens had "taken advantage" of "generous" U.S. immigration rules to attack it.[70] Comprehensive immigration reform was off the agenda. Relations with Mexico's Fox also cooled as Bush postponed any relaxation of immigration laws and Fox vigorously opposed the U.S.-led invasion of Iraq.

In the fall of 2003, the AFL-CIO supported hotel workers when they took the lead in organizing the Immigrant Workers Freedom Ride, a national mobilization intended to evoke the civil rights movement's 1961 freedom rides. Organized labor became a strong champion of legalizing undocumented workers in the late 1990s when it became clear that foreign-born union membership was growing sharply while native-born membership was dropping.[71] The Immigrant Workers Freedom Ride drew considerable media attention as roughly one thousand immigrant workers, most of whom were undocumented, rode buses across the country, held rallies in major cities, and ended their trip in Washington where they urged elected officials to enact a sweeping amnesty program. Reactions were decidedly mixed, as restrictionist groups, many conservative commentators, and prominent House Republicans pledged fierce opposition to legalization. Yet by December 2003, Democratic presidential candidates such as Representative Richard Gephardt (MO), Senator Joseph Lieberman (CT), and Governor Howard Dean (VT) endorsed "earned legalization" programs that would provide green cards for undocumented immigrants who had been in the country for five years, had a work history, and passed a background check. As Democrats described immigration reform as "another broken promise" by Bush in debates, word leaked to reporters that "the White House feels it's got to get its irons in the fire now" or risk losing ground with Latino voters in November.[72]

Wasting little time as he kicked off his reelection year, Bush unveiled a major immigration reform plan in the first week of January 2004 that made a new guest worker program its centerpiece. Designed by senior political adviser Karl Rove, in consultation with domestic policy staff, the Bush plan proposed granting three-year, renewable guest worker visas to undocumented immigrants who could find work. These permits were to serve as an eventual path toward citizenship and were designed to allow workers to return to their home countries and to provide them with Social Security benefits, minimum wage, and workplace benefits. The plan also promised tighter border controls, expanded use of technology and personnel at the border, and more stringent internal reporting requirements. "The President has long talked about the importance of having an immigration policy that matches willing workers with willing employers," White House press secretary Scott McClellan explained. "It's important for America to be a welcoming society."[73] Bush's own pleas on behalf of "millions of hardworking men and women condemned to fear and insecurity in a massive, undocumented economy"[74] were both impassioned and personal. "As a Texan I have known many immigrant families, mainly from Mexico, and I've seen what they add to our country," he told audiences. "They bring to America the values of faith in God, love of family, hard work and self-reliance."[75] Critics on both the left and right were unmoved.

From Democratic ranks, Howard Dean argued that the Bush plan helped large corporations who employed undocumented workers but made these workers "a permanent underclass" with no opportunities for upward mobility or full membership. AFL-CIO president John Sweeney echoed these concerns, warning that the guest worker program had "the potential for abuse and exploitation of these workers while undermining the wages and labor protections for all workers."[76] House Democrats led by Nancy Pelosi (D-CA) endorsed a system of "earned legalization" that they described as avoiding the exploitation and abuses of guest worker programs.[77]

Yet the harshest criticism came from congressional restrictionists of the president's own party. Tancredo chided Bush for rewarding people who break the law, while Gallegly said the White House was becoming "the Mexican Department of Social Services."[78] At a Republican retreat in Philadelphia later in the month, Karl Rove got an earful from outraged members of Congress who claimed that their constituents were overwhelmingly opposed to the Bush proposal and that "Hispandering" for votes would create a voter backlash within the party's base.[79] Yet the president's closest advisers were convinced that his immigration proposal would help with Latino voters without sacrificing support from his conservative base. "It's more conservative pundits than conservatives," one adviser observed of conservative radio, television, and print commentators versus rank-and-file voters. Grover Norquist, president of the conservative Americans for Tax Reform and a key pro-business advocate of the president's guest worker program, agreed that immigration reform was a safe strategy to win Latino votes without threatening the Republican base. "It's not a vote-moving issue for any bloc of the center-right coalition," he asserted. "People vote on guns. They vote on taxes. They vote on being pro-life."[80] By March of 2004, a truce was called between immigration restrictionists and expansionists in the Republican Party, as Bush quietly put his immigration proposal aside for the rest of the campaign. Congressional Democrats were not going to give Bush a legislative victory in an election year, and Republican border hawks in both houses made it clear that they would fight reform tooth and nail. That summer, a compromise Republican platform opposed amnesty but not the Bush plan.[81]

The 2004 election returns validate Rove's calculation that courting Latino voters with pro-immigrant rhetoric and a relatively expansive reform proposal could be done without losing ground among voters in the Republican base. Bush's reelection bid produced unprecedented mobilization and support from his partisan base, and it *also* yielded a GOP record 40 percent of the Latino vote.[82] Had Bush stopped here, content to leave immigration reform on the back burner, we might justly conclude that his controversial proposal was driven by the pursuit of an important new constituency for his electoral coalition. And we may conclude that his political gamble proved well worth the risk. Yet the White House did not abandon immigration reform upon reelection, but instead it became the centerpiece of his second term's domestic agenda from day one. Bush's decision to press forward with his polarizing initiative clearly reflected additional factors, including personal faith in the soundness of his policy plan, an eagerness to promote policies that served the labor needs of the business community, and the belief that public opinion was fluid and could be led on the issue.

Soon after the election, Bush met privately with Senator John McCain (R-AZ) to discuss reviving the derailed White House plan for a new guest worker program that would grant legal status to millions of undocumented immigrants. In the House, the administration coordinated with three other western Republicans: Christopher Cannon of Utah and Jeff Flake and Jim Kolbe of Arizona. Immigration reform became the key postelection talking point of Secretary of State Colin Powell, DHS Secretary Tom Ridge, and chief strategist Karl Rove, the latter telling reporters that it was striking that Bush did not lose votes among his conservative base in the election.[83] Press Secretary McClellan added that immigration reform was "a high priority" that the president "intends to work with members on to get moving again in the second term. It's something he believes very strongly in." Restrictionists were aghast. FAIR president Dan Stein doubted that Republican lawmakers would follow the administration "over a cliff" on the issue.[84] He was right. In late November, House Republicans blocked an intelligence overhaul bill to signal Bush that his immigration initiative would split the party and stall action in his second term.[85] Tancredo scorched the White House as abandoning conservative law-and-order values, proclaiming that "their amnesty plan was dead on arrival . . . in January, and if they send the same pig with lipstick back to Congress next January, it will suffer the same fate."[86] His views were echoed by many Republicans leaving a House Republican conference the same month. One Republican leader anonymously observed that it was "highly unusual for the administration to use their political capital that was given by the base against the base."[87]

Polls indeed found that most conservative Republicans disapproved of plans for granting legal status to undocumented immigrants. In truth, however, the business base of the Republican Party was a zealous and unwavering supporter of the president's guest worker plans throughout his two terms in office. The most active business lobbyists favoring the Bush initiatives formed the Essential Worker Immigration Coalition (EWIC), an alliance of immigrant-dependent industry associations headed by the U.S. Chamber of Commerce. The coalition would bring together powerful associations such as the American Health Care Association, the American Hotel and Lodging Association, National Council of Chain Restaurants, the National Retail Federation, and the Associated Builders and Contractors. EWIC was initially formed by meatpacking conglomerates to advocate for expansion of guest worker programs and counts many of the nation's largest employers as members, including Wal-Mart, Tyson Foods, and Marriott.[88]

Illegal immigration and insecure borders were hot-button issues for many Main Street Republicans, and their disquietude was fueled by local and national talk radio, television commentators such as Lou Dobbs and Pat Buchanan, and restrictive politicians such as Tancredo and his House Immigration Reform Caucus. New citizen patrols also propped up along the U.S.-Mexican border. In 2004, an accountant and decorated former Marine, James Gilchrist, founded the all-volunteer Minuteman Project to patrol the Arizona border armed with binoculars and cell phones. Former California schoolteacher Chris Simcox established the separate Minutemen Civil Defense Corps as an extension of this citizen patrol movement.[89] Described as "vigilantes" by Bush, surveys showed that most ordinary citizens approved of the Minuteman movement.[90]

In the winter of 2005, HB 4437, a punitive bill focused on border enforcement, narrowly passed the Republican-controlled House of Representatives. It proposed for the first time to make illegal presence in the United States a felony and made it a crime for any persons or organizations to lend support to undocumented immigrants. The bill was also a direct attack on day laborer centers. From March through May 2006, demonstrations against the bill by largely Latino immigrants and their supporters, unprecedented in number and size, took place in a wide array of cities and towns across the United States.[91] These nationwide rallies, protests, and boycotts drew negative reactions from most Americans: just 24 percent offered a favorable view of people who marched and protested for immigrant rights in major cities, while 52 percent expressed unfavorable opinions.[92] Overall, however, public opinion remained open to varied policy solutions: majorities favored legal status and earned citizenship for undocumented immigrants, stricter employer penalties, and tougher enforcement.[93] National pollsters concluded that most Americans supported the nation's immigrant heritage and granting legal options to undocumented immigrants but that they also wanted better enforcement.[94] Opinion was far from locked in either a restrictive or expansive position. If the Bush administration hoped that the president would be able to lead public views on the issue, they were disappointed that only 39 percent of Americans supported the president's approach on immigration reform (with 47% opposed) in the spring of 2006. Strikingly, 60 percent of Republicans backed Bush's plan, a number that would dwindle steadily in coming months.[95]

Three distinct Senate bills emerged in the spring of 2006: the first a bipartisan effort of Edward Kennedy (D-MA) and John McCain (R-AZ), the second from the Judiciary Committee chaired by Arlen Specter (R-PA), and a third from two border-state Republicans—John Cornyn (R-TX) and Jon Kyl (R-AZ). The McCain/Kennedy and Judiciary bills both attempted to satisfy disparate camps by including tough new language on border and interior enforcement, employment verification and an expanded guest worker program along with earned legalization for millions of undocumented, a reduction of the family immigration backlog, and a modified version of AgJOBS, a bill that provided legal status for a significant portion of undocumented agricultural workers. The AFL-CIO ended up opposing all three bills, reiterating its opposition to an expanded guest worker program, while the Service Employees International Union (SEIU) and the Hotel Employees and Restaurant Employees International Union (HERE) supported McCain/Kennedy and the Judiciary committee bills.[96] The Senate Judiciary bill passed the full Senate that spring but died in the House. With a majority of the House supporting a law-and-order approach to the issue while the Senate favored a more liberal bill, immigration reform was tabled until after the election. In November, Democrats gained control of both the House and Senate. President Bush, viewing the new Congress as an opportunity, began speaking of "a bipartisan effort" on immigration reform.

As the federal debate intensified, the Bush administration turned up the pressure for legislative action. ICE, after having all but abandoned large-scale workplace raids as an enforcement strategy since 1999,[97] launched an aggressive worksite enforcement campaign. The number of undocumented workers arrested on administrative immigration violations during worksite enforcement investigations increased from 485 in FY 2002 to 3,667 in FY 2006 and five months into 2007 had already reached 3,226.[98] The president also made overtures to enforcement-minded conservatives by proposing to put six thousand National Guard troops on the Mexican border. If the Bush administration's increased enforcement efforts and overtures were designed to dramatize the need for comprehensive immigration reform, it fueled grassroots opposition led by restrictionist groups and right-wing talk show hosts who were angered by the huge spring marches for immigrant rights. In the fall, Bush endorsed the Secure Fence Act of 2006 that authorized the construction of a 700-mile fence along the 2,000-mile U.S. border with Mexico. Signed just twelve days before the midterm elections, Bush used the occasion to urge moderation to assembled House and Senate Republicans. "There is a rational middle ground between granting an automatic path to citizenship for every illegal immigrant and a program of mass deportation," he observed, "and I look forward to working with Congress to find that middle ground."[99]

The midterm elections gave Democrats control of the House and Senate, but many of the new Democrats were moderates who won in culturally conservative swing districts that favored enforcement first. Surveys also showed that conservative white Republicans were the most hostile to the Bush administration's plans to provide a path to legal status for undocumented immigrants, and that they overwhelmingly favored mass deportations, denial of public benefits for immigrants, and a constitutional amendment depriving birthright citizenship to the children of undocumented immigrants. At the same time, polls showed that Bush and the Republican brand had lost considerable ground with Latino voters since the 2004 election, with most concluding that Democrats could be more trusted to handle the threshold issue of immigration.[100] The Bush plan was at once splitting and narrowing his base.

In March and April of 2007, Kennedy resubmitted the Judiciary bill as a starting point for Senate discussion, while Representative Luis Gutierrez (D-IL) submitted his own immigration bill. Both were liberal Democrats, and Kennedy had long been labor's leading ally in the Senate, yet both men incorporated guest worker programs in their proposals despite AFL-CIO opposition and Democratic control of Congress. The Gutierrez bill included earned legalization for the 12 million undocumented immigrants, as well as a large new temporary worker program. Nevertheless, it was embraced as a starting point by SEIU, HERE, the National Council of La Raza, the National Immigration Forum, and other allies. The White House also promulgated a proposal, although not in legislative form. By May, a bipartisan Senate coalition led by Kennedy negotiated behind the scenes and eventually put forward the Border Security and Immigration Act of 2007, a "grand bargain" that had the support of President Bush and became the focus of all meaningful subsequent discussion.[101]

Emerging in June 2007, the grand bargain included significant new funding for border security and other interior enforcement measures. It imposed criminal penalties for illegal entry, which had previously been a misdemeanor offense, and proposed to replace the current family- and employment-based admissions system with a "merit-based" system. The bill provided a new Z visa for undocumented immigrants that covered "a principal or employed alien, the spouse or elderly parent of that alien and the minor children of that alien" currently living in the United States, provided that they pay fees and penalties that could total as much as $8,000, and a "touchback provision" requiring the leader of the household to return home before applying for legal permanent residency status. It also contained a temporary Y worker program of about 200,000 that would allow workers to be admitted for a two-year period that could be renewed twice as long as the worker spent a period of one year outside of the United States between each admission (which eventually had a five-year sunset provision). Incorporating the White House proposal, the bill contained triggers to be met before the Z or Y visas could begin. These triggers included 18,000 border patrol hired, construction of 200 miles of vehicle barriers and 370 miles of fencing, resources to detain up to 27,500 persons per day on an annual basis, and the use of secure and effective identification tools to prevent unauthorized work.

Subject to intense media scrutiny and commentary, the public response to the compromise Senate immigration plan ranged from hostile to tepid. Many members of Congress were deluged with angry phone calls, e-mails, and letters from constituents and other activists. Surveys indicated that most Republicans, Democrats, and Independents opposed the measure, with only 23 percent in favor. Significantly, most Americans opposed the initiative not because they opposed "amnesty" or other proposals for legalizing millions of undocumented immigrants in the country (roughly two-thirds supported earned citizenship options over deportation), but rather because they had little trust that it would provide genuine border security. More than 80 percent in surveys said that they did not believe that the Bush-Senate compromise bill would reduce illegal immigration or enhance border control.[102]

This profound cynicism born of past implementation failures was a powerful theme for many lawmakers of both parties who lined up against the "grand bargain." Senator Byron Dorgan (D-ND) recalled believing the promises of the Simpson-Mazzoli Act when he was in Congress in 1986, only later discovering that "none of them were true, and three million people got amnesty. There was no border security to speak of, no employer sanctions to speak of, and there was no enforcement." Robert Byrd (D-WV) vowed "not to make the same mistake twice," while Charles Grassley said, "I was fooled once, and history has taught me a valuable lesson."[103] Dorgan and Grassley would be among dozens of senators proposing amendments designed to derail or fundamentally alter the fragile compromise bill that brought together EWIC and other business lobbies, the NCLR and various ethnic and civil rights groups, the ACLU, and labor unions such as the SEIU, HERE, and the United Farm Workers.

In late June, angry constituents, organized interests from the AFL-CIO to restrictionist lobbies, and both conservative and liberal lawmakers successfully blocked cloture on the Senate bill and thereby dashed hopes of avoiding killer amendments.[104] Fox News polling reaffirmed that conservatives were bitterly opposed to the bill and disenchanted with Bush, while a Democratic poll conducted by Stan Greenburg showed Democratic identifiers to be split 47 percent for and 47 percent against the bill.[105] With the measure close to death, the White House and a small bipartisan group of senators worked behind the scenes on a last-ditch effort to save the compromise plan.

Although insulated discussions saved the Immigration Reform and Control Act in 1986, private negotiations drew fire from all sides in the summer of 2007. "The process has been orchestrated by a handful of people behind closed doors," Senator Bob Corker (R-TN) observed, "and they are paying a price for that."[106] In truth, closed-door negotiations represented the primary means that an unpalatable compromise could be brokered among disparate interests. Yet the forces arrayed against this last-ditch effort were overwhelming, from the grassroots to the halls of Congress. Ultimately, the "grand bargain" developed by Bush, Kennedy, and McCain fell fourteen votes short of the sixty needed to force a final vote. Fifteen Democrats were among those who helped kill the bill, including freshman senators from swing states such as Claire McCaskill (MO), Jon Tester (MT), and Jim Webb (VA). Even if the bill had survived the Senate, it faced a steep climb in the House. Democrats like Jason Altmire, a freshman from a socially conservative district in Western Pennsylvania, served notice that they and other party centrists saw immigration reform as an electoral problem and said they "wouldn't want this to be viewed as a Democratic initiative." The House Republican Conference chair, Adam Putnam of Florida, dared the Speaker to champion the measure. "If Pelosi takes up the Senate bill and moves it further to the left," he told reporters, "it will convert our biggest political liability into a motivating force for our base."[107] Against this backdrop, Pelosi informed the White House that she would not even begin to consider taking up the bill unless at least seventy House Republicans committed to support the effort. Her demand proved unnecessary. On June 28, 2007, the grand bargain was defeated in the Senate for the second and final time.[108]

Bush had pursued comprehensive immigration reform out of a strong personal conviction that the best solution to the bedeviling problems associated with unauthorized flows was an expansive guest worker program that matched willing employers and willing laborers. He also believed that stricter enforcement of employer sanctions, improved efforts at the border, and earned citizenship for undocumented immigrants were necessary features of an effective compromise package. He and his advisers also were convinced that public opinion could be swayed on the issue, that his conservative base would hold and not rebel, and that his compassionate pragmatism on immigration reform would draw unprecedented numbers of Latino voters into the Republican fold. Tellingly, whatever inroads were made in 2000 and 2004 with Latinos and other new immigrant voters were forgotten by 2008 when another immigrant-friendly Republican stood atop the ticket. Consistent with trends that began in 2005 when Latinos soured on Bush's immigration plan and on House Republicans viewed as anti-immigrant, Barrack Obama and Democrats dominated the Latino vote in 2008 with more than two-thirds support in crucial battleground states from Florida to the Southwest. Equally troubling to Republicans was the fact that Latino turnout increased to 11 million voters (9% of the total) in 2008, double the turnout in 2000.[109] Bush's gamble on immigration reform also sealed the fate of his second-term domestic agenda; he had no political capital left to expend on Capitol Hill.

Conclusion

The Clinton administration elected *not* to propose significant immigration policy initiatives, first seeking to keep the issue in abeyance and then choosing to selectively validate or repudiate legislation shepherded by Republicans in the House and Senate. In contrast to the Clinton White House's preference for inaction or defensive reaction, the Bush administration made immigration reform a centerpiece of its domestic policy agenda before the terrorist attacks of September 11, 2001, and again from 2004 to 2007. Ironically, Clinton ultimately signed two laws in 1996 with major implications for immigrant admissions and rights, while Bush's determined pursuit of immigration reform ended in frustration and essentially sounded the death knell for his domestic policy leadership. When immigration reform exploded for the last time in the summer of 2007, Bush had virtually no political capital left either to mobilize his own base to support new domestic reforms or to build bipartisan coalitions behind pragmatic initiatives. Finally, the implications of fractious immigration politics for the political coalitions of Clinton and Bush stand in sharp contrast. Whereas the Clinton administration deftly (and ironically) translated its lethargy and defensive opportunism on immigration policy into electoral gains for the Democrats among Latinos and Asians, the aftermath for the Bush White House was a rebellious and unmanageable party base both within and beyond Washington and lost ground among new immigrant voters. These competing presidential choices and strategies for addressing one of the nation's most formidable modern policy dilemmas have had profound implications for their partisan coalitions.

The Early Obama Years

Undaunted by Bush's quixotic struggles for comprehensive immigration reform only a few years before, Barack Obama ran for president pledging to win a bipartisan compromise package that would enhance border control while extending legal status to roughly 12 million undocumented immigrants. In the two previous presidential elections, both major-party candidates touted strong pro-immigration credentials as they courted immigrant and co-ethnic Latino and Asian voters. During the 2008 campaign, however, Obama's position on immigration distinguished him from his Republican opponent, John McCain, who assumed a tough enforcement stance. McCain, once committed to comprehensive reform and guest worker programs, became an eleventh-hour border hawk during the primaries to appease a partisan base adamantly opposed to extending legal status to unauthorized immigrants no matter how long they lived in the country. When the dust settled, Obama's pro-immigration appeals helped him garner 67 percent of the Latino and 64 percent of the Asian vote in 2008. Yet neither this support nor his broader popularity upon entering office, the new president believed, was sufficient to propel major policy innovation. Even in an era of partisan polarization, few issues rivaled illegal immigration for how great the divide was between the Democratic and Republican base—ideological distance replicated in Congress.[110] Moreover, conflicts *within* each party on how to govern immigration remained profound. Obama's promise to secure sweeping immigration reform in his first year won cheers from the Democratic base on the campaign trail, but it loomed as a tall order for an untested administration.

Soon after entering office, the Obama White House announced that an immigration initiative would have to come after more looming priorities such as health care, energy, and financial regulatory reform.[111] Its determination to push the issue off its action agenda was influenced by two crucial coalitional realities. First, the Obama team could not find more than one Republican senator and a handful of Republican House members willing to work across the aisle on immigration reform. Major immigration policy innovation has long hinged on uneasy bipartisan compromises, but Republican lawmakers were in no mood to contradict hard-liners in the conservative media or to antagonize fervent anti-immigrant activists in their base. Second, the administration understood well that congressional Democrats from swing states and districts were politically exposed by the issue, with many publicly opposing any deal that included a "path to earned citizenship" for undocumented immigrants. These daunting impediments to building a majority coalition only compounded the bedeviling practical policy choices and broader public cynicism about comprehensive immigration reform. It is within this context that the Obama administration decided that the subject was too politically explosive to tackle at the outset. Instead, Obama reassured restive Latino and immigrant rights groups that he was ready to lead a "difficult" fight for reform when the time was right.

However, the administration learned that it was not so easy to change the subject. Claims that undocumented immigrants would benefit from health care reform became a prominent feature of vituperative town hall meetings during the summer of 2009. They elicited a strong rebuke from Obama in his health care speech to a joint session of Congress the following fall, serving as the impetus for Representative Joe Wilson's infamous outburst, "You lie!" At the first national Tea Party Convention in Nashville, Tennessee, during the winter of 2010, immigrants and immigration reform were major topics of speeches heard by assembled delegates of the grassroots movement. In one of the most prominent keynote addresses, the failed 2008 GOP presidential candidate and former representative Tom Tancredo was cheered when he fulminated that Obama was elected by naturalized immigrants and other people "who can't even spell the word 'vote' or speak English." Warning rapt delegates that "our culture is at stake," he then made headlines by lamenting, "we do not have a civics, literacy test before people can vote."[112] The next day, Tancredo joined Roy Beck, executive director of the restrictionist Numbers USA, to argue that cracking down on illegal immigration, discouraging "chain migration" from developing countries by cutting family preferences in legal admissions, and denying birthright citizenship (jus soli) to the children of undocumented mothers were keys to solving the nation's deep social and economic woes.[113] In the months that followed, the lone Republican senator who had been willing to work with Obama on immigration reform, Lindsey Graham of South Carolina, responded to pressure from his conservative base by announcing that he would seek to amend the Constitution to deny birthright citizenship to the children of undocumented immigrants. "People come here to have babies," Graham told Fox News. "They come here to drop a child. It's called, 'drop and leave.' To have a child in America, they cross the border, they go to the emergency room, have a child, and that child's automatically an American citizen. That shouldn't be the case."[114] A bipartisan deal on immigration reform was chimerical.

During the heat of the 2010 election, illegal immigration was again center stage. In races across the country, Republican candidates railed against "illegal aliens who take our jobs" and increase taxes by placing strains on "health care, criminal justice, and the educational system."[115] During the hotly contested Nevada Senate campaign, Republican challenger Sharron Angle ran negative ads blaming incumbent senator Harry Reid for "millions of illegal aliens, swarming across our border, joining violent gangs, forcing families to live in fear." By contrast, Obama sought to rally Latino voter support during the waning stages of the election by renewing his pledge to secure comprehensive immigration reform. In an interview with a popular Univision radio show in October 2010, Obama told the audience that the chief obstacle to reform was Republican intransigence on the issue. At every turn, Obama explained, he met resistance from "anti-immigration" Republicans "who are supportive of the Arizona law, who talk only about border security, . . . who are out there engaging in rhetoric that is divisive and damaging." He also reaffirmed his commitment to legalization. "I deeply believe that we've got to solve our immigration problem so that we're both a nation of immigrants and a nation of laws so that people can come out of the shadows . . . [and] that people who are productive and otherwise law-abiding are able to get on a pathway to citizenship." Further, Obama told the audience that he nevertheless was "committed to making it happen. We're going to get it done."[116]

While Angle's anti-immigrant attacks cost her dearly on election night, fellow Arizona Republican Janet Brewer easily won reelection as governor largely by touting her key role in enacting the nation's toughest law on illegal immigration, SB 1070. This controversial statute granted police broad power to question and to detain those they suspected were undocumented aliens. More significantly for national policymaking, the new House Judiciary Committee chair Lamar Smith (R-TX) and Immigration Subcommittee chair Steve King (R-IA) are longtime supporters of restrictive immigration measures. Both ardently oppose legalization for undocumented immigrants or birthright citizenship for their children, and they endorse "Arizona-style immigration enforcement," a crackdown on sanctuary cities, and reductions in legal immigration. King gained notoriety for advocating an electrified fence spanning the U.S.-Mexican border because "we do this with livestock all the time."[117] Like anti-immigration reformers of the early twentieth century, contemporary border hawks like Smith and King hope to win broad support by linking their restrictionist agenda to jobs, cultural protection, and national security. For some Republican leaders and key business constituencies who employ newcomers, however, affixing the Republican brand to perceived anti-immigrant causes poses grave long-term electoral and economic consequences.[118]

The Obama administration has fewer degrees of freedom on immigration than its predecessors. "If a fight starts, watch the crowd," E. E. Schattschneider advised us nearly fifty years ago. He was reflecting on how political conflicts are profoundly shaped by their scope, and bystanders may enter the fray and alter the power dynamics among those politically engaged on an issue.[119] The scope of conflict in American politics over illegal immigration and the future of undocumented aliens is greater now than it has been for decades, if not ever. Against this backdrop, Obama has not had the luxury to be as cautiously opportunistic as the Clinton White House was. Yet, thus far, he also has rejected Bush's unflinching pursuit of reform before lining up his congressional ducks. Given his campaign promises and his courtship of Latino, Asian, and immigrant voters, Obama has strong incentives to vigorously champion comprehensive immigration reform while avoiding the political traps that derailed the Bush plans. How Obama navigates this political minefield will have profound implications for his reelection, his transformative policy aspirations, and future party politics as American democracy adapts to new demography.

NOTES

1. This tendency for legal immigration policymaking to present opportunities for distributive politics and to raise few initial costs in an era of budget austerity is discussed most explicitly in my analysis of recent legal reform in Daniel J. Tichenor, *Dividing Lines: The Politics of Immigration Control in America* (Princeton, NJ: Princeton University Press, 2002). For a powerful cross-national model of this sort of distributive politics and interest group lobbying, see Gary Freeman, "Modes of Immigration Politics in Liberal Democratic States," *International Migration Review* 29, no. 4 (Winter 1995): 881–902.

2. On the redistributive character of illegal immigration politics, see James Gimpel and James Edwards, *The Congressional Politics of Immigration Reform* (New York: Longman, 1998).

3. See Daniel Tichenor, "Strange Bedfellows: The Politics and Pathologies of Immigration Reform," *Labor: Studies in Working-Class History*, Summer 2008, 39–60.

4. In thinking about presidential leadership and the emergence, articulation, and decline of partisan coalitions, a powerful theoretical and empirical foundation is provided by Stephen Skowronek, *The Politics Presidents Make* (Cambridge, MA: Harvard University Press, 1997).

5. T. H. Marshall, *Citizenship and Social Class and Other Essays* (Cambridge: Cambridge University Press, 1950).

6. Douglass is quoted in Adrian Cook, *The Armies of the Streets* (Lexington: University Press of Kentucky, 1974), 205.

7. The views of both of these labor leaders are discussed extensively in Tichenor, *Dividing Lines*, chap. 5.

8. Janice Fine and Daniel Tichenor, "A Movement Wrestling: American Labor's Enduring Struggle with Immigration, 1866–2007," *Studies in American Political Development* 23 (2009): 84–113.

9. U.S. Commission on Immigration Reform, *U.S. Immigration Policy: Restoring Credibility* (Washington, DC: Government Printing Office, 1994).

10. Lisa Caruso, "Splits on the Left," *National Journal*, June 30, 2007.

11. Andrew Carnegie, *Triumphant Democracy* (New York, 1887), 34.

12. Lowell is quoted in Tichenor, *Dividing Lines: The Politics of Immigration Control in America*, 38.

13. Patrick Buchanan, "State of Emergency: The Third World Invasion and Conquest of America" (New York: St. Martin's Press, 2006).

14. The arduous path to the Simpson-Mazzoli legislation in 1986 is discussed in depth in Tichenor, *Dividing Lines*, chap. 9.

15. On the politics of blame avoidance, see R. Kent Weaver, "The Politics of Blame Avoidance," *Journal of Public Policy*, October–December 1986, 371–98.

16. Luis Gutierrez interview, Democracy Now Radio and Television, May 2, 2006, transcript.

17. Marc Rosenblum, "A 'Path to Citizenship' or Current Illegal Immigrants?," Online Debate, Council of Foreign Relations website, April 1, 2007.

18. Carol Swain, "Introduction," in *Debating Immigration*, ed. Carol Swain (New York: Cambridge University Press, 2007), 1–16.

19. Lou Dobbs, "Big Media Hide Truth about Immigration," CNN.com, April 25, 2007.

20. George W. Bush, Address to the Nation on Immigration Reform, May 15, 2006.

21. See Tom Tancredo, *In Mortal Danger* (Nashville: WND Books, 2006).

22. Alan Dean Foster, "Garden Variety Javelinas," *New York Times*, August 7, 2010; Daniel B. Wood, "Opinion Polls Show Broad Support for Tough Arizona Immigration Law," *Christian Science Monitor*, April 30, 2010; Randal C. Archibold, "Arizona Law Is Stoking Unease among Latinos," *New York Times*, May 28, 2010.

23. Andrew Biemiller to Peter Rodino, September 8, 1972; Biemiller to Rodino, March 23, 1973; Rodino to Biemiller, May 15, 1973, Papers of the Legislation Department of the AFL-CIO, Box 71, Folder 28, George Meany Archives.

24. See, e.g., *New York Times*, December 31, 1974.

25. *Congressional Record*, September 12, 1972, 30164, 30182-83; National Council of La Raza documents made available to the author by the national office of the NCLR.

26. White House Statement, August 4, 1977, Patricia Roberts Harris Papers.

27. "Memorandum to Interested Parties from the Mexican-American Legal Defense and Education Fund: Statement of Position regarding the Administration's Undocumented Alien Legislation Proposal," November 11, 1977, Papers of the Leadership Conference on Civil Rights, Container 23, "Issues: Alien Civil Rights" Folder.

28. Ngai, *Impossible Subjects: Illegal Aliens and the Making of Modern America* (Princeton, NJ: Princeton University Press, 2005).

29. Author's anonymous interviews with Reagan administration officials, 1996; see also U.S. Commission on Immigration Reform, *U.S. Immigration Policy: Restoring Credibility* (Washington, DC: Government Printing Office, 1994), 95.

30. Ibid.

31. Alan Simpson to Lawrence Fuchs, January 24, 1991, Correspondence Files of Lawrence Fuchs, made available to the author by Fuchs.

32. See, e.g., Kitty Calavita, *Inside the State: The Bracero Program, Immigration, and the I.N.S.* (New York: Routledge, 1992).

33. Jorge Durand and Douglas Massey, eds., *Crossing the Border* (New York: Russell Sage, 2004).

34. Author's interviews with FAIR staff, California Save Our State movement leaders, and local activists.

35. William Jefferson Clinton, "Remarks and an Exchange with Reporters on Immigration Policy," *Weekly Compilation of Presidential Documents*, August 2, 1993.

36. Author's interview with Harold Ezell and anonymous staffer of SOS.

37. *Los Angeles Times*, October 29, 1994.

38. One can track the steady increase in restrictionist sentiment in Gallup Poll, *Public Opinion* (Wilmington, DE: Scholarly Resources, 1994), 250–51, and the American National Election Studies (Ann Arbor: University of Michigan Press, 1994).

39. NBC News/*Wall Street Journal* poll, October 14, 1994.

40. Gallup/Chicago Council of Foreign Relations Poll, October 7, 1994, in *American Public Opinion and U.S. Foreign Relations, 1995*, ed. Jack Reilly (Chicago: Chicago Council of Foreign Relations, 1995), 32.

41. Jack Citrin, Donald Green, Christopher Muste, and Cara Wong, "Public Opinion toward Immigration Reform," *Journal of Politics* 59, no. 3 (1997): 858–81.

42. Author's interviews with Republican House members; see also Dan Carney, "GOP Casts a Kinder Eye on 'Huddled Masses,'" *Congressional Quarterly Weekly Reports*, May 15, 1999, 1127–29.

43. Quoted in David Reimers, *Unwelcome Strangers: American Identity and the Turn against Immigration* (New York: Columbia University Press, 1999), 134.

44. U.S. Commission on Immigration Reform, *Restoring Credibility*.

45. U.S. Commission on Immigration Reform, *Legal Immigration: Setting Priorities* (Washington, DC: Government Printing Office, 1995).

46. *New York Times*, May 25, 1995.

47. See the comments of Chris Smith and Mark Souter, *Washington Times*, March 20, 1996.

48. Author's anonymous interviews with interest group leaders and lobbyists; see also John Juddis, "Huddled Elites," *New Republic*, December 23, 1996, 23–26.

49. *Wall Street Journal*, June 9, 1995; *Congressional Quarterly Weekly Reports*, November 25, 1995, 3600.

50. *Congressional Quarterly Almanac, 1995* (Washington, DC: Congressional Quarterly Press, 1996).

51. Kenneth Lee, *Huddled Masses, Muddled Laws* (Westport, CT: Greenwood Press, 1998), 108–9.

52. *New York Times*, December 8, 1994.

53. *Congressional Quarterly Weekly Reports*, March 23, 1996, 798.

54. *Congressional Quarterly Weekly Reports*, April 15, 1995, 1071.

55. Statement on Signing Executive Order on Illegal Immigration, *Weekly Compilation of Presidential Documents*, February 19, 1996.

56. Quoted in Reimers, *Unwelcome Strangers*, 143.

57. Dick Kirtschten, "Politicking Takes a Bill to the Brink," *National Journal*, September 21, 1996, 2015.

58. See FAIR advertisement, *Washington Times*, August 25, 1996.

59. Author's interviews with congressional members; see also 1996 Republican views of immigration as a "wedge" issue in *Congressional Quarterly Weekly Reports*, May 15, 1999, 1127–29.

60. *Congressional Quarterly Weekly Reports*, May 15, 1999, 1127.

61. William Schneider, "Immigration Issue Rewards Democrats," *National Journal*, November 30, 1996, 2622.

62. See *Hispanic Magazine*, January–February 2001; on earlier Republican adjustments, see Dick Kirschten, "Trying a Little Tenderness," *National Journal*, January 10, 1998, 54.

63. Robert Suro, Richard Fry, and Jeffrey Passel, "Hispanics and the 2004 Election," Pew Hispanic Center Report, June 27, 2005.

64. E.g., see Dan Balz, "Incumbent Reaches beyond His Base," *Washington Post*, January 8, 2004, 1.

65. Slobhan Gorman, "Reframing the Debate," *National Journal*, March 2, 2002, 618.

66. Mike Allen, "Immigration Reform on Bush Agenda," *Washington Post*, December 24, 2003, 1.

67. On the unsettled character of public opinion on how to deal with illegal immigration during the Bush years, see, for instance, Rasmussen Reports, "Immigration Issue Remains Divisive," March 30, 2006.

68. Gorman, "Reframing the Debate," 618.

69. Mike Allen, "Immigration Reform on Bush Agenda," *Washington Post*, December 24, 2003, 1.

70. Ibid.

71. Immigrant Union Members Numbers and Trends Migration Policy Institute Immigration Facts, May 2004, no. 7. See also Fine and Tichenor, "A Movement Wrestling," 89–114.

72. Allen, *Immigration Reform on Bush Agenda*," 1.

73. James Lakely and Joseph Curl, "Bush Will Propose Plan on Illegals," *Washington Times*, January 6, 2004, 1.

74. Doug Saunders, "Bush Plans Amnesty for Illegal Workers," *Globe and Mail*, January 8, 2004, 17.

75. Balz, "Incumbent Reaches beyond His Base," 1.

76. Richard Stevenson and Steven Greenhouse, "Bush on Immigration," *New York Times*, January 8, 2004, 28.

77. Amy Fagan, "Democrats Offer Plan on Aliens," January 29, 2004, *Washington Times*, 1.

78. Wayne Washington, "Campaign 2004: Bush Upsets Part of Conservative Base," *Boston Globe*, January 9, 2004, 1.

79. Ralph Hallow and James Lakely, "GOP Slams Bush Policies at Retreat," *Washington Times*, 1.

80. Washington, "Campaign 2004," 1.

81. Ralph Hallow, "GOP to Finesse the Immigration Issue," *Washington Times*, August 23, 2004, 4.

82. Suro et al., "Hispanics and the 2004 Election." See also "The Latino, Asian, and Immigrant Vote: 2004," National Immigration Forum Backgrounder.

83. Bill Sammon, "Bush Revives Bid to Legalize Illegal Aliens," *Washington Times*, November 10, 2004, 1; Daren Briscoe, "Immigration—A Hot Topic," *Newsweek*, November 22, 2004, 10.

84. Ibid.

85. Stephen Dinan, "House Shuns Illegals Proposal," *Washington Times*, November 11, 2004, 1.

86. Sammon, "Bush Revives Bid to Legalize Illegal Aliens."

87. Dinan, "House Shuns Illegals Proposal."

88. Fine and Tichenor, "A Movement Wrestling," 98–114.

89. Jim Gilchrist and Jerome Corsi, *Minutemen: The Battle to Secure America's Borders* (Los Angeles: World Ahead, 2006).

90. "Immigration Issue Remains Divisive," *Rasmussen Reports*, March 30, 2006 (containing earlier survey results).

91. See Victor Narro, Kent Wong, and Janna Sahdduck-Hernandez, "The 2006 Immigrant Uprising: Origins and Future," *New Labor Forum* 16, no. 1 (December 2007): 49–56, and Bill Ong Hing and Kevin R. Johnson, "The Immigrant Rights Marches of 2006 and the Prospects of a New Civil Rights Movement," *Harvard Civil Rights–Civil Liberties Law Review* 42 (2007).

92. "24% Have Favorable Opinion of Protestors," *Rasmussen Reports*, May 1, 2006.

93. "Immigration Rallies Fail to Move Public Opinion," *Rasmussen Reports*, May 3, 2006.

94. "Politicians Missed Key Point on Immigration Debate," *Rasmussen Reports*, May 7, 2006.

95. "39% Agree with President on Immigration," *Rasmussen Reports*, May 17, 2006.

96. Other unions within the Change to Win coalition, including the Laborers and the United Food and Commercial Workers, also objected to the guest worker provisions in the bills and, like the AFL-CIO, refused to support them.

97. Workplace enforcement policy has shifted over the years. During the Clinton years, additional resources were allocated to interior enforcement efforts, including employment eligibility verification and workplace enforcement, and between 1995 and 1998 the INS carried out large numbers of workplace raids, resulting in thousands of arrests. But in 1998, the INS, responding to complaints about agency tactics during raids, altered its approach to focus on working with employers to improve their compliance with employment eligibility requirements and to target criminal employer cases in which there was a clear pattern of knowingly hiring the undocumented, as well as engaging in abusive treatment of workers and violating labor and employment laws. In 1999, the INS targeted the meatpacking industry. Operation Vanguard subpoenaed all the I-9 forms and employment records of workers in all the meatpacking plants in Nebraska and others in Iowa and South Dakota, checked these records against INS and Social Security databases, and identified workers whose work authorization could not be verified. The lists were given to employers, who then "arranged interviews" for the workers with the INS. There was a strong political backlash against Operation Vanguard, and it was discontinued. See "Immigration Enforcement within the United States," Congressional Research Service (CRS) Year 2006, 37–40; see also Worksite Enforcement Fact Sheet, U.S. Immigration and Customs Enforcement, June 12, 2007.

98. Historically, many more resources had been committed to border enforcement: according to the CRS, U.S. Border Patrol resources close to doubled between FY 1997 and FY 2003, while interior enforcement activities increased only slightly and the number of inspection hours went down. "Furthermore, focusing on interior enforcement, in FY 2003, the largest amount of staff time was devoted to locating and arresting criminal aliens (39%), followed by administrative and non-investigative duties (23%) and alien smuggling investigations (15%). Only 4% was devoted to worksite enforcement (i.e. locating and arresting aliens working without authorization, and punishing employers who hire such workers)." Worksite Enforcement Fact Sheet, U.S. Immigration and Customs Enforcement, June 12, 2007.

99. "Bush OKs 700 Mile Border Fence," *CNN.com*, October 26, 2006.

100. Thomas Edsall and Zachary Goldfarb, "Bush Is Losing Hispanics' Support," *Washington Post*, May 21, 2006.

101. Robert Pear and Jim Rutenberg, "Senators in Bipartisan Deal on Immigration Bill," May 18, 2007, A-1.

102. "Support for Senate Immigration Bill Falls," *Rasmussen Reports*, June 6, 2007; "Why the Senate Immigration Bill Failed," *Rasmussen Reports*, June 8, 2007.

103. Robert Pear, "'86 Law Looms over Immigration Fights," *New York Times*, June 12, 2007; Stephen Dinan, "Grassley Admits Amnesty Mistake," *Washington Times*, June 22, 2007.

104. On June 8 (34 Y–61 N) a majority composed of conservative Republicans and liberal Democrats opposed the bill.

105. Carolyn Lochhead, "Democratic Poll Finds Tepid Support for Immigration Bill," *San Francisco Chronicle*, June 20, 2007; Angus Reid, "Americans Pick Enforcement in Immigration Debate," *Global Monitor*, June 11, 2007.

106. Gail Russell Chaddock, "Senate Makes a New Try for Immigration Bill," *Christian Science Monitor*, June 21, 2007.

107. Jonathan Allen, "Bar Is Set High for Immigration Bill in the House," *Congressional Quarterly*, June 21, 2007.

108. The actual vote was on invoking cloture, and it was 46 Y–53 N.

109. "Latino Vote Fueling Introspection for Republicans," *America's Voice*, November 11, 2008.

110. Nolan McCarty, Keith Poole, and Howard Rosenthal, *Polarized America: The Dance of Ideology and Unequal Riches* (Cambridge, MA: MIT Press, 2006).

111. Ginger Thompson and David Herszenhorn, "Obama Set for First Step on Immigration Reform," *New York Times*, June 25, 2009; Michael Farrell, "Obama Delays Immigration Reform—at Great Risk," *Christian Science Monitor*, August 11, 2009.

112. Brian Kates, "Tea Party Convention's Racial Brouhaha," *New York Daily News*, February 5, 2010.

113. Ibid.

114. E. J. Dionne, "Is the GOP Shedding a Birthright?" *Washington Post*, August 5, 2010.

115. James Coburn, "Candidates Sound Off on Illegal Immigration," *Edmund Sun*, July 12, 2010; Josh Kraushaar, "Tennesee Republicans Feud over Immigration," May 25, 2010, *Politico*.

116. "Univision Transcript: Piolin Interview with President Barack Obama," October 26, 2010.

117. Elise Foley, "House Immigration Policy Now in the Hands of GOP," *Washington Independent*, November 3, 2010.

118. Author's anonymous interviews with eight GOP officials, strategists, and congressional staffers, November 2010; see also "Dream Act's Failure Could Drive Latino Voters," *USA Today*, December 20, 2010.

119. E. E. Schattschneider, *The Semi-Sovereign People* (New York: Holt, Rinehart & Winston, 1960).

CHAPTER FOUR

Embracing the Third Rail?
Social Security Politics from Clinton to Obama

R. Kent Weaver

Social Security has long been known as the "Third Rail of American Politics"—touch it and you die. This image is misleading: both Bill Clinton and George W. Bush proposed significant Social Security initiatives and lived to tell the tale; indeed, President Bush put Social Security reform on the agenda not once but *twice*. While both presidents encountered major political difficulties with Congress and the public during their terms in office, Social Security was not anywhere close to the main source of those difficulties. Moreover, both were reelected to a second term. But while both presidents survived Social Security initiatives, the initiatives themselves did not; Social Security pensions emerged from the Clinton and G. W. Bush presidencies almost untouched. Barack Obama pursued a much more cautious approach to Social Security reform in his first two years in office but nevertheless suffered a major electoral rebuff in the 2010 midterm congressional elections.

This chapter uses Social Security policymaking to address three theoretical questions. The first concerns presidential initiatives: when and why do presidents propose initiatives that appear to deviate from the preferences of median voters—for example, that appeal to their political base or to a constituency that the president is hoping to attract to his political coalition—rather than putting forward proposals that hew closely to median voter positions or simply proposing nothing? Second, what determines the fate of these initiatives: under what conditions do they win enactment, in a form that is either close to the president's preferences or significantly different from the president's preferences, and when do they fail to be enacted at all? Third, how do policy initiatives by presidents (or, more rarely, legislative party leaders in Congress), whether successful or unsuccessful, contribute to the efforts of presidents and other political actors to build and manage stable, winning political coalitions over time?

Different theoretical perspectives on decision making suggest different empirical puzzles flowing from these research questions—indeed, whether the facts found in the case of Social Security are puzzles at all. From the median voter perspective, the puzzle is why President Bush *twice* put Social Security reform on the agenda when its potential political risks were clear. That the initiative failed is not much of a puzzle at all from this perspective. In a contrasting view popularized by Jacob Hacker and Paul Pierson in their book *Off Center*, a cohesive Republican Party in Congress (with majorities in both chambers in early 2001 and in 2005) fueled by strong leadership and base pressure had very strong agenda control. Moreover, they enjoyed what Hacker and Pierson call "backlash insurance": strong capacity to frame issues and alternatives "so that ordinary voters have difficulty correctly understanding policy effects or attributing responsibility for them," and shaping payoffs from policy initiatives to reward their political base and major donors while minimizing the negative effects of those initiatives and thus their political costs.[1] Public focus on national security issues after September 11, 2001, gave Republicans additional advantages for enacting their policy preferences. Thus, it is not surprising that Republicans would propose an initiative that was "off-center"; the puzzle is why this initiative, unlike the Republican tax cuts of 2001, failed to win enactment.

The median-voter-seeking and "Republican advantage" perspectives do not exhaust all possibilities, it should be noted. For example, politicians may also try to expand their political base by looking for "target of opportunity" constituencies that can be added to their political "base" if they can do so while diffusing or avoiding imposition of highly visible losses on identifiable constituencies. In the Social Security case, for example, this "coalition-building" perspective suggests that politicians might be tempted to appeal to younger voters anxious about whether Social Security will "be there" for them by proposing individual accounts while "grandfathering" people who are at or near retirement under the current system. Whether politicians actually propose such an initiative is likely to depend on the information available to them regarding the positions of various groups of voters, their assessments of how changeable those positions are, their assessment of the risks of calculating incorrectly, and their tolerance for risk. On all of these issues, there is likely to be a high degree of uncertainty.

The first section of the chapter briefly outlines some arguments about the strategic calculus of agenda setting and coalition management, with a focus on the Clinton and G. W. Bush presidencies. In particular, I argue that politicians (especially the president and his political and policy advisors) believe they can use several strategies to affect important aspects of their political environment in ways that will improve their prospects for achieving their preferred policy objectives, their objectives in building winning electoral coalitions, or both. However, they confront great uncertainty about many aspects of the political and policy environment, as well as how successful their own efforts and those of their political rivals will be in using strategies such as issue framing and agenda control to alter that environment. These uncertainties are useful in explaining why presidents expend resources on failed initiatives and on initiatives that undermine rather than enhance coalition-building efforts.

The second section of the chapter outlines the Social Security policy "regime" that confronted Presidents Clinton and G. W. Bush in the years between 1993 and 2008. The third through fifth sections of the chapter outline the Clinton administration's initiative and the two major Bush administration initiatives in Social Security and explain why they took the forms that they did and why none won enactment, focusing on policymakers' strategies to shape and control their political and policy environments. The sixth section briefly considers the first two and a half years of the Obama administration. The concluding section returns to the broader question of why politicians propose initiatives that depart from positions that are broadly acceptable to the public and/or fail to win enactment, and it asks whether there are ways to make the Social Security "third rail," if not more inviting to politicians, at least somewhat more susceptible to policy change in the future.

Strategic Politicians

Analytical frameworks that take strategic politicians as their starting point have much in common, but they also differ in their complexity and their basic assumptions. In what follows, I will differ from the simplest politician-centered models by assuming that most politicians have multiple objectives: while election and reelection are paramount in the calculations of most politicians operating in democratic political systems, they are generally not the exclusive objective. Other objectives may include policy preferences derived from ideology or personal experience (e.g., a passion for disability issues stemming from the experience of a family member) or their "place in history." Second, a politician's electoral calculus may vary depending on time perspective: politicians may have to trade off short-term electoral consequences of offending one constituency in the service of long-term coalition building and maintenance.

Third, the importance of electoral constraints on politicians' behavior is not invariant across politicians or over time. Politicians who believe that their chances of suffering electoral defeat in the near term are low and those who have longer term lengths (e.g., six years for senators vs. two years for House members) may also feel somewhat less constrained by the views of constituents and attentive interest groups. Timing in the electoral cycle may also matter—politicians may be somewhat more willing to take unpopular stands shortly after an election rather than immediately before one. And, of course, politicians who are not running for reelection face no direct electoral stake at all.

Fourth, politicians (including presidents) prefer to limit the policy agenda to items that make them better off on some or all of their objectives and worse off on none ("Pareto optimality"). Of course, politicians—even presidents—do not have complete control over their agendas. Sometimes issues like terrorism force their way onto the agenda, and presidents have to try to use those issues to their political and policy advantage if they can, or neutralize them if they cannot. Moreover, as one set of politicians may try to avoid politically contentious issues, their political opponents may be trying just as hard to force those issues onto the agenda if they see a political profit in it for themselves. Changed circumstances may also make costs higher and/or success less likely after an issue is put on the agenda—for example, rising food prices may change the political dynamic of biofuels policy and politics.

From this perspective, policy initiatives by presidents that are closer to the positions of their party's political base than to the positions of median voters may have several roots. Presidents may, for example, value policy objectives above electoral ones. Presidents may also believe that long-term coalition-building objectives, including keeping the political base happy and building support among new constituencies, are worth short-term political costs. Presidents may face weak electoral constraints, or not plan on running for reelection. Term lengths and electoral cycles may also matter: presidents may engage in more risk taking early in their terms if voters are myopic—but House members may be less likely to engage in risk taking in voting on those initiatives. Presidents may also propose initiatives that they do not expect to succeed in hopes of gaining credit with a particular constituency (usually their political base) for championing their cause. But they are likely to devote relatively few of their limited resources to actually pushing the initiative through.

Politicians, and especially presidents, confront five critical political tasks in deciding whether to undertake a policy initiative or to hold back.

1. *Agenda control* involves the prioritizing of issues considered for policy action, as well as the timing of consideration of the issue. Presidents in particular are generally successful in getting issues that they consider their top priorities both discussed by the media and given at least perfunctory attention by Congress.[2] Political leaders may try to manipulate at what point in the electoral cycle an issue is considered, giving prominence to those that provide visible benefits (e.g., Medicare prescription drug benefits) in the run-up to an election. Political leaders may also try to remove an issue from the set of issues currently being debated, "changing the conversation" if the political costs of proceeding with an initiative are perceived to be too high and they need to limit negative political consequences.

2. *Issue framing* involves efforts to portray a proposal in ways that are likely to maximize support for that proposal, usually by appealing to values that a broad swath of voters already strongly believe and that are strongly rejected by very few. Political leaders may use what Jacobs and Shapiro have called "crafted talk" to change the public's mind about the stakes in the policy sector and how it relates to values that they already hold.[3] Negative issue framing of the status quo and of alternatives to the president's preferred option can be another important strategy for moving a presidential initiative forward.

3. *Interest mobilization* refers to the array of organized interests that may seek to influence the policymaking process. Presidents and other political

leaders may try to mobilize existing and new constituencies to change public opinion, as well as to exert grassroots and advertising pressure and lobby legislators to change their position on a policy initiative.

4. *Legislative coalition building* involves the strategies used by presidents (or in some cases legislative coalition leaders) to win congressional majorities for their initiatives. In particular, coalition leaders may seek to build majorities exclusively on legislators from their own party, try to win a few defectors from the other party, or pursue a largely bipartisan strategy from the outset. As discussed below, which strategy is pursued will depend heavily on whether the party of the initiative's sponsor has control of both chambers of Congress and how cohesive those majorities are.

5. *Venue control* refers to efforts to influence which institutions (e.g., Congress, courts, regulatory agencies, subnational governments, or special ad hoc commissions) make the authoritative decisions during policy formulation and adoption. Political leaders may try to "venue shop" to ensure that policies are considered in decision-making venues that are most likely to be favorable to their own position and exercise venue control to try to keep issues out of decision-making venues that are likely to be hostile to their positions. They may even try to create new venues or procedures like special commissions, although in most policy sectors creation of new venues is likely to be more practical during the policy formulation and alternative consideration phase of policymaking than when authoritative policy decisions require legislative approval. Having policy formulated in favorable venues may allow political leaders to limit the range of options that are considered as alternative policy packages are developed, giving an advantage to those they favor and keeping others from obtaining serious consideration. Indeed, a president faced with a Congress controlled by the opposing party may prefer to avoid legislation wherever possible, using executive orders and regulatory agency decisions to limit congressional authority.

Given limited political resources, we might expect that presidential initiatives will be undertaken only when they confront a relatively favorable environment with respect to most or all of these tasks. When they face an unfavorable environment, presidents not only will not launch initiatives but may be willing to devote substantial political resources to keep that issue off the agenda. But clearly this does not always happen in practice. To understand why presidents may introduce politically risky initiatives, and why presidential initiatives may fail, it helps to employ two additional insights, both having to do with uncertainty. The first is that in many cases, presidents may face *environmental uncertainty*. For example, it may be unclear in what policymaking venue an issue will be decided. It may also be unclear which groups will be active in the policymaking process, as well as what positions those groups will take and what political clout they will bring to the policymaking process. The issue-framing environment may also be unclear. Presidents may be especially uncertain about the issue-framing environment if an issue is currently of low salience for most voters, so that they do not have well-defined positions. Uncertainty over issue framing may also be high if the public holds positions that contradict one another (e.g., favoring creation of individual accounts in Social Security but only if it can be done without cuts in guaranteed benefits or increasing revenue).

In addition to this environmental or exogenous uncertainty, presidents may also experience what can be called *endogenous uncertainty*, stemming from the fact that politicians are strategic actors who believe that they can, at least to some degree, reshape the environments in which they operate rather than simply responding to them on each of the five dimensions outlined earlier (agendas, issue framing, interest mobilization, legislative coalition building, and venue control). But it is rarely clear in advance exactly how successful those strategies will be.

Thinking of presidents as strategic actors who face uncertainty in and try to reshape their environments offers several insights into why they may overreach and why presidential initiatives may fail. First, presidents may overestimate their ability to reframe the issue, mobilize groups, and control venues. They may fail to anticipate alternative framings or misestimate their resonance with the public. And having taken a gamble that they no longer believe is likely to pay off, they may cut their losses and "change the conversation" when a proposal is failing. Believing that they can "change the conversation" may increase the probability that they undertake initiatives with a low probability of success, especially if they believe that doing so involves relatively low reputational costs and opportunity costs in terms of other initiatives.

Uncertainty about and consequent miscalculation of costs, risks, or the capacity of the president and his/her opponents based on imperfect information about the policymaking environment may therefore lead to both non-median-voter initiatives and their failure. In short, analyzing both the strategic position of presidents and the level of uncertainty surrounding specific potential policy initiatives can help to understand why presidents make the strategic choices that they do and why those initiatives may fail.

Characteristics of the U.S. Public Pension Regime

Old Age and Survivors Insurance (OASI), commonly known as Social Security, was created by the Social Security Act of 1935 and today covers the vast majority of the U.S. workforce.[4] The system, like public pension systems in most other countries, operates largely on a pay-as-you-go (PAYGO) basis, meaning that most of the money raised in current contributions is used to pay current beneficiaries, rather than being invested to pay the future benefits of current workers. The Social Security program has a progressive benefit formula that has a higher "replacement rate" (i.e., the percentage of earnings averaged over the best thirty-five years of employment that is replaced by a retiree's initial Social Security benefit) for workers with low incomes than for high-income workers.

Unlike the public pension systems in many other wealthy industrialized countries, Social Security was until 2011 financed almost entirely through payroll tax contributions, rather than having a significant element of general revenue financing. (In 2010, temporary cuts in the employee share of Social Security payroll taxes were enacted for 2011, with the shortfall made up by contributions from the Treasury—which is to say by increased debt.) Thus, Social Security faces a particularly direct financing problem from population aging: taxation levels that are sufficient with 2.9 workers for every Social Security beneficiary in 2011 (the ratio was even higher in earlier years) will not be sufficient in 2030, when there are expected to be only 2.1 workers to support every beneficiary—or in later years, when the ratio of workers to beneficiaries falls even further.[5] This means that there is a strong action-forcing mechanism to promote either benefit cuts or taxes when the "trust fund" (accumulated surpluses of revenues over contributions, plus the interest accrued on those surpluses) is getting close to being empty, because if nothing is done, checks cannot go out. This has happened twice in the past: major retrenchment in Social Security was enacted in both 1977 and 1983 as trust funds came close to running dry. There was a long-term reduction in replacement rates in 1977. The response in 1983 was more complex: there was an ad hoc indexation cut that resulted in a permanent benefit decrease for current recipients, plus the introduction of benefit taxation for upper-income recipients and a delayed (phase-in did not begin until 2001) and gradual increase in standard retirement age from 65 to 67, with a simultaneous increase in penalties for early retirement.

The OASI trust fund and its companion Disability Insurance (DI) trust fund enjoyed substantial short-term surpluses of contributions over expenditures after 1983, as the baby boom generation entered its peak earning years before retirement. These surpluses totaled more than $33 billion in 2009 alone, not including interest earned on prior surpluses.[6] But as the baby boom retires, Social Security is expected to have serious long-term deficits. Those deficits will hit sooner and be more severe as a result of the severe economic crisis that hit the United States in 2008, and they will be more severe the longer the economic downturn lasts. The cash flow from contributions and taxation of benefits relative to benefit payouts turned negative temporarily in 2010 because of the economic downturn and is expected to do so permanently around 2016, meaning that the federal government will have to start coming up with funding to pay those benefits, since it has no assets other than government securities to liquidate to pay for benefits.[7] Very large long-term deficits are expected after 2036, when accumulated OASI plus DI "reserves" (Treasury securities held by the Social Security trust funds) are exhausted.[8] Revenues are expected to be sufficient to cover only about 77 percent of promised benefit entitlements in 2036 and 74 percent in 2085.[9]

It should also be emphasized, however, that the Social Security funding problem is much more manageable than that for Medicare: the Social Security trustees estimated in 2011 that balancing total income and expenditure over the seventy-five-year projection period for the Social Security program would require an immediate and permanent 2.15 percent payroll tax increase or 13.8 percent benefit reduction. The longer we wait to address the problem, the more serious it becomes: by 2085 there is estimated to be a 4.24 percent of payroll gap between income and expenditures if nothing is done.[10] Projections in the "out" years are, of course, highly uncertain because they depend on projections about fertility and immigration rates, economic growth rates, mortality, and other factors that cannot be known in advance.

The policymaking dilemma at the heart of Social Security politics is the combination of short-term funding surpluses and long-term deficits.[11] This combination means that acting quickly will lower the long-term need to raise payroll taxes or cut benefits, but there is no action-forcing mechanism to make politicians do so in the near term. Indeed, Social Security surpluses have allowed politicians to fund deficit spending in the rest of the budget now by "borrowing" those surpluses. It takes a courageous and skillful politician to convince the public—or even to *try* to convince the public—that swallowing bitter medicine now will mean that they will have to swallow less bitter medicine in the future.

Multiple options have been proposed for restoring long-term solvency to the Social Security system in the United States. Incremental reforms use retrenchment and refinancing mechanisms to bring revenue and spending into balance. For example, eligibility for benefits could be further reduced by raising the standard retirement age to 70, or "replacement rates" (the percentage of former earnings replaced by Social Security benefits) could be reduced. On the revenue side, general payroll tax rates could be raised, or the payroll tax ceiling above which Social Security taxes are paid could be raised or abolished altogether. General revenues could be used to pay part of the costs of the Social Security system, as is done in many other countries. The political problem is that all of the potential cutbacks on the expenditure side are fiercely resisted by liberals, labor unions, and major interest and advocacy organizations for the elderly, while revenue increases are resisted just as fiercely by conservatives. Increasing returns on the holdings of the Social Security trust funds by investing in assets other than Treasury securities is another option that has intermittently been considered. It has the additional advantage of evening out the cash flow transition after 2017 (because those assets could be sold to pay benefits), but it also sparks deep opposition among conservatives who worry about the potential for government interference in markets and political pressures to bail out failing firms and make other politically motivated investments. In any case, the collapse of financial markets that began in the fall of 2008 will probably keep this issue off the policy agenda for the foreseeable future.

In addition to these incremental reforms, there has been a growing debate in the last two decades over changing Social Security to include individual investment accounts based on "defined contribution" principles—meaning that retirement benefits received would not be based directly on workers' earnings history but on their contributions to their retirement accounts and the investment return on those accounts before the money was withdrawn. Individual retirement accounts have the advantage that they do not create a long-term funding liability for governments: workers get whatever they have saved in their accounts, plus market returns on those accounts. But individual accounts create a number of other problems. Workers face increased investment risk: if their investments do poorly, because of either bad investments or simply bad luck in retiring during a downturn in the business cycle, they may end up with very poor retirement incomes. Workers with low lifetime earnings are also likely to have inadequate retirement incomes if they rely solely on individual investment accounts with no additional help from government. But the greatest problem is how to finance such a system: since current contributions are being used largely to finance current recipients, taking part of those contributions to put into individual accounts would cause the current PAYGO system to run out of money much sooner. Asking current workers to "double pay" (for their own retirement and those of current retirees) is neither fair nor politically viable. And borrowing the money to pay current beneficiaries and paying it back over several generations will add to an already high U.S. federal debt burden.

The Social Security "discussion agenda" of possible reforms in the world of academia, think tanks, opinion columnists, and other members of the chattering classes has been quite broad over the past two decades, incorporating both individual accounts and collective investment of trust fund surpluses, as well as more parametric reforms. Conservative organizations, notably think tanks such as the Cato Institute and Heritage Foundation, have been particularly persistent in pressing for the introduction of individual accounts as part of Social Security.[12] Presidential initiatives on Social Security have been intermittent, however, and congressional action beyond committee hearings has been even more limited. The contrast between a broad discussion agenda and actual policy change has been even more striking: the United States has been unique in the advanced industrial world in the absence of any major policy change in its public pension program for the more than a quarter of a century since 1983.[13]

To understand why there have been these immense gaps between the broad discussion agenda, presidential initiatives, and actual policy change, it is helpful to think in terms of the strategic calculus and the uncertainties outlined in the first part of this chapter. Any presidential initiative on Social Security proposing benefit cuts faces the certainty that opponents of any reform package will frame that initiative as harmful to seniors and those nearing retirement, even if there are provisions "grandfathering" them against some or all of the impact of cuts. Agenda setting is also critical: given the necessity to impose painful losses in any realistic Social Security reform plan, the president will have a better chance of getting a plan through if it can be done shortly after an election rather than in the heat of a midterm election campaign. Presidential initiatives on Social Security reform also have no alternative venues for final policy adoption: a Social Security reform package requires congressional approval, and it would be very difficult if not impossible to get around Senate rules requiring 60 percent approval to invoke cloture on debate—in effect requiring supermajority approval in that chamber. As we will see when we get to President Bush's 2001 initiative, there are opportunities to try to privilege positions favored by the president during policy formulation— but their prospects for success are dubious at best.

Presidential Social Security initiatives also face great uncertainty with respect to issue framing. Prior to the financial crisis in autumn 2008, proponents of individual accounts could hope that the increasing familiarity of 401(k) retirement accounts and defined contribution employer plans, combined with very high returns to those accounts in the Wall Street boom of the late 1990s, might make individual accounts acceptable to the public. But the transition costs of a shift to a Social Security system including sizeable individual accounts—the "double payment problem"—are immense. Another question mark concerns younger voters, who tend to be much more skeptical than older voters about whether promised Social Security benefits will in fact be paid. Will they embrace the idea of individual accounts, and even if they do, will they view it as sufficiently salient to offset likely opposition from seniors, who are also more likely to vote? Much depends on the details of the proposal.

Also uncertain about Social Security initiatives is the balance of interest group pressures for Social Security reform. The greatest known quantity in any proposal over the past thirty years is that AARP, formerly the American Association of Retired Persons, will be a big player. With more than 35 million members and a powerful lobbying operation, AARP is certain to oppose most benefit cutbacks and a move to individual accounts funded by a carve-out from current contributions, which it sees as undercutting both the financial viability of and political support for the current Social Security system. Less certain in recent rounds, however, was whether the financial services industry, which potentially had much to gain in management fees from individual accounts, would mobilize in support of the idea of individual accounts. Personal accounts could bring not just increased management fees but also increased government regulation and potentially the market power of a monopsony purchaser (if individuals were limited to a choice of a few government-approved plans awarded by competitive bidding). Even if financial services firms supported the idea in principle, would they put their full muscle behind it, or just give lukewarm support?[14] Much would presumably depend on the details of a reform proposal and the way that the political winds were blowing. We will see in the following sections that recent presidential administrations in the United States have taken not only very different substantive approaches to restructuring Social Security but also different strategic approaches, with Presidents Clinton and Obama more cautious and defensive and President G. W. Bush more aggressive and focused on the values of the party's base and efforts to broaden that base with appeals to young people and minorities.

Strategic Action in Social Security Reform
The Clinton Administration

President Clinton's approach to Social Security reform was initially very cautious. His budget and tax package enacted in 1993 included an increase in taxation of Social Security benefits for upper-income recipients but otherwise left the program essentially untouched. The administration's top priorities when it came into office—the budget, NAFTA, health care reform, and welfare reform—were all controversial, and adding Social Security into the mix was unlikely to make the administration's political path any easier.

After the loss of Democratic control of Congress in the 1994 elections, President Clinton was in a very weak bargaining position, affecting both the administration's goals and its strategy. Putting Social Security on the agenda could potentially result in a Republican-dominated Congress passing proposals far more conservative than the president's own preferences, as happened with welfare reform. But Republicans also had reason to be cautious, given Social Security's "third rail" reputation. Indeed, House Republicans explicitly steered clear of Social Security in their 1994 "Contract with America" proposals because of the perceived risks.

Nor did Clinton have much opportunity to manipulate the policy formulation process through the use of special ad hoc commissions or other vehicles. Indeed, the recent history of commissions as a vehicle to guide policy formulation for Social Security reform has been mixed at best. The 1981–83 Social Security reform commission appointed by President Reagan and congressional leaders came close to deadlock, but it eventually provided a vehicle for an inner group of moderates to reach a deal among themselves and then sell it to the rest of the commission, Congress, and the president.[15] Later experiences with commissions as a mechanism to guide the policy formulation process were not as productive. A commission on entitlement and tax reform appointed by President Clinton in 1993 (largely as the price for getting Senator Robert Kerrey to vote for his 1993 budget package) was unable to reach agreement on any reform package. The quadrennial Advisory Council on Social Security appointed by President Clinton included broad representation of interests, including three members each from business and labor; it too failed to agree on a proposal in its 1997 report, with its members splitting among a proposal that called for incorporating individual accounts, one that focused on shoring up the current system, and a "middle road" proposed by the group's chair, Edward Gramlich of the University of Michigan.

With President Clinton facing an extremely hostile Republican-majority Congress, Social Security became part of a broader White House effort to use issue framing to set down political markers that would define the Democratic Party as defenders of popular middle-class entitlement programs and prevent Republican tax cuts that would defund government. In his 1998 State of the Union speech, President Clinton called on Congress to "Save Social Security First." In his January 19, 1999, State of the Union address, Clinton presented a more detailed proposal, calling for legislation that would reserve 62 percent of the federal budget surplus that was then anticipated to occur over the next fifteen years to bolstering the Social Security (OASI) trust fund. Approximately one-fifth of this amount would be invested in equities—collectively rather than individually—through a mechanism insulated from government influence. In addition, another 11 percent of the anticipated surplus was to be reserved for government subsidies to new "Universal Savings (USA) Accounts"— new retirement savings accounts through which the federal government would match individual retirement savings accounts. Subsidies would be skewed toward low-income workers. These accounts would help individuals prepare for retirement based on personal choice and individual accounts, as privatizers prefer, but they would not have taken money out of existing payroll taxes or be part of the basic OASI system. Thus, they would not require additional cuts in existing benefits of the OASI system, and government commitments to subsidize the new accounts could be scaled back when government budget surpluses shrank.

It would be hard to imagine a less propitious set of conditions for moving toward a bipartisan agreement on Social Security reform. The president's State of the Union speech occurred in the middle of his Senate impeachment trial. Partisan divisions were intense, and Republicans would not want to give the president a major legislative victory that would add some luster to his second term. On the other hand, congressional Republicans did not want to appear obstructionist either.[16]

Overall, Clinton's proposal was carefully tailored to appeal to median voters, and initial public opinion surveys on most of its components were primarily positive.[17] The option of investment of Social Security trust funds in the stock market as a way to help finance Social Security quickly proved to be a political nonstarter, however. Congressional Republicans were overwhelmingly opposed, and public opinion polls showed that the public was opposed as well.[18] In a deliberate framing echo of the 1993 health care battle, Bill Archer (R-TX), chair of the House Ways and Means Committee, argued, "If you thought a government takeover of health care was bad, just wait until the government becomes an owner of private-sector companies."[19] Alan Greenspan, the powerful and widely respected chairman of the Federal Reserve Board, was also a highly vocal critic of government investment in equities markets. Greenspan argued that no mechanisms to insulate investment managers from political pressures would be adequate.[20] The Social Security proposal that the president sent to Congress in October 1999 dropped the idea of investing surpluses in Social Security in capital markets, focusing instead on paying off the entire U.S. public debt by 2015 (and transferring interest saved to the Social Security trust funds) as a way to create additional fiscal room for Social Security reform.[21]

Also inhibiting a deal was the fact that Republicans were becoming more united around the idea that a Social Security reform plan must include some form of individual accounts. In addition, Republicans and Democrats became entangled in partisan bickering over which party offered the more secure "lockbox" to prevent "raids" on the Social Security trust funds, with Republicans attempting to use the lockbox idea both to resist specific Democratic spending initiatives and to frame Democrats as fiscally irresponsible.[22] In this environment, the debate over Social Security became much less about enacting a policy initiative than about solidifying favorable images of your own party and framing the other party as untrustworthy in protecting retiree incomes. The result was stalemate and policy inaction.

Bush 2001

How and how much to restructure Social Security was an important issue in the 2000 presidential election campaign in the United States. Republican candidate George W. Bush proposed allowing workers to divert part of their Social Security payroll taxes to individual accounts, but he did not spell out a detailed plan. The roots of the president's position are long-standing and appear to flow from personal policy conviction rather than political calculation.[23] From the outset, there was a framing battle, with his Democratic opponent, Al Gore, suggesting that such a plan constituted "stock market roulette."[24] The Bush campaign responded that "Governor Bush trusts Americans; Gore trusts big government."[25]

Bush entered the Social Security fray from a relatively weak strategic position, however. The public is very mistrustful of Social Security's prospects—especially the young. But attitudes toward individual accounts tend to be significantly lower as potential downsides of those accounts are pointed out, even among those who initially support the idea. The risk for the president was that unless he could maintain a near monopoly on issue framing—which he almost certainly could not—alternative frames would undermine diffuse support for the idea of individual accounts.

In fact, President Bush pursued two quite different strategies in his 2001 and 2005 initiatives, focusing on control of which alternatives were considered during the policy formulation process in 2001 and issue framing and interest mobilization in 2005. Neither was successful. Since there was substantial overlap in political dynamics of the two episodes, I will focus in this section on the policy formulation process and hold the discussion of issue framing and interest mobilization until the section on the 2005 round.

After the 2000 election, the new president decided to wait on Social Security until after his top priority, a tax cut, had made it through Congress. Instead, President Bush decided to appoint a commission on how best to implement an opt-out plan.[26] But perhaps because of the unhappy history of commissions under President Clinton, President Bush took a different approach. He appointed all of the members of the commission, although members were drawn from both political parties in equal number. More importantly, all appointees had to agree in advance to support a set of principles established by the White House, which included no increase in the Social Security payroll tax; no change in Social Security benefits for retirees or near retirees; a requirement that individually controlled, voluntary personal retirement accounts be included; and no investment of the Social Security trust fund in equities.

Thus, the Bush administration essentially chose to increase its control over the policy formulation process at the risk that the process would not be perceived as legitimate. The president's commission eventually decided to present a menu of three policy options rather than a single plan, featuring varying combinations of cutbacks in "traditional" Social Security benefits to future retirees (especially those who were many years away from retirement), including those who do not opt out into individual accounts, as well as optional individual accounts financed with carve-out of part of the Social Security payroll tax, and transfers from general revenues to make up shortfalls in Social Security trust funds. Not surprisingly, the response from congressional Democrats and other supporters of the traditional Social Security system was hostile.[27]

The decision not to offer a single plan was intended in part to shield the administration from criticism over the benefit cuts that would be required to fund a Social Security opt-out: a single plan would produce a single (very large) estimate of cutbacks.[28] Stock market declines in 2001 and 2002 also dampened, at least temporarily, support for partial privatization of Social Security. Perhaps most important, the quick disappearance of federal budget surpluses after September 11 and the 2001 Bush tax cut made financing a transition to opt-out advance-funded individual accounts more difficult.[29] The collapse of the Enron Corporation and the loss of retirement benefits by many Enron retirees whose retirement funds were invested primarily or entirely in Enron stock stimulated public nervousness about creating individual accounts that could be invested in the stock market—a concern that Democratic congressional leaders sought to stoke.[30] Congressional Republicans and the White House agreed to postpone consideration of the commission proposals as the 2002 congressional midterm election approached. Indeed, Republican candidates in the 2002 congressional election were encouraged by the party to distance themselves from the notion of "privatization" because of its perceived political risks, and the issue returned to the back burner for the final two years of Bush's first term. [31]

Bush 2005

The 2005 Bush round of Social Security reform involved much more direct presidential involvement, but it was equally unproductive in terms of legislative output. After his 2004 reelection, the president mounted a major public relations campaign touting the need for a major restructuring of Social Security. But after several months of presidential speeches, public opinion polls showed that the public had little appetite for Social Security reform and little confidence in the Bush administration as a source of Social Security reform proposals.

The president certainly made full use of his agenda-setting powers on Social Security in 2005. Individual accounts for Social Security were a centerpiece of his 2005 State of the Union address, and he further put his personal prestige on the line with a series of carefully controlled public "forums" and managed events in early 2005 to push the idea of individual accounts.[32]

The Bush administration also devoted much attention to trying to reframe the Social Security issue. The administration needed to do three major things in issue framing: establish a message that had broad appeal across groups and that lacked credible counterattacks, establish its own legitimacy as the paramount issue framer, and dominate the messages that were being received by the public. With respect to the content of the framing, the administration repeatedly pushed the idea that Social Security was effectively bankrupt, noting back in 2000 that "there are a lot of people younger than you and me who don't think that they'll ever see a dime of Social Security money."[33] In his 2005 forums, he repeated the claim that there would be no money for young people when they retired—despite consistent Social Security trustee projections that over 70 percent of benefits could be paid if no changes were made in the program. The president and his allies also argued that there was a compelling need to address problems now rather than later, when any cutbacks would have to be much greater. Social Security was criticized as unfair to younger generations. Reform proponents also stressed the advantages of individual ownership and inheritability of accounts, while downplaying framing individual accounts as "privatization." Proponents of personal accounts also argued that minorities were "shortchanged" because their average life spans are shorter than those of whites. (Opponents of reform quickly struck back, arguing that when Social Security disability and survivors' benefits are included, minorities do better than whites).[34] And the Bush administration portrayed Democrats as irresponsible in not presenting an alternative proposal, with the president arguing in March 2005, "I think politicians need to be worried about not being a part of the solution."[35]

Issue "counter-framing" by opponents of the Bush approach had several important themes. They emphasized the riskiness of investing in the stock market, and they sought to maintain the issue framing of personal accounts as "privatization." Issue framing by opponents also focused on potentially high administrative costs that could erode benefits and the potential for "Wall Street rip-offs."[36] The president was almost constantly playing defense on this and other Social Security issues, trying in his 2005 State of the Union speech to allay these fears by promising that under his plan "your earnings are not going to be eaten up by hidden Wall Street fees."[37] Liberal groups targeting the young argued that "privatization" would force young people to be the first generation to have the "unfair" burden of paying for their own generation and that of the generation preceding them.[38] Opponents also criticized "scare-mongering" by the Bush administration about the financial status of the Social Security program—a charge that the administration played into with its exaggerated claims that there would be no money for young workers, when the reality of serious benefit cuts without a Social Security fix was bad enough.[39]

Not surprisingly, given the general polarization of opinion toward the president (and the war in Iraq) evident by 2005, opponents of the president's Social Security reform package also sought to portray the president as a mendacious political manipulator and as the problem rather than the solution. AARP ran ads comparing Bush's plan to knocking down a house because the kitchen sink was clogged.[40] And while the administration's advocacy allies spent a lot of money on advertising, so did opponents of the plan.

In an effort to increase the salience of the Social Security issue, Bush administration officials began a "60 Stops in Sixty Days" campaign in March 2005 to raise both the issue's salience and the visibility of their specific issue framing. But these events came under criticism for being heavily stage managed and excluding anyone who was not a supporter of the president's plan.[41] Moreover, opposition groups quickly adapted, staging rallies and press conferences at many of the administration's "Sixty Days" events. Since these events were also covered by the media, the administration's efforts to have a "clear shot" in portraying their issue framing were undercut.[42]

In short, the Bush administration failed at all three of the things it needed to do in issue framing. First, the administration was constantly having to play defense against credible counterattacks by opponents. Second, its credibility as a messenger of the need for change was damaged by reports criticizing its stage managing of Social Security forums and by opposition events at those forums in the "Sixty Stops in Sixty Days," as well as the president's own sagging popularity. Third, it failed to dominate the messages that were being received by the public as opposition groups spent millions of dollars on counterattacks. The administration's failure in its efforts to use issue framing to gain support for its Social Security proposals is evident in table 4.1. Public support for individual accounts actually trended slightly downward from 2002 through the middle of 2005. As table 4.2 shows, public confidence in the president's capacity to handle the Social Security issue also declined in this period despite the intense White House effort and support from allied interest groups.[43]

The Bush administration was also much less successful than it had hoped on the interest group front. Several broad coalitions of business interests were formed, notably the Alliance for Worker Retirement Security (AWRS), which included most of the major business associations (e.g., the Chamber of Commerce, Business Roundtable, and National Association of Manufacturers), and the related Coalition for Modernization and Protection of Americans' Social Security (COMPASS), to provide lobbying support and advertising in support of the president's personal accounts initiative.[44] Conservative organizations that had backed President Bush in the 2004 election, such as Progress for America and the Club for Growth, joined in this effort. But business support for Social Security individual accounts proved less than solid, in part because of strong actions by organized labor. The AFL-CIO in particular targeted bro-

Table 4.1   Trends in support for individual accounts in Social Security reform, 2002–5

Month and year	Good idea	Bad idea
October 2000	50%	42%
June 2001	48	46
January 2002	54	39
November 2002	48	46
November 2004	49	45
January 2005	45	50
April 2005	45	49
June 2005	45	50

Source: CBS / New York Times.
    Note: Responses were to the question, "Do you think that allowing individuals to invest a portion of their Social Security taxes on their own is a good idea or a bad idea?"

Table 4.2 Trends in public confidence in President Bush's handling of Social Security

Month and year	Gallup / CNN / *USA Today* [a]	
	Approve	Disapprove
February 2005	44%	50%
March 2005	40	53
July 2005	29	62
	CBS News / *New York Times* [b]	
	Confident	Uneasy
February 2005	31%	63%
June 2005	27	66

[a]Responses were to the question, "Do you approve or disapprove of George W. Bush's approach to addressing the Social Security system?"
[b]Responses were to the question, "Do you have confidence in George W. Bush's ability to make the right decisions about Social Security, or are you uneasy about his approach?"

kerages and financial services firms with Internet criticisms and occasionally direct protests, causing at least one brokerage firm to leave AWRS in February 2005.[45] The pharmaceutical giant Pfizer, which depends heavily on sales to seniors, left AWRS a week later.[46] Union pension fund trustees also put pressure on investment firms to end their firms' support for or membership in organizations that support individual accounts, while making an implicit threat to withdraw funds if they failed to do so.[47]

Spelling more trouble for the president, opposition groups proved extremely resilient, with deep pockets as well. AARP was of course the 800-pound gorilla, using both paid advertisements and town hall meetings to oppose personal accounts. But the AFL-CIO was also a strong opponent as noted above, and a variety of other liberal organizations also joined in the campaign.[48] And like the pro-reform groups, those opposed to the Bush reforms formed a broad coalition, Americans United to Protect Social Security, to coordinate strategy across groups and with Democratic leaders.[49] Moreover, efforts by a conservative, pro-Bush group called USA Next to discredit AARP by falsely charging it with promoting a gay rights agenda backfired badly. USA Next's chairman Charlie Jarvis, who had mounted the Swiftboat Veterans for Truth campaign against John Kerry in 2004, argued that AARP is "the boulder in the middle of the highway to personal accounts. We will be the dynamite that removes them."[50] The brief USA Next campaign garnered lots of media attention, but almost all of it was scornful and dismissive.

The Bush administration also faced a fundamental conundrum on policy formulation and venue control on Social Security in 2005: a monopoly of policy formulation was *not* in their interests. To maximize their prospects for passing legislation, they needed to (1) be vague for as long as possible on their own proposal, to avoid spelling out the size of benefit cuts, and (2) limit the range of options under discussion to proposals that included individual accounts. But they also needed to (3) have Democratic alternatives so that the debate would be on the relative merits of the two parties' plans and which proposal did a better job of protecting particular demographic groups and age cohorts, rather than on the costs imposed by the Republican plan. They succeeded on none of these. After being criticized for vagueness on how they were going to pay for their proposal, the administration decided to back price (rather than wage) indexing for calculating the initial benefits of high-income workers, which, analyses showed, would produce sharply lower benefits for those workers. Every new detail simply gave opponents of the administration's package something new to shoot at.

Democrats had no incentives to cooperate on either limiting proposals to those that included individual accounts or offering their own alternatives— indeed, precisely the opposite. So long as only agreement to oppose was required, Democrats were able to remain unusually unified: all but one Democratic senator had pledged to oppose diversion of Social Security tax revenues into individual accounts by April 2005—enough to block an individual account bill from being brought to a Senate vote.[51] The president repeatedly tried to get congressional Democrats to make a concrete counterproposal, but Democrats, knowing that any credible alternative that addressed Social Security's funding shortfall would inevitably involve proposing cutbacks or tax increases or both, refused to do so until the president took individual accounts off the table.[52] And while administration officials sometimes said that "everything is on the table," taking individual accounts off the table would clearly signal a presidential defeat and alienate the president's most conservative allies in Congress and the interest and advocacy communities, with no guarantee that the Democrats would in fact play along.[53]

The president's main problem, in short, was with congressional Republicans. They would need to provide most if not all of the votes to pass the president's plan. Most of them were deeply opposed to any sort of tax increase that would likely be necessary to get Democrats to negotiate seriously, and many were also opposed to the government borrowing that would be required to finance such an individual accounts plan. Moreover, most congressional Republicans did not share the president's enthusiasm for touching the third rail. Their fears were many. Some feared creating a new cohort of "notch babies" (a cohort of workers who were made worse off than slightly older workers by the 1977 Social Security rescue package and have been a consistent irritant to legislators with their calls for redress) among today's middle-aged voters who would not have an opportunity to contribute to individual accounts over their entire working lives.[54] Back in their home districts, many Republican legislators tried to play down the issue and make clear that they were not personally committed to Bush's reform,[55] while several Democratic House members attended or held town meetings on Social Security in the districts of neighboring Republicans.[56] And the closer the 2006 midterm elections got, the more nervous congressional Republicans could be expected to get. Republican leaders in the House of Representatives sought to have the Senate move first, not wanting to have their members go out on a limb with a series of potentially costly party-line roll call votes that would have no policy payoff if Republicans in the Senate decided not to move a bill because they did not have the votes needed to pass it.[57] But the Senate bill would have to pass through the Finance Committee, where the Republicans had only a one-vote majority, and where Senator Olympia Snowe (R-ME) had already declared her opposition to personal accounts.

Without backing from congressional Republicans, Bush backed away from Social Security reform by the middle of 2005—but after possible long-term effects on the president's popularity and major opportunity costs for a second-term domestic agenda.[58] Prospects for reform declined even further once Republicans lost control of both chambers of Congress in the 2006 elections. The new Democratic congressional majority was very hopeful of recapturing control of the White House in 2008 from a Republican Party with a very tarnished brand, and they had no incentive to negotiate with President Bush and congressional Republicans in the interregnum.

The Early Obama Years

The dramatic push for Social Security reform of 2005 was not repeated in the initial two years of Barack Obama's presidency. Indeed, President Obama, facing an extraordinarily difficult economic and fiscal climate and a pledge to enact health care reform, essentially took Social Security off the policy agenda for his first two years by appointing a bipartisan deficit reduction commission that would not report until after the November 2010 election. This freed the administration to concentrate on its key domestic priorities and removed the need to put forward an inevitably loss-imposing Social Security initiative that could worry older voters, while creating the aura that bipartisan action might be possible later.

A deteriorating economy and extraordinarily high level of partisan rancor over health reform and most other issues meant that senior issues were never far from the surface, however. In the run-up to the midterm elections, President Obama and the Democrats warned that Republicans still wanted to privatize Social Security in a bid to mobilize senior voters. This time, however, the Republicans had an even more effective counter-message: that the president's recently enacted health care legislation was financed in large part by cost savings (labeled as "cuts") of about $500 billion in planned spending for Medicare. This claim had the advantage of being partially true (though there were many offsetting new benefits for seniors) and being based on official reports of the Congressional Budget Office. Seniors' share of the electorate swelled from about 16 percent in 2008 to about 23 percent in 2010, and they swung heavily against the Democrats.

If the 2010 election reinforced politicians' concerns about imposing losses on the elderly, other developments have heightened environmental uncertainty. The president's deficit reduction commission did report after the election recommending a number of cuts in Social Security, including an increase in the retirement age and cuts in benefits for upper-income workers, but no increases in broad payroll tax rates or carve-out individual accounts. The budget deal reached between President Obama and congressional Republicans in August 2011 left Social Security untouched, however. That legislation also created a congressional "super-committee" to recommend additional deficit reduction, with painful cuts in discretionary programs triggered if no deal was reached. While this in theory offers a mechanism to get around the "first mover" problem in proposing painful Social Security changes, the past record of such mechanisms in promoting Social Security change does not suggest much room for optimism. And the ferocious insistence of the Tea Party wing of the Republican Party on massive expenditure cuts combined with rejection of any sort of revenue increases makes a balanced approach to Social Security's long-term financing problem less likely rather than more. Moreover, the inclusion in 2010 legislation extending the Bush-era tax cuts of a provision temporarily lowering the employee Social Security tax rate (with reimbursement from the Treasury) creates a precedent that worries both liberals (who fear defunding of Social Security) and conservatives (who fear that injection of general revenues into the program will reduce pressures to lower benefits). How this precedent plays out in the future remains to be seen.

Conclusion

This chapter began with three questions: Why do presidents sometimes propose policy initiatives that appear to be different from the preferences of median voters? Why do presidential initiatives sometimes fail to win enactment or achieve other presidential objectives? What consequences do presidential initiatives have for presidential efforts to build and maintain winning political coalitions?

Regarding the first question, the evidence from the three presidential administrations suggests that decisions to undertake or forego a presidential initiative are usually complex rather than mono-causal, and they can differ substantially across cases. In the two cases of President Bush's decision to propose an apparently "off-center" Social Security initiative, the most important factor was almost certainly a personal belief in the position as good public policy. But there were other contributing factors as well. In particular, there was a perceived opportunity to widen the base of the party (e.g., younger voters on Social Security) *and* simultaneously appeal to the business base of the party and its base among free-market proponents. Public opinion was uncertain (notably with respect to the degree of crisis in the current system and the desirability of individual accounts) and potentially could be influenced by "crafted talk." These factors helped to make a Social Security reform initiative focused on individual accounts more plausible, especially given the administration's apparent success in framing issues during the 2004 presidential campaign. Moreover, the Bush administration enjoyed potential advantages in controlling the issue during policy formulation (2001) and in building coalitions based on Republican congressional majorities (2005). The Bush administration was also able to "change the conversation" in mid-2005 without the devastating reputational effect that Bill Clinton's defeat on health care reform in 1994 had on his administration.

Other conditions may lead presidents to launch initiatives even when there is a low probability of success, however. For example, initiatives may be mounted when political capital expended and expectations for getting legislation adopted are both relatively low, as was the case with Bill Clinton and Social Security in 1998 and 1999. Those failed initiatives staked out a credit-claiming and blame-generating opportunity for future elections.

Regarding the failure of presidential initiatives, many of the "usual suspect" explanatory variables clearly apply. Divided government during Clinton's initiative and most of Bush's first initiative made policy gridlock more likely, and its frequency helps to explain the general absence of major Social Security policy change since 1983.

Thinking of presidents as strategic politicians trying to use policy management strategies to advance their political and policy objectives in the face of uncertainty offers several additional insights into why they may overreach and why their initiatives may fail. First, as suggested above, presidents may overestimate their ability to mobilize groups and control venues. They may also overestimate their capacity to use venue and agenda control to insulate their party's legislators from blame-generating pressures when losses are being imposed. Failure of an initiative is more likely when there are visible losses to be allocated, when there is no way to insulate your party's legislators from those losses in a political system of decentralized political accountability, and when the status quo is still a viable option for political opponents to defend, at least in the short term.

Presidents and their advisors may also overestimate their ability to reframe the issue and fail to anticipate alternative framings or estimate their resonance with the public. President Bush's second Social Security initiative suggests that even when a president has a congressional majority, "base-centered" initiatives are likely to fail when there are alternative framings at least as plausible as the president's and when those framings have resourceful carriers.

The Social Security case also suggests some broader lessons about building and maintaining political coalitions in the contemporary United States. In particular, it suggests that adding new "target" groups to a political coalition is extremely difficult. It is most likely to occur either when there is a traumatic event that shapes the identity or perceived interests of a large group of people (like the Great Depression, the civil rights movement, or perhaps a major war) or when an issue clearly and directly plays into values that are already part of a group's identity and that are constantly reinforced by other groups to which individuals belong, as in the case of opposition to abortion and gay rights solidifying an alliance between social conservatives and the Republican Party. The Bush administration's efforts to appeal to young people on the basis of individual accounts did not have such advantages.

In addition, the Social Security case suggests that there is an inherent tension in maintaining political coalitions between groups' desire to support (and, more importantly, not undermine) politicians who are generally their allies and their desire to show that they cannot be taken for granted just because their interests are generally aligned and supporting the opposing party is not a viable political option. Showing "base" groups that you are truly committed to their cause is probably not enough to cause a president to undertake an initiative that is a certain loser, but in the case of the Bush Social Security privatization initiatives, solidifying links with the business community may have added weight to the case for undertaking an initiative that should have been seen by the administration as a high-risk proposition.

The Social Security case also suggests that politicians are vulnerable to hubris related to their own persuasive powers: politicians' belief in the power of their own "crafted talk" to reframe an issue and move public opinion may lead them to undertake initiatives in the face of uncertainty where prudence would suggest otherwise. In the face of conflicting issue-framing campaigns, negative images of any reform proposal raise the spectre of losses vis-à-vis the status quo, and these images are likely to be the most powerful ones.

A final lesson suggested by recent experience with presidential Social Security initiatives is perhaps the most sobering one of all for an era in which partisan divides are high and divided party control of government is the norm: it is difficult for presidents to engage the opposition party in serious policy dialogue when losses are being allocated. Incentives to generate blame against the president and his party are high, and incentives to compromise are weak when the next election may strengthen your party's institutional leverage. Thus, any loss-imposing deal on Social Security is likely to be very difficult until the checks are about to bounce.

NOTES

1. Jacob S. Hacker and Paul Pierson, *Off Center: The Republican Revolution and the Erosion of American Democracy* (New Haven, CT: Yale University Press, 2006), 12–13.

2. Matthew Eshbaugh-Soha and Jeffrey S. Peake, "Presidential Influence over the Systemic Agenda," *Congress and the Presidency* 31, no. 2 (Autumn 2004): 161–81.

3. On crafted talk, see Lawrence Jacobs and Robert Y. Shapiro, *Politicians Don't Pander: Political Manipulation and the Loss of Democratic Responsiveness* (Chicago: University of Chicago Press, 2000).

4. The main exceptions are many (but not all) state and local government employees and most federal civil servants hired before 1984.

5. Board of Trustees, Federal Old-Age and Survivors Insurance and Disability Insurance Trust Funds, *The 2011 Annual Report of the Board of Trustees of the Federal Old Age and Survivors Insurance and Disability Insurance Trust Funds*, House Document 112-23, May 13, 2011, 53. The ratio includes recipients under disability insurance as well.

6. This figure is for OASI only and includes both contributions and taxation of benefits but excludes net interest on the trust fund of $108 billion in 2008, system administrative costs, and transfers to the Railroad Retirement account. See *The 2010 Annual Report of the Board of Trustees of the Federal Old Age and Survivors Insurance and Disability Insurance Trust Funds*, 23.

7. Ibid., 142–43.

8. The OASI fund is expected to be exhausted in 2038 and the DI Trust Fund in 2018. *2011 Annual Report*, 20.

9. Ibid., 20–21.

10. Ibid., 3. These projected figures are for the combined OASI and DI funds.

11. On this problem, see Alan M. Jacobs, "The Politics of When: Redistribution, Investment and Policy Making for the Long Term," *British Journal of Political Science* 38 (2008): 193–220.

12. See, e.g., Daniel Beland and Alex Waddan, "From Thatcher (and Pinochet) to Clinton? Conservative Think Tanks, Foreign Models and US Pensions Reform," *Political Quarterly* 71, no. 2 (April–June 2000): 202–10.

13. See R. Kent Weaver, "Public Pension Reform in an Age of Austerity," in *Trans-Atlantic Policymaking*, ed. Martin Levin and Martin Shapiro (Washington, DC: Georgetown University Press, 2005), 64–99.

14. For a discussion of the role of the financial services industry, see Robert Dreyfuss, "Wall Street Is Putting Money into Privatization Efforts, but Doing It Quietly," *Nation*, February 8, 1999.

15. See Paul Light, *Still Artful Work: The Continuing Politics of Social Security Reform*, 2nd ed. (New York: McGraw Hill, 1995).

16. See Alexis Simendinger, "Can Clinton Lead?," *National Journal*, January 2 and 9, 1999, 28–29.

17. See Pew Center on People and the Press, "Support for Clinton, but Not Social Security Funds in Market," January 26, 1999, http://people-press.org/reports/pdf/70 .pdf, 9; and *Los Angeles Times* Poll Study #421, "National Survey: State of the Union & Impeachment Trial," January 1999, www.latimesinteractive.com/pdfarchive/stat _sheets/la-timespoll421ss.pdf, 7.

18. Pew Center on People and the Press, "Support for Clinton," 9; *Los Angeles Times* Poll Study #421, 8.

19. Quoted in Amy Goldstein and George Hager, "President Ties Social Security's Future to Stocks," *Washington Post*, January 20, 1999, A1.

20. For Greenspan's views, see, e.g., Richard W. Stevenson, "Fed Chief Warns of Painful Choices on Social Security," *New York Times*, January 29, 1999, A1.

21. Richard W. Stevenson, "Clinton Abandons Idea of Investing Retirement Funds," *New York Times*, October 29, 1999.

22. Amy Goldstein, "House Backs 'Lockbox' for Retiree Fund," *Washington Post*, May 27, 1999, A1; Stevenson, "Clinton Abandons Idea."

23. A conservative activist who met with Bush in 1998 described him as already convinced on the principle of private accounts and concerned primarily about how to overcome political hurdles. See Richard W. Stevenson, "For Bush, a Long Embrace of Social Security Plan," *New York Times*, February 27, 2005.

24. Alice Ann Love, "Bush, Gore Spar over Social Security," Associated Press newswire, May 3, 2000, retrieved from Lexis-Nexis; Kevin Sack, "Gore and Bush Trade Jabs on Pensions and Spending; Vice President Sees Threat to Future of Social Security," *New York Times*, November 2, 2000, A1.

25. Love, "Bush, Gore Spar."

26. For a discussion, see Amy Goldstein, "Bush Plans Panel to Study Overhaul of Social Security," *Washington Post*, February 27, 2001, A1, and Sara Fritz, "Proof of Bush's Social Security Intentions Will Be in the Panel," *St. Petersburg Times*, April 2, 2001, 3A.

27. Criticisms of the Bush Commission's proposals included a lack of clarity on where general revenues would come from, substantial cuts in traditional benefits, and disability provisions that did not appear to meet the president's mandate.

28. President's Commission to Strengthen Social Security, *Strengthening Social Security and Creating Wealth for All Americans* (Washington, DC: Commission, December 2001).

29. Richard Morin and Claudia Deane, "Poll Shows New Doubts on Economy; President's Tax Cut, Policy Are Questioned," *Washington Post*, March 27, 2001, A1.

30. Glen Kessler, "Democrats View Social Security as Election Issue," *Washington Post*, February 23, 2002, A2; Ron Hutcheson, "President Plugs Retirement Plan; Republicans Worry about Enron Anxiety," *Miami Herald*, March 1, 2002.

31. Jim Vanderhei and Juliet Eilperin, "Bush's Plan for Social Security Loses Favor," *Washington Post*, August 13, 2002, A1; Amy Goldstein, "Action on Social Security Debated," *Washington Post*, November 15, 2002, A16. President Bush's 2003 State of the Union address gave Social Security reform a scant two sentences of mention—a strong indicator that the administration did not intend to make the issue a legislative priority in the new Congress. Stephen Dinan, "Social Security Accounts off Agenda," *Washington Times*, February 3, 2003, A9.

32. George C. Edwards III, *Governing by Campaigning*. Chaps. 7 and 8 of Edwards's book contain an excellent history and analysis of Bush's 2005 Social Security initiative.

33. Jackie Calmes, "Bush's Social Security Plan Has Democrats Wondering," *Wall Street Journal*, May 8, 2000, A44.

34. See, e.g., Peter Wallsten and Tom Hamburger, "Blacks Courted on Social Security," *Los Angeles Times*, February 28, 2005.

35. Quoted in Adriel Bettelheim, "Bush's Rough Choice: Backtrack or Take Flak," *CQ Weekly*, March 7, 2005, 550–51.

36. On framing of individual accounts as beholden to Wall Street financial interests, see, e.g., Jill Zuckman, "Social Security Fight Expands to State Races," *Boston Globe*, May 15, 2000.

37. State of the Union transcript.

38. "MTV Generation Takes on Social Security," AP Newswire, April 4, 2005.

39. Warren Fieth and Richard Simon, "President Casts Doubt on Trust Fund," *Los Angeles Times*, April 6, 2005.

40. David Rosenbaum, "Few See Gains from Social Security Tour," *New York Times*, April 3, 2005; Andrew Taylor, "Weighing Nip, Tuck vs. Total Makeover," *CQ Weekly*, April 4, 2005, 841–43.

41. On the administration's management of the "Sixty Days" campaign, see Edwards, *Governing by Campaigning*, chap. 7.

42. See Richard Benedetto, "Protesters of Overhaul Dog Bush," *USA Today*, May 25, 2005, 8A. A study of local media newspaper coverage of the Bush Social Security campaign found that it generated more positive coverage than parallel coverage of the *Washington Post*, but that coverage was more descriptive of local events than focused on the substance of the issue and thus was unlikely to change voters' minds on the issue. See Matthew Eshbaugh Soha and Jeffrey S. Peake, "'Going Local' to Reform Social Security," *Presidential Studies Quarterly* 36, no. 4 (December 2006): 689–704.

43. For a detailed discussion of public opinion movement in this period, see Edwards, *Governing by Campaigning*, chap. 8.

44. AWRS and COMPASS shared the same executive director, Derrick Max. See Bennett Roth, "Social Security Lobbying War Is On," *Houston Chronicle*, February 14, 2005, A1.

45. See Jeffrey H. Birnbaum, "Brokerage Leaves Coalition," *Washington Post*, February 12, 2005, E1.

46. AWRS removed its corporate membership list from its website after the AFL-CIO began its campaign. See Peter Wallsten and Tom Hamburger, "Pfizer Is Neutral on Bush Plan," *Los Angeles Times*, February 21, 2005.

47. Jeffrey H. Birnbaum and Ben White, "Social Security Tactics Escalate," *Washington Post*, February 23, 2005, E2.

48. Roth, "Social Security Lobbying War."

49. See Jeffrey H. Birnbaum, "Groups to Coordinate Attack on Bush Plan," *Washington Post*, February 25, 2005, A19.

50. Jarvis is quoted in Ronald Brownstein, "Attack on AARP, Like 'Religious War,' Built on Either/Or Fallacy," *Los Angeles Times*, February 28, 2005. See also Vieth, "Campaign-Like Attacks Turn Up the Volume on Social Security Debate."

51. Rosenbaum, "Few See Gains."

52. Some Senate Republicans, notably Rick Santorum of Pennsylvania, even expressed a willingness to have payroll tax rates on the table in negotiations with Republicans, but since that was rejected by House Republicans and the Bush administration, it was not sufficient to lure Democrats into negotiations. Joel Havemann, "Santorum Puts Tax Rate on the Table," *Los Angeles Times*, February 28, 2005.

53. The "everything is on the table" quote is from Treasury Secretary John Snow on March 2, 2005, quoted in Bettelheim, "Bush's Rough Choice."

54. See William E. Gibson, "Middle-Aged Fear Losing Out under Social Security Reform," *South Florida Sun-Sentinel*, February 23, 2005.

55. See, e.g., Jon Sawyer, "Many Republicans Aren't Talking about Social Security," *St. Louis Post-Dispatch*, February 26, 2006; Alex Wayne, "Lawmakers Find Social Security Plan a Tough Sell," *CQ Today*, February 25, 2005; Rosenbaum, "Few See Gains";

and Mike Allen and Peter Baker, "Hill Takes a Back Seat on Social Security," *Washington Post*, April 6, 2005, A4.

56. Glen Johnson, "Democrats Hit Road in Social Security War," AP Newswire, April 3, 2005.

57. Rosenbaum, "Few See Gains"; Alex Wayne, "Rally against Bush Plan Will Coincide with Finance Panel's Hearing," *CQ Today,* April 19, 2005.

58. See, e.g., Jacob Weisberg, "The President Has Lost on Social Security, How Will He Handle It?," *Slate*, March 31, 2005.

CHAPTER FIVE

The Bush Administration and the Politics of Medicare Reform

Jonathan Oberlander

The addition of prescription drug coverage to Medicare stands out as one of George W. Bush's signature domestic policy accomplishments.[1] It also stands out as one of the Bush administration's more puzzling legacies: how did an avowedly conservative, Republican president opposed to government-run health care end up, with support from a Republican Congress, expanding the federal government's largest health insurance program? Heritage Foundation policy analyst Robert Moffitt captured the frustration of many conservatives with his comment: "I don't know what in the name of God anybody among Republicans is thinking."[2]

The Bush administration's Medicare legacy is all the more incongruous given its record in other health policy domains of resisting even incremental proposals (including expanding the State Children's Health Insurance Program) that would have increased government's role in providing health insurance. Medicare thus represents a "strange case" in the Bush presidency.[3]

As this essay explains, the puzzle of the Bush administration's support for expanding Medicare is largely explained by electoral motivations. The Bush administration had both short- and long-term political reasons to push for a

Medicare drug benefit. In the short term, it hoped to improve the president's reelection prospects by neutralizing an issue that favored Democrats, while picking up votes from elderly Medicare beneficiaries and from independents drawn to the administration's "compassionate conservatism." In the long term, the White House hoped that Medicare reform would move more seniors into the Republican coalition. That shift would in turn help the administration realize its larger goal: creating an enduring Republican majority. Adopting Medicare drug coverage was a policy choice that, above all else, served the Bush administration's political interests.

However, the Bush administration's support for a Medicare prescription drug benefit is not just a story about a political party moving to the center for electoral gain or trying to broaden its base by using public policy to attract a new constituency. From the beginning, the administration had an important policy goal: remake Medicare into a more conservative program by promoting competition and private insurance. It consequently attempted to use enactment of the drug benefit as an opportunity to advance conservative reforms to restructure Medicare. In other words, the Bush administration simultaneously wanted to expand Medicare and privatize it; even as the administration embraced a liberal goal for political gain, it sought to do so on conservative terms. Bush's pursuit of a Medicare drug benefit is, then, also a story about how the administration balanced those competing motivations.

This chapter explores the Bush administration's political and policy goals in Medicare reform. The chapter starts by providing background about Medicare. Next, I analyze the political opportunities and constraints that the Bush administration faced as it pursued Medicare reform during 2001–3. I then discuss the circumstances that led to enactment of the 2003 Medicare Prescription Drug, Improvement, and Modernization Act (MMA). Finally, I explore the political and policy legacies of the Bush administration's Medicare reform and compare that effort with health care reform during the Obama presidency.

Background

Enacted in 1965, Medicare is a federal health insurance program for elderly Americans, persons with disabilities, and kidney disease patients who require dialysis or transplantation. Most Medicare beneficiaries are enrolled in an insurance program operated by the federal government, often referred to as traditional Medicare. Beneficiaries can alternatively choose to join private insurance plans that contract with Medicare.

Medicare is divided into four components.[4] Medicare Part A provides insurance for hospital services, and Medicare Part B covers the costs of physician services. Medicare Part C, also known as the Medicare Advantage program, encompasses the private insurance plans that contract with the government to provide medical care to Medicare beneficiaries. Part D is Medicare's prescription drug benefit.

Medicare has always provided a limited benefits package rather than comprehensive insurance for all medical care costs. Yet despite gaping holes in its insurance coverage, benefit expansions have been rare in Medicare.[5] Historically, Medicare did not cover the costs of prescription drugs obtained outside the hospital, a particular burden for elderly Americans who commonly take multiple medications.

There were few serious efforts to expand Medicare to cover prescription drugs during 1965–2000.[6] In part, that was because Medicare beneficiaries turned to other sources of prescription drug coverage. Lower-income Medicare beneficiaries acquired drug coverage through Medicaid (a public insurance program jointly funded by federal and state governments). Other Medicare beneficiaries had supplemental insurance policies sponsored by former employers, purchased coverage on their own, or obtained coverage by enrolling in private insurance plans that contracted with Medicare. As beneficiaries' access to drug coverage increased, the political pressures for expanding Medicare benefits diminished.

In addition, many policymakers long viewed Medicare, in the words of Senator Russell Long, as a "runaway program" whose rising costs threatened the federal budget and triggered intermittent alarms over the impending "bankruptcy" of its trust fund.[7] Cost control thus dominated the Medicare policy agenda, further reducing political enthusiasm for expanding program benefits. The political influence of advocacy groups like AARP remained largely defensive.[8] Elderly advocacy groups could help fend off proposals they didn't like, but they lacked the political clout to push through reforms that would substantially expand Medicare benefits.

The one successful effort to add prescription drugs to Medicare ironically ended in stunning failure. In 1988 the Reagan administration (looking to soften the administration's image with the elderly and recover from the Iran-Contra crisis) and the Democratic majority in Congress (looking for any opportunity to expand social programs in a political environment bounded by federal deficits) agreed on legislation expanding Medicare, including a new prescription drug coverage program. Congress, though, repealed the Medicare Catastrophic Coverage Act just sixteen months after its enactment.[9] Repeal followed a backlash by seniors angered by the program's financing arrangements. The costs of new benefits were to be paid entirely by the Medicare population without any subsidy from other taxpayers and with income-related premiums that imposed a significant new tax on more affluent beneficiaries. The backlash was fueled by widespread confusion among Medicare beneficiaries about who would have to pay the new surtax, confusion largely attributable to misleading mailings sent by interest groups opposed to the program.[10] After the political trauma of catastrophic health insurance, Congress had little appetite for expanding Medicare benefits, though the Clinton administration proposed a new Medicare drug benefit as part of its ill-fated health care reform plan in 1993.[11]

Prescription drug coverage reemerged as an issue in 1999, when President Clinton called for expanding Medicare to cover outpatient medications and Democratic members of the National Bipartisan Commission on the Future of Medicare pushed for the benefit as an essential component of any program reforms.[12] The rising political fortunes of a Medicare drug benefit were closely linked to a dramatic change in fiscal conditions. In 1998, for the first time in three decades, the Congressional Budget Office announced a federal budget surplus, forecast at $131 billion by 2000 and projected to grow during the ensuing decade. The surplus triggered a debate over how projected excess federal funds should be spent. A Medicare prescription drug benefit emerged as a popular destination for that potential windfall. Developments in the insurance market also prompted the renewed drive for a Medicare drug benefit: in response to skyrocketing costs, private health plans were limiting or dropping their drug coverage for Medicare beneficiaries.[13]

By 2000, Medicare prescription drug coverage had become a first-order political issue and figured prominently in that year's presidential campaign between Al Gore and George W. Bush. Gore made Medicare drug coverage a central item in his proposed domestic agenda, while Bush, after suffering politically earlier in the campaign without a proposal, eventually countered with his own plan. The two presidential candidates offered competing visions of Medicare reform. Gore favored making the benefit available to all beneficiaries as part of the traditional Medicare program, while Bush proposed a more limited benefit focused on helping lower-income beneficiaries to purchase private insurance. The chasm between Democratic and Republican plans in the 2000 election foreshadowed just how difficult it would be for the Bush administration and Congress to enact a Medicare prescription drug benefit in coming years.

Opportunities: Inoculation and Realignment

When the Bush administration took office in January 2001, it saw political opportunity in Medicare reform. In the short term, the administration hoped to inoculate the president and the Republican Party against an issue that favored Democrats, thereby improving Bush's' reelection chances.[14] Republican pollster Bill McInturff explained that Medicare prescription drug coverage could do for the Bush administration "what welfare reform did for [Bill] Clinton."[15] President Clinton's signing of welfare reform legislation aided his 1996 reelection bid and helped neutralize an issue that favored Republicans. Voters had long viewed Democrats as the party of Medicare. By passing a Medicare drug benefit, the GOP would embrace "a cause that [the Republican Party] once resisted and in so doing turns a vulnerability into a strength."[16]

The administration obviously hoped that expanding Medicare benefits would help Bush add elderly voters to his column in 2004. Bush had narrowly lost with voters over age 65 (50%–47%) to Al Gore in the 2000 election. Adopting a prescription drug benefit that would be popular among seniors was an especially enticing prospect given high voting rates among the elderly. In the 2000 election, 68 percent of Americans over age 65 reported voting.[17]

However, the political benefits of pursing Medicare reform were not limited to seniors. Opinion polls showed that younger voters also strongly supported adding prescription drug coverage to Medicare.[18] Enacting Medicare drug coverage could enhance Bush's reputation as a "compassionate conservative," thereby winning over independents and swing voters.[19] The Bush campaign pursued a similar strategy in emphasizing education during the 2000 election.[20]

In sum, the Bush administration's short-term political calculus strongly favored enacting a Medicare drug benefit. That policy choice offered multiple political benefits: currying favor with elderly voters, neutralizing a Democratic Party issue, and attracting independent voters. As pollster McInturff noted, "Having a Republican president deliver on the largest expansion of

Medicare in two generations is an enormous advantage going into the 2004 election."[21]

Enacting Medicare reform also had the potential for a longer-term payoff. Senior adviser Karl Rove believed that the Bush administration could forge a political realignment that would ensure a "permanent" Republican majority.[22] Since political conditions did not appear to favor realignment—Bush took office having won a minority of the popular vote and with the Senate evenly divided between Republicans and Democrats—Rove argued that the administration had to make its own history by transforming the political environment through policymaking. Electoral realignment is often thought of as a cause of policy change, but Rove sought to turn that formulation on its head by attempting to use policy change to trigger realignment. As David Mayhew has convincingly documented, realignment is a highly problematic, mythic concept.[23] Nonetheless, since Rove believed in it, realignment is crucial to understanding the political motivations behind the administration's policy choices.

The Bush administration's realignment strategy rested on a number of policy initiatives, including education reform, immigration reform, and Social Security privatization, each aimed at weaning core constituencies and swing voters away from the Democratic Party to expand the Republican Party base. Medicare reform was an important part of that realignment strategy.[24] As Robert Novak wrote, "The [Medicare] drug plan was an audacious effort to co-opt the votes of seniors, reflecting Rove's grand design of building on the electoral majority by adding constituency groups."[25] Given population aging—Medicare's enrollment is projected to nearly double from 40 million in 2000 to 78 million in 2030 as the baby boomers reach retirement age[26]—the political benefits of adding more elderly voters to the Republican coalition were clear. Moreover, seniors represented a "swing group that [was] in play for both political parties" as the generation socialized to politics during the New Deal was replaced by a new cohort of potential voters.[27] Indeed, elderly Americans have not always voted for Democrats despite the party's political strength on Medicare and Social Security. Republican candidates won the over-60 vote in presidential elections from 1980 to 1988 and lost it by a margin of only 4 percentage points in both 1996 and 2000.[28]

Medicare reform also afforded the Bush administration an opportunity to realign the program to better reflect conservative philosophy. Many Republicans have long disliked Medicare's liberal elements—its universalism, social insurance and defined benefit structure, entitlement status, embrace of government-operated health insurance, and resemblance to single-payer health systems (like Canada's national health insurance system). Former Medicare administrator Tom Scully, who served under President George W. Bush, colorfully expressed the desires of many would-be Medicare reformers on the right: "I hate this whole G-damn system. I'd blow it up if I could, but I'm stuck with it. . . . If it were up to me I'd buy everyone private insurance and forget about it."[29]

Republicans have accordingly promoted policies to make Medicare more market-friendly by strengthening private insurers' role in the program, and those policies rose on the agenda after Republicans won majority control of the House and Senate in 1994. During the 2000 campaign George W. Bush unveiled a plan to transform Medicare into a market of competing insurance plans under the rubric of "modernization."[30] If enacted, that plan could, in turn, generate additional political benefits. Rove believed that "if you could recast major government programs to make them more susceptible to market forces, broader support for the Republican party would ensue."[31] In other words, Democrats' identification with and traditional advantage on Medicare could be weakened if the program's identity changed to embody conservative principles. Conservative Medicare reforms, when combined with similar efforts to remake Social Security, would enable Republicans to shake the "twin pillars of countless Democratic campaigns."[32]

Republican majority control of the House and Senate during Bush's first term—interrupted only when Vermont senator James Jeffords left the Republican Party in May 2001 to become an independent, putting Senate Democrats back in majority control until the 2002 elections—enhanced the administration's opportunity to restructure Medicare into a more conservative program.[33] In fact, Bush's first term marked the first time in Medicare's history that the program had operated under unified Republican government. That gave conservative reformers arguably the best chance they ever had to remake Medicare in their own image. If efforts to expand Medicare to include prescription drugs could successfully be linked to policies that shifted Medicare beneficiaries into private insurance, then expanding Medicare would paradoxically enable the Bush administration to privatize it (an outcome also desired by the insurance industry).

Constraints and Pressures: The Risky Politics of Medicare Reform

While the Bush administration hoped to earn considerable political rewards from Medicare reform, they confronted no shortage of political pressures and constraints. Unified Republican control meant that Republicans were accountable if Medicare reform failed. In that event, Republican pollster Bill McInturff warned that Democrats would run ads in the 2004 election with a simple message: "President Bush promised in the last campaign to provide a Medicare drug benefit, but even with Republicans in control of the White House, Senate and the House, they failed to deliver. Vote Democratic for prescription drugs."[34] Now that Medicare expansion had emerged on the national political agenda, failure to deliver Medicare prescription drug coverage carried a significant political cost.[35]

Yet success on Medicare reform was hardly assured. The administration had to rely on slim Republican congressional majorities. As previously noted, Republicans lost majority control of the Senate only four months into Bush's first term, and even after the 2002 elections, they held only fifty-one Senate seats. In the House of Representatives, Republicans won 221 seats in the 2000 election and 229 seats in 2002.[36] Adopting major Medicare reform, especially reform aimed at restructuring Medicare into a more conservative program, was no easy task given the congressional balance of power. Moreover, as the administration discovered with unsuccessful attempts at Social Security and immigration reform, having a Republican Congress did not guarantee that it would embrace the administration's domestic policy agenda.

Further complicating the political picture, many members of Congress split into two opposing groups on Medicare reform. Conservative Republicans preferred *structural reform without expansion.* They wanted to restructure Medicare to incorporate market competition so more beneficiaries obtained health insurance from private insurers rather than the government. Many conservatives also believed that it was fiscally irresponsible to expand Medicare by creating a new entitlement to prescription drugs given foreboding estimates of Medicare's fiscal future.

Meanwhile, liberal Democrats preferred *expansion without structural reform.* They wanted Medicare to adopt a comprehensive prescription drug benefit without altering Medicare's traditional structure, and they opposed any policies that privatized Medicare or altered the program's entitlement status. They also disputed the claim that forecasts of Medicare's future financing shortfalls compelled radically restructuring.

In order to secure enactment of a new Medicare drug benefit, the Bush administration had to navigate the cross-pressures from these two groups. After 2002 they also had to pursue Medicare reform without the benefit of budget surpluses. In the aftermath of 9/11, a recession, and large-scale tax cuts sponsored by the Bush administration, the projected budget surplus quickly disappeared. The Congressional Budget Office forecast a ten-year budget surplus of $5.6 trillion in 2001, but by 2002 the federal government was again running a deficit.[37] Legislation establishing a prescription drug benefit could no longer be financed "for free." Congress instead had to pay for expanding Medicare benefits by either raising taxes, finding offsetting cuts in other federal programs, or adding the Medicare drug coverage bill to the federal deficit.

Meanwhile, outside (and inside) of Congress, a host of interest groups had a stake in the Bush administration's Medicare reform strategy. Medicare politics is an arena filled with powerful stakeholders, including organizations representing doctors (the American Medical Association and assorted specialty groups), hospitals (the American Hospital Association and Federation of American Hospitals), insurers (America's Health Insurance Plans),[38] seniors (AARP, unions, and consumer groups like Families USA), and the drug industry (the Pharmaceutical Research and Manufacturers of America [PhRMA]). Because Medicare accounts for about 20 percent of all U.S. health care spending, any change in the program has important financial implications for medical providers and other stakeholders in the Medicare-industrial complex; their incomes depend in no small part on Medicare spending.[39] Many of these stakeholders are literally invested in maintaining the Medicare status quo and will resist reforms that promise to slow the flow of federal funds or that otherwise threaten their business interests and autonomy. The drug industry, for example, previously opposed Medicare coverage of prescription drugs because it worried that this would set the stage for system-wide price controls and reduced profits.[40] A Republican Congress was unlikely to vote for a drug bill opposed by both the drug and insurance industries.

Furthermore, any effort by the Bush administration to structurally reform Medicare and move Medicare beneficiaries out of the traditional program and into private insurance ran headlong into a crucial political reality: most Medicare beneficiaries were satisfied with their coverage. In fact, Medicare beneficiaries were more satisfied with their insurance than any other insured group in the United States.[41] Conservative reformers consequently confronted a fundamental political dilemma in trying to convert Medicare to a full-scale competitive model and dislodge beneficiaries from traditional Medicare.[42] Medicare was immensely popular with beneficiaries and the broader public, and unlike the Medicaid program that serves low-income Americans who have comparatively less political voice, it was politically impossible to compel Medicare beneficiaries to join private insurance plans. As former congressman Billy Tauzin quipped, "You couldn't move my mother out of Medicare with a bulldozer."[43] Any policies viewed as forcing Medicare beneficiaries out of the traditional program would be politically treacherous and risked alienating the very constituency that the Bush administration wanted to pry away from Democrats by adopting prescription drug coverage.

Medicare's short-term fiscal health provided another barrier to the Bush administration's desire to restructure Medicare. Major Medicare reforms have usually coincided with shortfalls in Medicare's trust fund for hospitalization insurance (HI), which is funded through earmarked payroll taxes.[44] Projected shortfalls in the HI trust fund have periodically triggered Medicare bankruptcy crises, providing policymakers extraordinary opportunities to push through reforms in the name of restoring Medicare's solvency.[45] The Bush administration, however, did not have the benefit of a similar trust fund crisis that would allow it to argue that structural reforms were necessary to save Medicare. In 2001, Medicare's HI trust fund projected to be solvent until 2029—in Medicare's thirty-six years of operation, that represented the best shape the Medicare trust fund had ever been in.[46] That comparatively sunny outlook prevented the Bush administration from framing reforms as a response to imminent bankruptcy. Perhaps the administration could mobilize longer-term projections of a Medicare shortfall to build support for program reforms, but longer-term projections generate less political urgency than short-term bankruptcy crises.[47]

A final dilemma for the Bush administration and other advocates of adding prescription drug coverage was that most Medicare beneficiaries already had drug coverage through Medicaid, employer-sponsored retiree health insurance, or other private insurance plans. If efforts to cover the Medicare population that was uninsured for prescription drugs threatened to disrupt or worsen the existing coverage that many Medicare beneficiaries carried, seniors' support for reform could evaporate and the new benefit could even trigger a political backlash from its intended beneficiaries, as catastrophic health insurance did during 1988–89. The Bush administration had much to gain from the enactment of Medicare prescription drug coverage and much to lose if it did not pass before the 2004 elections. But it also ran the risk of serious political fallout if Congress passed, in beneficiaries' eyes, the wrong legislation.

Enacting the Medicare Modernization Act

The political drama surrounding enactment of the Medicare Modernization Act has few rivals.[48] The final bill passed the House of Representatives at six on the morning of November 22, 2003, by a 220–215 margin, but only after Republican leaders held open the vote for three hours—the longest recorded vote in House history—in order to persuade a few GOP congressmen to reverse their positions and support the bill when it appeared headed to defeat (an initial vote had the bill losing 218–216). It then passed the Senate 54–44, having earlier survived a budgetary point of order by one vote. The slim majorities held off opposition from both the right and left. Conservatives objected to the bill as an expensive entitlement that did too little to overhaul Medicare and control costs, consequently exacerbating federal budget deficits. Liberals denounced the bill for inadequate benefits, too much privatization, and as a sellout to drug companies and private insurers.[49]

The drama did not end with the bill's enactment. In ensuing months, there were allegations of vote buying (a Republican congressman was allegedly offered $100,000 "to help his son run for his seat on the condition that he switch his vote"[50] and support the legislation); revelations that the Bush administration had concealed from Congress estimates by the federal Medicare actuary that projected substantially higher program costs than it had given during the MMA debate (the actuary charged that the Medicare administrator threatened to fire him if he disclosed the estimates);[51] and controversy over the administration's use of fake news stories to promote the new benefit (an action subsequently deemed illegal by the General Accounting Office).[52] Still, the bottom line is that the Bush administration succeeded in its goal of enacting a Medicare prescription drug benefit before the 2004 election. How did Bush do it?

Perhaps most importantly, the Bush administration demonstrated a willingness to compromise conservative principles in order to achieve political goals; expanding Medicare is, after all, a liberal cause. The administration's original proposals for a Medicare drug benefit were much more limited than the program that ultimately emerged from Congress. The Bush administration initially proposed offering comprehensive drug coverage only to low-income Medicare beneficiaries and enrollees who left traditional Medicare for private insurance.[53] Those plans were consistent with conservatives' general preference for means-tested benefits over universal programs and for private plans over government insurance. Yet the MMA established a much broader benefit than the Bush administration envisioned, a benefit universally available to all Medicare beneficiaries regardless of income and regardless of whether they joined a private Medicare plan or remained in the traditional program. Simply put, the Bush administration accepted a Medicare drug benefit as the political price for reelection and, having made that decision, then accepted a substantially larger program than they wanted as the price for enacting the drug benefit.

The Bush administration also deferred to Congress. After its initial drug benefit proposals floundered, the administration released a general Medicare reform framework but left the job of working out the actual legislation to congressional leaders (at their urging).[54] That enabled the White House to distance itself from a proposal sure to draw conservatives' fire, as well as from intra-Republican fights within Congress.[55] House Republicans passed legislation in June 2003 (it passed the House by a single vote) containing a provision that would transform Medicare into a full-fledged competitive market with a greatly enhanced role for private insurers, while their Senate colleagues produced a bipartisan bill (it garnered seventy-six votes) lacking that provision.

When Medicare reform threatened to stall because of difficulties reconciling the House and Senate bills in conference committee—"at one point Ways and Means Committee Chairman Bill Thomas (R-CA) stormed out of the Capitol" in the midst of negotiations—Senate Majority Leader Bill Frist (R-TN) and House Speaker Dennis Hastert (R-IL) intervened to craft a compromise plan and ensure its passage. Even if congressional Republicans did not share Karl Rove's realignment vision, many of them were up for reelection as well in 2004. The Republican leadership consequently believed that "the price of failure on the proposed Medicare revision would be too high."[56]

The administration agreed and lobbied hard at the end of the process to secure enough Republican votes to pass the bill. Ultimately, both the Bush administration and Republican congressional leadership relied on largely partisan majorities to enact the MMA. In a final vote that Tom Oliver and colleagues aptly termed "upside-down politics,"[57] 89 percent of House and 82 percent of Senate Republicans voted for legislation creating a new Medicare prescription drug benefit, and 92 percent of House and 76 percent of Senate Democrats voted against it.[58] Political motivations help explain why so many Republicans voted to add an expensive new benefit to an entitlement program they already regarded as unaffordable. But those motivations dot no fully account for Republican support for the MMA or Democratic opposition. That upside-down pattern is also explained by the fact that the MMA was, in crucial respects, conservative legislation that promoted Medicare privatization.[59]

For the first time in program history, the MMA created a Medicare benefit only available through private plans. Under the legislation, Medicare beneficiaries could choose to purchase prescription drug coverage from numerous private plans. But the federal government did not, unlike Medicare insurance for hospital or physician services, directly offer its own Medicare drug plan. The MMA effectively privatized drug coverage in Medicare, a policy strongly favored by a drug industry that feared greater federal involvement in regulating pharmaceutical prices.

In addition, the law provided a series of financial subsidies and payment increases designed to attract private insurers to the Medicare market and established a demonstration project (scheduled to start in 2010) that would put Medicare in direct competition with private insurance plans. That competitive system could raise costs for beneficiaries who stay in the traditional program, accelerating Medicare enrollees' movement into private insurance plans. The demonstration project represented an effort to mollify House Republicans who wanted Medicare fully converted into a market system. Additional provisions aimed to increase enrollment in private Medicare plans in rural areas.

The MMA also created Health Savings Accounts (HSAs), a move popular with conservatives.[60] HSAs are tax-preferred accounts that are paired with high-deductible health insurance. The idea is that persons (or their employers) can deposit money into HSAs and then use the money to pay for medical services below the deductible.[61] Since the deductible is high and HSA funds can accumulate, HSA advocates argue that enrollees will face financial incentives to use fewer medical services. Conservatives consequently regard HSAs as an important alternative to conventional health insurance and as a potential consumer-driven solution to rising health care costs.[62]

The MMA incorporated a number of conservative provisions intended to enhance the position of private plans in Medicare, lure Medicare beneficiaries away from the traditional program and into private insurance, and move the health care system toward less comprehensive insurance models. And if drug coverage had to be added to Medicare, conservatives and the drug industry much preferred relying on private plans rather than on the federal government to deliver the benefit.

Those provisions helped the Bush administration and Republican leadership secure enough GOP votes to pass the MMA, though they also ensured that most Democrats would oppose the MMA.[63] From the beginning, the Bush administration pursued a strategy of linking a new Medicare drug benefit to conservative reforms that would restructure Medicare. While the legislation did not go nearly as far in adopting those reforms as many conservatives wanted—some conservatives derided the demonstration project as a "fig leaf"[64] intended to cover up the Republican leadership's failure to push through bolder reforms—it still incorporated significant new policies that appealed to Republicans skeptical about expanding Medicare. Even if those policies disappointed, the electoral calculus (adopt prescription drug coverage or risk losing the 2004 elections) provided a compelling motivation for Republicans to vote for the MMA. The administration consequently won enactment of the MMA without losing much of the conservative Republican base in Congress.

Although conservative reforms were crucial to amassing Republican votes to pass the MMA, the Medicare drug benefit also depended on the rejection of conservative budgeting principles. There is no more important factor in the MMA's enactment than the fiscal permissiveness that enabled the Bush administration and Republican Congress to pay for the Medicare drug benefit by simply adding the bill to the growing federal deficit.[65] The Bush administration, which took office with a surplus, showed scant interest in cutting the deficit once it reappeared. Their economic policies prioritized tax cutting, and they made no serious effort to implement large-scale spending cuts. It is striking that while the three presidents preceding George W. Bush all supported major reforms that reduced the rate of growth in Medicare spending, the Bush administration did not sponsor similar measures. As Joe White notes, "the administration clearly did not care enough about the budget to restrain spending."[66] The Republican Congress also displayed little interest in budget deficits and let pay-as-you-go (PAYGO) budgetary rules, which required that Congress offset increased entitlement spending or tax cuts by adopting corresponding tax increases or spending cuts, expire in 2002.[67]

Fiscal permissiveness allowed the administration and congressional leadership to buy interest group support for the MMA, enhancing its political prospects. It is hard to find a group or parochial interest that did not benefit from the bill. The MMA left virtually no interest group behind. Pharmaceutical companies won freedom from Medicare price controls—the legislation prohibited the federal government from directly negotiating drug prices, ensured that the drug benefit was provided through the private sector, and neutralized the threat of reimported drugs from Canada and other nations. Managed care plans and private insurers secured a larger role in Medicare—by serving as the insurers for Part D—and larger subsidies to participate in Medicare's growing insurance market. Employers gained over $70 billion in tax-free subsidies to maintain retiree insurance for prescription drugs that they were already providing. Physicians had a scheduled 4.5 percent cut in payment rates reversed and instead received a 1.5 percent increase. Hospitals won higher reimbursements and a temporary moratorium on the construction of new specialty hospitals that they feared could divert profitable patients and procedures. Rural areas gained higher Medicare payments. The National Federation of Independent Businesses and conservative advocates of consumer-driven health care lobbied successfully for the inclusion of HSAs. And on it went.[68]

The triumph of interest group politics in the MMA contrasts with the politics of cost containment that had dominated Medicare politics for the previous twenty years. Budget deficit pressures in the 1980s and 1990s led policymakers to adopt a series of reforms that strengthened federal regulatory authority and reduced payments to medical providers.[69] Such was the influence of deficit politics that even conservative Republicans friendly to provider interests and averse to regulation—including Ronald Reagan—signed off on the expansion of Medicare's regulatory and price-setting powers in order to contain program spending on hospitals and doctors.

In contrast, Congress enacted the MMA in 2003 amidst an environment of fiscal permissiveness. It thus afforded an array of groups, many of whom had unrequited agendas deferred by past Medicare cost containment efforts, an extraordinary opportunity to pursue their aims. And with no regard for the deficit, the Bush administration and Republican Congress could afford to buy as much stakeholder support as they wanted for the legislation.[70]

While the MMA offered something to just about everyone in Medicare policy, support from one group—AARP, formerly the American Association of

Retired Persons—proved especially crucial to the legislation's passage. Historically, AARP's leadership had "consisted mostly of Democrats committed to
maintaining Medicare as a strong government-run program."[71] However, the
Bush administration and congressional Republicans (led by Majority Leader
Frist and Speaker Hastert) actively courted AARP, knowing that its opposition
could imperil the bill.[72]

AARP believed that the MMA was flawed, but also that the opportunity to
commit $400 billion to a Medicare drug benefit was too good to pass up, espe-
cially given a growing federal budget deficit; the program could be improved
over time once the new benefit and funding were locked in. AARP also worked
to ensure enhanced coverage for low-income beneficiaries and to "defang"
the bill of provisions they deemed harmful to traditional Medicare,[73] though
some congressional Democrats believed that AARP struck an overly generous
bargain with Republicans.

Ultimately, the administration and Republican leadership won AARP's
backing for the MMA, providing them with cover against Democratic charges
that the bill sold out elderly beneficiaries to the drug industry and undercutting Senate Democrats' effort to filibuster the legislation.[74] AARP ended up
running an advertising campaign on behalf of the MMA.[75] If they had instead opposed the legislation and run ads against it, the MMA may well never
have become law, a reminder that the outcome of Medicare reform was highly
contingent. For all the Bush administration's electoral incentives and political strategies, this was a legislative battle they nearly lost.

Policy Legacies

How have the Bush administration's Medicare reforms fared in practice? Medicare's prescription drug program (known as Medicare Part D) has a mixed record to date. On the positive side, enrollment has been strong (in 2010, almost
28 million Medicare beneficiaries were enrolled in Part D plans, and 90% of all
beneficiaries had prescription drug coverage). Private plan options for Medicare drug coverage have been much more numerous than expected, and beneficiary premiums for that coverage (as well as overall program costs) were initially lower than anticipated.[76]

The Medicare prescription drug market also has been relatively stable. Few
plans have dropped out of the program, minimizing disruptions for beneficiaries. Moreover, during 2006–8 only 6 percent of Part D enrollees voluntarily

switched plans. There also has been no large-scale erosion of employer-provided drug coverage for Medicare beneficiaries (Medicare pays subsidies to employers who continue drug coverage for their retirees). Furthermore, 76 percent of seniors enrolled in Medicare drug plans report a very positive or somewhat positive experience with their plan.[77]

On the other hand, there were serious problems with the program's initial implementation, including the mishandling of low-income beneficiaries' switch to Medicare drug coverage—Medicaid had previously covered some low-income Medicare enrollees' drug costs—which resulted in interrupted treatment, relapses, and hospitalization for some enrollees with severe mental illness. Moreover, many Medicare beneficiaries continue to incur high drug costs because of Part D's limited benefits. Medicare beneficiaries also face a bewildering array of coverage options: in virtually all states, Medicare beneficiaries must choose from at least thirty different stand-alone drug plans in addition to numerous Medicare Advantage plans. The sheer number of options and the many dimensions that plans can differ on make it difficult for beneficiaries to detect meaningful differences between plans and make a good choice.

In addition, many Medicare beneficiaries who are eligible for a low-income subsidy that provides them with comprehensive coverage are not enrolled in the program. There have also been marketing abuses reported, with seniors duped into signing up for private plans whose benefits and restrictions they don't understand, as private insurers look to profit from their Medicare business. Finally, during 2006–11 premiums for stand-alone Part D drug plans rose by 57 percent.[78]

However, the drug benefit is not the MMA's only policy legacy. Conservatives criticized the law's market-oriented provisions as a "fig leaf," but those provisions, at least in the short run, pushed Medicare further down the path toward privatization. Conservatives' long-term goal is to transform Medicare by moving beneficiaries out of the traditional program and into private insurance plans. There are three ways to accomplish that aim. The first, simply closing the traditional program and mandating beneficiaries to join private insurers, is not politically feasible. The elderly are too popular a group for that. A second means to that end is to replace the current system with a competitive insurance market where traditional Medicare has to compete with private plans. That is what House Republicans wanted to do in 2003, but there was not sufficient support in the Senate to include that plan in the final legislation. A third method of increasing private insurance enrollment is an indirect strategy: give private plans financial subsidies so they can offer beneficiaries generous benefits and thereby induce them to leave traditional Medicare. That strategy amounts to loading the dice in favor of private insurers.

The Bush administration and congressional Republicans embraced the loading-the-dice strategy in the MMA by creating new private plan options and especially by increasing federal payments to private plans. After the payment increases, private Medicare Advantage plans were paid 112 percent of what it would have cost to care for beneficiaries in the traditional Medicare program.[79] In other words, the federal government subsidized private insurance plans so they could offer better benefits than the federal government. As Joe Antos put it, "The strategy of the MMA is to make MA [Medicare Advantage] plans so attractive that most beneficiaries will voluntarily switch out of traditional Medicare."[80] Higher payments were reinforced by administrative decisions that further aided private plans, including protecting them against risk-adjustment formulas that would have lowered federal payments to reflect the fact that private plans enrolled healthier-than-average Medicare beneficiaries.[81]

Those strategies successfully strengthened the position of private insurers in Medicare. In 2010, 11.1 million Medicare beneficiaries (24%) were enrolled in Medicare Advantage plans, up from 5.3 million in 2003 before the MMA was passed, representing the highest private plan enrollment in Medicare history.[82] That enrollment gain was a significant victory for conservatives who wished to privatize Medicare insurance, despite the fact that the scheduled demonstration in Medicare competition never got off the ground. Yet it represented a defeat for fiscal discipline since the extra payments mean that the federal government is losing money on beneficiaries who enroll in private plans (which ironically were originally promoted in Medicare for their cost-saving potential).

That boost to privatization was a crucial legacy of the MMA and the Bush administration's Medicare reform efforts. If enrollment in Medicare Advantage plans continued to grow at a rapid rate, then traditional Medicare would erode without Congress having ever enacted a full-fledged competitive insurance system. However, as the final section in this chapter explains, this legacy is far from secure as the Obama administration and congressional Democrats subsequently have targeted Medicare's excess payments to private plans.

Political Legacies

Regardless of the policy outcomes, the Bush administration pushed for a Medicare drug benefit largely for political reasons. Did its Medicare strategy pay off?

In the short run, the Bush administration and congressional Republicans benefited. If the Medicare drug legislation had failed to pass after rising so high on the public agenda and coming so close to enactment, Republicans could well have lost votes in the 2004 election, though the scope of those losses is uncertain. In addition, adopting the Medicare drug benefit allowed the 2004 Bush campaign to focus on politically advantageous issues like national security, while depriving Democrats of an issue that played to their favor. Furthermore, George W. Bush improved his standing with elderly voters in 2004. According to exit polls, 52 percent of Americans over age 65 voted for Bush in 2004 compared with 47 percent in 2000.[83]

However, Bush also improved his standing among voters under 65 in 2004 (by 3 percentage points), and only 8 percent of all exit poll respondents named health care as the most important issue in the 2004 election. It is thus impossible to know precisely what role the Medicare drug benefit legislation had, as opposed to other issues like terrorism, in generating more elderly votes for Bush in 2004.[84]

The controversy surrounding the Medicare drug benefit probably limited the ability of Bush and congressional Republicans to leverage political benefits from the MMA. Adopting a new benefit for a popular program should have provided ample opportunity for credit claiming. But, as previously noted, the MMA vote was polarized along partisan lines, with Democrats charging that the legislation provided an inadequate drug benefit, sold out seniors to the drug and insurance industries, and privatized Medicare. The program's bizarre benefit design—the standard plan initially covered 75 percent of beneficiaries' drug expenses up to $2,250 and then stopped providing any coverage in its infamous "doughnut hole" before covering 95 percent of expenses after $5,100— also attracted substantial media coverage.

Not surprisingly, the program drew weak public support. As President Bush signed the MMA into law, an ABC News/*Washington Post* Poll found that only 26 percent of seniors approved of the new bill, with 47 percent disapproving. Among all Americans, the bill hardly earned a ringing endorsement: 38 percent of public respondents disapproved, 32 percent approved, and a sizable 30 percent—no doubt reflecting widespread confusion over what the MMA did for and to Medicare—had no opinion.[85] Two weeks before the 2004 election, only 27 percent of seniors had a favorable view of the legislation, while 44 percent of seniors had an unfavorable view.[86]

Remarkably, the Bush administration managed to enact the most expensive benefit expansion in Medicare history in a way that alienated, if only in the short term, many members of the very constituency that the administration aimed to impress. The administration and congressional Republicans avoided blame for not enacting any legislation. But the legislation they did enact probably reduced the potential political benefits. Of course, it could have been worse. Despite its visible flaws, the MMA did not provoke the vehement post-enactment opposition that led to repeal of the 1988 Medicare Catastrophic Coverage Act, partly because policymakers applied lessons from that experience to the MMA (by providing a temporary benefit—a drug discount card—immediately; relying on a general revenue subsidy rather than Medicare beneficiaries alone to finance the benefit; and making enrollment and thus the extra premium payment for drug coverage voluntary).[87]

What about the long-term political benefits of adopting Medicare prescription drug coverage? The Bush administration wanted to use Medicare reform to shift more seniors to the GOP and thereby expand the Republican Party base. Medicare policymaking became an instrument of coalition building. The administration's chief political strategist, Karl Rove, believed that the Medicare policy initiative, along with other initiatives in education, Social Security, and immigration, would trigger a realignment that produced a permanent Republican majority.

Rove's vision suffered major blows when Democrats won majority control of both the House and Senate in 2006 and then in 2008 won the White House and expanded their congressional majorities. The Democratic victory in 2008 came despite the fact that John McCain won the over-65 vote (53%–45%). McCain's margin among senior voters was greater than that enjoyed by Bush in 2004, but that almost certainly had little to do with Medicare. Even as they have increased their share of the elderly vote, Republicans' overall electoral performance worsened, a sign of their political troubles among other demographic groups. Polls taken after the MMA's enactment showed that Democrats maintained a sizable advantage over Republicans on prescription drugs for the elderly and on health care reform.[88]

The Medicare case, along with other Bush administration initiatives such as Social Security and immigration, suggests the limits of seeking realignment and expanding the party coalition through policy reform.[89] Permanent majorities were always more a product of Karl Rove's political imagination than a likely outcome of Bush administration policies.[90] Policy reforms can impact partisan identification and voting patterns. Leveraging those reforms, though, to produce enduring changes in the American political landscape is extraordinarily difficult.

Efforts to expand a party's political coalition through policymaking can fail to produce the desired political benefits in numerous ways: Congress may not adopt the policy; the adopting party may not get credit from voters (a particular risk in a fragmented political system); new policies may not reshape public opinion or overcome the other party's long-term identification with a particular program; the policy can be adopted under contested circumstances that undermine its political appeal; poor implementation can cast the policy in a bad light or initial policy successes may not be sustained; the policy can, when enacted, turn out to be less popular, successful, or politically consequential than anticipated; and even if a policy successfully adds one group to a party coalition, if additional policies or conditions lead other groups to leave that party, then that gain can be negated.[91] The Bush administration's foray into Medicare illustrates that even when politicians enact major reforms for electoral gain, there is no guarantee they will reap lasting benefits.

The 2003 MMA had one final political legacy. The rise of the Tea Party movement and conservatives' renewed crusade against federal spending during 2009–10 arguably was a reaction not just against the expansion of government during the presidency of Barack Obama but also against the fiscal excesses of George W. Bush's compassionate conservatism. The Medicare drug benefit—an expensive, unfunded entitlement sponsored by Republicans—came to embody the idea that the GOP had lost its way and needed to return to core conservative values of limited government, balanced budgets, and welfare state retrenchment.

The Early Obama Years

Barack Obama, like George W. Bush, made health care a signature issue of his presidency. Yet whereas Bush focused on the (comparatively) politically easier task of extending Medicare benefits, Obama set out to overhaul the U.S.

health care system by extending insurance coverage to the uninsured, mandating larger employers to offer health insurance to their workers, requiring most Americans to obtain insurance or pay a penalty, and much more.[92] Another contrast is evident: while the Bush administration pursued Medicare reform largely because of the potential electoral payoff in luring voters outside the party's base, the Obama administration pushed forward with risky health reform more as a matter of ideological conviction and political commitment to the Democratic base (and also to take advantage of an opportunity created by the economic crisis). Furthermore, Obama's task was complicated by a financial constraint that the Bush administration chose to ignore: Democrats reinstated PAYGO principles, so Obama's health reform plan—at a cost of over $900 billion during 2010–19—had to be fully paid for and could not worsen the federal deficit, necessitating both tax increases and cuts in payments to the health care industry.

While the goals and scope of the Bush and Obama health reforms diverged widely, there are some parallels between the 2003 Medicare Modernization Act and the 2010 Patient Protection and Affordable Care Act (ACA). Like the MMA before it, the ACA built on a model of competing private insurance plans. The defeat of the public insurance option meant that many Democrats reluctantly embraced a health reform model that had something in common with the Bush administration's Medicare framework. Moreover, the Obama administration chose, as the Bush administration did in Medicare, to defer key decisions on the substance of health reform legislation to congressional leaders (though Obama was much more involved in the details than Bush had been). Democrats in 2009–10 took another page from the 2003 Republican playbook in co-opting interest groups to improve the odds of passing controversial health care legislation. Obama attempted to neutralize opposition and win support for reform where possible from the health care industry—a direct reaction to the Clinton administration's unsuccessful two-front war against the insurance industry and small business lobby during 1993–94, a clash that helped doom the Clinton health plan to defeat.[93] The strategy of co-opting health industry groups, which stood to gain financially from the expansion of private insurance coverage, mostly paid off (though insurers still campaigned against the law and particularly the public option). Just as Republicans benefited from AARP running ads endorsing the MMA in 2003, in 2009 Democrats benefited from ads in support of health reform sponsored by PhRMA, the pharmaceutical industry's chief lobbying organization.

The Obama administration, as well as Senate Democrats, also tried, in effect, to build a coalition to pass health reform legislation that reprised the one that enacted the MMA: overwhelming support from the president's own party, with some backing from the opposition to give the reform a bipartisan imprimatur. Obama, though, never seriously sought Republican votes in the House. The administration initially did seek a handful of Republican votes in the Senate (Maine's Olympia Snowe was one target). The quest for bipartisanship was largely instrumental. Key Democratic leaders such as Max Baucus—chair of the Finance Committee—and conservative Democrats such as Ben Nelson insisted (wrongly as it turned out) that health care legislation could not pass the Senate, particularly given the supermajority necessary to circumvent a filibuster, on a party-line vote without any Republican support.

The Obama administration ultimately failed to put together even a semblance of a bipartisan coalition. The final health reform legislation passed the House and Senate in March 2010 without a single Republican vote. Yet Obama faced a much more difficult task than Bush had in assembling an interparty coalition. Unlike 2003, when Democrats agreed with the goal of adding prescription drug coverage to Medicare even if they didn't like how Republicans were doing it, congressional Republicans in 2009–10 did not agree with Obama's goal of dramatically expanding health coverage to the uninsured.

How did the 2010 health reform law impact Medicare and the political and policy legacies of the Bush administration? The 2010 law paid for extending health coverage to the uninsured in large part by reducing projected future spending in Medicare by over $400 billion during the next decade. Democrats targeted private Medicare Advantage plans for cuts, taking away excess payments the Bush administration had introduced to expand private insurers' role in Medicare. If those cuts hold, then Medicare's drift toward private insurance will slow (though if Republicans regain the White House and win congressional majorities in 2012, they will likely try again to boost private plans in Medicare).

Democrats' reliance on Medicare to fund coverage for the uninsured also helped to create a new, unusual political dynamic. During the health reform debate, Republicans repositioned themselves as the party of Medicare, defending it against alleged Democratic plans to undermine the program. Indeed, Republican scare talk about the impact of health reform—the specter of "death panels" and "pulling the plug on grandma"—was aimed squarely at seniors. The health reform law actually contained significant improvements in basic

Medicare benefits—including gradually filling in the notorious gap in prescription drug coverage. The Obama administration and congressional Democrats may have hoped that expanding Medicare benefits would help sell seniors on health reform. If so, that strategy failed miserably. The administration failed to explain to Medicare beneficiaries—and indeed, more generally to insured Americans—how the new law would help them. Talk of "death panels" and other imaginary reform specters overshadowed real improvements in Medicare coverage. Only 48 percent of Americans surveyed in September 2010 knew that the health reform law closed Medicare's prescription drug "doughnut hole"; meanwhile, 30 percent falsely believed that the ACA allowed a government panel to make decisions about end-of-life care for Medicare beneficiaries.[94] According to exit polls, Republicans enjoyed a 16-point advantage over Democrats in the 2010 congressional election among voters age 65 and older, and seniors' unhappiness with health reform probably contributed to the shift toward the GOP.

No sooner had Republicans taken up the mantle of defending Medicare than they proceeded to squander the advantage. The party that had reaped political benefits from Tea Party activists' warning that Democrats should "keep their hands off my Medicare" stunningly set out to remake the program. In 2011, the new Republican majority in the House passed a controversial Medicare reform plan authored by Wisconsin Congressman Paul Ryan. The Ryan plan proposed to eliminate the traditional Medicare program and instead subsidize beneficiaries to purchase private insurance. Republicans were, once again, pushing to privatize Medicare. But this time, in the context of soaring federal budget deficits, they were intent on saving money. The Ryan proposal would have firmly limited federal spending on Medicare, establishing a de facto program budget, though only by shifting the burden of rising health care costs to beneficiaries. The plan, which failed to clear the Senate, predictably triggered intense opposition from congressional Democrats, the Obama administration, and seniors. Polls showed substantial public opposition. Republicans' campaign to become the party of Medicare had imploded.

The political failure of the Ryan plan appeared to offer a cautionary tale. If expanding Medicare didn't produce much in the way of electoral benefits for either the Bush or Obama administrations, then contracting Medicare seems, just as the share of Americans over age 65 is set to grow significantly, like an even riskier political prospect for future administrations and congresses. Medicare savings will not come absent controversial increases in what Medicare beneficiaries pay for medical care, reduced benefits, or further cuts in what the government pays hospitals, doctors, and other medical service providers. Nor will it be easy to raise the Medicare payroll tax. Such policy choices offer the prospect of substantial political pain, but not much gain. Medicare reform offers a set of policy choices that, based on short-term calculations, both parties could perceive as a threat to their electoral futures. Avoidance is consequently an appealing (non-)option in Medicare policy.[95]

But the rise of deficit politics following the 2010 elections has changed the political calculus. The long-term deficit is seen in Washington largely as a health care spending problem. Pressures to cut the deficit—exacerbated by the specter of international debt crises and fears that such a crisis could happen in the United States—thereby generate strong pressures to find Medicare savings. Tellingly, during 2011 negotiations with Speaker of the House John Boehner over a "grand deal" to reduce deficits by $4 trillion and raise the debt ceiling, President Obama reportedly agreed to $250 billion in Medicare savings over the next decade, including a gradual increase in the Medicare eligibility age. The negotiations failed, with Congress and the administration instead agreeing to over $900 billion in initial deficit reduction that exempted Medicare. It was left to a bipartisan congressional "super committee" to come up with additional savings or face the prospect of automatic cuts that would include steep reductions in defense spending and reductions in Medicare payments to medical care providers (Medicare benefits were left untouched).

At this writing, the outcome of that process is unclear. But a Democratic president's willingness to consider a highly controversial change in Medicare's eligibility age (even at the cost of squandering his party's political advantage in the aftermath of the Ryan plan) suggests that significant Medicare reforms are on the table. Could deficits and debt motivate interparty action? There is precedent for bipartisan Medicare policy. During the 1980s and 1990s, Democrats and Republicans collaborated on Medicare reform, supporting measures that significantly reduced Medicare payments to the health care industry. The question now is whether political leaders from either party can assemble another bipartisan coalition given the level of partisan and ideological polarization in Congress and the legacy of a health reform debate that (wrongly) defined any cut in Medicare spending as a threat to elderly Americans. Debt pressures could overcome those barriers and catalyze Medicare reform, although the partisan divide on Medicare is unlikely to disappear and could widen.

Medicare politics has shifted dramatically. Less than a decade after a projected budget surplus helped spur enactment of a Medicare prescription benefit, debate over program policy is now driven by deficits, debt, and proposals to control program spending. The stakes for Democrats and Republicans in Medicare are higher than ever, and both parties will have to navigate a risky political environment where Medicare reform is increasingly equated with reducing benefits.

NOTES

1. For overviews of the Bush presidency, see Colin Campbell, Bert A. Rockman, and Andrew Rudalevige, eds., *The George W. Bush Legacy* (Washington, DC: Congressional Quarterly Press, 2007), and George C. Edwards III and Desmond S. King, eds., *The Polarized Presidency of George W. Bush* (New York: Oxford University Press, 2007).

2. Quoted in William W. Welch, "Conservatives Sound Warning over Medicare Plan; Bush-Backed Prescription Benefit Creating Rift with Political Base," *USA Today*, July 13, 2003.

3. Douglas Jaenicke and Alex Waddan, "President Bush and Social Policy: The Strange Case of the Medicare Prescription Drug Benefit," *Political Science Quarterly* 121 (2006): 217–40.

4. For a detailed description of Medicare's benefits, eligibility rules, and financing arrangements, see Marilyn Moon, *Medicare: A Policy Primer* (Washington, DC: Urban Institute Press, 2006).

5. Jonathan Oberlander, *The Political Life of Medicare* (Chicago: University of Chicago Press, 2003): 36–53.

6. For a comprehensive history of these efforts, see Thomas R. Oliver, Philip R. Lee, and Helene L. Lipton, "A Political History of Medicare and Prescription Drugs," *Milbank Quarterly* 82 (2004): 283–354.

7. Oberlander, *Political Life of Medicare*, 47.

8. Robert H. Binstock, "The Old Age Lobby in a New Political Era," in *The Future of Age-Based Public Policy*, ed. Robert B. Hudson (Baltimore: Johns Hopkins University Press, 1997), 56–74.

9. Richard Himelfarb, *Catastrophic Politics: The Rise and Fall of the Medicare Catastrophic Coverage Act of 1988* (University Park: Pennsylvania State University Press, 1995).

10. Ibid., 76–77.

11. Oliver et al., "Political History of Medicare," 301–2.

12. Oberlander, *Political Life of Medicare*, 189–93.

13. In 2000, spending on prescription drugs rose by 15%. See Kaiser Family Foundation, *Prescription Drug Trends* (May 2007), http://kff.org/rxdrugs/3057.cfm.

14. Oliver et al., "Political History of Medicare"; Jaenicke and Waddan, "President Bush and Social Policy"; Andrea Louise Campbell and Kimberly Morgan, "The Shifting Line between Public and Private: The Politics of the 2003 Medicare Modernization

Act and Prescription Drug Reform" (paper presented at the Social Science History Association Annual Meeting, Portland, Oregon, November 3–6, 2005).

15. Quoted in Elisabeth Bumiller, "A Final Push in Congress: The White House; For White House, 2 Bills Offer Route to Political High Ground," *New York Times*, November 23, 2003.

16. Robin Toner, "Revamping Medicare: The Context; G.O.P Steals Thunder," *New York Times*, June 28, 2003.

17. Voting data are from the U.S. Census Bureau: www.census.gov/prod/2002pubs /p20-542.pdf.

18. A September 2000 *National Survey on Prescription Drugs* by the Kaiser Family Foundation, Harvard School of Public Health, and the NewsHour found that 87% of respondents under age 65 favored a "proposal to guarantee prescription drug coverage to everyone on Medicare," compared with the 79% of respondents age 65 and older who favored that proposal. A total of 76% of all respondents favored guaranteeing drug coverage for all Medicare beneficiaries even if it meant more government spending. http:// kff.org/rxdrugs/loader.cfm?url=/commonspot/security/getfile.cfm&PageID=13545.

19. Dan Balz, "GOP Aims for Dominance in '04 Race; Republicans to Seek Governing Majority by Feeding Base, Courting New Voters," *Washington Post*, June 22, 2003.

20. Joseph Curl, "Bush Usurps Democrats on Road to '04 Election," *Washington Times*, July 6, 2003.

21. Quoted in Bumiller, "Final Push in Congress."

22. Joshua Green, "Rove Presidency," *Atlantic Monthly*, September 2007, 52–72.

23. David R. Mayhew, *Electoral Realignments: A Critique of an American Genre* (New Haven, CT: Yale University Press, 2004).

24. Green, "Rove Presidency," 56.

25. Robert Novak, "Blame Karl Rove for Medicare Drug Blunder," *Human Events Online*, January 8, 2006, www.humanevents.com/article.php?id=11339.

26. Kaiser Family Foundation, *Medicare Chart Book* (July 2005), www.kff.org/medi care/7284.cfm.

27. Campbell and Morgan, "Shifting Line between Public and Private," 13–14; Robin Toner, "Shift by Older Voters to G.O.P is Democrats' Challenge in 2000," *New York Times*, May 31, 1999.

28. Exit poll data are from http://elections.nytimes.com/2008/results/president /exit-polls.html.

29. Quoted in Rick Mayes, *The Elusive Quest for National Health Insurance* (Ann Arbor: University of Michigan Press), 161.

30. Alison Mitchell, "Bush Spells Out Major Overhaul in Medicare Plan," *New York Times*, September 6, 2000; Oliver et al., "Political History of Medicare," 306–7.

31. Green, "Rove Presidency," 56.

32. David S. Broder, "GOP May Get a Boost with Seniors," *Washington Post*, June 28, 2003.

33. Jaenicke and Waddan, "President Bush and Social Policy," 220.

34. Quoted in David S. Broder, "GOP's Wins: Close, Costly," *Washington Post*, November 30, 2003.

35. Oliver et al., "Political History of Medicare," 328; Jaenicke and Waddan, "President Bush and Social Policy," 227.

36. http://clerk.house.gov/member_info/electionInfo/index.html.

37. Congressional Budget Office, *The Budget and Economic Outlook: An Update* (August 2003), www.cbo.gov/doc.cfm?index=4493.

38. In 2003, this organization was known as the American Association of Health Plans.

39. Bruce C. Vladeck, "The Political Economy of Medicare Reform," *Health Affairs* 18 (1999): 22–36.

40. Marilyn Moon, *Medicare: Now and in the Future* (Washington, DC: Urban Institute Press, 1996): 128–29.

41. Karen Davis, Cathy Schoen, Michelle Doty, and Katie Tenney, "Medicare versus Private Insurance: Rhetoric and Reality," *Health Affairs* Web exclusive (October 9, 2002): w311–24.

42. Jonathan Oberlander, "Through the Looking Glass: The Politics of the Medicare Prescription Drug, Improvement, and Modernization Act," *Journal of Health Politics, Policy and Law* 32 (April 2007): 187–219.

43. Quoted in Robert Pear and Robin Toner, "Bush Medicare Proposal Urges Switch to Private Insurers," *New York Times*, March 4, 2003.

44. Medicare Part B also has a trust fund. However, since it is funded from general revenues and beneficiary premiums that are adjusted annually to meet program expenditures rather than from an earmarked payroll tax like Part A, historically it has not generated bankruptcy concerns.

45. On trust fund politics generally, see Eric Patashnik, *Putting Trust in the U.S. Budget: Federal Trust Funds and the Politics of Commitment* (Cambridge: Cambridge University Press, 2000). On trust fund politics in Medicare, see Oberlander, *Political Life of Medicare*, 74–106.

46. www.cms.hhs.gov/reportstrustfunds/.

47. Long-term projections of health care spending are highly unreliable but politically useful since programs can be indicted on the basis of their projected futures, rather than their present performance and financial condition. See Joseph White, *False Alarm: Why the Greatest Threat to Social Security and Medicare Is the Campaign to Save Them* (Baltimore: Johns Hopkins University Press, 2001), 99–113, and Oberlander, *Political Life of Medicare*, 74–106.

48. Oliver et al., "Political History of Medicare," 321. This section draws on Oberlander, "Through the Looking Glass."

49. John K. Iglehart, "The Medicare Prescription Drug Benefit—a Pure Power Play," *New England Journal of Medicine* 350 (2004): 826–33.

50. Oliver et al., "Political History of Medicare," 321.

51. Robert Pear, "Medicare Official Testifies on Cost Figures," *New York Times*, March 25, 2004.

52. Amy Goldstein, "GAO Says Bush Administration Broke Laws with Medicare Videos," *Washington Post*, May 24, 2004.

53. The Bush administration's plan to limit drug coverage to Medicare beneficiaries who joined private plans was panned in Congress by both parties. Among other problems, many Medicare private plans did not operate in rural areas, so members of Congress from rural areas objected to leaving their constituents without drug coverage. See Campbell and Morgan, "Shifting Line between Public and Private," 23.

54. Oliver et al., "Political History of Medicare," 309.

55. Bumiller, "Final Push in Congress."

56. Amy Goldstein, "For GOP Leaders, Battles and Bruises Produce Medicare Bill," *Washington Post*, November 30, 2003.

57. Oliver et al., "Political History of Medicare," 285.

58. Jaenicke and Waddan, "President Bush and Social Policy," 237–38.

59. Ibid., 225–30; Campbell and Morgan, "Shifting Line between Public and Private"; Oberlander, "Through the Looking Glass," 200–207; Joseph White, "Protecting Medicare: The Best Defense Is a Good Offense," *Journal of Health Politics, Policy and Law* 32 (April 2007): 236–37; Jacob Hacker and Theodore Marmor, "Medicare Reform: Fact, Fiction, and Foolishness," *Public Policy and Aging Report* 13 (2004): 20–23.

60. Oliver et al., "Political History of Medicare," 312; Jaenicke and Waddan, "President Bush and Social Policy," 228–29.

61. Beth Fuchs and Lisa Poetz, *The Fundamentals of Health Savings Accounts and High Deductible Health Plans*, April 23, 2007, National Health Policy Forum.

62. Timothy Stoltzfus Jost, *Health Care at Risk: A Critique of the Consumer-Driven Movement* (Durham, NC: Duke University Press, 2007).

63. Jaenicke and Waddan, "President Bush and Social Policy," 227–31.

64. Amy Fagan, Bush Pushes Prescription-Drug Bill; Negotiators Want More than Pep Talk," *Washington Times*, October 20, 2003.

65. Part D was financed primarily from general revenues, with beneficiary premiums accounting for 25% of costs.

66. White, "Protecting Medicare," 237.

67. In 2007, the House adopted a new PAYGO rule. See Peter R. Orszag, "Issues in Reinstating a Statutory Pay-As-You-Go Requirement," Statement before the Committee on the Budget, U.S. House of Representatives, July 25, 2007; Richard Kogan, *The New Pay-As-You-Go Rule in the House of Representatives*, Center on Budget and Policy Priorities, January 12, 2007.

68. Michael T. Heaney," Brokering Health Policy: Coalitions, Parties, and Interest Group Influence," *Journal of Health Politics, Policy and Law* 31 (2006): 887–944; Iglehart, "Pure Power Play."

69. Oberlander, *Political Life of Medicare*, 107–35; Rick Mayes and Robert A. Berenson, *Medicare Prospective Payment and the Shaping of U.S. Health Care* (Baltimore: Johns Hopkins University Press, 2006); Jacob Hacker and Paul Pierson, *Off Center: The Republican Revolution and Erosion of American Democracy* (New Haven, CT: Yale University Press, 2005), 85–93.

70. Some Republicans, especially in the House, voiced concerns over the program's cost and advocated strict spending controls for Medicare Part D, though most House Republicans ultimately voted for the legislation without those controls.

71. Barbara Dreyfus, "The Seduction: The Shocking Story of How AARP Backed the Medicare Bill," *American Prospect*, May 12, 2004.

72. Goldstein, "Battles and Bruises Produce Medicare Bill."

73. Telephone interviews with John Rother, Director of Legislation and Public Policy for AARP, July 19, 2006, and September 23, 2006; Iglehart, "Pure Power Play," 831.

74. Robin Toner, "A Final Push in Congress; News Analysis; An Imperfect Compromise," *New York Times*, November 25, 2003; Campbell and Morgan, "Shifting Line between Public and Private," 26–27.

75. Oliver et al., "Political History of Medicare," 319.

76. Patricia Neuman and Juliette Cubanski, "Medicare Part D Update—Lessons Learned and Unfinished Business," *New England Journal of Medicine* 361 (2009): 406–14.

77. Kaiser Family Foundation, *Fact Sheet: The Medicare Prescription Drug Benefit*, February 2008; Dana P. Goldman and Geoffrey F. Joyce, "Medicare Part D: A Successful Start with Room for Improvement," *JAMA* 299 (2008): 1954–55; Kaiser Family Foundation / Harvard School of Public Health, *Seniors and the Medicare Prescription Drug Benefit*, December 2006.

78. Patricia Neuman et al., "Medicare Prescription Drug Benefit Progress Report: Findings from a 2006 National Survey of Seniors," *Health Affairs* 26 (2007): w630–43; Robin Toner, "Rival Visions Led to Rocky Start for Drug Benefit," *New York Times*, February 6, 2006; Robert Pear, "For Recipients of Medicare, the Hard Sell," *New York Times*, December 17, 2007; Robert Pear, "Medicare Audits Show Problems in Private Plans," *New York Times*, October 7, 2007; Robert Pear, "States Intervene after Drug Plan Hits Early Snag," *New York Times*, January 8, 2006; Robert Pear, "Medicare Woes Take High Toll on Mentally Ill," *New York Times*, January 31, 2006; Jane Zhang, "Time to Review Seniors' Drug Options," *Wall Street Journal*, November 8, 2008.

79. Kaiser Family Foundation, *Medicare Fact Sheet*, June 2007.

80. Joseph R. Antos, *Will Competition Return to Medicare?* Working Paper No. 125 (Washington, DC: American Enterprise Institute, 2006), www.aei.org/paper/23843.

81. White, "Protecting Medicare," 236–37; Oberlander, "Through the Looking Glass," 204–7.

82. Kaiser Family Foundation, *Medicare Advantage Fact Sheet*, September 2010.

83. Exit poll data for the 2000 and 2004 elections are available at www.cnn.com /ELECTION/2004/pages/results/states/US/P/00/epolls.0.html and http://observation alism.com/2008/11/09/selected-exit-poll-comparisons-2000-2004-2008/.

84. Campbell and Morgan, "Shifting Line between Public and Private," 33–34.

85. Oliver et al., "Political History of Medicare," 285; ABC News / *Washington Post* Poll, December 8, 2003, http://abcnews.go.com/images/pdf/883a37Medicare.pdf.

86. Robert J. Blendon et al., "Voters and Health Care in the 2004 Election," *Health Affairs* Web exclusive, March 1, 2005 (w5), 86–96.

87. Oliver et al., "Political History of Medicare," 338.

88. In a May 2006 poll, respondents in a *New York Times* / CBS News poll favored Democrats by a 61%–18% margin as the party most likely to make prescription drugs for the elderly more affordable; that margin was almost identical to a 2002 poll taken a year before the MMA's enactment. In a February 2007 *New York Times* / CBS News poll, 62% of respondents ranked the Democratic Party as most likely to improve health care, with 18% selecting the Republican Party. www.nytimes.com/packages/pdf/poli tics/20060509_POLL_RESULTS.pdf; http://graphics8.nytimes.com/packages/pdf/na tional/03022007_poll.pdf.

89. Realignment itself is a highly problematic concept, though politicians may still strive to achieve it. See Mayhew, *Electoral Realignments*.

90. Green, "Rove Presidency."

91. I thank Tom Burke for this point. See also Joe Soss and Sanford F. Schram, "A Public Transformed? Welfare Reform as Policy Feedback," *American Political Science Review* 101 (2007): 111–27.

92. Jonathan Oberlander and Theodore Marmor, "The Health Bill Explained at Last," *New York Review of Books* 57, no. 13 (August 19, 2010): 61–63.

93. Jonathan Oberlander, "Long Time Coming: Why Health Reform Finally Passed," *Health Affairs* 29 (2010): 1112–16.

94. Kaiser Family Foundation, *Kaiser Health Tracking Poll*, October 2010.

95. R. Kent Weaver, "The Politics of Blame Avoidance," *Journal of Public Policy* 6 (1986): 371–98.

CHAPTER SIX

A Solution for All Seasons

The Politics of Tax Reduction in the Bush Administration

Tim Conlan and Paul Posner

Tax cuts were the centerpiece of George W. Bush's domestic agenda. In one sense, this was merely "politics as usual." Cutting taxes has become the central tenet of Republican domestic policy. As former Congressional Budget Office (CBO) director and McCain adviser Douglas Holtz-Eakin has observed, "It's the brand, and you don't dilute the brand."[1]

This branding became the touchstone for Republican policy positioning in the 1980s, when Ronald Reagan made large-scale individual tax cuts the core of his fiscal policy approach. Eugene Steurele, who served in the Treasury Department during the Reagan years, subsequently labeled the 1980s the "tax decade," owing to successive political battles over a series of major laws that first cut, then raised, and then reformed federal taxes.[2] Yet, the central role of tax policy in American politics and policymaking did not fade away with the 1980s. Rather, the tax "decade" stretched on for over a quarter century, driving partisan identification, electoral campaigns, and legislative agendas. Today, both parties routinely vie over competing proposals for middle-class tax cuts, compete to offer the most generous assortment of new tax expenditures, and struggle to construct sensible budgets without tapping new sources of revenue.

Yet, as central as the politics of taxation had become, the structure and marketing of the Bush administration's tax proposals went beyond politics as usual. Tax policy in the Bush administration underscored the deepening interplay between policy design and political strategy.[3] Taken as a whole, the composition of the administration's tax policies served to satisfy and solidify the Republican base. Key elements of President Bush's 2001 tax legislation were chosen purposefully for their strong appeal to core Republican constituencies, including the sizable reduction of top marginal rates and the phaseout of the estate tax. Others were selected for their appeal to interest group supporters of the administration, although the corporate agenda was largely delayed until 2003 so that strategic goals could be addressed first. Still other provisions, such as eliminating the so-called marriage penalty and expanding tax credits for children, had broad appeal to middle-class voters regardless of party affiliation.

Given this diversity of goals, a variety of coalition-building approaches was employed to advance tax legislation in the Bush administration, including partisan mobilization, pluralist interest aggregation, symbolic valence politics, and expert consensus building. In the process, patterns of executive-legislative relations were established that would reappear in other policy realms throughout the administration. These included the discipline to focus on big-picture strategy, a willingness to rely on narrow and polarized partisan coalitions in Congress in order to maximize policy outcomes, and a tolerance for legislative tinkering with smaller tax provisions that provided electoral benefits to individual members and stabilized the majority coalition.

Regardless of these shifts in coalition-building strategies and despite broad changes in the economic and political context of tax policymaking, tax reduction never moved far from the core of President Bush's agenda throughout his administration. The rationales advanced for tax cuts changed over time, from reducing the anticipated surplus in 2000 and early 2001, to providing countercyclical economic stimulus in 2001 and 2002, to promoting investment and long-term economic growth, to reducing progressivity and "double taxation" in the tax code. But the commitment to a policy output of lower taxes and to the political goals this policy served remained a bedrock of the Bush administration's approach to governance.

It also established the parameters for Obama administration policies. President Bush sought but failed to permanently extend his tax cut policies. Both as a candidate and as president, Barack Obama promised to extend the "middle-class" tax cuts—the individual rate reductions on income below $250,000 (on joint returns). But he proposed to allow the highest tax brackets to return to their pre-2001 levels. This issue became the focal point of tax policy debates during President Obama's first two years in office.

The Historical, Political, and Economic Context of Bush's Tax Policy

Tax policy lay at the core of Ronald Reagan's domestic agenda, and tax cuts came to be viewed as the key to continued Republican electoral success.[4] This lesson was particularly resonant with George W. Bush. He, and many others, viewed his father's failure to keep his "no new taxes" pledge as being responsible for his electoral defeat in 1992.[5] In addition to expanding the party's appeal to blocs of middle-class voters, tax cuts provided essential glue for holding together an increasingly diverse Republican coalition. Neo-, social, and economic conservatives all supported aggressive tax cut initiatives, whereas the coalition was often strained over other issues of social and foreign policy.[6]

Tax Cuts in the 2000 Election

George W. Bush and Al Gore both advocated tax reduction plans during the 2000 presidential election. Bush's proposal was substantially larger than Gore's more targeted approach, but both candidates modified and increased the size of their plans over the course of campaigning, largely in response to the growing federal surplus. Bush originally proposed multiyear tax cuts totaling $486 billion. This increased by the fall of 2000 into a multi-part proposal totaling $1.6 trillion over ten years.[7] Al Gore originally proposed tax cuts totaling about $250 billion over ten years. His package was expanded to about $500 billion over ten years by mid-2000.[8]

These differences in size reflected stark differences in design of the proposed tax cut packages. Gore's proposals were aimed primarily at those earning less than $50,000. The most costly component was a refundable tax credit designed to supplement a new program of retirement savings plans for those earning under $100,000. Gore also proposed an expanded deduction to reduce the marriage penalty and new tax credits to promote energy efficiency, health care, education, and child care. A portion of the cost of these provisions was to be borne by a twenty-five-cent increase in cigarette taxes.[9]

In contrast, the core of Bush's approach consisted of reductions in individual income tax rates. The top rates of 39.5 percent and 36 percent would be lowered to 33 percent, the 31 percent and 28 percent rates would come down to 25 percent, and, while the 15 percent rate would remain, a new rate of 10 percent would be established for the lowest-income taxpayers. In addition, Bush proposed doubling the per-child tax credit, ending the marriage penalty, and allowing non-itemizers to deduct charitable donations.[10] Finally, Bush advocated abolishing the estate tax. Because the reductions in the top income tax rates and the elimination of the estate tax primarily benefited the wealthiest taxpayers, the distributional effects of Bush's plan were very different than Gore's. An estimated 43 percent of the benefits of Bush's proposals would go to the top 1 percent of income earners.[11]

Opinion polling during and after the election demonstrated considerable, though not determinative, public support for tax cuts. This was particularly true when taxes were considered in isolation. Thus, in a September 2000 *Newsweek* poll, about half (47%) of respondents indicated that it was "absolutely necessary" that they agree with candidates on taxes in order to vote for them. Forty-three percent said that it would be "important but not absolutely necessary," while only 6 percent said taxes were "not important" in casting their vote.[12] Similarly, a Gallup/CNN/*USA Today* poll in January 2000 found 29 percent of the public saying that the amount Americans pay in federal taxes would be "extremely important" in determining their vote in the presidential election. Another 43 percent said taxes would be "very important," and only 27 percent said taxes would be "somewhat" or "not too" important.[13] A comparable poll for the same organizations six months later found 33 percent of respondents saying taxes were "extremely important," 44 percent "very" important, and 22 percent "somewhat" or "not" important.[14]

On the other hand, taxes ranked less high in polling designed to assess the relative importance of different, and possibly competing, issues on the public agenda. A January 2000 ABC News/*Washington Post* poll found that taxes ranked fifth among respondents asked to indicate the "single most important issue in deciding whom to support for president." Education (21%), Social Security and Medicare (21%), the economy (19%), and health care (13%) all ranked higher than taxes (9%) in this survey.[15] Taxes also tied for fifth place in a similar question asked by Gallup in July 2000. The economy, education, health care, and Social Security again ranked higher than taxes as "the single most important issue," which in this poll tied with abortion and gun issues among a longer list of options.[16] In fact, Hacker and Pierson conclude that the Bush tax cuts lacked a significant popular base at the time of their passage.[17]

Not surprisingly, polling did find differences among partisan identifiers on this question. Taxes were ranked as the second most important issue among Republican respondents (including independents who leaned Republican) in a February 2000 ABC News/*Washington Post* poll. "Moral values" ranked highest among this subpopulation at 33 percent, taxes ranked second at 18 percent, and Social Security/Medicare and education were ranked third and fourth, at 15 percent and 14 percent, respectively. In contrast, Democratic identifiers in this survey (including leaners) ranked taxes sixth overall, after the economy (21%), Social Security and Medicare (21%), education (20%), health care (17%), and world affairs (7%).[18]

Given the higher salience of taxes among Republican voters, it is not surprising that George W. Bush enjoyed greater public confidence to deal with issues of taxation. A Battleground survey of likely voters in early 2000 found that 53 percent of respondents had greater confidence in Bush on the issue of taxes, 30 percent said Al Gore, and 18 percent said both, neither, or had no opinion.[19] A subsequent survey in March 2000 produced similar findings, with 49 percent of respondents expressing greater confidence in Bush on the issue of taxes, 36 percent choosing Gore, and 14 percent in the remaining categories.[20] On the other hand, centrist voters appeared to prefer Gore's emphasis on targeted tax expenditures that focused on salient, individual needs such as health care and retirement savings. Consequently, in the general election, George Bush's campaign rhetoric de-emphasized his very expensive individual rate reductions—which he had touted "almost exclusively" while running against John McCain during the Republican primary—and placed greater focus on the more broadly popular tax credits and deductions.[21]

The Economic Context

Among the factors contributing to public opinion on taxes during the 2000 election was the upward trend in levels of federal taxation. Federal revenues as a percentage of GDP reached a post–World War II high of 20.9 percent in 2000, up from 17.5 percent in 1992 (much of it reflecting growth in incomes from capital and bonuses accruing from the booming "dot-com" economy).

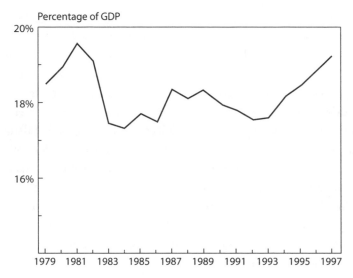

Figure 6.1. Federal revenues as a percentage of GDP.
Source: Congressional Budget Office.

The previous peak in federal revenues as a share of the economy occurred in 1981, coterminous with the tax cut initiatives of Ronald Reagan (see fig. 6.1).[22] Moreover, a CBO study of trends in federal tax rates found that average effective tax rates had returned to pre-1981 tax levels by 1997. The rebound in federal tax rates was particularly noticeable for the highest-income quintile and, even more, the top 1 percent of income earners.[23] Although this trend of rising tax rates reflected the growing concentration of income at the upper levels, as well as policy changes during the Clinton administration, this growth in the federal tax burden contributed to the political environment of tax policy during this period.

Fiscal and budgetary trends also shaped the context of tax policy decisions over the course of the Bush administration. Initially, Bush's tax cuts were premised on reducing the size of the anticipated federal surplus. The growing surpluses in the federal budget prompted both parties to embrace some form of tax cuts in the 2000 elections, and when in early 2001 CBO projected surpluses totaling $5.6 trillion over the coming decade, sizable tax cuts were made more likely (see fig. 6.2). Federal Reserve Board chairman Alan Greenspan provided further validation and political energy to the movement toward tax reductions when he expressed worry that the surpluses would cause the

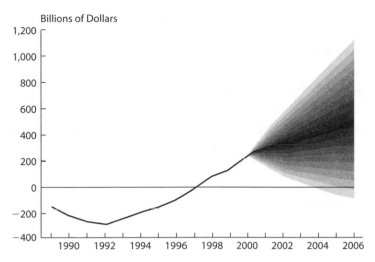

Figure 6.2. Projected federal surplus (in billions of dollars), 2001.
Source: Congressional Budget Office.

federal government to eventually run out of debt and become a net investor on Wall Street.

A slowing economy in late 2000 and early 2001 prompted the incoming Bush administration to rapidly shift its rationale for tax cuts, however. The new cause became the need for economic stimulus. Subsequent economic recovery forced the rationale for additional tax cuts—and for making the 2001 tax cuts permanent—to shift once more. Promoting long-term economic growth and avoiding the disruption of a rapid rise in tax rates in 2011 became the rationale du jour.

The Political Dynamics of Tax Policy in 2001

Following up on its campaign proposals, the Bush administration developed a tax reduction package estimated to cost $1.6 trillion over ten years.[24] The centerpiece remained a package of individual income tax rate cuts, with the bottom rate sliced from 15 percent to 10 percent and the two highest rates pared in stages from 39.6 percent and 36 percent down to 33 percent. The total cost of these rate reductions was estimated at $724 billion over ten years. However, because they were gradually phased in, the estimated cost of the rate cuts in the second decade was expected to be much larger still. The next most costly item was the phaseout and ultimate repeal of the estate tax, with an estimated ten-year cost of $236 billion. Other provisions in the administration's tax package included doubling the child care tax credit ($162 billion), a reduction in the "marriage penalty" ($88 billion), allowing non-itemizers to deduct charitable contributions ($80 billion), and making the research and development (R&D) tax credit permanent ($23 billion).

Although this package closely mirrored the president's campaign proposals, its design and political packaging were the subject of considerable debate between the new administration and its Republican congressional allies. Given the close margins of Republican control in the House (221 to 211, with two independents) and the Senate (50–50, with ties broken by Vice President Dick Cheney), congressional leaders initially wanted to advance the package in pieces, with the most popular components taken up first.[25] Provisions to reduce the marriage penalty and to phase down the estate tax had already passed during the 106th Congress (and were vetoed by President Clinton), and this approach demonstrated an ability to garner both Democratic and public support. As the spokesman for House Speaker Dennis Hastert put it, "The American people don't understand $1.3 trillion. . . . They do understand that they want to get rid of the marriage penalty. They do understand that they want to get rid of the death tax."[26] In contrast, across-the-board rate cuts seemed to many legislators to be a bridge too far, since they were both very costly and politically polarizing. Bush's election strategy actually reflected this. Once the campaign shifted from the primary to the general election, he had played down the rate cuts and emphasized the more popular middle-class provisions.[27]

On the other hand, conservative activist groups maintained pressure for an expansive and aggressive tax-cutting approach once Bush won the election. Groups such as Grover Norquist's Americans for Tax Reform (ATR) and the Club for Growth viewed lowering the top rates down to 33 percent and eliminating the "death tax" as "litmus tests" of administration tax policy.[28] Once the White House, at the prodding of the president's chief political advisor Karl Rove, decided to adopt a "base"-focused political strategy for moving forward administration legislative proposals, satisfying such conservative tax groups became a top priority.[29] "There isn't an us and them with this administration," observed ATR chief Grover Norquist. "They is us. We is them."[30]

The incoming Treasury secretary, Paul O'Neill, also found the president to be immovable on the size and design of the administration's tax cuts. Bush had committed to this plan in the election, he told O'Neill, and was "not going to negotiate with myself. . . . You've got to pursue what you said you're going to pursue."[31] As a result, potential competing formulations, such as devising tax policies to promote savings over consumption or to resolve the emerging Alternative Minimum Tax (AMT) problem gathering on the horizon, were rejected or given short shrift. Similarly, proposals and legislative strategies that showed greater potential to generate bipartisan support were shelved in order to maximize outcomes pleasing to the president's conservative base.

A final part of the political calculation in the design of Bush's 2001 tax cuts concerned whether reductions aimed at corporations and business investment would compose a major component of his initial proposal. In the end, the business community was largely frozen out of the administration's first tax package, except for the R&D credit. But this was not for want of trying. There were early reports of a corporate feeding frenzy as groups engaged in a "bidding war" for favorable tax treatment. Various business groups and trade associations were seeking tax credits for telecommunications infrastructure, exemptions for income from stock options, favored treatment of retirement savings, and other goals. But with the administration already committed to a huge package of individual tax reductions, business lobbyists were told their day would come later. They should stand aside and make way for broad-based tax cuts with broader political appeal.[32]

A Legislative Steamroller in the House

The legislative politics of tax cuts in 2001 were characterized by a highly partisan process in the House and an unevenly bipartisan approach in the Senate. Tax cut legislation began in the House, which quickly adopted four distinct bills that incorporated different elements of the president's tax reduction package. Anticipating subsequent problems in the Senate, some House Republican leaders pushed for even larger cuts than the president proposed, in order to enhance their negotiating position. This required aggressive tactics, however, which set the stage for often bitter partisan conflict.

The very fast start for tax cuts in the House reflected, in part, the belief by administration officials and House leaders that rapid congressional adoption of the president's tax cut agenda would build political capital for subsequent successes.[33] In addition, this political strategy was reinforced by growing economic concerns. By late 2000 and early 2001, the economy appeared to be softening. Federal Reserve chairman Alan Greenspan, who was already on record supporting tax cuts to limit the size of federal surpluses, stated in January testimony before Congress that tax cuts, if adopted, should pass "sooner rather than later." "Should economic weakness spread," Greenspan testified, "having a tax cut in place may, in fact, do noticeable good."[34]

Although Greenspan's testimony lent further momentum to the tax cut juggernaut, neither the president's package nor congressional legislation was substantially altered to reflect this new concern for countercyclical stimulus. Apart from a willingness to make some cuts retroactive to the beginning of the year, the administration still favored long-term approaches, such as phasing in permanent rate cuts and gradually phasing out the estate tax, rather than restructuring the package for rapid economic stimulus. In a pattern to be repeated in subsequent years, the rationale for tax cuts was altered to fit political circumstances, but the commitment to a policy of tax cuts for any problem remained remarkably stable.

Following through on House Majority Leader Tom DeLay's promise to pursue tax cuts "in an aggressive manner," Republicans began pushing the president's proposals through the House just two days after he formally unveiled them before a joint session of Congress, and before Congress adopted the budget resolution.[35] This jeopardized chances for bipartisan support for the legislation, since the conservative "blue dog" Democrats—who wished to avoid a return to federal deficits—insisted on passing the budget first. Nevertheless, the White House and Republican leaders were "determined to maintain the momentum for passage." "The victory is to get it done, to get it passed," proclaimed Speaker Hastert.[36]

Consequently, House leaders decided to move the legislation in four separate tax bills. A modified version of the president's plan for rate reductions was taken up first and quickly passed the House Ways and Means Committee on a party-line vote of 23–15, on March 1, 2001.[37] The bill passed the full House on March 8 by a vote of 230–198. Upset by the procedures used and the lack of opportunities for minority-party input, only ten Democrats supported the bill. No Republications opposed it.

The remaining three bills included the Marriage Penalty and Family Tax Relief Act, a bill that expanded child care tax credits and addressed the "marriage penalty" issue; the Death Tax Elimination Act, which phased out the federal estate tax over a ten-year period; and the Comprehensive Retirement Security and Pension Reform Act of 2001, which increased the contribution limits for IRAs and the deferral of income invested in 401(k) and other retirement plans.[38] Each was even more expansive than the president proposed, and House Ways and Means Committee Democrats complained about their lack of input into legislative design. Nevertheless, the concepts had bipartisan support, and the first two passed with approximately one-third of House Democrats voting in favor, and the last passed by a margin of 407–24.[39]

A Compromise in the Senate

The real challenge facing the Bush administration was in the Senate, where Republicans controlled the evenly divided chamber only because Vice President Cheney broke the tie vote to organize the Senate. In addition to Republicans' lack of a working majority, many Senate moderates of both parties had qualms about the size of the president's proposed tax cuts, especially in light of the prospect for a return to federal budget deficits. Consequently, unlike the House, Senate strategy was built around the budget process. This entailed including the tax reductions in the budget resolution and in a subsequent reconciliation package that was immune from filibuster, thereby requiring only fifty votes for passage in a chamber that was evenly divided.

Even assembling a simple majority in the Senate was a daunting task, however. Democrats favored tax cuts totaling roughly $800 billion, about half the size of Bush's request. Several moderate Republicans shared concerns about the size of the administration's tax cut package, and they feared that a slowing economy would erode projected surpluses. Many favored the idea of making future tax cuts contingent on a trigger mechanism, which would delay or defer the phase-in of future tax cuts if anticipated surpluses failed to materialize.[40] This concept was given a boost when Federal Reserve chairman Alan Greenspan endorsed it.[41]

The Bush administration opposed the trigger concept (although Treasury Secretary O'Neill quietly favored it), arguing that investment decisions require predictability.[42] Moreover, the president remained firm in his insistence that the tax cuts total 1.6 trillion. This amount was "just right" and not negotiable.[43] But this insistence began to unravel when the Senate's most liberal Republican, Senator Lincoln Chafee (R-RI), defected and refused to support a tax cut that large.[44] Ultimately, he was joined by two other Republican moderates, who voted with Democrats on a key amendment to the Senate budget resolution limiting the tax cuts to $1.2 trillion, plus another $85 billion in retroactive tax cuts for economic stimulus. These defectors were Senators Arlen

Specter (R-PA) and James Jeffords (R-VT), both of whom favored greater spending on health and education programs in the budget in lieu of larger tax cuts.[45]

This reduction in the size of the tax cut package was fiercely opposed by the White House and its conservative allies. House leaders had declared that $1.6 trillion was the minimum they would accept, while many conservatives pressed for larger cuts.[46] Conservative groups began demanding that Senator Chaffee be punished by the Senate Republican conference. Moreover, groups such as ATR and the Club for Growth began running TV ads back in wavering members' districts and threatening future primary challenges if moderates did not toe the line.[47] President Bush also began to campaign for his larger tax cut package in the districts of moderate and conservative Democrats from states that Bush had carried in the election. This included the ranking Democrat on the Senate Finance Committee, Max Baucus of Montana.[48]

In the end, however, these campaigns were unable to alter the necessary votes, and a Democratic amendment to the budget resolution limiting the tax cuts to $1.2 trillion passed the Senate by a vote of 51–49.[49] This forced administration strategy to shift to the conference committee on the congressional budget resolution. The waffling Republican moderates were excluded from the conference and leading Democrats were largely frozen out of the key negotiations. Instead, working only with a pair of Democratic moderates, John Breaux (D-LA) and Ben Nelson (D-NE), the administration was able to boost the tax cut target to $1.35 trillion in the final budget resolution adopted by the full Congress.[50]

Passage of the budget resolution established the maximum size of tax cuts, but the actual legislation to reduce taxes became part of the subsequent budget reconciliation bill. The House had already passed its tax legislation prior to adopting the budget, but it readopted legislation reducing tax rates to demonstrate its seriousness about top rate reductions and for parliamentary reasons.[51] The key negotiations on the tax reconciliation bill were held between the White House, the Republican chairs of the Senate Finance and House Ways and Means Committees, and Democratic senators Max Baucus and John Breaux. Although Senate moderates had successfully forced compromises in the budget resolution that reduced the overall size of the tax cut package, the chair of the Finance Committee, Senator Charles Grassley (R-IA), was under great pressure to accommodate the president's original goals within the smaller fiscal window. This was achieved through a variety of budgetary gimmicks, which made the final 2001 tax bill a testament to the uneasy marriage of tax policy and budgetary gamesmanship.

Specifically, the final legislation contained most of the major features of the president's proposal, but with lower revenue estimates. These lower revenue targets were met by such strategies as back-loading the tax cuts (by phasing in marginal tax rate reductions and other costly provisions more slowly). In addition, many of the bill's tax reductions were designed to sunset in the final year. For example, the per-child tax credit was gradually raised from $500 to $1,000 over the period from 2001 to 2010, but it was then scheduled to fall back to $500 in 2011.[52] Similarly, the marriage penalty, estate tax, and retirement plan contribution provisions became progressively more generous through 2010 but returned back to 2001 levels in 2011.

These sunsets were driven by the "Byrd rule" prohibition against including provisions in a budget bill that caused increased deficits following a ten-year period. The administration could have avoided the use of sunsets by moderating its tax proposals to accommodate enough moderates and Democrats to assemble a sixty-vote Senate majority that could override a Byrd rule objection. However, it chose not to further dilute its tax proposals, in the hope that sunsets could be abolished in the future. Consequently, most major provisions were designed to expire in December 2010 as a result.

Although denounced by most independent analysts as a "joke" and an "outright fraud,"[53] the sunsetting provided Senate moderates with the illusion of fiscal responsibility while serving the president's political objectives, rewarding upper-income voters in the Republican base (see table 6.1).[54] It also provided a ready-made agenda of future battles to make the tax cuts "permanent."

Table 6.1 Share of tax cuts received by various groups under 2001 tax bill (when fully phased in)

Estate tax calculation by:	Percentage received by:						
	Top 1%	Next 4%	Next 15%	Fourth 20%	Middle 20%	Second 20%	Lowest 20%
Center for Tax Justice	35.0%	9.8%	24.8%	14.7%	8.9%	5.7%	1.0%
Treasury Department	29.3	13.6	26.5	14.9	8.9	5.7	1.0

Source: Center for Budget and Policy Priorities.

The Political Dynamics of Tax Policy in 2003

Traditional tax legislation often resembles the archetypical example of pluralist policymaking, in which each sliver of industry and each segment of the population seeks and often receives preferences under the tax code. Computer manufacturers want credits for research and development, extractive industries seek special depreciation rules, nonprofit groups want favorable treatment of charitable contributions, parents and colleges support deductions for educational expenses, multinational corporations seek favorable treatment of overseas income, and so forth. Members of Congress author amendments and embrace provisions that serve their constituents and supporters, and they lobby for transition rules that provide selective benefits for specific local projects.

In 2001, this model of tax policymaking was largely sidelined in favor of a bold partisan agenda. Although interest groups began that year compiling shopping lists of tax preferences they would like to see included in forthcoming legislation, the feeding frenzy was dampened under pressure from the White House and congressional leaders.[55] The administration sought to keep attention focused on publicly salient proposals aimed directly at voters, and they feared that group infighting or a bloated corporate Christmas tree might undermine the legislation. Business lobbyists were told, including in a personal meeting with the president, that they were expected to hold off on corporate provisions and lobby in support of individual tax cuts in 2001. Their day would come later.

That day was first expected to come in 2002, but the 9/11 terrorist attacks and subsequent war in Afghanistan—along with divided party control of the House and Senate—sidetracked major tax legislation. A modest set of business tax cuts was passed in early 2002 as part of an economic stimulus package. It combined provisions allowing businesses to write off certain expenses more quickly with an extension of unemployment benefits. The House also sought to make the 2001 tax cuts permanent, but this proposal died in the Senate, where Democratic leaders proposed trimming back the 2001 cuts.

Consequently, a new day of reckoning was anticipated to arrive in the form of a corporate tax bill in 2003. A strange thing happened on the way to the tax trough, however. The Bush administration once again sought a bill with electoral appeal to broader constituencies of voters rather than one narrowly tailored to corporations and trade associations. The centerpiece of the administration's 2003 proposal was a plan to eliminate the taxation of corporate dividends, as well as an accelerated phase-in of rate reductions from the 2001 law. The dividend proposal had political appeal to individual investors, and it was favored by many tax professionals as a means of promoting efficiency in the system. It eliminated the double taxation of corporate income and reduced the problems caused by differential tax treatment of corporate and individual income.

The reaction from Congress and the business community ranged from hostile to unenthusiastic, however. Congressional conservatives generally favored alternatives, such as reducing taxes on capital gains. Democrats generally opposed the plan because of its high cost and its distributional biases; an estimated 59 percent of the benefits would go to the wealthiest 12 percent of the population.[56] Senate moderates, including a key group of Republican senators, opposed the plan because of its cost. They were deeply concerned about the return of large federal deficits and the prospects for mounting debt during a time of war.[57] Finally, much of the business community was divided over the plan. Many small businesses would not benefit, and many larger ones paid little in dividends. The proposal was costly—thus crowding out revenues for other, more targeted tax benefits—and it would tend to reduce the value of many existing corporate preferences by encouraging the payout of dividends rather than use of specialized tax credits to offset retained earnings.[58]

Such divisions inside and outside of Congress meant that the administration's hopes for adopting its tax proposals would again hinge on using the budget process, to prevent the use of filibusters and unlimited amendments in the Senate. The scope of the challenge was symbolized by Senator Tom Daschle (D-SD), the Senate Democratic leader, who had pronounced the president's plan "dead on arrival."[59] Moreover, the budgetary impacts were substantial. Bush's proposed tax cuts were estimated to cost $726 billion over ten years: $396 billion for eliminating federal taxes on dividends, $264 billion for accelerated phase-in of the 2001 tax cuts, and $66 billion for small business and AMT relief.[60] Although the House-passed version of the budget resolution accommodated tax cuts of this magnitude, the Senate refused to go along. Three Republican moderates—Senators Chafee (R-RI), Snowe (R-ME), and Voinovich (R-OH)—joined all but one Senate Democrat to support an amendment by John Breaux (D-LA) limiting tax cuts to $350 billion. The amendment passed by a vote of 51–48.[61]

Because the Senate's $350 billion budget cap was well below the cost of the president's proposal—and less than the cost of the dividend proposal alone—the move set off furious lobbying in conference over the budget resolution. Ultimately, the House and Senate conferees split the difference and agreed to a budget cap of $550 billion for tax cuts, which could be enough to allow passage of some version of the president's proposals if supplemented with offsets that raised revenues by closing other tax preferences. This conference report passed the House on a largely party-line vote of 216–211, but Senate moderates refused to go along. They refused to vote for any bill allowing more than $350 billion in new tax cuts, and they had the power to block action in the Senate. Eventually, Senators Voinovich and Snowe agreed to support the conference resolution after extracting a promise from the chairman of the Senate Finance Committee, Senator Charles Grassley (R-IA), to report no tax bill costing more than $350 billion. This promise allowed the budget resolution to squeak through on a vote of 51–50, with Vice President Cheney casting the tie-breaking vote. Only a single Democrat, Zell Miller (D-GA), supported the budget resolution; two Republicans, Lincoln Chaffee (R-RI) and John McCain (R-AZ), voted against it.[62]

Adoption of the resolution paved the way to the construction and passage of a tax bill as part of reconciliation. The House passed a $550 billion tax cut on a largely party-line vote on May 9, 2003.[63] The bill reduced taxes on dividends as well as capital gains, but it did not eliminate them as the president proposed. It also sped up the phase-in of portions of the 2001 tax cuts (raising the amount of income subject to the 10 percent and 15 percent tax brackets, increasing the child care tax credit, and accelerating marriage penalty adjustments to the standard deduction). The task of designing a bill that could pass the Senate was much more difficult for Senate Finance Chairman Grassley. He could not adopt deep cuts in dividend or capital gains taxes unless the bill included revenue offsets (i.e., selective tax hikes), which were deeply opposed by affected interest groups. The White House sent President Bush to campaign for his proposals in Ohio, hoping to force Senator Voinovich to relent from his opposition to a larger tax cut bill. Conservative antitax groups also ran ads in Maine, hoping to do the same with Senator Snowe. But both moderates refused to cave in to the "high-pressure sales pitch" and continued to insist on the smaller tax cut target.[64]

Consequently, the business lobby was deeply split on the proposal, and many in Congress were noncommittal. Although the Senate passed a version of the president's proposal, it sought to reduce the budgetary impact by eliminating selected tax preferences already on the books. House Republicans favored a reduction in the tax on capital gains instead, something that would benefit a broader array of business interests and which had been on their policy agenda for many years. As one House Republican put it, "People hold assets they want to sell. There's wide support in rural areas for a capital gains cut. Ranchers could cut inventory by selling cattle. It would benefit the sale of any kind of asset, or any business."[65] Reflecting such sentiments, Ways and Means chairman Bill Thomas pushed through a bill that cut both the capital gains and corporate dividends tax rates to 15 percent and accelerated the personal rate cuts.

Such Republican and business defections made the partisan coalition strategy of 2001 untenable for the administration, and the final bill resembled the House solution, though with a new round of sunsets and phaseouts to obscure the true budgetary impact. The policy result also showed the continued influence of election strategy on policy design, though from a legislative perspective rather than the White House strategy.

Tax Reform in the Bush Administration

The administration was in control of tax policy with its congressional allies for the first four years of the new decade. Following the two major tax cuts of 2001 and 2003, the administration focused its priorities on consolidating its gains by pushing to make the tax cuts permanent in 2005, far ahead of their scheduled expiration in 2010. As budget deficits cast a longer shadow over the policy agenda, however, congressional actors faced growing fiscal pressures that limited their freedom to enact additional tax cuts. Deficits ballooned to over $400 billion as a result of the tax cuts, the 2001 recession, and higher discretionary spending on defense and homeland security. By the end of 2004, federal tax receipts as a percentage of net national income had plummeted to 16.3 percent of GDP, which was the lowest level since 1959, owing to a combination of the Bush tax cuts and economic recession. As noted above, the reemergence of deficits already made it difficult to pass the 2003 tax cuts through the Senate, signaling opposition to lower taxes that would surely undermine tax reform proposals cast as tax cuts.

Building on his earlier tax victories, the president announced a new thrust in fall of 2004 to reform the tax system. Similar to the model followed by

President Reagan twenty years earlier that culminated in the successful 1986 tax reform act, Bush announced his intent to achieve a revenue-neutral simplification and rationalization of the tax code following major tax cuts, a project that received wide endorsement from many tax professionals across the political spectrum. Like Reagan, he deferred the development of a detailed proposal until after the presidential election. However, unlike Reagan, who relied on his Treasury secretary and staff, Bush appointed a commission with bipartisan and expert credentials to lead the development of proposals, a process that would enable him to distance himself from the report should the political fallout be too intense. The revenue neutrality principle was an important constraint for this new effort, an acknowledgement by the administration that the prospects for tax reform could be advanced best by separating its fate from the increasingly vexing politics of budget deficits.

The new tax reform panel was also structured with a bipartisan cast, cochaired by two former senators—Republican Connie Mack from Florida and the moderate Democrat John Breaux of Louisiana. Among its nine members were leading experts on tax policy and administration, including James Poterba, a leading public finance economist from MIT, and Charles Rosotti, a highly respected former commissioner of the IRS.

The difficult challenges facing the panel were magnified by the growing presence of the AMT in tax policy. Originally designed in the 1960s to reach wealthy individuals who paid no taxes, this tax loomed like a gathering cloud over the middle class. Its projected growth was scheduled to cover over 50 million Americans over ten years—partly because the thresholds triggering the tax were not inflation adjusted. The AMT not only constituted a new source of burden and complexity for many taxpayers but threatened to undermine the tax reductions achieved by the 2001 and 2003 tax cuts.

However, even this administration could not simply eliminate the AMT. It had grown to become a revenue foundation for the budget, and its elimination would open a $1 trillion gap in the ten-year deficit. Given the growth of the deficit as a political issue, the administration would have to pursue eliminating the AMT through a revenue-neutral strategy.

This fiscal reality was seized by the panel and economists inside the Treasury as a trigger to initiate a broader sweeping review of the economic efficiency of tax expenditures and other features of the tax code. The report they issued recommended paying for the repeal of the AMT with a series of major reforms in the federal tax treatment of health care, mortgage interest, and state and local taxation.[66] These tax expenditures were the largest among the 120 tax expenditures in the income tax system and drew widespread condemnation by economists owing to their distortionary effects on economic investment choices.

The report itself received wide praise in the expert community, and its recommendations have perennially been supported by experts. For instance, the health care exclusion had grown to become the largest tax expenditure and one that was widely acknowledged to prompt firms to establish enriched health care insurance plans for their employees, adding to the explosive cost growth in our health care system. The report proposed to transform this exclusion into a credit that would not only reverse the incentives but make the subsidy more widely shared across income groups. The report also proposed to limit the size of the mortgage deduction, following the long-standing views of economists that this tax preference was responsible for raising prices of real estate beyond their pure economic value. The state and local deduction was already recaptured for high-income taxpayers by the AMT, so the panel reasoned that the objections to its elimination would be less intense. However, these tax expenditures were also among the most politically sensitive items in the tax code.

Predictably, perhaps, the commission report fell on hard times. Its recommendations were quickly swallowed up and spit back by a wide range of interest groups, from the real estate lobby to health care insurance groups to unions. The president failed to support his experts and all but abandoned the report within a short period after its issuance. It is always more difficult to pass tax reform under revenue-neutral rules, since new tax benefits can only be adopted if others sacrifice existing benefits. The political difficulties are only magnified when promising vaguely perceived or tenuous future gains in exchange for the loss of current tangible benefits. The 1986 tax reform act, also revenue neutral, was able to overcome this obstacle because the pain of losing tax expenditures for specific taxpayers was offset by politically compelling tax rate reductions that nearly all taxpayers could appreciate. The tax expenditure eliminations recommended by the Bush panel, on the other hand, were offset by the elimination of the AMT in the future—a prospect that most taxpayers were only dimly aware of, if at all.[67]

Tax policy largely quieted down after the reform commission fizzled. The budget deficit was gaining more attention, and further tax cuts were largely off the table prior to the election season of 2008. Even though the expiration of President Bush's earlier tax cuts loomed in December 2010, tax cut advocates were on their heels as the president's popularity declined and Democrats regained control of Congress in the 2006 elections. Ironically, the sunsets that were adopted in 2001 as a "gimmick" designed to lower the projected costs of the tax cuts became a troubling feature for tax cut proponents. Extending the cuts was considered to be new policy requiring offsets under the PAYGO regime established in congressional rules when Democrats returned to the majority in 2007. Advocates of continuing the cuts engaged Democrats in negotiations to extend the cuts in modified form, but they had little success prior to Bush's departure.

One final action was taken early in 2008, however—the passage of a stimulative tax rebate. In a throwback to earlier political eras, the new tax cut was passed in record time on a bipartisan basis as a symbolic response by the administration and Congress to the housing crisis and market downturn, even in the absence of an officially defined recession. When viewed against the backdrop of a polarized Congress and an administration that had used tax policy as a wedge issue to appeal to its extreme wing, such an action was an ironic bipartisan epitaph to a highly partisan tax policy decade.

Bush's Policies in Political Perspective: The Pathways of Tax Policymaking

Tax policy in the Bush administration took a variety of different forms, often with quite distinctive electoral implications. These political considerations in turn give rise to different strategies for framing issues, for attracting political support, and for building coalitions in Congress. In *Seeking the Center*, we introduced a framework of "policy pathways" to describe the process of tax policymaking in the 1980s and 1990s, and we believe that it continues to illuminate the politics of tax policymaking during the Bush administration as well.

This typology, summarized in table 6.2, distinguishes four policy pathways, which are differentiated by the *scale* of political mobilization and the *method* of mobilization. By the scale of mobilization, we draw on E. E. Schattschneider's insight that the dynamics and outcomes of political contests are affected by the scope of the audience and the scale of political participation. The politics of highly specialized issues or those that address only narrow political and economic interests are very different from those that engage a

Table 6.2   Pathways of tax policymaking (with prototypical examples listed)

Form of mobilization	Scope of mobilization	
	Specialized	Mass
Ideational	Expert (tax reform 1986)	Symbolic ("death" tax)
Organizational	Pluralist (tax reform commission)	Partisan (2001 tax cuts)

broad public audience. By the method of political mobilization, we mean to contrast the politics of building coalitions principally through the actions of organizations, especially political parties or interest groups, versus garnering support and building coalitions principally through the politics of ideas.

Clearly, these four strategies are not mutually exclusive, and the four pathways are not meant to represent independent and discrete policy types. Rather, they are distinctive approaches to coalition building: dynamic and changeable strategies by which political actors can seek to build support for their proposals. While it is often accurate to characterize the politics of a particular bill as "mostly" partisan or "chiefly" pluralist, others resist being pigeonholed so neatly. Three or four can be in play simultaneously, as different actors pursue strategies most favorable to their objectives and political resources. Moreover, tax policy can switch tracks from one piece of legislation to the next. Changes in the electoral context, the economic climate, the interest group environment, and the chief actors' agendas all contribute to policymakers choosing one path over another.

Pluralist Pathway

As noted earlier, the traditional pattern of U.S. tax politics closely fit a pluralist-incremental model. The federal income tax system has grown enormously in size and complexity since its creation in 1913, but its basic structure has remained intact, as have key elements of tax politics. John Witte described the standard pattern of tax law change as beginning with "marginal adjustments to the existing structure. . . . Applicable rates, bracket changes, exemption levels, standard deductions, depreciation percentages, investment credits, depletion allowances—the list of changes that can be accomplished by simply altering a number is very long. . . . Tax laws can also be easily and marginally altered by expanding or contracting eligible groups, actions, industries, commodities, or financial circumstances."[68] Moreover, the creation and expansion

of tax preferences, which is among the more obvious "incremental" addi-
tions and changes, has traditionally been attributed to the influence of organized beneficiary groups.[69]

We would argue that this pattern of tax politics continues to persist, although it was largely overshadowed by partisan politics in 2001 and 2003. Indeed, an interest group "feeding frenzy" of specialized tax breaks threatened
to overwhelm the politics and structure of the 2001 tax bill until the White
House intervened forcefully to hold off the assault. Interest groups nonetheless
helped to shape the education, retirement, investment, and estate tax provisions in 2001, and they had somewhat more success in 2003, when they helped
House tax writers replace the president's dividend proposal with a tax cut for
capital gains as well as dividends. As the old terminology of "veto groups" suggests, interest group politics can be even more effective in blocking as opposed
to enacting legislation. Aggressive lobbying by affected interests helped kill the
Senate's revenue-raising offset provisions in 2003, as well as the president's tax
reform commission proposals in 2005. In fact, the prospect of major opposition from real estate and health care interest groups played an important role
in President Bush's decision to forgo a major tax initiative in his second term.

Partisan Pathway

While pluralist politics played a secondary role, the partisan pathway lay at
the center of tax policymaking in 2001. In the classic form of partisan policymaking, a new president sweeps into office with a mandate and party majorities in both chambers of Congress, mobilizes the resources of office to construct a coherent legislative program, and rallies the public and party followers
behind it. Bush hardly won a landslide victory in 2000, and Republicans had
only tenuous control over the Senate, but there is little question that his administration attempted to govern in 2001 as if he had won a rousing mandate
in his election.[70] Consistent with what legislative scholars have termed the
conditional party government model, Bush and House leaders structured
their proposals and built their House coalition on an explicitly partisan
model, in hopes of furthering the party's reputation and its future electoral
success.[71] In contrast to the pluralist model, most business-oriented interest
groups were explicitly sidelined in the process and had surprisingly little say
over the principal contours of the legislation.

Because of the narrow Republican margin in the Senate, as well as the nature of Senate representation and rules, it was not possible to rely solely on a

partisan mobilization strategy in the Senate. Centrists of both parties, and the interests they represented, had far more influence in the upper chamber. Nevertheless, when all was said and done, the major outlines of the tax legislation adopted in 2001 strongly reflected the president's original proposals and the initial strategy of partisan coalition building. On critical votes in both 2001 and 2003, only a tiny handful of senators voted with the opposition party, and Vice President Cheney preserved Republican control on several occasions by breaking tie votes on key provisions.

Expert Pathway

Whereas the pluralist and partisan models of policymaking are familiar standbys in American politics, contemporary scholarship has placed great emphasis on the politics of ideas. The pathways framework affirms this emphasis but argues that the politics of ideas comes in two very different flavors. One form is the expert pathway, associated with the politics of deregulation and the tax reform act of 1986.[72] Expert policymaking reflects the truism in complex fields of modern governance that "knowledge is power." Policies shaped in this pathway reflect the influence of highly committed policy professionals, often organized in communities and networks of experts and often holding positions of considerable importance. Most of these participants share a commitment to a specific view of what constitutes "good" or "sound" policy, as well as an opportunity to pursue it owing to the needs of other policy actors.

Both the influence and the limitations of the expert pathway were seen in the makeup and approach of Bush's tax reform commission, as well as in the taxation of dividend income. Tax experts were able to shape a policy response in both cases that was consistent with the professional norms of improving equity and efficiency in the income tax system. To effect legislative change, however, experts need help from elected leaders. In the case of AMT and tax reform, the president chose not to pursue a major reform of the system in the face of mobilized interest groups and congressional reluctance. In the case of dividend taxation, the president embraced the expert's solution but House Republicans were unwilling to do the same. Nevertheless, experts are typically influential behind the scenes in a technically complex field like tax policy. When elected officials need to know how to accomplish their policy goal, or to find a source of revenue to pay for a favored proposal, they are forced to rely on tax experts who can often craft the answers in ways consistent with their professional norms.

Symbolic Pathway

Not all ideas in politics meet professional muster, even when the policy experts are in agreement on the makeup of good policy. Bad ideas as well as good ones become law—in tax policy as elsewhere.[73] They often do so through what we term the symbolic pathway. By symbolic, we refer to the style of coalition building rather than the policy outcome. Symbolic coalition building can drive important and consequential legislation as well as trivial posturing and position taking.

Successful use of the symbolic pathway requires more than just issue framing. Most political communication efforts today attempt to frame issues in the most favorable light. In order to serve as the principal pillar of coalition building, however, symbolic policies must strike a rich existing vein of sympathy, often appealing to broadly shared, commonsense narratives of understanding. But their advocates need not possess a reservoir of power, expertise, or resources for bargaining with a broad array of interests. A single, but single-minded, policy entrepreneur may accomplish the task. So long as the attention of Congress and the country can be focused on some widely shared (or greatly feared) legislative aim—rather than on more complex questions of program design, policy instruments, and implementation approaches—coalition building can be greatly simplified. Such proposals may ultimately reach the floor in a form that essentially compels approval, in a way that no one can afford to oppose. As former New York City mayor Ed Koch said in explaining why he voted as a congressman for many federal mandates he later decried as mayor, "As a member of Congress . . . the bills I voted for in Washington came to the House floor in a form that compelled approval. After all, who can vote against clean air and water, or better access and education for the handicapped?"[74]

In the 2001 tax bill, the transformation of the estate tax into the "death tax" provides a case in point. From the standpoint of most tax policy experts, the successful drive to eliminate the tax made little sense. There were few beneficiaries from this change, and the fiscal consequences were substantial. The debate itself seemed utterly removed from reality. Many of the strongest advocates for the change would have been little affected by it, and many others could have been exempted from the tax by adjusting its thresholds for inflation. But a successful campaign to transform what had been a technical provision of the tax law for many decades into a morally repugnant assault

Table 6.3   Tax policy regimes over time

Year	Initiative	Pluralist	Partisan	Expert	Symbolic
1981	ERTA		•		
1982	TEFRA			•	
1986	TRA			•	
1993	OBRA		•		
1997	TRA				•
1998	IRS				•
2001	CUTS		•		
2003	CUTS		•		
2009	ARRA		•		

on basic American values dramatically altered the political playing field. Voters perceived a problem, and politicians responded.[75]

Ultimately, the choice of policy pathway reflects both the character of the policy in question and the political strategies involved. The pluralist pathway, which is salient to and mobilizes smaller political audiences, is often best suited to the electoral incentives of individual legislators. Pluralist policies can often be tailored to the specific politics of particular districts and provide the sort of divisible benefits attractive to electorally minded legislators. Policies capable of producing large-scale electoral effects—perhaps contributing even to party realignment—generally need to travel the partisan or symbolic pathways, combining high salience and high potential with high risk. But, as table 6.3 illustrates, the successful use of policy pathways is highly variable, even in a single policy realm like taxation. A successful strategy for one bill in one context may not succeed in another.

The Early Obama Years
The Bush Legacy and Tax Policy in the Obama Administration

President Bush's highest-profile tax policy accomplishments—marginal rate cuts for top earners and elimination of the estate tax—were placed in jeopardy when he left office. Ironically, the administration's budgetary strategy, which permitted enactment of deeper and more sweeping tax cuts by disguising the long-term costs through the use of phaseouts and other gimmicks, came back to haunt its advocates. The marginal rate cuts were accelerated but never made permanent, and they became vulnerable on both political and fiscal grounds when President Obama assumed office in the midst of an economic crisis.

Barack Obama had campaigned on a pledge to extend the Bush tax cuts for the "middle class": individuals earning under $200,000 and couples earning under $250,000. But he favored allowing the top two rates, applying to income above those amounts, to return to pre-2001 levels, and he advocated restoring the estate tax to 45 percent on estates valued over $7 million. These policies were not immediately pursued upon his inauguration, however, because the economy was already in a deepening recession and teetering on the brink of a collapse of the financial system. Thus, President Obama's first order of fiscal business became a bold plan to stimulate the economy. The countercyclical rationale for tax cuts and other stimulative policies, which had been so prominent during the 2001 debate, returned in full force in 2009.

Tax cuts composed approximately one-third of President Obama's $787 billion stimulus program, which was ultimately passed as the American Recovery and Reinvestment Act (ARRA). The principal tax provisions consisted of an increase in the Earned Income Tax Credit for low-wage workers and families; a "Making Work Pay" tax credit for earners under $75,000 ($150,000 for joint filers); relief from the AMT; an increase in the child tax credit; a variety of tax credits for education, energy, and first-time home buyers; and a range of tax benefits for corporations and businesses.[76] Congressional Republicans had wanted a larger share of the stimulus program to be composed of tax cuts, including some wishing to make the 2001 cuts permanent. However, the administration and most economists believed that federal spending programs, particularly an extension of unemployment benefits and flexible aid to state and local governments to forestall layoffs of teachers and other employees, would constitute more effective economic stimulus. Hence, $285 billion of ARRA funds were provided in the form of grants to states and localities, roughly half of which was provided in the form of flexible funding for education and health care, and the remainder composed of funding for federal projects in the national parks, federal infrastructure improvements, health care IT, and so forth. The ARRA's tax cut provisions, though substantial, were sufficient to attract only three Republican votes in the Senate—just enough to avoid a Republican filibuster. In a reprise of the hyperpartisan politics of the 2001 tax cut, the Recovery Act passed the House on a party-line vote without a single Republican voting yea.

The battle to extend the Bush-era tax cuts began in earnest in 2010. Many assumed that the Democrats would use their large majorities in the House and Senate to extend only the middle-class tax cuts in the spring of 2010. However, these plans were complicated by the death of Senator Edward Kennedy and the Democrats' loss of their filibuster-proof majority in the Senate. As the health care reform battle extended into March of 2010, and as support for Democrats eroded in public opinion polls, more vulnerable Democrats in the House and Senate began to oppose voting on tax cut extensions until after the November elections. Although public opinion polls consistently showed support for the Democrats' position of extending only the tax cuts on income under $250,000, Democratic defections made their success uncertain.[77]

Delay proved to be no help to nervous congressional Democrats, who surrendered control of the House of Representatives with a loss of sixty-three House seats and six Senate seats. This gravely complicated plans to extend the 2001 tax cuts before they expired on December 31. An extension could be accomplished in the lame-duck session of Congress following the election, in which Democrats still retained their majorities in the House and Senate. But partisans on both sides of the aisle were dug into their positions. Republicans insisted on extending all of the 2001 tax cuts, knowing that their position had been strengthened by the election and coming control over the House of Representatives. Democratic liberals sought to hold firm on extending only the lower rates on incomes below $250,000, feeling that Republicans would be blamed if the cuts expired. For its part, the Obama White House feared the economic impact of even a temporary rise in taxes during a lingering recession, and the president believed that his position would fare worse in the coming Congress.

Consequently, President Obama and his top aides negotiated a compromise with Republican leaders. This compromise extended all of the 2001 and 2003 tax cuts until 2012, along with an extension of the estate tax at 35 percent on estates over $5 million; a temporary reduction in the Social Security payroll tax; an extension of the earned income, tuition, and child tax credits; extension of the "patch" for the AMT; rapid depreciation (expensing) of business investments; and an extension of unemployment benefits for the long-term unemployed. All told, it was a surprisingly large $858 billion package that gave Republicans a temporary extension of all of the Bush-era tax cuts while providing the economy (and Obama administration) with a large dose of additional economic stimulus with the payroll tax reduction, lower income tax credits, the extension of unemployment benefits, and the business expensing provisions.[78] After initial resistance from liberal Democrats, who felt that the president had caved in to Republican demands, the compromise passed the Senate on a vote of 81–19 and the House on a bipartisan vote of 277–148.[79]

Pathways to the Future

As the twenty-first century enters its second decade, tax policy is increasingly being viewed through the prism of federal deficits. The federal deficit exceeded 10 percent of GDP in FY 2010, and while this is projected to decline as the U.S. economy improves, large deficits are embedded in the federal budget as it is currently structured. The long-term fiscal imbalance posed by an aging society and the escalating costs of health care programs is poised to become a fiscal emergency within the next decade. Controlling the federal deficit emerged as an issue in the 2010 midterm elections, and the issue ranks high on the agenda for the 112th Congress.

Solutions to this deficit problem will inevitably involve tax policy as well as reductions in federal spending. Three bipartisan national commissions issued reports and recommendations for dealing with federal deficits in late 2010, and all recommended major revisions to the federal tax code and ideas for raising new federal revenues.[80] In particular, each recommended broadening the federal income tax base by eliminating or restricting major tax expenditures for health insurance, home mortgage interest, and state and local taxes. This could raise additional federal revenues while still allowing for some reduction in federal income tax rates.

The political challenges confronting tax increases of any kind remain daunting, however. For all of the conservative talk of "socialism" and Democrats' hopes for a "new New Deal" under President Obama, much of the tax policy legacy—and fiscal public philosophy—of Ronald Reagan remains remarkably resilient. No successful Democratic presidential candidate has taken on the challenge of arguing for a reversal of fiscal approach—and particularly the need for tax increases—since Walter Mondale's crushing defeat in 1984. Far from it. Democrats since that time have voiced repeated calls of "me too" on taxes. Bill Clinton advocated a middle-class tax cut in 1992, and Democrats were punished at the polls in 1994 in part because of a failure to live up to this promise in his 1993 budget. Al Gore took up the pledge for substantial middle-class tax cuts in his 2000 presidential campaign, and Barack Obama made repeated and firm promises to cut the taxes of 95 percent of taxpayers during his electoral campaign. What is more, Democrats from Clinton to Obama have enthusiastically embraced tax expenditures as an attractive means of providing subsidies and incentives for favored policy goals. Although the Recovery Act and health care reform appeared to mark a return to the traditional Democratic option of direct grants and subsidies, President Obama returned to a tax cut strategy for economic stimulus in his compromise with Republican leaders in December 2010. Thus, much of the political landscape of unsustainable tax policy remains unchanged at the midpoint of Barack Obama's first term, despite all of the drama of the Bush years and its subsequent fiscal and political wreckage.

The continuing evolution of tax policy pathways may open new avenues of change, however. The tax story of the Bush and early Obama years shows that the partisan pathway gained unusual ascendancy over other competing pathways. In contrast with the traditional battle between Treasury professionals and pluralistic forces in Congress, which dominated tax policymaking before 1980, the Bush years accelerated the ascendance of partisan control over tax policy that began in 1981. Bush's first term, in particular, witnessed the unusual combination of an ideological administration dedicated to enacting policies appealing to its base and a compliant Congress eager to serve as parliamentary actors in promoting this same agenda by linking their fortunes to a popular president.

Recent changes in policymaking institutions further accentuated the role played by party leaders in tax policy. Changes in congressional budgeting increased the power of central congressional party leaders over policy machinery involving both budget and tax policy. As tax and budget policies become increasingly intertwined, the centrally dominated arenas of congressional budgeting have increasingly intruded on the specialized domains of tax policy committees in the Congress, placing constraints and policy dictates on tax policy actors through such vehicles as budget reconciliation packages and PAYGO offset rules.

Yet this dominance of the partisan pathway is both unusual and historically unstable. The other pathways are alive and well and remain vital sources of ideas and energy that will continue to churn tax policy changes going forward. The bipartisan nature of the Tax Relief, Unemployment Insurance Reauthorization, and Job Creation Act of 2010, as well as the multiple deficit reduction commissions, underscores the point. This openness may provide needed avenues to new tax policy alternatives, coming in the side door through a process of issue reframing and alternative mobilization.[81] For example, increased future revenues might come from a broadened tax base, new taxes on energy or health care, or a value-added tax. In short, the sources of needed revenues in our future may arise from other policy arenas—energy, environment, health care, and national security—and follow very different policy pathways than those seen in the past thirty years.

NOTES

1. Douglas Holtz Eakin, quoted in Joe Klein, "The McCain Tax Increases—Continued," *Time* (September 12, 2008), http://swampland.time.com/2008/09/12/ the _mccain_tax_increasescontin/.

2. C. Eugene Steuerle, *The Tax Decade: How Taxes Came to Dominate the Public Agenda* (Washington, DC: Urban Institute Press, 1992); see also C. Eugene Steuerle, *Contemporary U.S. Tax Policy* (Washington, DC: Urban Institute Press, 2004).

3. Jacob S. Hacker and Paul Pierson, *Off Center: The Republican Revolution and the Erosion of American Democracy* (New Haven, CT: Yale University Press, 2005).

4. Bryan D. Jones and Walter Williams, *The Politics of Bad Ideas* (New York: Pearson Longman, 2008), ix.

5. Dan Balz, "Bush Takes Pledge against Tax Hikes," *Washington Post*, June 9, 1999, A6; Donald Lambro, "Bush Signals the Right," *Washington Times*, January 18, 2001, A15.

6. For one analysis of these tensions, see Michael D. Tanner, *Leviathan on the Right* (Washington, DC: Cato Institute Press, 2007).

7. Ron Suskind, *The Price of Loyalty: George W. Bush, the White House, and the Education of Paul O'Neill* (New York: Simon & Schuster, 2004), 34.

8. Steven Thomas, "Plan to Cut Taxes Bit by Bit Is GOP's Strategy for 2000," *Philadelphia Inquirer*, July 24, 2000, A1.

9. Robert S. McIntyre, "Tax Wars: Winners and Losers from the Bush and Gore Tax Plans," *American Prospect*, October 23, 2000, 23–24.

10. Since the standard deduction may be taken in lieu of itemizing individual deductions—including charitable donations—this proposal was comparable to deducting charitable contributions twice.

11. McIntyre, "Tax Wars," 24.

12. *Survey by Newsweek and Princeton Survey Research Associates, September 7– September 8, 2000.* Retrieved August 4, 2008, from the iPOLL Databank, The Roper Center for Public Opinion Research, University of Connecticut.

13. *Survey by Cable News Network, USA Today and Gallup Organization, January 13–January 16, 2000.* Retrieved August 4, 2008, from the iPOLL Databank, Roper Center for Public Opinion Research.

14. *Survey by Cable News Network, USA Today and Gallup Organization, July 25–July 26, 2000.* Retrieved August 4, 2008, from the iPOLL Databank, Roper Center for Public Opinion Research.

15. *Survey by ABC News/Washington Post, January 13–January 16, 2000.* Retrieved August 4, 2008, from the iPOLL Databank, Roper Center for Public Opinion Research.

16. *Survey by Cable News Network, USA Today and Gallup Organization, July 25–July 26, 2000.*

17. Hacker and Pierson, *Off Center.* See also Jacob S. Hacker and Paul Pierson, "Tax Politics and the Struggle over Activist Government," in *The Transformation of American Politics,* ed. Paul Pierson and Theda Skocpol (Princeton, NJ: Princeton University Press, 2007), 258.

18. *Survey by ABC News/Washington Post, February 3–February 6, 2000.* Retrieved August 4, 2008, from the iPOLL Databank, Roper Center for Public Opinion Research.

19. *Survey by The Tarrance Group & Lake, Snell, Perry & Associates, January 3–January 5, 2000.* Retrieved August 4, 2008, from the iPOLL Databank, Roper Center for Public Opinion Research.

20. *Survey by The Tarrance Group & Lake, Snell, Perry & Associates, March 12–March 13, 2000.* Retrieved August 4, 2008, from the iPOLL Databank, Roper Center for Public Opinion Research.

21. Terry M. Neal, "Whither Bush's Big Tax Cut Vow? Republican Candidate Shifts Campaign Focus to Smaller, Targeted Breaks," *Washington Post,* June 17, 2000, A4.

22. U.S. Office of Management and Budget, *Historical Tables: The Budget of the United States Government, Fiscal Year 2008,* 24.

23. Congressional Budget Office, *Historical Effective Tax Rates, 1979–1997* (Washington, DC: Congressional Budget Office, 2001), 15, 21.

24. The administration originally estimated that its proposals would cost $1.3 trillion over ten years, but Congress's Joint Committee on Taxation pegged the cost at $1.6 trillion. The administration, following custom, accepted this figure for legislative purposes.

25. Mike Allen, "Bush to Forge Ahead with Agenda: Taxes, Education Big Priorities," *Washington Post,* December 14, 2000, A1.

26. Quoted in Heidi Glenn, "U.S. Democrat Miller Joins Gramm to Introduce President Bush's Tax Cut," *Tax Notes International,* February 5, 2003, 639. See also Glenn Kessler and Eric Pianin, "Tax Cuts Gaining, in Pieces: Breaking Up Wins Democrats," *Washington Post,* July 9, 2000, A1.

27. Neal, "Whither Bush's Big Tax Cut Vow?," A4.

28. Glenn Kessler, "Tax Cut Compromise Reached," *Washington Post,* May 2, 2001, A1.

29. Lambro, "Bush Signals the Right," A15.

30. "Red Hot Quotes," *Hill,* March 21, 2001, np.

31. Quoted in Suskind, *Price of Loyalty,* 28.

32. John Maggs and Peter H. Stone, "Tax Cut Fever," *National Journal,* February 3, 2001, 326, 329.

33. Suskind, *Price of Loyalty*, 45.

34. Quoted in Lori Nitschke, "Writing Size of a Cut in the Budget Looms as Tax Turning Point," *CQ Weekly*, January 27, 2001, 220.

35. Quoted in Juliet Eilperin, "Few Democrats Are Likely to Back House Tax Bill," *Washington Post* (March 6, 2001), A8; see also George W. Bush, "Address before a Joint Session of the Congress on Administration Goals, February 27, 2001," *Weekly Compilation of Presidential Documents* 37, no. 9, 351–57.

36. Eilperin, "Few Democrats," A8.

37. U.S. House Committee on Ways and Means, H. Rpt. 107-7, *Economic Growth and Tax Relief Act of 2001*.

38. House Committee on Ways and Means, H. Rpt. 107-051—Part 1, *Comprehensive Retirement Security and Pension Reform Act of 2001*.

39. *2001 CQ Almanac*, 18-7.

40. Stephen Norton, "A Bruised Bush Tax Plan Heads into Middle Innings on Hill," *National Journal's Congress Daily*, April 25, 2001, 16.

41. Susan Crabtree, "Centrists 'Trigger' Bush Tax Problem," *Roll Call*, March 5, 2001, 1.

42. Suskind, *Price of Loyalty*, 131.

43. Ibid., 134; Glenn Kessler and Helen Dewar, "Senate Scales Back Bush's Tax Cut," *Washington Post*, April 7, 2001, A1.

44. Susan Crabtree and Mark Preston, "Chafee Giving GOP Heartburn," *Roll Call*, April 2, 2001.

45. Kessler and Dewar, "Senate Scales Back," A1; *2001 CQ Almanac*, 5–9. Importantly, Jeffords also revealed his plans to leave the Republican Party and allow Democrats to assume control of the Senate as soon as the tax and budget legislation was completed.

46. Susan Crabtree, "Tax Rhetoric Divides GOP," *Roll Call*, March 19, 2001.

47. Dan Morgan, "No Recess in Political Ad Season: Issue Spots Follow Lawmakers Home," *Washington Post*, April 14, 2001, A1; Alexander Bolton, "State Leaders Pressure Senators," *Hill*, May 9, 2001, 1.

48. Mike Allen and Glenn Kessler, "Bush to Back Larger Retroactive Tax Cut," *Washington Post*, March 22, 2001, A6.

49. *2001 CQ Almanac*, 5-9.

50. Susan Crabtree, "Shut Out Senate Democrats Denounce Behind-the-Scenes Budget Compromise," *Roll Call*, April 23, 2001.

51. Barbara Sinclair, *Unorthodox Lawmaking: New Legislative Processes in the U.S. Congress*, 3rd ed. (Washington, DC: CQ Press, 2007), 256.

52. U.S. Congress, Joint Committee on Taxation, *General Explanation of Tax Legislation Enacted in the 107th Congress*, Joint Committee Print JCS-1-03 (Government Printing Office, January 24, 2003), 10.

53. Clive Crook, "How to Take a Flawed Tax Bill and Turn It into a Joke," *National Journal*, June 9, 2001, 1707–8.

54. Robert Greenstein and Isaac Shapiro, "Who Would Benefit from the Tax Proposal before the Senate?," Center for Budget and Policy Priorities, May 21, 2001.

55. Maggs and Stone, "Tax Cut Fever," 324–29.

56. Jill Barshay and Alan K. Ota, "White House Must Keep Delicate Balance When Drafting Latest Tax Cut Package," *CQ Weekly Online*, January 4, 2003, 31.

57. Jill Barshay and Alan K. Ota, "White House Tax Cut Package Gets a Wary Hill Reception," *CQ Weekly Online*, January 11, 2003, 68–69.

58. Alan K. Ota, "Bush Encounters Ill Wind from Republicans on Dividend Tax Cut," *CQ Weekly Online*, February 8, 2003, 335.

59. Alan K. Ota, "Investor Class Flexes New Political Clout in Debate over Bush's Dividend Tax Cut," *CQ Weekly Online*, February 1, 2003, 248.

60. Alan K. Ota, "Uncertain Future in Conference Awaits Bush Tax Cut Package," *CQ Weekly Online*, April 19, 2003, 935–37.

61. Ibid.

62. Ibid.

63. The Jobs and Growth Reconciliation Tax Act of 2003 (H.R. 2).

64. Alan K. Ota, "Committee Chairmen Step Up to Tackle Tax Cut Issue." *CQ Weekly Online*, April 26, 2003, 991–92.

65. Quoted in Alan Ota, "For Business, Tax Conference Will Be Damage Control," *CQ Weekly*, May 17, 2003, 1171.

66. President's Advisory Panel on Tax Reform, *Final Report* (Washington, DC: U.S. Treasury Department, November 1, 2005).

67. "U.S. Panel's Final Report Kicks Off Tax Reform Season," *Tax Analysts*, November 1, 2005.

68. John F. Witte, *The Politics and Development of the Federal Income Tax* (Madison: University of Wisconsin Press, 1985), 244–45. For a recent analysis of the politics of tax expenditures, see Christopher Howard, *The Hidden Welfare State: Tax Expenditures and Social Policy in the United States* (Princeton, NJ: Princeton University Press, 1997).

69. Stanley S. Surrey, "The Congress and the Tax Lobbyist: How Special Tax Provisions Get Enacted," *Harvard Law Review* 70 (May 1957): 1145–82.

70. Suskind, *Price of Loyalty*.

71. David W. Rohde, *Parties and Leaders in the Post Reform Congress* (Chicago: University of Chicago Press, 1991).

72. Martha Derthick and Paul J. Quirk, *The Politics of Deregulation* (Washington, DC: Brookings Institution, 1985); Timothy J. Conlan, Margaret T. Wrightson, and David R. Beam, *Taxing Choices: The Politics of Tax Reform* (Washington, DC: CQ Press, 1990).

73. Bryan Jones and Walter Williams, *The Politics of Bad Ideas* (New York: Pearson Longman, 2008).

74. Edward Koch, "The Mandate Millstone," *Public Interest*, Fall 1960, 44.

75. Michael Graetz and Ian Shapiro, *Death by a Thousand Cuts: The Fight over Taxing Inherited Wealth* (Princeton, NJ: Princeton University Press, 2005).

76. Shawn Fremstad, *The Tax Provisions in the American Recovery and Reinvestment Act* (Washington, DC: Center for Economic and Policy Research, 2009).

77. Richard Rubin, "Leaders Caught in Tax Turmoil," *CQ Weekly*, September 20, 2010, 2170–71.

78. "Highlights of the Tax Cut Deal," *CQ Weekly*, December 13, 2010, 2865.

79. Lori Montgomery and Shailagh Murray, "Liberal Concerns Delay House Vote on Tax-Cut Deal," *Washington Post*, December 16, 2010; Lori Montgomery, Shailagh Murray, and William Branigin, "Obama Signs Bill to Extend Bush-Era Tax Cuts for Two More Years," *Washington Post*, December 17, 2010.

80. *The Moment of Truth: Report of the National Commission on Fiscal Responsibility and Reform*; Bipartisan Policy Center, *Restoring America's Future*; *Getting Back in the Black: A Report of the Peterson-Pew Commission on Budget Reform*.

81. E. E. Schattschneider, *The Semi Sovereign People* (New York: Holt, Rinehart & Winston, 1960).

CHAPTER SEVEN

The Bush Administration and the Uses of Judicial Politics

Thomas F. Burke and Nancy Scherer

Most of the chapters in this book tell stories of fiascos, political misadventures in which the Bush administration grievously miscalculated in its quest to build a permanent Republican majority. The administration's strategy of placating the Republican base while adding new constituencies through the enactment of Social Security reform, a new Medicare drug benefit, immigration legalization, and other such policies backfired completely, and as in the case of Iraq, part of the challenge in telling these stories is to diagnose what led administration policymakers so far astray.

This chapter offers a contrast, a small yet significant island of success in a sea of failure. We call that island "judicial politics," though it goes beyond the federal judiciary to include all the ways in which the Bush administration used controversies over law and the legal system to achieve its ends. In this realm the administration found strategies that successfully achieved its twin goals of satisfying its base of interest group supporters and committed partisans while also reaching out to that fabled personage in political science, the median voter. In some significant cases the Bush administration was able to "get past no" despite the strong opposition of Democrats, but on other issues "no"—or at least "no action"—was precisely what the administration wanted: on many cultural issues judicial politics served to divert attention from troublesome political conflicts in issue areas such as abortion, gay rights, and health care by reframing them as the product of a judiciary run amok.

For the Bush administration, judicial politics was almost always a plus. For Barack Obama it has proven more mixed terrain, in which juggling the demands of base and median has proven more difficult. Both Bush and Obama were able to play to their base through judicial nominations, "scoring points" (Scherer 2005) by placing judges approved by their respective constituencies on the federal bench. But for Bush, judicial politics had another dimension: he was able to use law and judiciary as villains, reframing difficult political issues by castigating "activist judges" and "runaway litigation" as the source of the nation's difficulties. Obama famously tried this strategy himself in his State of the Union address, criticizing Supreme Court justices to their faces for their decision in *Citizens United*, the corporate campaign spending case, but the relationship of Obama and the Democratic Party to the legal system is too complex for this attack to have had much resonance. Bush, by contrast, could draw on anti-law and anti-judge themes that have been built up over decades by conservatives and so have become quite familiar to the public. Beating up on plaintiff lawyers and "runaway litigation" as a cause of the nation's economic ills is a technique that was first nurtured in the Nixon administration and reached maturity in the George H. W. Bush administration (Burke 2002). Castigating "judicial activism" and promoting "strict construction" of the Constitution are rhetorical techniques that go much further back.

These judicial politics strategies may have been particularly important for George W. Bush. Ronald Reagan famously argued that "government is not the solution to our problem, government is the problem" (Reagan 1981). Reagan's presidency capped the ascendancy of an antigovernment conservatism within the Republican Party. The Bush administration's attempt to create a Republican majority, however, was founded on much different premises. Bush's embrace of "compassionate conservatism," and of ambitious government policies such as No Child Left Behind and Medicare Part D, simply underlined that Bush, in both philosophy and practice, was a big government conservative. For Bush this weakened a rhetorical resource central to Reaganism, the ascription of problems in the economy and society to big government and government bureaucracies. Political movements need enemies, both to rally supporters and to construct persuasive narratives about social problems. Often in political narratives the starring role is played by a villain, as in Bush's claim that "everyone pays more for health care" because of "excessive litigation" (Bush 2003), or that "activist courts" are discouraging Americans who have "deep concerns about our culture" (Bush 2006). Of course, for Bush the main enemy was found offshore; antiterrorism was used to justify policies foreign and domestic. But Bush also used judges and avaricious lawyers as his scapegoats, to a degree that observers, focused on the big-ticket items in his presidency, often missed.

Admittedly this was mostly small-bore politics; it certainly did not have the sweep or resonance of Reagan's call to get the government off the backs of the people. Nonetheless, judicial politics proved a durable resource, as lawyers and activist judges effectively took the villainous roles previously assigned to overweening government bureaucrats and welfare queens.

The balance of the chapter describes three ways in which the Bush administration used judicial politics and the results the administration achieved. In the final section we offer a brief comparison with Barack Obama's approach to judicial politics. We argue that for the Obama administration, judicial politics has often been a source of difficulty rather than the useful political tool it proved for Bush.

Supporting Business and Professional Constituencies

Presidents need to pay off their constituencies, and Republican presidents in particular need to find ways to reward business and professional supporters. The main mechanisms by which the Bush administration helped out business constituencies were the old-fashioned ones—subsidies, tax breaks, and favorable regulations. These all incurred costs, usually budgetary but also political, as when the administration controversially imposed tariffs on imported steel (Washington 2003) or championed energy legislation replete with subsidies to the oil, gas, and nuclear industries (Adams 2005).

The administration's judicial politics strategies, by contrast, proved relatively costless, both fiscally and politically. In both of his terms, Bush embraced "tort reform," the effort to reduce the size and frequency of personal injury damage claims, mostly against businesses, insurers, and profession-als. Among business and professional groups, tort costs have become a perennial issue. Tillinghast, a consulting group, estimates that in 2005 the tort system absorbed about $261 billion in costs, roughly 2 percent of GDP (Towers Perrin Tillinghast 2006). There are reasons to question Tillinghast's methodology in arriving at this figure (Chimerine and Eisenbrey 2005), but in the business community it is widely accepted that tort is a substantial problem, limiting innovation and impairing productivity. For the past three decades, an array of business and professional groups have spent mil-lions of dollars on lobbying, research, public relations, and campaign con-tributions in the quest to reform the system. Their efforts are to some ex-tent coordinated through the American Tort Reform Association and the U.S. Chamber of Commerce Institute for Legal Reform, which both special-ize in the issue (Burke 2002).

For Bush, as for his Republican predecessors, tort reform was safe ground. Outside of a few academics and the main plaintiff lawyer organization, the American Association for Justice, few contest the narrative of a tort system out of control and constricting the economy. Tort reformers have largely won the war of public opinion (Haltom and McCann 2005). Thus, "tort talk" for Bush was an unmitigated positive. Bush advertised tort reform as one of his main accomplishments as governor of Texas, and in his 2000 campaign he regularly denounced plaintiff lawyers for sucking the life out of the economy. The 2000 Republican Party platform called for an array of tort reforms, including sanctions for attorneys who file frivolous suits, caps on damages, special protections for educators, and changes in medical mal-practice and product liability law (Republican Party 2000). Bush endorsed tort reform in each of his State of the Union addresses, contending that "our economy is held back" by irresponsible litigation (Bush 2005c) and asking Congress to protect business "from junk and frivolous lawsuits" (Bush 2003).

Bush was particularly focused on medical malpractice reform, an attractive policy because it promised to address the pressing issue of health care costs without cutting the incomes of health care providers or the options available to patients. Bush suggested an array of mostly small-bore health policies in his State of the Union addresses and in his presidential debates, but medical mal-practice reform was the one constant. In 2005 Bush even traveled to Southern

Illinois, which he identified as "the number one place for trial lawyers to sue," to disparage malpractice lawyers:

> Many of the costs that we're talking about don't start in an examining room or an operating room. They start in a courtroom. What's happening all across this country is that lawyers are filing baseless suits against doctors. . . .
>
> Because junk lawsuits are so unpredictable, they drive up insurance costs for all doctors, even for those who have never been sued; even for those who have never had a claim against them. When insurance premiums rise, doctors have no choice but to pass some of the costs on to their patients. That means you're paying for junk lawsuits every time you go to see your doctor. That's the effect of all the lawsuits. It affects your wallet. If you're a patient, it means you're paying a higher cost to go see your doctor. If part of the national strategy has got to be to make sure health care is available and affordable, health care becomes less affordable because of junk lawsuits. (Bush 2005b)

Variations on this theme could be found throughout the Bush presidency. A particularly memorable formulation came during the 2004 presidential campaign, when Bush told a Missouri crowd, "Too many good docs are getting out of business. Too many OB-GYNs aren't able to practice their love with women all across the country" (Milbank 2004). In a career filled with verbal missteps, it was perhaps Bush's most hilarious gaffe.

Unfortunately for the caring OB-GYNs and the other purported victims of tort litigation, Bush was unable to do much for them: he proved much better at cheerleading for tort reform than delivering. His main proposal, a bill to limit noneconomic damages in medical malpractice cases to $250,000, was blocked by the threat of filibuster in the Senate. A grand bipartisan compromise on asbestos litigation never came together (Barnes 2011). A bill reforming class action lawsuits was bottled up in the Senate until 2005, when Republicans, having expanded their majority in the 2004 elections, were able to attract enough Democratic votes to reach cloture. This gave Bush his one major tort reform victory, enactment of the "Class Action Fairness Act," whose main feature was to move some class action lawsuits from state to federal court, in some cases a more favorable venue for business interests. The bill was watered down in order to get through the Senate, but it was hailed by business groups, particularly the Chamber of Commerce, which spent a reported $168 million to campaign for it (Labaton 2005).

For Bush, then, tort politics proved an easy way to rally the troops, at little cost to himself.

Reframing Cultural Issues

Republicans came to power in large part by knitting together their traditional antitax constituency with a new group, cultural conservatives repelled by the Democrats' embrace of gender equality, abortion, and, later, gay and lesbian rights. The challenge for Bush, as for his father and for Ronald Reagan, was to manage the tensions this alliance created. If he went too far in pleasing cultural conservatives, he risked alienating swing voters attracted to the low-tax stance but more moderate on cultural issues. If he did too little, he risked a right-flank rebellion. Bush resolved this dilemma by reframing cultural issues as matters of judicial overreaching, a ground on which his voters could come together.

On abortion Bush temporized. Unlike Reagan, he did not promise a frontal attack on *Roe*. In the 2000 presidential debates he outlined his approach:

> Surely we can find common ground to reduce the number of abortions in America. This is a very important topic, and it's a very sensitive topic because a lot of good people disagree on the issue. I think what the next president ought to do is promote a culture of life in America. As a matter of fact, I think a noble goal for this country is that every child, born and unborn, ought to be protected in law and welcomed into life. What I do believe is, we can find good common ground on issues like parental notification or parental consent. ("2000 Unofficial Debate Transcript," October 3, 2000)

Illegalizing abortion is a "noble goal," placed in a distant and hazy horizon. In the interim Bush promised only to work on secondary issues, partial-birth abortion and parental consent, on which the median voter was firmly on his side.

This by itself might not have been enough to assuage cultural conservatives, but Bush had a more substantial promise, that he would pack the federal judiciary with judges who would overturn *Roe*. Yet again, stating this too baldly risked alienating swing voters, so Bush framed his approach to the federal courts carefully, using language that more attentive cultural conservatives could recognize. He criticized judges who "insist on forcing their arbitrary will upon the people" and rule by "the whim of the gavel" rather than "the letter of the law" (Bush 2004b, 2008). When asked during the 2000 campaign which justice he most admired, Bush picked Scalia and Thomas; his opponent, Al Gore, contended that these were "code words" for judges who would be anti-*Roe* (Lewis 2000). In talking about the judiciary, Bush repeatedly found language that would not alarm moderates yet reassure his Christian conservative supporters. When, during the presidential debate in 2004, Bush was asked what kind of justice he would nominate, he turned the question around, explaining what kind of judge he *wouldn't* want:

> I wouldn't pick a judge who said that the Pledge of Allegiance couldn't be said in a school because it had the words "under God" in it. I think that's an example of a judge allowing personal opinion to enter into the decision-making process as opposed to a strict interpretation of the Constitution.
>
> Another example would be the Dred Scott case, which is where judges, years ago, said that the Constitution allowed slavery because of personal property rights. ("2004 Debate Transcript")

The recently decided Pledge of Allegiance case was an understandable citation, but what made Bush go all the way back to Dred Scott for an example of judicial activism? Among constitutional scholars it was a particularly puzzling example, because some believe that Dred Scott was in fact decided according to the interpretive method favored by Bush's favorite judges, original meaning (Graber 2006). To them the reference seemed a non sequitur, but for evangelical Christians, it made perfect sense. Within their circle, *Roe v. Wade* was often framed as another *Dred Scott v. Sanford*, a trampling of basic human rights. Bush's message was not so hard for evangelicals to decipher, notwithstanding his renunciation, a few sentences later in the debate, of any litmus test for nominees (Kirkpatrick 2004).

Bush's debate performance nicely illustrated, in miniature, his ability to have it both ways on abortion, sending reassuring messages to both base and median voters. It is not easy to know the extent to which this was the result of Bush's background as a Christian conservative, which gave him the language and the credibility to connect easily with antiabortion supporters, or a more self-conscious product of polling and focus group technologies. The formulation "a culture of life," employed relentlessly during the Bush years, seems an example of "crafted talk," the use of poll-tested, focus-grouped language to reframe political issues, a technique ubiquitous in national-level politics today (Jacobs and Shapiro 2000; Luntz 2006). But Bush's mention of Dred Scott suggests an even more sophisticated method, of coded appeals, in which a message is sent to a target audience wrapped in an innocuous rhetorical package. Christian conservatives knew exactly what Bush meant by his reference to Dred Scott, but it likely flew by the median voters Bush also wanted to attract. Research suggests that coded appeals may be more effective than more open statements of support, because as they bypass potential opponents they reinforce a bond with the target audience. When Bush said in his 2003 State of the Union address that "there is power—wonder-working power—in the goodness and idealism of the American people," he was using a phrase, "wonder-working power," well known to some Christians. One study found that among those raised as Pentecostals, this statement was more powerful in attracting support than a more openly religious appeal (Albertson 2006).

Whether through the conscious use of coded appeals, crafted talk, or just good political instincts, Bush largely defused the abortion issue, but he faced a more difficult problem with gay and lesbian rights. Here again, the root of the problem was the tension within the Republican alliance, but initially, at least, Bush had no *Roe* to lean on. Legislation on discrimination in employment, for example, posed a real dilemma: a stance against it might persuade moderates that Bush was too closely tied to Christian conservatives, but an endorsement would offend the base. Bush's response was to bob and weave, giving hope to both sides. During the 2000 presidential campaign, he met with a small group of Log Cabin Republicans, a gay organization, and his administration continued to enforce a ban on discrimination in federal employment. Yet when Bush was asked during the 2000 presidential debate about discrimination against gays and lesbians, his response was to rule out providing "special rights," though he did say that personally "I don't hire and fire somebody based on their sexual orientation" ("2000 Unofficial Debate Transcript," October 11, 2000). The equivocating pattern continued through both terms. An administration appointee for a time refused to enforce the federal employment discrimination policy, and the administration threatened to veto legislation banning sexual orientation discrimination, though it was never forced to follow through—the legislation never got out of the Senate (Herszenhorn 2007).

Bush was largely bailed out of his troubles on gay rights by the Supreme Judicial Court of Massachusetts. The Court's 2003 ruling in *Goodridge v. Department of Public Health* allowed Bush to reframe the issue of gay rights as a matter of judicial activism, and from then on this was how he described it, as in his 2004 State of the Union address: "Activist judges . . . have begun redefining marriage by court order, without regard for the will of the people and their elected representatives. On an issue of such great consequence, the people's voice must be heard. If judges insist on forcing their arbitrary will upon the people, the only alternative left to the people would be the constitutional process. Our nation must defend the sanctity of marriage" (Bush 2004b). Same-sex marriage was deeply unpopular among both cultural conservatives and moderates, so in talking about the decision Bush did not have to worry about splitting his alliance. Bush's endorsement of a constitutional amendment defining marriage as between a man and a woman was less popular, but the president took care to portray it as the only recourse left to the people by "activist courts" that "are presuming to change the most fundamental institution in the country" (Bush 2004a). The constitutional amendment never went very far. Yet in the 2004 election and several that followed, states across the country amended their own constitutions to stop same-sex marriage, a process that may have benefited Republican office seekers, including Bush himself. Lost in the furor over same-sex marriage was that Bush quietly endorsed civil unions, a position that would have been considered liberal at the beginning of his term (Bumiller 2004). In any event, the *Goodridge* ruling turned what had been a problematic issue into a winner. As in the case of abortion, Bush employed judicial politics to defuse tensions between base and median voter.

Bush was not nearly so adroit in his handling of the Terri Schiavo controversy, where he seemed a victim of events. Bush found himself caught up as evangelical Christians mobilized and demanded congressional intervention to overturn unfavorable federal and state court rulings. Indeed, the Schiavo controversy neatly reversed the Bush strategy: it was a case in which the public lined up with the legal system against Congress, and Bush himself, and in which the elected politicians appeared "activist," reaching beyond their normal roles to intervene where they were unwanted (Kohut 2005).

Schiavo was the exception. Bush was largely successful at managing his party's cultural politics. For this he had the judiciary to thank. In a post-*Roe* world Bush would have been forced to confront the core issue of abortion more squarely, and in a world without the same-sex marriage rulings, his endorsement of civil unions would have been far more salient and troublesome to cultural conservatives. As he was excoriating judges for their activism, Bush might have added a word of thanks.

Scoring Points with Cultural Conservatives

Bush could not reward his cultural conservative supporters with major legislation, but he could give them the kind of judges they desired. Here again, though, the Bush administration faced a problem: in a system of judicial independence with lifetime appointment, how can a president guarantee to his supporters that his judicial nominees, once appointed, will reliably vote the party line?

Bush came to power after several decades of conservative frustration with Republican judicial appointees stretching back to the 1950s. President Eisenhower famously expressed regret over his appointments of Earl Warren and William Brennan to the Court. Though both Republicans, they ultimately became the core of the Warren Court, the source of a series of liberal rulings that transformed constitutional law. Richard Nixon ran in large part on the backlash against the Warren Court, promising to appoint "law and order" judges that would ratchet back a series of decisions protecting criminal suspects. From Nixon on, presidential candidates, both Democratic and Republican, articulated litmus tests on the campaign trail designed to signal to their base as to the type of judges they would appoint to the federal courts once elected (Goldman 1997; Scherer 2005).

In the 1980s, Presidents Reagan and George H. W. Bush pronounced their commitment to appoint judges who "believe in the sanctity of human life"—a not-so-subtle signal to their core constituents that they intended to seek out judges who would overturn *Roe v. Wade*. But, despite their best efforts, and five nominations to the Supreme Court between them, these Republican presidents ultimately failed to live up to their campaign promises. Confronted with a case, *Planned Parenthood v. Casey*, in which the justices specifically considered overturning *Roe*, three of the five Reagan/H. W. Bush Supreme Court appointees (O'Connor, Kennedy, and Souter) formed the pivotal swing group that voted to uphold the right to an abortion.

How to avoid such unpleasant surprises? By the beginning of the Bush presidency, Republican leaders figured out a judicial selection system that virtually guaranteed that their judicial nominees would be stalwart conservatives. Integral to this strategy is a conservative organization known as the Federalist Society. As Senate Judiciary Committee member Richard Durbin (D-IL) observed, "As we try to monitor the legal DNA of President Bush's nominees, we find repeatedly the Federalist Society chromosome" (Benac

2005, quoting Durbin). Or as Karl Rove, Bush's political strategist, put it, "One of George W. Bush's greatest contributions as president will be the changes he's brought about in our courts and our legal culture, and those changes would have been impossible were it not for the Federalist Society" (Rove 2005). Thus, any examination of Bush's appointment strategy must begin with the mission of the Federalist Society and the role it has come to play in Republican presidential administrations.

The Federalist Society was founded at Yale Law School in 1980 and began strictly as a law student organization (Bossert 1997; Hicks 2006). From its inception, the Federalist Society sought to provide a counterbalance to the "liberal jurisprudence" that prevailed in the nation's law schools at that time. While Federalist Society members declaim the notion that they are united around a particular philosophy (Teles 2008), many were associated with a method of constitutional interpretation variously referred to as "textualism" or "original meaning." The Society's executive director, Eugene Meyer, explained this approach: "If a word meant 'x' when the Constitution was passed, and it means 'y' today . . . you presumably want to stick with the meaning it had before" (Meyer 2002). Society members contend that judges should practice "judicial restraint," that is, unelected jurists should not interject their personal policy preferences when interpreting the Constitution: "Is the court interpreting the text and meaning of the Constitution? If it is, and they [the judges or justices] are doing the best they can do . . . their judgment might be off, but there is not a structural problem. If the court is saying, 'gee, we don't like the direction policy is going in this country [and w]e want to change the direction of policy' . . . that is not a proper role for the courts" (Meyer 2002). The rhetoric of originalism aligns neatly with conservative positions on constitutional questions on abortion and gay rights. Critics point out that conservatives are typically not so intent on following "original meaning" in areas such as affirmative action, executive powers, freedom of speech, and federalism where, it seems, their policy views might not mesh so neatly with historical research on the origins of the relevant constitutional provisions (Rosen 2006). But these subtleties of legal doctrine, while much debated within the academy, are lost in the larger public debate over "judicial activism," which tends to focus on the most salient controversies, over abortion and same-sex marriage. Because the philosophies of Federalist Society members were broadly in line with conservative political policy goals, and because their positions on both constitutional interpretation and the role of unelected

Table 7.1 Federalist Society members nominated to U.S. Supreme Court and the U.S. Courts of Appeals by administration (1989–2007)

Name	Court	Year questionnaire submitted	Membership acknowledged
George H. W. Bush			
Samuel Alito	3rd Circuit	1990	Yes
Lillian Bevier*	4th Circuit	1991	Not available
Dennis Jacobs	2nd Circuit	1992	Yes
Francis Keating*	10th Circuit	1991	Not available
Michael Luttig	4th Circuit	1991	No
Sheldon Plager	Federal Circuit	1989	Yes
John Roberts*	D.C. Circuit	1992	Not available
Clarence Thomas	D.C. Circuit	1989	No
Clarence Thomas	Supreme Court	1991	No
George W. Bush			
Samuel Alito	Supreme Court	2005	Yes
Carlos Bea	9th Circuit	2003	Yes
Janice Brown†	D.C. Circuit	2003	Yes
Jay Bybee†	9th Circuit	2001	Yes
Michael Chertoff	3rd Circuit	2003	No
Edith Clement	5th Circuit	2001	Yes
Steven Collonton	8th Circuit	2003	Yes
Deborah Cook†	6th Circuit	2001	No
Jennifer Elrod	5th Circuit	2007	Yes
Miguel Estrada*	D.C. Circuit	2001	Yes
E. Duncan Getchell*	4th Circuit	2007	Not available
Thomas Griffith†	D.C. Circuit	2004	No
Neil Gorsuch*	10th Circuit	2006	Yes
Raymond Gruender	8th Circuit	2003	Yes
Harris Hartz	10th Circuit	2001	Yes
William Haynes†	4th Circuit	2003	Yes
Kent Jordan	3rd Circuit	2006	Yes
Brett Kavanaugh†	D.C. Circuit	2003	Yes
Peter Keisler*	D.C. Circuit	2006	Yes
Carolyn Kuhl*	9th Circuit	2001	No
Steve Matthews*	4th Circuit	2007	Not available
Michael McConnell	10th Circuit	2001	Yes
David McKeague†	6th Circuit	2001	Yes
Stephen Murphy*	6th Circuit	2006	Not available
William Myers*	D.C. Circuit	2003	Yes
Priscilla Owen†	5th Circuit	2001	No
Gene Pratter*	3rd Circuit	2007	Not available
William Pryor†	11th Circuit	2003	Yes
John Roberts†	D.C. Circuit	2001	No

Table 7.1   (continued)

Name	Court	Year questionnaire submitted	Membership acknowledged
John Roberts	Supreme Court	2005	No
John Rogers	6th Circuit	2001	Yes
Rod Rosenstein*	4th Circuit	2007	Not available
Henry Saad*	6th Circuit	2001	Yes
N. Randy Smith	9th Circuit	2005	Yes
William Smith*	1st Circuit	2007	Not available
Leslie Southwick	5th Circuit	2006	Yes
Shalom Stone*	3rd Circuit	2007	Not available
Jeffrey Sutton†	6th Circuit	2001	Yes
Diane Sykes	7th Circuit	2003	Yes
Timothy Tymkovich†	10th Circuit	2001	Yes
Michael Wallace*	5th Circuit	2006	Yes

*Not confirmed.
†Confirmed in subsequent congressional session.

judges aligned as well, the Society soon found itself enmeshed in Republican administrations.

The association between the Federalist Society and the executive branch began during the Reagan administration, expanded during the George H. W. Bush administration, but reached a new level under George W. Bush. Table 7.1 is a list of all Federalist Society members nominated by Presidents George H. W. Bush and George W. Bush to the Supreme Court and the U.S. Courts of Appeals. While George H. W. Bush nominated eight Federalist Society members to the appellate courts to fill forty-four vacancies (18.1%), George W. Bush nominated thirty-nine Society members to fill seventy-nine vacancies (49.4%).[1] The George W. Bush administration used Society members to fill almost half of all nominations to the courts of appeals and Supreme Court. At the Supreme Court level, one of George H. W. Bush's two nominees, Thomas, came from the Federalist Society; the other was Souter, a profound disappointment to conservatives. George W. Bush's two successful nominees, Roberts and Alito, were both Society members.

George W. Bush relied on Federalist Society members because they were seen as a "sure thing." Unlike Justices Kennedy, Souter, and O'Connor, Society members were virtually guaranteed to vote conservatively once on the bench because their membership signals an allegiance to the principles of constitutional interpretation laid down by the Society. A study by Scherer and Miller

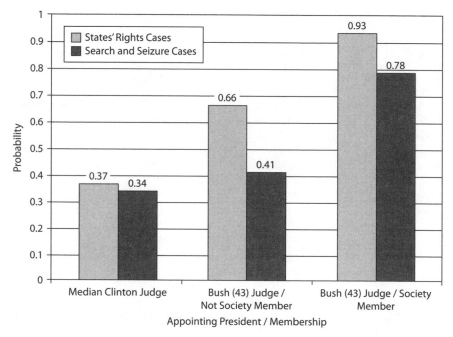

Figure 7.1. Probability of a conservative vote in cases addressing (1) state's rights and (2) search and seizure, 1995–2006.

(2009) confirms that, once on the bench, Society members are much more likely to cast conservative votes than fellow non-Society Republican colleagues, as well as Democratic-appointed judges. As shown in figure 7.1, judges appointed by George W. Bush who are members of the Federalist Society are 27 percent more likely than nonmember Bush-appointed jurists to take the conservative position in states' rights cases and 36 percent more likely to rule against a criminal defendant in search and seizure cases.

This pattern also occurs at the Supreme Court level, where political ideology scores developed by political scientists suggest that Society members are much more conservative than their fellow nonmember Republican justices and far more conservative than their Democratic counterparts. As shown in figure 7.2, Federalist Society members Thomas, Alito, and Roberts are on the far right of the ideological spectrum, with Republican, non-Society nominees Miers and Souter toward the center. As one would expect, the two Democrats appointed in this period, Ginsberg and Breyer, appear on the left side of the ideological continuum.

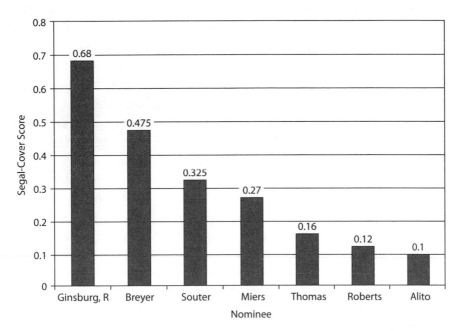

Figure 7.2. Segal-Cover ideology scores of Supreme Court nominees, 1989–2007. Segal-Cover scores range from 0 to 1; 0 indicates most conservative and 1 most liberal.

The one great exception to Bush's reliance on Federalist Society members at the Supreme Court level was his failed nomination of Harriet Miers. This represents perhaps the only time in his presidency that Bush made an appellate nomination that appealed to moderates, and the only time conservative activists opposed a Bush nominee. Thus, this episode invites closer examination.

When Justice O'Connor announced her intention to retire on July 1, 2005, the White House was quick to name D.C. circuit judge John Roberts as her replacement. Well known in conservative legal circles for his work in the Justice Department during the Reagan and George H. W. Bush administrations, Roberts's nomination thrilled conservative activists (Purdham 2005). Roberts's record during his days at the Justice Department and at the Solicitor General's Office was solidly conservative. As deputy solicitor general, Roberts had argued that *Roe* "was wrongly decided and should be overruled" (Reichmann 2005).

When Chief Justice Rehnquist passed away in the fall of 2005, Bush, undoubtedly influenced by the popularity of the Roberts nomination with conservative groups, renominated Roberts for the chief justice position. This left the O'Connor seat open. At this point in his presidency, Bush's political capital was rapidly waning. His approval ratings hit an all-time low of 41 percent in the wake of his mishandling of Hurricane Katrina (Zogby American Survey 2005) and the war in Iraq (Toner and Connelly 2005).[2] With so many political disasters with which to contend, Bush wanted to avoid another political setback, this time at the hands of Senate Democrats, over his next Supreme Court nomination. Bush anticipated two concerns of Democrats about the nomination. The first was the desire to appoint a woman to fill O'Connor's seat. Not only were Democratic-affiliated interest groups pressuring the president and Senate Democrats to ensure a second woman remained on the Court (National Organization for Women 2005), but even the First Lady, Laura Bush, publicly endorsed the nomination of a woman to fill the vacancy left by O'Connor (Bumiller 2005). Second, Senate Democrats would likely assess the nominee's willingness to overturn *Roe v. Wade*. While Roberts, an anti-*Roe* justice, had replaced another anti-*Roe* justice (Rehnquist), Bush's second nominee to the Court would be replacing a justice who declined to overturn *Roe*.[3]

Upon O'Connor's announced retirement, many Court watchers assumed that Bush would appoint an ultraconservative woman to replace O'Connor— someone who, like Roberts and the majority of Bush's courts of appeals nominees, was affiliated with the Federalist Society. But Bush struggled to find such a woman. Before Rehnquist's death, when there was only one vacancy on the Court, Bush had considered nominating one of the women on his original short list for Supreme Court justices (Epstein and Segal 2005, 53–55) but ultimately concluded that these women were unconfirmable. For example, both Priscilla Owen (Fifth Circuit) and Janice Rogers Brown (D.C. Circuit) faced staunch opposition from Democrats during their lower court confirmation proceedings. The Democrats argued that these women's decisions while serving as state court judges were out of the mainstream (Scherer 2005, 150–51).[4] Another female appellate judge affiliated with the Federalist Society and on Bush's short list, Edith Clement (Fifth Circuit), was considered for a time to be a front-runner to replace O'Connor because she had not faced stiff opposition from Senate Democrats when Bush appointed her at the beginning of his first term in office (Bumiller and Stout 2005). But apparently her interview with the president had not gone well, and so she was crossed off the list (Ertelt 2005). Moreover, other unidentified female candidates for the nomination asked the White House not to be considered for the O'Connor seat because of "the ordeal of going through the confirmation process" (Baker and Babington 2005, citing Scott McClellan).

With few female options remaining, Bush ultimately decided to go with a "stealth" candidate, Harriet Miers, a personal friend who was serving as White House Counsel. Miers was not an easy target for liberals. She had never served as a judge so she had no voting record; her views on *Roe* and on constitutional interpretation more generally were not well known. Moreover, even before her nomination, Miers already had an important Democratic ally in the Senate: Democratic leader Harry Reid had suggested to the president that Miers should be considered to replace O'Connor (Reid 2005). Miers was attractive also because of the many "firsts" listed on her resume: first woman to be hired by a major Dallas law firm, first woman to be named managing partner of a major Texas law firm, first woman to head the Dallas Bar Association, and first woman to be elected president of the Texas Bar Association (Bush 2005a). She was also named one of the top fifty woman lawyers in the nation (Bush 2005a).

While Miers may have been a stealth candidate to outsiders, Bush's close relationship with Miers, dating back to their days in Texas politics, gave him an insider's advantage. Bush did not worry that Miers would be "another Souter," a traitor to the conservative cause. The president was sure he knew Miers's positions on *Roe* and other controversial legal issues[5]—and that they were in line with the president's conservative agenda. Yet Bush also calculated that Miers would be seen by Democrats as a moderate choice, someone who could potentially serve as a swing vote on the Court, much like O'Connor.

The president did not anticipate the backlash to Miers that erupted from his own Republican base (Coats 2007). Still stinging from the Souter appointment fifteen years earlier, conservative Republican leaders and interest groups were not willing to take another chance on a stealth candidate (Coats 2007). Bush's plea to his base "to trust him" about Miers proved insufficient to turn the tide (Coats 2007). In fact, the conservative Republican base was so intent on not repeating the mistakes of the Souter nomination that, following the struggle over Miers, the party inserted into its 2008 platform a clause denouncing the nomination of "stealth" candidates to the federal bench: "We oppose stealth nominations to the federal bench and especially to the Supreme Court, whose lack of a clear and distinguished record leaves doubt about their respect for the Constitution or their intellectual fortitude. Nominees must have a record of fidelity to the U.S. Constitution and the rule of law" (Republican Party 2008, 20).

Conservatives insisted that the president nominate someone with a proven written record of opposition to *Roe* and a stated commitment to interpret the Constitution according to Federalist Society principles, in particular the theory of original meaning. The Republican base did not care about the appointment of another woman to the bench; in fact, some accused Bush of engaging in classic liberal affirmative action policies by nominating a less qualified woman over the plethora of qualified men to fill the O'Connor vacancy (O'Beirne 2005). And, so, with growing opposition within the Republican base over her nomination, Miers withdrew her name from consideration.

Bush would not repeat his miscalculation with his second nomination. He chose Samuel Alito to fill O'Connor's seat—a Federalist Society member with an extensive written record from fourteen years of experience as a judge on the Third Circuit, a record that demonstrated his commitment to interpreting the Constitution according to its original meaning and his hostility toward *Roe*.[6]

Taken together, the failed nomination of Miers and the successful nominations of both Roberts and Alito suggest the great value to Republican presidents of the Federalist Society. Federalist Society membership solves the problem that daunted Republican presidents since at least Nixon, how to get reliably conservative judges onto the bench, and how to reassure conservative activist groups that these judges will remain loyal to the cause once appointed.

But while placating the Republican base, Bush also had to be careful not to alienate moderates. Did Bush pay a price with the median voter for his nomination of extremely conservative judges? Political scientists have long observed that the broad public knows little about the Supreme Court and virtually nothing about the lower federal courts. George W. Bush's ultraconservative appointments to the U.S. Courts of Appeals undoubtedly went largely unnoticed by the average American voter; only his political base was paying attention (Scherer 2005). Not surprisingly, then, there is no publicly available polling data on voters' views of George W. Bush's appellate appointments.[7] We do, however, have polling on the public's views of the president's Supreme Court appointments.

The polls suggest a high level of misperceptions about nominees to the Court. Despite Roberts's and Alito's unequivocal conservative records, including skepticism about *Roe*, independent voters—the median voters—overwhelmingly supported their confirmations. Yet this same group also

Table 7.2   *Washington Post* / ABC News Poll, July 21, 2005
(500 respondents, margin of error ±4%)

Party	Uphold	Overturn	Unsure
		Roe v. Wade[a]	
Republican	~50%		
Independent	~66		
Democrat	~80		
Overall	~65%	32%	4%
	Should	Confirm Roberts[b] Should not	Unsure
Republican	84%		
Independent	58		
Democrat	41		
Overall	59%	23%	17%

[a]Responses were to the question, "The Supreme Court legalized abortion 32 years ago in the ruling known as *Roe versus Wade*. If that case came before the court again, would you want Roberts to vote to uphold *Roe versus Wade*, or vote to overturn it?"
[b]Responses were to the question, "Do you think the U.S. Senate should or should not confirm Roberts's nomination to the Supreme Court?"

told pollsters that they opposed judicial nominees who wanted to overturn *Roe*. The contrast was demonstrated in a July 2005 poll taken as Roberts's nomination was being considered (table 7.2). A large majority of respondents overall, including the independents, wanted Roberts to uphold *Roe*. Nonetheless, despite Roberts's statements opposing *Roe*, an almost equally large majority supported his confirmation.

A poll on Alito demonstrated a similar pattern (table 7.3). Opinion about Alito was divided equally among the supportive, the opposed, and the unsure. But a large majority of respondents, including the independents, said they would oppose Alito if they knew he would strike down *Roe*.

Another study conducted by the Annenberg Foundation in 2005 provides further confirmation of citizens' confusion over support for Supreme Court nominees antagonistic toward *Roe*. The Annenberg Supreme Court study asked respondents whether Bush's nominees to the Supreme Court should hold the same position on *Roe* as respondents' positions: 67 percent of independents surveyed said it was very important (36%) or somewhat important (31%) that Bush's nominations to the Supreme Court were in sync with the positions on *Roe* held by these respondents (Bartels and Johnston 2008).

Table 7.3   Harris Poll, December 9–14, 2006 (1,961 respondents, ±2%)

Party	Confirm Alito[a]		
	Should	Should not	Unsure
Republican	65%	9%	26%
Independent	34	38	28
Democrat	14	48	38
Overall	34%	31%	34%

	If Alito would make abortion illegal[b]	
	Favor	Oppose
Republican	56%	44%
Independent	26	74
Democrat	14	86
Overall	31%	69%

[a]Responses were to the question, "President Bush has nominated Samuel Alito to be an Associate Justice of the U.S. Supreme Court. Do you believe he should be confirmed by the Senate?"

[b]Responses were to the question, "If you thought that Judge Alito, if confirmed, would vote to make abortions illegal, would you favor or oppose his confirmation?"

Two other polls taken at about the same time as the Roberts and Alito nominations are also telling. A Gallup poll in July 2005 found that 63 percent of the public opposed overturning *Roe* (Gallup 2005), and a CNN/*USA Today*/Gallup poll conducted in January 2006 showed that 56 percent of the public would oppose Alito's confirmation if he were unwilling to uphold *Roe* (CNN/*USA Today*/Gallup Poll 2006). Collectively, these polls suggest that the majority of citizens should have been opposed to both Alito and Roberts but were not.

Thus, though independents favored *Roe*, and both Roberts and Alito opposed *Roe*, independents nonetheless went along with the confirmation of both. This suggests that independents pay little attention to the judicial branch of government, giving the president a free hand to make appointments that pleased his base. Moreover, if Alito and Roberts do one day strike down *Roe*, Bush will be far from the scene and immune from the wrath of the median voter.

Judicial appointments are by far the most significant and long-lasting reward Bush has given to cultural conservatives who supported him. For all his talk about a "culture of life" and his rhetorical opposition to same-sex marriage, Bush's achievements in this arena were modest at best. Congress did enact a partial-birth abortion law (upheld narrowly by the Court), and Bush issued some antiabortion executive orders, but the administration never reached further. Although Bush did endorse a constitutional amendment to stop same-sex marriage, he also endorsed civil unions, and during his two terms the gay rights movement marched forward without any serious federal intervention. "Faith-based initiatives," the rhetorical heart of Bush's compassionate conservatism, in practice turned out to be much less than promised (Kuo 2007; Kuo and Dillio 2008). To the extent that cultural conservatives made any lasting progress on his watch, it was in the federal judiciary.

Anti-Government/Anti-Judiciary

On several fronts, then, the Bush administration used judicial politics to manage tricky political problems, satisfying cultural conservatives and business interests without alienating median voters. Liberal legalism in its various guises has been the target of Republican presidents at least since Nixon, but before Bush, anti-governmental themes loomed much larger. Under Bush those themes receded, making judicial politics strategies all the more significant. In Bush's rhetoric, activist judges and greedy plaintiff lawyers replaced government bureaucrats and foolish government programs as the cause of social ills.

The contrast is nicely illustrated by two passages from State of the Union addresses. Consider first Ronald Reagan in 1984:

> The problems we're overcoming are not the heritage of one person, party, or even one generation. It's just the tendency of government to grow, for practices and programs to become the nearest thing to eternal life we'll ever see on this Earth. And there's always that well-intentioned chorus of voices saying, "With a little more power and a little more money, we could do so much for the people." For a time we forgot the American dream isn't one of making government bigger; it's keeping faith with the mighty spirit of free people under God.

Compare George W. Bush in 2006:

> In recent years, America has become a more hopeful nation. Violent crime rates have fallen to their lowest levels since the 1970s. Welfare cases have dropped by more than half over the past decade. Drug use among youth is down 19 percent since 2001. There are fewer abortions in America than at any point in the last

three decades, and the number of children born to teenage mothers has been falling for a dozen years in a row.

These gains are evidence of a quiet transformation—a revolution of conscience, in which a rising generation is finding that a life of personal responsibility is a life of fulfillment. *Government has played a role.* Wise policies, such as welfare reform and drug education and support for abstinence and adoption have made a difference in the character of our country. . . .

Yet many Americans, especially parents, still have deep concerns about the direction of our culture, and the health of our most basic institutions. They're concerned about unethical conduct by public officials, *and discouraged by activist courts that try to redefine marriage.* (emphasis added)

Government has been a force for good, Bush argues, but activist courts threaten the progress the culture has made. Of course, Bush also criticized government at times and invoked standard claims about the need to reduce government waste and inefficiency. But he never soared to Reaganesque heights in denouncing government. Only the legal system attracted his sustained ire.

The moment when a national Republican leader would say that "government has played a role" in resolving social issues and in the moral improvement of the citizenry quickly passed, and Bush's "big government" conservatism looks in retrospect like an anomaly. The events of 2008–12, particularly the controversies over government bailouts, the stimulus package, and health care reform, together with the rise of Sarah Palin, Michelle Bachmann, and the Tea Party, seem to have buried the "big government" version of conservatism. Republicans have once again made antigovernment rhetoric the centerpiece of their politics. The Bush administration's pro-government policies, to the extent that they were acknowledged by Republicans after 2008, were treated as a betrayal of the conservative movement.

Will the anti-law and anti-judiciary rhetoric of the Bush administration also fade? Increasingly, the unpopular decisions federal courts make are in a conservative direction, raising the possibility of a reversal, in which liberals attack—and conservatives defend—the judicial branch. President Obama's 2010 State of the Union address featured just such an attack. Obama, speaking "with all due deference to separation of powers," nevertheless criticized the Supreme Court's decision in *Citizens United*, which struck down regulations on corporate spending in election campaigns. With the justices he was criticizing sitting just a few feet away, Obama predicted that their decision

would "open the floodgates for special interests—including foreign corporations—to spend without limit in our elections" (Obama 2010b). But Obama's
celebrated attack was more a one-off than the opening salvo in a struggle
against judicial conservatism. He didn't connect *Citizens United* to other
"activist" decisions made by the Supreme Court, nor did he move beyond the
particulars of the decision to locate the decision in a broader context of conservative judicial activism. In academic circles, critiques of conservative judicial activism are common (Keck 2004), but they have failed to break through
to the popular culture. Even the prospect of a judicial decision overturning
Obama's signature legislative accomplishment, health care reform, seems unlikely to revert the American political universe to its pre-*Brown* alignment,
with liberals fulminating against "judicial activism" and urging courts to defer to the elected branches. The main barrier to this reversion is the salience
of two cultural issues, abortion and gay rights, which more than cancels out
a host of significant but less resonant decisions. As long as the Court's liberal
decisions on abortion and gay rights loom largest in the political culture,
they will orient the public's understanding of judicial politics. Thus, whatever the reality of the federal judicial decision making, Republicans should
be able to decry liberal judicial activism for years to come.

The Early Obama Years

For the Bush administration, judicial politics often served as a resource, a way
to preserve the uneasy coalition that brought the Republican Party to power,
satisfying both the conservative base and the median voters Bush needed to
be reelected. For the Obama administration, however, judicial politics has not
provided a neat solution to the problem of appealing to both base and
median.

Take, for example, the arena of gay rights. Strangely enough, Obama entered office with the same position on the most prominent gay rights issue as
his predecessor, favoring civil unions but opposing marriage. Aside from this
issue, though, Obama pledged to be a "fierce advocate" for gay rights, to repeal
"Don't Ask Don't Tell," to enact a federal nondiscrimination law, and to overturn the restrictions on federal benefits to same-sex couples in the Defense of
Marriage Act (Stolberg 2010). Of these pledges, the Obama administration had
by the end of his first two years in office fulfilled only one, the repeal of Don't
Ask Don't Tell, and along the way had been criticized repeatedly for its

cautious handling of gay rights. When, for example, gay and lesbian rights organizations brought lawsuits challenging the constitutionality of the Defense of Marriage Act, the Obama Justice Department at first energetically defended the law, angering gay and lesbian rights supporters. The administration argued that it had a legal responsibility to defend the constitutionality of the law until it was repealed (Condon 2010). In 2011, however, the Obama administration reversed course and announced that it would no longer defend the law, concluding that it was unconstitutional (Savage and Stolberg 2011). On Don't Ask Don't Tell, an issue on which he clearly had support from the median voter, Obama took a go-slow approach that nearly ran aground; the Senate enacted the repeal law in the last possible moments before the Republicans took over the House in 2010. On gay marriage, meanwhile, Obama said, nearly two years into his term, that he was "wrestling with" his position and observed that "attitudes evolve, including mine." Yet Obama has continued to stick to his official position against same-sex marriage (Reeve 2010). Obama's wobbling on gay rights issues looked in some respects like a mirror image of the bobbing and weaving that characterized the Bush administration's approach in its first term. Both administrations attempted to placate an intense base while acting so as not to arouse more moderate voters. But when the *Goodrich* decision was handed down, Bush gained a resource Obama lacked, the ability to deflect attention from troublesome issues and bring his coalition together in an attack on "judicial activism." Obama instead appeared to have relied on the proper use of tempo, calculating that he could go slow enough on gay rights so as not to offend moderates, but just fast enough not to cause a rebellion from liberal supporters.

On terrorism the Obama administration also struggled to find a middle ground and was repeatedly criticized by civil liberties groups for its caution. Although Obama barred torture and fundamentally reformed the system for detaining suspected terrorists, civil liberties groups complained of the administration's use of the "state secrets privilege" to defend lawsuits seeking redress for torture and, more broadly, the administration's failure to investigate possible war crimes of Bush administration officials. Above all, Obama was criticized for failing in his campaign pledge to close the Guantanamo prison camp, though he was thwarted mainly by Congress, which barred the use of government funding to bring Guantanamo prisoners to the United States (Cole 2010).

Even judicial appointments proved difficult terrain, though here the Obama administration had some big successes, particularly at the Supreme Court level.

Like all presidents in the modern political era, Obama used his judicial appointments to curry favor with the base of his party and sympathetic political activists. Bush accomplished this goal through the use of a litmus test—does the nominee interpret the Constitution according to the principles of textualism?—validated by the Federalist Society "brand." Obama followed the playbook of previous Democratic presidents, beginning with Carter, who used the appointment of minority and female judges to "score points" with identity interest groups and minority elites in the Democratic Party (Scherer 2005).

Obama did, however, make a rhetorical shift in his approach to judicial appointments that appeared to be designed to comfort median voters. Instead of promising, as his predecessors did, simply to increase minority and female presence on the bench, Obama emphasized the experiences of his appointees and connected those experiences with their decision making. In describing his philosophy of Supreme Court nominations, Obama asserted, "We need somebody who's got the heart, the empathy, to recognize what it's like to be a young teenage mom. The empathy to understand what it's like to be poor, or African American, or gay, or disabled, or old—and that's the criterion by which I'll be selecting my judges" (Whelan 2008). President Obama thus suggested that members of marginalized groups are likely to have struggled in life, making them better situated to understand the plight of average citizens who come before the courts. In praising Sonya Sotomayor's qualifications for the Supreme Court, President Obama emphasized her background of hardship but did not stress her ethnicity or gender, saying she had "experience being tested by obstacles and barriers, by hardship and misfortune; experience insisting, persisting, and ultimately overcoming those barriers. It is experience that can give a person a common touch of compassion; an understanding of how the world works and how ordinary people live. And that is why it is a necessary ingredient in the kind of Justice we need on the Supreme Court" (Obama 2010a). Obama moved away from a "descriptive representation" justification for his appointments, in which the racial and gender makeup of an institution is constructed to reflect that of the nation, and from an emphasis on remedying past discrimination. Both of these justifications, invoked by previous Democratic presidents, can be tied in the public mind to the imposition of racial and gender quotas, which are in disrepute. By shifting the focus away from identity politics and toward a neutral standard of empathy, President Obama may have hoped to quell conservative objections to his pattern of appointment.[8] Indeed, it appears that President Obama's empathy approach may have found traction with the American public; a recent study found that 67 percent of the public believes that judges should be empathetic (Gibson 2010).

Whatever the rationale, there can be no doubt about the Obama administration's commitment to diversifying the federal bench. Far fewer than half the nominees in the first two years of Obama's presidency were white men. At the end of his first two years in office, besides his two female appointments to the Supreme Court, Obama had nominated twenty-four people to the courts of appeals, of which 21 percent were white males, and sixty-five to the district courts, of which 35 percent were white males. Sixteen of the appeals court nominees and forty-four of the district nominees were confirmed.[9]

The Obama administration struggled to fill spots on the federal judiciary, leaving an increasing number of positions vacant. This was due in large part, of course, to the many obstacles—holds, delays, and threats to filibuster—that Senate Republicans created to block the administration's nominees. Perhaps because of this determined opposition, or because of the effort put into the administration's two successful Supreme Court nominations, the administration was also slow to nominate candidates at the appellate and district court levels. By the second year of his presidency, Obama had made one-third fewer nominations than Bush did at roughly the same point,[10] a record deeply disappointing to his liberal supporters (Fletcher 2009; Stern 2010). The pace of nominations may have reflected an administration that was careful about vetting potential nominees lest they became objects of controversy, as happened during the Bush and Clinton administrations. After all, a nominee who can be portrayed as "extreme," or who can be tied to some scandal, can damage a president's standing with median voters. In a highly polarized climate, with congressional Republicans ready to seize on any misstep by the Obama administration, the cost of a "nomination gaffe" may have led the administration to be particularly cautious. Whatever the cause of the slow pace, on judicial nominations, as on judicial politics generally, where the Bush administration was frequently on the attack, the Obama administration was often on the defensive.

NOTES

1. One-third of these, however, were blocked in the Senate, where controversy over the Bush nominations for a time nearly reached the "nuclear" stage: Republicans con-

sidered eliminating the use of the filibuster for judicial nominations, a move Democrats suggested would lead to all-out war in the Senate.

2. Of course, Bush's poll numbers would plummet further in the balance of his presidency, reaching 22% in October 2008 (Nagourney and Thee 2008).

3. See *Planned Parenthood of Southeastern Pennsylvania v. Casey*, 505 U.S. 833 (1992).

4. The two female nominees, after years of awaiting confirmation, were seated on the appellate bench only after the "Gang of 14"—seven Democrats and seven Republicans in the Senate who joined forces to break the deadlock over judicial nominations—brokered a bipartisan deal to allow some of Bush's stalled nominees (including Owens and Brown) to be confirmed, while forcing other controversial nominations to be withdrawn (Babbington and Edsall 2005).

5. E.g., Bush knew that Miers would be a strong proponent of expansive executive power (Savage 2005), an issue with which the Court had been grappling in the aftermath of September 11 and which a majority of the Court had been unwilling to grant the president. See *Boumediene v. Bush*, 553 U.S. 723 (2008); *Hamdan v. Rumsfeld*, 548 U.S. 557 (2006); and *Hamdi v. Rumsfeld*, 542 U.S. 207 (2004).

6. See *Planned Parenthood of Southeastern Pennsylvania v. Casey*, 942 F2d 682 (3d Cir. 1991) (Alito, dissenting).

7. There was, however, one relevant poll conducted by the New Democrat Network that received some attention in the press (*Washington Times* 2003), which highlights voters' lack of attention to even high-profile appellate court appointment battles. The poll asked eight hundred Hispanic voters whether they supported the nomination of Miguel Estrada, a Bush nominee to the D.C. Circuit who had been embroiled in a long-standing confirmation fight with Senate Democrats since first nominated in May 2001. Sixty-one percent of respondents said they never heard of Estrada. Moreover, although 21% said they supported the Estrada nomination, interviews indicated that many of these respondents were confusing Miguel Estrada with the actor Erik Estrada, the star of the 1970s television program CHiPS (*Washington Times* 2003).

8. See Scherer (2011). As numerous public opinion polls indicate, a majority of whites favor "affirmative action," but once the question is reframed as one about "quotas" or "preferences," support precipitously drops. See, e.g., Plous (1996). Polls that give respondents only two choices on the affirmative action issue (keep affirmative action "as it currently exists" or "no affirmative action whatsoever") are flawed; when given in-between options, a *Time*/CNN Poll found that 80% of the public wants to continue affirmative action in some form (Shelton and Minor 1995, citing Harris Poll, conducted March 16–18, 1995; Quinnipiac University Polling Institute 2009).

In addition, two Supreme Court rulings between the Clinton and Obama presidencies made the government's use of benign race preferences subject to strict scrutiny standards. See *Grutter v. Bollinger*, 539 U.S. 306, 343 (plan to admit undergraduate university students based in part on race held unconstitutional); *Parents Involved in Community Schools v. Seattle School Dist. No. 1*, 551 U.S. 701, 748 (2007) (plan to assign children to elementary public schools based in part by race held unconstitutional).

9. For the courts of appeals, the gender, race, and ethnicity breakdown for Obama's judicial nominees is as follows: five black men (four confirmed), one black woman (confirmed), two Hispanic men (one confirmed), one Hispanic woman (confirmed), two Asian men (one confirmed), eight white women (four confirmed), and five white men (four confirmed). For the district courts, the gender, race, and ethnicity break-

down is as follows: six black men (four confirmed), seven black women (seven confirmed), three Hispanic men (one confirmed), three Hispanic women (one confirmed), two Asian men (one confirmed), four Asian women (four confirmed), seventeen white women (twelve confirmed), and twenty-three white men (fourteen confirmed).

10. By the end of his second year in office, Bush nominated thirty-two courts of appeals judges, compared with Obama's twenty-four (66.7% of Bush's total). As for district courts, Bush nominated a total of ninety-eight people, and Obama sixty-five (66.2% of Bush's total). See www.thomas.gov/home/nomis.html (107th and 111th Congresses).

WORKS CITED

Adams, Rebecca. 2005. "Hard-Fought Energy Bill Clears." *Congessional Quarterly Weekly Report*, August 1, 2005.

Albertson, Bethany. 2006. "Dog-Whistle Politics, Coded Communication and Religious Appeals." Unpublished manuscript.

Babbington, Charles, and Thomas B. Edsall. 2005. "Conservative Republicans Divided over Nominee." *Washington Post*, October 4, 2005.

Baker, Peter, and Charles Babbington. 2005. "Role of Religion Emerges as Issue." *Washington Post*, October 13, 2005. Available at www.washingtonpost.com/wp-dyn/content/article/2005/10/12/AR2005101201381.html.

Barnes, Jeb. 2011. *Dust-Up: Asbestos Litigation and the Failure of Commonsense Reform.* Washington, DC: Georgetown University Press.

Bartels, Brandon L., and Christopher D. Johnston. 2008. "How Should Supreme Court Selection Processes Be Conducted?" Paper presented at the 2008 Annual Meeting of the American Political Science Association, Boston, MA.

Benac, Nancy. 2005. "Group Becoming Must for Some Conservatives." Associated Press, July 18, 2005. Available at www.law.yale.edu/documents/pdf/Student_Organizations/Fed_Soc_Group_Becoming_a_Must.pdf.

Bossert, Rex. 1997. "Conservative Forum Is a Quiet Power." *National Law Journal*, September 8, 1997, A1.

Bumiller, Elizabeth. 2004. "Bush Said His Party Was Wrong to Oppose Gay Civil Unions." *New York Times*, October 26, 2004.

———. 2005. "Pillow-Talk Pressure for a Woman in O'Connor's Robe." *New York Times*, July 18, 2005.

Bumiller, Elizabeth, and David Stout. 2005. "Bush Nominating John G. Roberts Jr. to Supreme Court." *New York Times*, July 19, 2005.

Burke, Thomas F. 2002. *Lawyers, Lawsuits and Legal Rights*. Berkeley: University of California Press.

Bush, George W. 2003. State of the Union Address, January 28, 2003.

———. 2004a. "President Calls for Constitutional Amendment Protecting Marriage." Washington, D.C., February 24, 2004. Available at www.whitehouse.gov/news/releases/2004/02/20040224-2.html.

———. 2004b. State of the Union Address, January 20, 2004.

———. 2005a. Judicial Nominations—Harriet Miers, October 3, 2005. Available at www.whitehouse.gov/infocus/judicialnominees/miers.html.

————. 2005b. "President Discusses Medical Liability Reform." Collinsville, IL, January 5, 2005. Available at www.whitehouse.gov/news/releases/2005/01/20050105-4.html.

————. 2005c. State of the Union Address, February 2, 2005.

————. 2006. State of the Union Address, January 31, 2006.

————. 2008. State of the Union Address, January 28, 2008.

Chimerine, Lawrence, and Ross Eisenbrey. 2005. "The Frivolous Case for Tort Law Change: Opponents of the Legal System Exaggerate Its Costs, Ignore Its Benefits." *Economic Policy Institute Briefing Paper #157.* Washington, DC: Economic Policy Institute.

CNN/*USA Today*/Gallup Poll. 2006. "Majority Would Oppose Alito If He Would Overturn Roe" (January 10). Available at http://edition.cnn.com/2006/POLITICS/01/09/alito.poll/.

Coats, Dan. 2007. "Anatomy of a Nomination: A Year Later, What Went Wrong, What Went Right and What We Can Learn from the Battles over Alito and Miers." *Hamline Journal of Public Law and Policy* 28:405–30.

Cole, David. 2010. "Breaking Away: Obama's War on Terror Is Not 'Bush Lite.'" *New Republic*, December 30, 2010.

Condon, George E. 2010. "Judgment Calls on Gay Rights." *National Journal*, October 16, 2010.

Epstein, Lee, and Jeffrey A. Segal. 2005. *Advice and Consent: The Politics of Judicial Appointments.* New York: Oxford University Press.

Ertelt, Steven. 2005. "Pro-Life Women Judges Likely Top President Bush's Supreme Court List. LifeNews.com, September 16, 2005. Available at: http://freerepublic.com/focus/f-news/1485432/posts.

Fletcher, Michael. 2009. "Obama Criticized as Too Cautious, Slow on Judicial Posts." *Washington Post*, October 16, 2009.

Gallup Poll. 2005. Available at www.gallup.com/poll/1576/Abortion.aspx.

Gibson, James L. 2010. "Expecting Justice and Hoping for Empathy." June 20, 2010. Available at www.miller-mccune.com/legal-affairs/expecting-justice-and-hoping-for-empathy-17677.

Goldman, Sheldon. 1997. *Picking Federal Judges: Lower Court Selection from Roosevelt through Regan.* New Haven, CT: Yale University Press.

Graber, Mark A. 2006. *Dred Scott and the Problem of Constitutional Evil.* New York: Cambridge University Press.

Haltom, William, and Michael McCann. 2005. *Distorting the Law: Politics, Media and the Litigation Crisis.* Chicago: University of Chicago Press.

Herszenhorn, David. 2007. "House Approves Broad Protections for Gay Workers." *New York Times*, November 7, 2000.

Hicks, George W. 2006. "The Conservative Influence of the Federalist Society on the Harvard Law School Student Body." *Harvard Journal of Law and Public Policy* 29:625–717.

Kirkpatrick, David. 2004. "Speaking in the Tongue of Evangelicals." *New York Times*, October 17, 2004, D15.

Jacobs, Lawrence R., and Robert Y. Shapiro. 2000. *Politicians Don't Pander: Political Manipulation and the Loss of Democratic Responsiveness.* Chicago: University of Chicago Press.

Keck, Thomas M. 2004. *The Most Activist Supreme Court in History: The Road to Modern Judicial Conservatism.* Chicago: University of Chicago Press.

Kohut, Andrew. 2005. "A Political Victory That Wasn't." *New York Times,* March 23, 2005.

Kuo, David. 2007. *Tempting Faith: An Inside Story of Political Seduction.* New York: Free Press.

Kuo, David, and John J. DiIulio Jr. 2008. "The Faith to Outlast Politics." *New York Times,* January 29, 2008, A28.

Labaton, Stephen. 2005. "Quick Early Gains Embolden Business Lobby. *New York Times,* February 17, 2005, C1.

Lewis, Neil. 2000. "The 2000 Campaign: The Judiciary." *New York Times,* October 8, 2000.

Luntz, Frank. 2006. *Words That Work: It's Not What You Say, It's What People Hear.* New York: Hyperion.

Meyer, Eugune. 2002. Telephone interview with Nancy Scherer. Tape recording, July 30. East Hampton, NY.

Milbank, Dana. 2004. "A New Problem, or the Wrong Word." *Washington Post,* September 7, 2004, A06.

Nagourney, Adam, and Megan Thee. 2008. "Poll Finds Obama Gaining Support and McCain Weakened in Bailout Crisis." *New York Times,* October 2, 2008.

National Organization for Women. 2005. "Save the Supreme Court—Save Women's Lives." Available at www.now.org/issues/judicial/supreme/womannominee .html.

Obama, Barack. 2010a. "Obama Introduces Sotomayor." *Blog of the Legal Times,* May 26, 2009. Available at http://legaltimes.typepad.com/blt/2009/05/transcript-obama -introduces-sotomayor.html.

———. 2010b. "Remarks by the President in the State of the Union Address." January 27, 2010. Available at www.whitehouse.gov/the-press-office/remarks-president-state -union-address.

O'Beirne, Kate. 2005. "Set-Aside Set-to: If You're Going to Practice Affirmative Action on the Court. . . ." *National Review,* November 7, 2005.

Plous, Scott. 1996. "Ten Myths about Affirmative Action." *J. Soc. Issues* 52, no. 4: 25, 27.

Purdham, Todd S. 2005. "In Pursuit of Conservative Stamp, President Nominates Roberts." *New York Times,* July 20, 2005.

Quinnipiac University Polling Institute. 2009. "New Poll: Overwhelming Opposition to Race Preferences." Available at www.discriminations.us/2009/06/.

Reagan, Ronald. 1981. "First Inaugural Address." Washington, D.C., January 20, 1981. Available at www.americanrhetoric.com/speeches/ronaldreagandfirstinaugural.html.

Reeve, Elspeth. 2010. "Is Obama Just Stringing Gay Rights Supporters Along?" *National Journal,* October 28, 2010. Available at www.nationaljournal.com/dailyfray/is-obama -just-stringing-gay-rights-activists-along—20101028.

Reichmann, Nan. 2005. "Bush Nominates Conservative Roberts for Supreme Court." Associated Press, July 19, 2005.

Reid, Harry. 2005. "From Energy to Katrina Relief, Reid Says Together We Can Do Better." Statement on the Senate floor. October 4, 2005. Available at http://democrats .senate.gov/2005/10/04/.

Republican Party. 2000. Republican Party Platform of 2000. July 31, 2000. Available at www.presidency.ucsb.edu/ws/index.php?pid=25849#axzz1VJbw9IF1.

———. 2008. Republican Party Platform 2008. Available at www.gop.com/2008Platform/.

Rosen, Jeffrey. 2006. *The Most Democratic Branch*. New York: Oxford University Press.

Rove, Karl. 2005. "Our Courts Are in Crisis." Address to the Federalist Society, Washington, D.C., November 10, 2005. Available at www.americanrhetoric.com/speeches/karlrovefederalist.html.

Savage, Charlie. 2005. "Miers Has Backed Wide Executive Role." *Boston Globe*, October 5, 2005.

Savage, Charlie, and Sheryl Gay Stolberg. 2011. "In Shift, U.S. Says Marriage Act Blocks Gay Rights." *New York Times*, February 23, 2011.

Scherer, Nancy. 2005. Scoring Points: Politicians, Activists and the Lower Federal Court Appointment Process. Stanford: Stanford University Press.

———. 2011. "Diversifying the Federal Bench: Is Universal Legitimacy for the U.S. Courts Possible?" *Northwestern Law Journal* 105:1–47.

Scherer, Nancy, and Banks Miller. 2009. "The Federalist Society's Influence on the Federal Judiciary." *Political Research Quarterly* 62:366–78.

Shelton, Melinda L., and Diane Minor. 1995. "Poll Supports NOW's Affirmative Action Position." Available at www.now.org/nnt/05-95/poll.html.

Stern, Seth. 2010. "Bench-Clearing Brawl Continues." *CQ Weekly*, September 27, 2010, 2212–14.

Stolberg, Sheryl Gay. 2010. "One Battle Finished, Activists Shift Sights." *New York Times*, December 20, 2010.

Teles, Steven. 2008. *The Rise of the Conservative Legal Movement*. Princeton, NJ: Princeton University Press.

Toner, Robin, and Marjorie Connelly. 2005. "Bush's Support on Major Issues Tumbles in Polls." *New York Times*, June 17, 2005.

Towers Perrin Tillinghast. 2006. *2006 Update on Tort Cost Trends*.

"2000 Unofficial Debate Transcript," First Gore-Bush Presidential Debate, University of Massachusetts–Boston, Boston, Massachusetts, October 3, 2000. Available at Commission on Presidential Debates website: www.debates.org/index.php?page=october-3-2000-transcript.

"2000 Unofficial Debate Transcript," Second Gore-Bush Presidential Debate, Wake Forest University, Winston-Salem, North Carolina, October 11, 2000. Available at Commission on Presidential Debates website: www.debates.org/index.php?page=october-11-2000-debate-transcript.

"2004 Debate Transcript," Second Bush-Kerry Presidential Debate, Washington University, St. Louis, Missouri, October 8, 2004. Available at Commission on Presidential Debates website: www.debates.org/index.php?page=october-8-2004-debate-transcript.

Washington, Wayne. 2003. "Bush Lifts Steel Import Tariffs Industry Angry; Trade War Averted." *Boston Globe*, December 5, 2003, A1.

Washington Times. 2003. "Hispanics Tune Out Estrada Filibuster." *Washington Times*, June 19, 2003. Available at www.washtimes.com/news/2003/jun/19/20030619-4622r/.

Whelan, Edwin. 2008. "Obama's Constitution: The Rhetoric and Reality." *Weekly Standard* 13, no. 26 (March 17, 2008). Available at www.weeklystandard.com/Content/Public/Articles/000/000/014/849oyckg.asp.

Zogby American Survey. 2005. "Bush Job Approval Hits 41%—All Time Low; Would Lose to Every Modern President; Public Rates All Levels of Government Poorly in Katrina Handling; Red Cross Rated Higher than Federal Government, 69%–17%" (September 5). Available at www.zogby.com/news/2005/09/08/.

CHAPTER EIGHT

A Feint to the Center, a Move Backward

Bush's Clear Skies Initiative and the Politics of Policymaking

David Emer

"In one respect, possibly no president in American history has surpassed George W. Bush," writes David Mayhew in his concluding chapter. Mayhew continues, "Bush stood out as an eyes-open promoter of a policy menu targeting, on the one hand, 'the party base' but also, on the other hand, 'the center' or 'the median voter' or voters who might 'expand the party coalition'" (see chap. 13).

The politics and policy of Clear Skies were part of the "difficult, dissonant game" where party leaders attempted to balance the views of base and median voters to win elections. Levin, DiSalvo, and Emer explain in the introduction that parties navigate the tensions between their base and the political center to try to maintain the election support of both groups. These groups, by their nature, have differing or conflicting policy preferences. The following partisan statement, made by President George W. Bush in a closed-door meeting with congressional Republicans, is an example of policy targeting. The president said, "We need clear-skies legislation, so that we can say our party has led to reasonable, sane environmental policy."[1] The intent is to use a major presidential policy initiative as a way to gain votes for the party.

Politically, air pollution is the subject of intense battles between the energy industry and environmental groups. The Bush administration's Clear Skies legislative proposal consisted of new "market-based" cap and trade programs to regulate sulfur dioxide, nitrogen oxides, and mercury that would replace "command and control" environmental permitting programs, among other programs.

The actions of the Bush administration on Clear Skies indicate that two groups were targeted. The substance of Clear Skies benefited the business base constituency because, on balance, it weakened air pollution policy. At the same time, in order to make the policy appeal to moderates, the administration cast Clear Skies as environmental policy reform (a "new generation of tools" for clean air) rather than a retreat from clean air. The moderate political rhetoric advancing Clear Skies constituted a feint to the center, while the base-oriented details of the policy constituted a move backward on air pollution policy.

Policy Choices and Their Consequences in the Context of the Clean Air Act

Air pollution policy choices are dependent on the politics and the policy regime of the 1970 Clean Air Act. The pathbreaking Clean Air Act, passed in 1970, set the goal of clean air for every American. Section 111 of the Clean Air Act requires the Environmental Protection Agency (EPA) to establish National Ambient Air Quality Standards (NAAQS) for air pollutants. The statute does not specifically define the pollutants to be regulated, leaving that discretionary authority to the EPA. A recent Supreme Court case declared that NAAQS lie at the very heart of the Clean Air Act.[2]

In *Clean Coal/Dirty Air*, William Hassler and Bruce Ackerman defined the Clean Air Act as an "agency-forcing statute." They explain that agency forcing provides a means for removing an issue from the general run of agency discretion and instead guiding policy in a particular direction. However, the statute's nature also signals congressional recognition that the issue requires the exercise of expert judgment that cannot be applied directly from Capitol Hill.[3] Under the Clean Air Act policy regime, the EPA is given discretion in setting regulations but only so far as it continually works toward the rights-based goal of clean air for every American.

In the 1977 Clean Air Amendments, a distinction was drawn between the areas of the country that had attained and those that had not attained the

NAAQS. Whether a particular area of the country meets the air quality standard determines the stringency of permitting for every industrial and power plant construction project. In areas of the country where the air quality standard is met, the Prevention of Significant Deterioration (PSD) program applies. It requires new or modified pollution sources to install Best Available Control Technology (BACT).[4] In areas of the country where the air quality standard has not been met, the Part D New Source Review (NSR) requires new pollution sources or modified sources to install less stringent Lowest Achievable Emission Rate (LAER) technology.[5] As a convention, both programs are together referred to as NSR.

In addition to the NSR program, cap and trade programs also regulate air pollution. A cap and trade program caps the emissions of a particular pollutant for a nation or region. It allows power plants to trade allowances to pollute, which are the "currency" of the total emission limit. Since all pollution sources must adhere to the predefined cap, old sources and new sources are treated more equally.

In 1990, a significant cap and trade program was established to address power plant sulfur dioxide pollution that causes acid rain. The program has been widely heralded for its ability to achieve a significant reduction in these emissions at a cost far lower than projected.[6] The reason for the lower cost of reducing pollution is that pollution sources were able to earn higher profits if they reduced pollution in the most cost-effective manner. For industry, pollution abatement was not something to be avoided, but rather something that could save money. The reductions came from a mix of added pollution control technologies and the use of low-sulfur coal. Specifically, approximately 40 percent of the reductions came from the use of scrubbers. Sixty percent of the reductions came from switching to low-sulfur coal—a switch that was greatly assisted by the deregulation of railroads, which made western low-sulfur coal cheaper to transport as railroad shipping rates became lower.[7]

The Clear Skies Strategy

The Bush administration's Clear Skies strategy involved changes to the 1970s-era NSR programs and the 1990 cap and trade program. The administration attempted to accomplish the goals of Clear Skies through both the legislative and regulatory policy levers. The administration's approach to air pollution was pursued concurrently and consistently through the eight years of the Bush administration. The legislative Clear Skies proposal would have weakened many of the command and control programs of the 1970 Clean Air Act, including NSR, and it would have replaced them with cap and trade programs that would not reduce air pollution as quickly as an unchanged Clean Air Act likely would have. The cap and trade programs of the Clear Skies Initiative would have built on the existing programs for sulfur dioxide and a nitrogen oxides cap and trade program started in 1998.

Clear Skies also would have created a new cap and trade program for mercury. The reason for the new mercury program was that the Clinton administration had declared mercury a hazardous air pollutant, which would subject it to stricter emissions limits than the Bush administration wanted to accept. The top policymakers at the EPA came to believe that the concerns over mercury were more political than scientific.[8] The Clear Skies Initiative would also have curtailed a number of regulatory provisions of the Clean Air Act, most notably the NSR permitting program.

Finally, the Clear Skies Initiative was significant for what it did not include: a cap and trade program for carbon dioxide, the pollutant that causes global warming. The president had pledged to cap carbon dioxide pollution during the 2000 campaign. This decision was the first reversal on any policy issue for the not-even-two-month-old administration.[9] The administration linked the California energy crisis and rolling blackouts to the global warming issue. In a letter to a group of Republican senators who had been advocating the reversal, Bush wrote, "At a time when California has already experienced energy shortages, and other Western states are worried about price and availability of energy this summer, we must be very careful not to take actions that could harm consumers. This is especially true given the incomplete state of scientific knowledge of the causes of, and solutions to, global climate change and the lack of commercially available technologies for removing and storing carbon dioxide."[10] These two sentences attempted to both emphasize the gravity of the energy shortages and give credence to skeptics of global warming. On *Meet the Press*, economic advisor Lawrence Lindsey put the issue in far starker terms, by saying, "We have a choice in this country of having the lights on or, at least in the short run, having more carbon dioxide."[11] The position reversal was permanent for the duration of the administration and became an obstacle to achieving a compromise on emission reductions during the Clear Skies congressional debate.

Through Bush's two presidential terms, the Clear Skies strategy also consisted of a series of Clean Air Act rules that attempted to accomplish most of the cap and trade expansions (once again excluding carbon dioxide) and NSR changes in the Clear Skies legislative proposal. One set of rules implemented cap and trade programs to address sulfur dioxide, nitrogen oxides, and mercury pollution that was very similar to the legislative proposal. The second set of rules changed NSR in a way that made it easier for utilities to upgrade their plants while maintaining their valuable grandfathered status. Both sets of rules were largely struck down by the courts as being inconsistent with the Clean Air Act. The courts ruled that they failed to accomplish the air pollution reduction goals of the Clean Air Act statute under which they were promulgated.

In defending Clear Skies legislation and the rulemakings, the Bush administration used the rhetoric of environmental regulation reform in a way that seemed to be aimed at convincing the median voter that the administration was seeking a reasonable environmental policy that would improve air quality. EPA administrator Christine Whitman, a New Jersey moderate Republican, testified before the Environment and Public Works (EPW) Committee, "Clear Skies is a powerful new tool for the next generation of air quality, building on the success of the Clean Air Act, while recognizing its original command and control methodology might not be the most efficient way to continue to improve our air."[12] In his 2005 State of the Union address, the president stated, "My Clear Skies legislation will cut power-plant pollution and improve the health of our citizens."[13]

An official NSR study committee published a report in the National Academies Press that suggests that the rhetoric of Clear Skies as an expansion of the Clean Air Act was incongruous with the substance of the signature environmental proposal. The report concluded that Clear Skies would have likely reduced pollution at a slower rate than an unchanged Clean Air Act would have.[14] A Congressional Research Service report also notes that the EPA's own analysis revealed that the Clear Skies Initiative would not achieve two air quality standards under Clean Air Act deadlines.[15] The Clear Skies policy benefited the energy industry of the business base. Martin Shapiro's chapter characterizes the energy industry as "the most inner circle" of the president's base. After all, the president and the vice president both were from the energy industry. There were more executives from energy than from any other industry group among President Bush's most elite fund-raisers, called

"Pioneers," who each generated more than $100,000 in donations during the 2000 election.[16]

Three Scenarios

From the perspective of the business base, the Clear Skies strategy could have led to three possible scenarios.

Scenario I: The Legislative Route. The first scenario would be successful enactment of the Clear Skies legislative proposal. Legislative success would have permanently recast air pollution policy by eliminating many Clean Air Act programs and would likely delay the rate of air pollution reductions.

Scenario II: The Regulatory Route. The second scenario would involve no statutory changes, but successful implementation of the regulations promulgated under existing Clean Air Act rulemaking authority. The Clean Air Act would not have been altered as fundamentally, but the change would have slowed down air pollution reductions for the time being.

Scenario III: Delay. The third scenario, in fact, occurred. The Bush administration failed to enact the legislative proposal and was blocked by the courts in enacting most of the regulatory changes. However, the absence of full implementation of the Clean Air Act during the Bush years was a valuable result for the business base.

As an environmental consultant who was heavily involved in developing alternative legislation to Clear Skies, Michael Bradley, argued, "The Bush administration bought the coal industry a pass for eight years. It was worth millions and millions."[17] Since the air pollution policy of the Clean Air Act mandated aggressive and timely reductions in air pollution, the Bush administration's strategy delayed air pollution reductions. Minimizing changes to the status quo air quality standard was valuable to energy interests. This consequence of delay satisfied the business base.

Looking Ahead

The conclusion to this chapter provides a realpolitik explanatory framework to this story. If Clear Skies had passed, it would have led to a reduction in air quality regulation. But if there was a deadlock and Clear Skies did not pass, there were still two possibilities that would satisfy business allies in the Bush administration. First, the rules that altered the Clean Air Act might be accepted by the courts. Second, the next possibility was that the courts would reject the rules, as they did. However, the time spent promulgating weaker rules than the statute called for contributed to delayed air quality improvements even though those rules were ultimately rejected by the courts. Battling out the details in court gave business eight years of relaxed environmental enforcement. Yet throughout the Clear Skies debate, the Bush administration consistently cast Clear Skies as a policy that reformed environmental regulation but expanded it too. The Bush administration produced changes in policy effects without changes in formal policies. The actions of the administration produced a free ride of no significant new standards for industry.

The Unsuccessful Pursuit of Scenario I: The Legislative Route

The Clear Skies Initiative did receive serious legislative attention in 2003 and then again in 2005. But, after its initial formal announcement on Valentine's Day in 2002, the Bush administration's decision not to release technical data related to Clear Skies delayed legislative action such that Clear Skies saw little attention in the 107th Congress. At the time, subcommittee chairman Joe L. Barton (R-TX) of the House Energy and Commerce Subcommittee on Energy and Air Quality said he wanted the analysis as soon as possible. "None of the staffers on the Hill have [any] idea what the technical basis is," which made it hard for Republicans to defend the Clear Skies proposal.[18] Even the legislative language was not released until August 3, 2002.[19] This was too late for any meaningful action on Clear Skies with the 2002 midterm elections looming.

The Clear Skies Initiative saw serious legislative attention during the 108th Congress in 2003 and the 109th Congress in 2005 when the Republicans were in control of both houses of Congress. The 2003 Clear Skies legislation was the administration bill. The 2005 Clear Skies was an amended version of the administration bill and was introduced by Senator James Inhofe, chairman of the EPW Committee. The two major changes in Senator Inhofe's version of Clear Skies were that mercury standards were made less stringent and an opt-in provision was created so that non-electricity generation pollution sources could join the cap and trade program. The opt-in provision was significant because it would make non-electricity-producing sources of pollution not subject to state and local regulation if these sources chose the federal standard. The 2003 version of Clear Skies was stalled when Republican senator

Lamar Alexander, a member of EPW, declined to support it. The 2005 Inhofe version failed after a 9–9 vote in the EPW Committee. Senator Lincoln Chafee (R-RI) and Senator Max Baucus (D-MT) were seen as the swing voters, and they both decided to side with the Democrats to stop the bill.

A major impetus behind the second attempt to pass Clear Skies was the looming June 2005 deadline for the Bush administration to promulgate mercury regulations under the Clean Air Act. This deadline was set into motion by Clinton EPA administrator Carol Browner's decision to declare mercury a hazardous air pollutant under the Clean Air Act. Passing Clear Skies would have removed the possibility that the Bush administration's controversial approach to mercury regulation would be overturned by the courts.

In determining why Scenario I was unsuccessful, I will address a major question of this volume, which is also directly posed in Kent Weaver's Social Security policymaking chapter: what determines the fate of base-oriented initiatives, under what conditions do they win enactment, either in a form that is close to the president's preferences or significantly different from the president's preferences, and when do they fail to be enacted at all? The likely reasons why Clear Skies failed to be enacted in a form close to the president's preferences was that there were credible Democratic alternative framings and alternative proposals. As Weaver suggests in his chapter, base-oriented initiatives are likely to fail when there are alternative framings at least as plausible as the president's and when those alternative framers have resourceful advocates. For Clear Skies, most of the framings of Clear Skies were dependent on one's view of the effectiveness of the Clean Air Act. Without passage of Clear Skies or a Democratic alternative proposal, the Clean Air Act still forces the EPA to keep working toward the goal of full attainment of clean air. The crux of the debate about Clear Skies was the disagreement over what rate air pollution would be reduced with an unchanged Clean Air Act. The Democrats and their environmentalist allies claimed that Clear Skies would allow air pollution to be reduced more slowly than an unchanged Clean Air Act would have.

On Clear Skies, the Bush administration framers presented Clear Skies as a regulatory reform initiative, meaning that it would continue to improve air quality like the Clean Air Act currently does, but it would do it in a more cost-effective way. From early on, environmentalists attacked Clear Skies as a sham that would permit more pollution than the Clean Air Act would permit unaltered. David Hawkins, climate change director at the Natural Resources

Defense Council (NRDC), said, "the administration plan would result in millions of tons more pollution than faithful enforcement of the current law."[20]

The administration was "surprised" by this line of attack. Deputy EPA administrator Jeffrey Holmstead expected criticism from environmental groups. He said, "All of us who worked on Clear Skies assumed that as soon as the President announced the proposal environmental groups would jump on it and say it didn't go far enough, quick enough—that was a fair debate." He continued, "But all of us were also completely unprepared for the charge that we were gutting the Clean Air Act. In our view, that accusation was pretty dishonest."[21]

The debate took on this unusual character because of the agency-forcing nature of the Clean Air Act.[22] Without Clear Skies, the Clean Air Act continues to force the EPA to work toward the goal of full attainment of clean air. Some environmental policy experts believe that this so-called total victory is impossible. Shep Melnick affirms the historical role of the Clean Air Act's deadlines as being political. Melnick explains that the deadlines are supposedly based on a point where the pollution level is "safe." Melnick writes, "Most scientists now agree that for most pollutants there is no health effects threshold, that is, a concentration below which there are no serious health effects and above which there are."[23] Melnick explains that environmentalists point to the Clean Air Act deadlines as a benchmark: any proposal that mandates slower reductions is pegged as anti-environment.

Nevertheless, the Clean Air Act gives the EPA discretion in attaining these goals, and supporters and opponents of Clear Skies disagreed over how EPA would be forced to use its discretion in the absence of a statutory change, such as Clear Skies or a Democratic alternative. David Hawkins claimed that the administration used a "Rip Van Winkle" scenario for what the EPA would do to continue reducing air pollution. In effect, Hawkins argued that the administration touted benefits in air quality under the assumption that the agency stops promulgating new rules to improve air quality. Given the complexity and uncertainty about what is required by the agency-forcing Clean Air Act, credibility was a major issue.

The administration's credibility was undermined by a PowerPoint presentation that Jeffrey Holmstead delivered to the Edison Electric Institute (EEI) that was released under a Freedom of Information Act request. In December 2001, the EPA told the EEI that if Clear Skies was not passed, an equivalent Maximum Achievable Control Technology (MACT) standard for power plants would reduce mercury emissions from 48 tons to 5 tons nationwide by the end of 2007.[24] By comparison, the administration's version of Clear Skies called for more lenient caps of 26 tons by 2010 and 15 tons by 2018. Senator Inhofe's version of Clear Skies called for an even more lenient cap of 34 tons by 2010 and 15 tons by 2018. The presentation provided apparent proof of the environmentalists' contention that Clear Skies weakened the current requirements of the Clean Air Act.

An irony of the situation was that the Bush administration likely never intended to use the MACT standard. One EPA career official who helped prepare the EEI presentation says that the agency basically "created the business-as-usual scenario [of what would happen under the Clean Air Act] out of whole cloth. To be honest, we wanted to scare the hell out of the utility industry."[25] The real motivation behind the EEI presentation appeared to be to garner industry support for Clear Skies.

The administration's credibility on Clear Skies as a piece of legislation truly designed to promote air pollution reduction was undermined by a number of other provisions as well. One issue was the ability of polluters to bank allowances to use in future years. By overcomplying with the caps in Phase I, sources of pollution can apply those extra allowances toward the Phase II reductions, pushing back the 2018 date when the Phase II cap on emissions would actually have been reached. John Graham, the so-called regulatory czar at the Office of Management and Budget, pointed out that the 70 percent uniform reduction levels of sulfur dioxide, nitrogen oxides, and mercury by 2018 were an important reason why the caps were set where they were in the development of the Clear Skies proposal.[26] In his 2003 State of the Union address, President Bush claimed that his air pollution plan "mandates a 70-percent cut in air pollution from power plants over the next 15 years."[27] This suggests that the 70 percent reduction would happen by 2018. However, Walke testified in 2005 that the "EPA and the Energy Department have told us plainly that this legislation will not achieve actual pollution reductions of 70 percent until sometime after 2025." Walke framed this issue as the "biggest lie behind the bill."[28] Shi-Ling Hsu, who criticizes NSR and advocates the concept of cap and trade, wrote, "President Bush's 'Clear Skies' pollution program, for example, proposes the use of cap and-trade programs, but the program is hopelessly unambitious, setting lenient pollution reduction targets that culminate in 2018. It would be misguided to blame the emissions trading concept, and not the administration, for this fecklessness."[29] The administration thought that these arguments were exaggerated. In a personal interview, Graham responded, "Early reductions against the Phase I cap did permit banking against the Phase II cap. I viewed this issue as minor because the Phase II cap was likely to be tightened again in the long run anyway."[30] Also, the issue of banking was not unique to Clear Skies. Despite being widely heralded as a success, the 1990 acid rain cap and trade program permitted utilities to transfer unused allowances to deficient utilities throughout the nation or to "bank" excess allowances and use or sell them in future years.[31] Nonetheless, the "banking" argument put forward by Walke did support the contention that "enforcing today's Clean Air Act will clean up power plant pollution more than a decade sooner than S.131 [Clear Skies], enabling 159 million additional Americans to breathe healthy air by the end of this decade." The "banking" aspect of cap and trade was a complex component of Clear Skies. The environmentalists and the Democrats utilized the ability of utilities to "bank" allowances to support their alternative framing that Clear Skies was a stealth measure with a misleading name. The administration and Senate Republicans thought that it was an unfair attack given that it is a known aspect of cap and trade and that the ability of utilities to "bank" allowances was not a stealth provision.

In addition to a credible alternative framing of Clear Skies, there also was a credible alternative proposal. There is an important distinction between these two concepts. As Weaver's chapter explains, an alternative framing is an opposing argument that frames an issue in such a way that a rational person could conclude that a presidential initiative should not be passed. An alternative proposal is an alternative bill to address the same public policy issue. On Social Security privatization legislation, the Democrats articulated an alternative framing to the issue. They suggested that Bush's plan would undermine Social Security. But they deliberately did not put forward an alternative proposal. For Democrats, the status quo was not just sufficient for Social Security; it was preferable. In clean air policy, for Democrats, the status quo was not only insufficient but retrograde, at least in the sense that Democrats believed that air quality needed to be improved dramatically.

In the Clear Skies debate, two major alternative proposals were put forward by the Senate Democrats: Senator Jeffords's bill (the Clean Power Act) and Senator Carper's bill (the Clean Air Planning Act) (see table 8.1). What they shared in common was that they both included mandatory caps on carbon dioxide, the pollutant that causes global warming, and they did not change NSR or any other major portions of the Clean Air Act.

Table 8.1 Clear Skies and Democratic alternatives

Pollutant	Clear Skies	Jeffords (Clean Power Act)	Carper (Clean Air Planning Act)
		108th Congress	
SO_2	2010: 4.5 2018: 3.0	2010: 2.25	2009: 4.5 2013: 3.5 2016: 2.25
NO_x	2008: 2.1 2018: 1.7	2010: 1.51	2009: 1.87 2013: 1.7
CO_2	Not covered	2010: 2.050 (507.2 MMTCE)	2009: 2006 emissions* (2.655 billion tons, 656.9 MMTCE) 2013: 2001 emissions* (2.454 billion tons, 607.2 MMTCE)
Hg	2010: 26 2018: 15	2010: 5 No Hg trading. Hg unit-specific emissions limitation of no greater than 2.48 g/1,000 MWh in 2009	2009: 24 2013: 10 Includes Hg unit-specific limit
(Birthday provision)		Facilities subject to BACT limits after 1/1/2014, or 40 years after commencement of generation, whichever comes later	Starting in 2020, affected units on which construction commenced before 8/17/1971 must meet performance standards for SO_2 and NO_x
		109th Congress	
SO_2	2010: 4.5 2018: 3.0	2010: 2.25	2010: 4.5 2015: 2
NO_x	2008: 2.2 2018: 1.8	2010: 1.51	2009: 1.9 (East) 2010: 1.9 (West)
CO_2	Not covered	2010: 2.050 (507.2 MMTCE)	2010: 2.65 2015: 2.45
Hg	2010: 34 2018: 15	2010: 5	2010: 19–23 2015: 7–8

Sources: Environmental Protection Agency, Office of Air and Radiation, *Multi-Pollutant Analysis: Comparison Briefing*, October 2005; Larry Parker and John Blodgett, "Air Quality: Multi-Pollutant Legislation," *Congressional Research Service*, May 2006.

Note: NO_x and SO_2 (millions of tons), CO_2 (billions of tons), Hg (tons).

*May be achieved using emissions offsets.

The Jeffords bill set more aggressive targets for pollution reduction than Senator Carper's bill did. It saw the most legislative action when Senator Jeffords was chair of the EPW Committee after he left the Republican Party, handing control of the Senate to the Democrats. On June 27, 2002, the EPW Committee approved Senator Jeffords's bill on a 10–9 party-line vote.[32] According to Frank O'Donnell of Clean Air Trust, Senator Lincoln Chafee and Senator Carper both voted for Jeffords's bill but would not support the bill on the Senate floor without significant modifications because they believed that its targets were too stringent. In other words, it was not a vote for Senator Jeffords's bill, but a party-line vote against Clear Skies.[33] No additional action was taken on the bill after the successful committee vote. After 2002, when the Democrats lost control of the Senate, the significance of the Jeffords bill was that it represented the left flank of potential courses of action on utility pollution.

Senator Carper's bill was more significant in defeating Clear Skies than Jeffords's bill because it was seen as a reasonable alternative by some Republicans, moderate Democrats, and some in the utility sector. Michael Bradley is an environmental consultant who helped develop Senator Carper's bill. He said, "It was credible, real, [and the goal was] to derail Clear Skies." Senator Carper's bill was similar to Jeffords's bill in that it did not make major changes to NSR or other regulatory provisions of the Clean Air Act. A second similarity to the Jeffords bill was that it included a cap on carbon dioxide. Most significant, though, was that the Carper bill would cost industry an amount that was comparable to the cost of Clear Skies. It was likely for this reason that industry was willing to support it, which marked the first time that utilities supported a cap on carbon dioxide emissions.

The Carper bill proved to be a political headache for the Bush administration. Senator Lamar Alexander (R-TN), whose refusal to support Clear Skies was seen as the nail in the coffin of the 2003 effort, announced that he would support Carper's bill. Senator Alexander said that Clear Skies "does not go far enough, fast enough in my back yard."[34] Senator Carper's bill allowed Senator Alexander to be seen as responsible on the environment in his "backyard" and to support a bill that was reasonable for industry. The EPA's refusal to release modeling of Senator Carper's bill also had a role in the defeat of Clear Skies because it gave political cover to those who voted against Clear Skies in the March 2005 committee vote. This was particularly true of the critical votes of Senator Baucus and Senator Chafee, who did not show their cards until late in the Clear Skies debate. However, the decision not to release complete findings on Senator Carper's bill was present as a factor in the 2003 Clear Skies debate and through the March 2005 committee vote. The EPA did an analysis of the Carper bill but only released a raw data printout of the finding. A summarized report, which indicated that the proposal had some advantages, was not released.[35] At a May 2, 2003, meeting with EPA employees, one of them told the *New York Times* that Holmstead wondered out loud, "How can we justify Clear Skies if this gets out?" Holmstead told the *Times* that he did not "recall making any specific remarks." The decision not to release the modeling was criticized by the credible figure of William D. Ruckelshaus, who served as the first EPA administrator under the Nixon administration and then again during the Reagan administration. Ruckelshaus said, "Whether or not analysis is released is based on at least two factors. Is the analysis flawed? That is a legitimate reason for not releasing it. But if you don't like the outcome that might result from the analysis, that is not a legitimate reason."

The Democrats were able to block a proposal that was "close to the president's preferences" because they were able to come up with both a plausible alternative framing of the issue and plausible alternative proposals. The reason why neither party was able to get past no to reach a legislative compromise appeared to be a lack of commitment on both sides. John Graham explained that Senator Baucus (D-MT) was the key to passage and that Senator Chafee's probable opposition would be an "annoyance." Graham points out that Senator Baucus had sided with the Bush administration on the 2001 tax cuts and 2003 Medicare reform. On environmental issues, Senator Baucus represents a coal state. Graham, therefore, says that it is "interesting" that the organized environmental groups and the Senate Democratic leadership were successful in persuading these moderate Democrats not to collaborate with President Bush in a serious effort to pass Clear Skies.[36] For Baucus, during the 2005 Clear Skies debate, concessions were even added to the bill for a Montana coal mining operation. Senator Baucus's response was that "there haven't been any honest-to-goodness final negotiations. . . . I have not seen the White House."[37] In her book, *It's My Party Too*, EPA administrator Christine Todd Whitman writes in reference to the 2003 Clear Skies debate, "Outside the EPA, there was not much commitment to Clear Skies."[38]

The Bush administration's reversal on capping carbon dioxide, the pollutant that causes global warming, also contributed to the difficulty in passing a multi-pollutant proposal. Graham called it "a negative complicating factor."[39]

Without a carbon dioxide cap, there was some hope of Senator Carper's bill passing. Andrew Wheeler, the top Republican staffer on the EPW Committee, explained that the Republicans were unwilling to include a carbon dioxide cap in the bill because they did not see it as an acute health hazard. He said that the Republicans asked Senator Carper if he would support his bill without carbon dioxide, and Senator Carper refused. Wheeler points out that it was unclear whether Chairman Inhofe and Senator Voinovich would have supported the bill without the NSR reforms anyway.[40] However, it is not fully clear whether a compromise was impossible solely as a result of the carbon dioxide cap issue. Three senators who ultimately voted against the bill—Max Baucus (D-MT), Barack Obama (D-IL), and Lincoln Chafee (R-RI)—said they were open to a compromise that addressed carbon dioxide without imposing strict caps.[41]

The Largely Unsuccessful Pursuit of Scenario II: The Regulatory Route

Even before the 2003 legislative push, the EPA initiated a simultaneous effort to implement much of the substance of the Clear Skies Initiative through the Clean Air Act rulemaking process. The rulemakings included changes to NSR and cap and trade programs for sulfur dioxide, nitrogen oxides, and mercury. This route would have accomplished most of the goals of Clear Skies in the short term. However, since the changes would not be statutory, a future administration would remain able to use the Clean Air Act to accelerate air quality improvements.

These rulemakings, most of which were struck down by the D.C. Circuit Court, were controversial within the Bush administration. Administrator Whitman wrote in her autobiography, "I pushed for using elimination of [NSR] as a carrot to help build support for Clear Skies."[42] In developing the Clear Skies legislative proposal, Deputy Administrator Jeffrey Holmstead explained that the EPA tried to remove the regulatory programs of the Clean Air Act that the EPA thought were "superfluous" in the context of Clear Skies.[43] The National Energy Policy Development Group, chaired by Vice President Cheney, wanted to take over the NSR rulemaking authority from EPA. Whitman said she had to fight "tooth and nail" to prevent Cheney's energy task force from handing over the job of reforming the NSR to the Energy Department, a battle she said she won only after appealing to White House Chief of Staff Andrew Card Jr. This was an environmental issue with major implications for air quality and health, she believed, and it shouldn't be driven by a task force primarily concerned with increasing production. The internal disagreement centered around the "holy grail" of NSR, which is the undefined routine maintenance repair and replacement (RMRR) exemption, which exempts RMRR activity from the NSR permit process. Whitman thought that the RMRR exemption needed to be clarified, but not in a way that undercut the ongoing Clinton-era NSR enforcement lawsuits—many of which had merit, she said.[44] At the time, the Department of Justice was continuing Clinton-era prosecutions of the utilities for making modifications without undergoing NSR. In fact, Justice Department lawyers said they intended to prosecute the cases "vigorously." The White House wanted to end the cases.[45]

In a controversial rule promulgated on August 27, 2003, two days before Labor Day, the EPA decided that utilities would be allowed to spend up to 20 percent of an electricity-generating unit's replacement cost, per year, without tripping the NSR threshold.[46] A power plant could sum the cost of the relevant activities performed at the source during the year, from least expensive to most expensive, to arrive at a yearly cost. If the total cost came within the allowance, all of the activities would be considered RMRR and exempt from NSR.[47]

The high number was justified in the rule's preamble, which stated that a restrictive RMRR exclusion in many instances will result in higher levels of pollution. The logic is that utilities forgo efficiency improvements that would reduce energy costs and pollution for fear of triggering NSR, which would require even greater pollution reductions, but at costs that are high enough that the efficiency improvement is no longer worthwhile. The 20% figure created significant controversy. The Congressional Research Service concluded that, unlike previous efforts to address NSR, the focus of the administration's proposed routine maintenance rule was not to reduce pollution but to facilitate electricity production.[48]

In *Transatlantic Policymaking in an Age of Austerity: Diversity and Drift*, R. Daniel Kelemen identified these NSR changes as part of the Bush administration's commitment to flexible and cooperative approaches to environmental issues. He explains that the environmental lobby strongly viewed a "flexible and cooperative" approach to environmental issues as a smoke screen for a deregulatory agenda.[49] Frank O'Donnell, executive director of the Clean Air

Trust, a nonprofit watchdog group, said, "It's a moron test for power companies." He continued, "it's such a huge loophole that only a moron would trip over it and become subject to NSR requirements."[50] Shi-Ling Hsu further pointed out an interesting consequence of the rule. Strict NSR requirements would still apply for new entrants to the market, but the grandfathered plants would see their competitive position strengthened. Hsu writes, "This is precisely what the industry side has wanted all along: New Source Review to lock out new entrants, and a hands-off regulatory policy that gives incumbents a free hand to revamp existing facilities without governmental oversight, further protecting them from competition."[51] Whitman acknowledged that she was unable to sign the new rule and that it was the reason for her resignation. "I just couldn't sign it," she said. "The president has a right to have an administrator who could defend it, and I just couldn't."[52]

The D.C. Circuit Court rejected the EPA's rule. The court pointed out that the purpose of the NSR is to limit emissions. The opinion read, "EPA's interpretation would produce a 'strange,' if not an 'indeterminate,' result: a law intended to limit increases in air pollution would allow sources operating below applicable emission limits to increase significantly the pollution they emit without government review."[53] The court rejected the administration's view that a less restrictive NSR would result in less pollution. (The court did uphold some less significant changes to the NSR program that affected when NSR is triggered.)

Two additional rulemakings attempted to implement the cap and trade elements of Clear Skies legislation. As table 8.2 shows, the two rules were very similar to the Clear Skies legislation. To address sulfur dioxide and nitrogen oxides, the Clean Air Interstate Rule (CAIR) was adopted. The CAIR program did go into effect but was overturned on February 8, 2008. The opinion of the court read, "All the policy reasons in the world cannot justify reading a substantive provision out of a statute."[54] According to the decision, the main provision that the Bush administration read out of the statute was that Section 110(a)(2)(D)(i)(I) of the Clean Air Act prohibits sources "within [a] State from emitting any air pollutant in amounts which will contribute significantly to nonattainment in, or interfere with maintenance by, any other State." Theoretically, sources in Alabama could purchase enough NO_x and SO_2 allowances to cover all their current emissions, resulting in no change in Alabama's contribution to Davidson County, North Carolina's nonattainment. CAIR only

Table 8.2   Rulemaking versus Clear Skies

		Clear Skies	
Pollutant	CAIR/CAMR/ CAVR	Inhofe/Voinovich	Administration
SO_2	2010: 3.6	2010: 4.5	2010: 4.5
	2015: 2.5	2018: 3.0	2018: 3.0
NO_x	2009: 1.5	2008: 2.2	2008: 2.1
	2015: 1.3	2018: 1.8	2018: 1.7
CO_2	Not covered	Not covered	Not covered
Hg	2010: 38	2010: 34	2010: 26
	2018: 15	2018: 15	2018: 15

assures that the entire region's significant contribution will be eliminated. It was the regional nature of the program that the court explained violated the state-by-state-oriented Clean Air Act.

In a footnote included in the decision, the case also made a revealing point about how the rules were based on the Clear Skies proposal rather than on the Clean Air Act statute that they were promulgated under. The footnote read, "EPA briefly summarized a series of analyses and dialogues with various stakeholder groups in which the participants considered 'regional and national strategies to reduce interstate transport of SO2 and NOx. See CAIR, 70 Fed. Reg. at 25,199.'" It continued, "The most recent of these, EPA's analysis in support of the proposed Clear Skies legislation, considered nationwide SO2 caps of, coincidentally, '50 percent and 67 percent from . . . title IV cap levels.'"[55] John Walke explains what this cryptic footnote in the decision means. He writes that the use of the word "coincidentally" meant that the court recognized that "the Bush Administration worked backwards from its Clear Skies legislative proposal to institute the emissions caps and design features of CAIR, rather than working forward from the Clean Air Act."[56] Walke's explanation is supported by the fact that CAIR's reduction levels are nearly the same as the Clear Skies reduction levels, which suggests that CAIR was a part of the administration's overall strategy to enact Clear Skies through regulation if not through legislation.

The Clean Air Mercury Rule (CAMR) was also vacated by the D.C. Circuit Court. The decision employed an allusion to *Alice in Wonderland* in explaining that the delisting of mercury as a hazardous air pollutant (HAP) violated the Clean Air Act. Circuit Judge Janice Rogers Brown, who was appointed by

President George W. Bush, wrote that the administration's promulgation of CAMR "deploys the logic of the Queen of Hearts, substituting EPA's desires for the plain text of section 112(c)(9). Thus, EPA can point to no persuasive evidence suggesting that section 112(c)(9)'s plain text is ambiguous."[57] Before delisting an air pollutant as an HAP, Section 112(c) requires the EPA to make a specific finding; EPA concedes that it never made such findings. The "specific findings" required by the statute are the determination that " 'emissions from no source in the category or subcategory concerned . . . exceed a level which is adequate to protect public health with an ample margin of safety and no adverse environmental effect will result from emissions from any source.' *Id.* § 112(c)(9)." It was this finding that the EPA failed to make before declassifying mercury as an HAP, and it was the reason that CAMR was struck down by the court. Since CAIR, CAMR, and most of the NSR changes were struck down by the courts, the Bush administration was not successful in getting Clear Skies adopted through regulation. As with Scenario I (the legislative route), Scenario II (the regulatory route) was largely unsuccessful.

The goal of Scenario II, promulgating rules in a manner that does not comport with the statute, is similar to the environmental policy pursued during the Reagan administration. Landy, Roberts, and Thomas's *The Environmental Protection Agency: Asking the Wrong Questions* is generally critical of the Clean Air Act's inflexible approach to air pollution. Nonetheless, the authors criticize the Reagan administration by noting, "By often ignoring the spirit, if not the letter, of environmental laws, the Reagan administration denied its accountability to the Constitution."[58] In using rulemaking authority to accomplish objectives that should have been addressed through a statutory change, the George W. Bush administration used the rulemaking process in a very similar manner. While the administration's formal attempts to change policy were rejected by the courts, failure to achieve a legislative change (Scenario I) and a change through the rulemaking process (Scenario II) still helped them achieve the goal of delay.

Scenario III: The Bush Administration Delayed Pollution Reductions

Achieving Scenario I (legislative victory) or Scenario II (successful rulemaking) would have been a better alternative for the business base because both options would have changed the Clean Air Act to slow down the drive toward clean air. Scenario I would have created statutory certainty under a new cap and trade program and would have weakened environmental permitting rules in a way that a future Democratic president could not undo without another statutory change. Scenario II would have created regulatory certainty for the time being, but those rules could have been undone by a future president with greater ease. Yet being blocked in the Congress and then in the courts on weak Clean Air Act rules was not a complete loss from the perspective of the business base. The eight-year absence of consistent action to reduce air pollution under the Clean Air Act did not change anything in a fundamental policy sense, but it was a valuable result for the business base.

Scenario III is an example of policy being made through inertia. Even though the Clean Air Act guided policy in the direction of higher air quality, the actions of the Bush administration and the responses of Congress and the courts produced a result that, all in all, added up to delay. As Jacob Hacker so persuasively argued, inertia can have significant policy consequences. In his fine essay "Reform without Change, Change without Reform: The Politics of U.S. Health Policy Reform in Cross-National Perspective," Hacker argued that health care in the 1980s and 1990s was characterized as reform without change and change without reform. In American health care at this time, this meant that the long-term working out of cost containment produced the contraction of private coverage by employers in spite of efforts to broaden coverage protection.

Environmental policymaking during the Bush years was also a case of change without reform. The mechanism of this type of change Hacker defined as policy "conversion and drift," which is "changes in policy effects without changes in formal policies."[59] With air pollution policy, through delay, the Bush administration produced changes in policy effect without changes in formal policies. Formal policy changes were not achieved, but the actions of the administration had an effect on environmental policy during those eight years. Namely, it was a free ride of no significant new standards.

A Realpolitik Explanatory Framework

A further advantage of the delay approach to environmental protection of the Bush administration over the direct and open opposition of Reagan was that it could masquerade as a pro-environmental stance while achieving the opposite result. The administration framed Clear Skies as an expansion of the

Clean Air Act. As objective sources, such as the Congressional Research Service and a nonpartisan committee of scientists, concluded, it was not an expansion, not even the same level of regulation as the Clean Air Act, but instead a reduction. If Clear Skies did not pass, then at least there would be deadlock, if not a reduction in government intervention. With or without Clear Skies, new regulations could undercut the goals of the Clean Air Act. If the regulations were judicially invalidated, it would also lead to deadlock. The pursuit of a simultaneous rulemaking strategy with the Bush administration's Clear Skies legislative proposal meant that the success or failure of the legislative proposal would only determine the degree of reduced environmental regulation. To the business base, this was a "sane and reasonable" policy.

The Early Obama Years

In the first two years of the Obama presidency, environmental policy appears to be following two strands. First, the EPA is working to address the court rulings that invalidated the Bush administration's implementation of the Clean Air Act standards. Second, a dynamic story is emerging on global warming with legislative proposals and EPA Clean Air Act rulemaking that serves as a foil to the story of the Bush administration's Clear Skies Initiative.

Addressing the Bush-Era Clean Air Act Court Rulings

Under court order, the Obama EPA is working to bring the Bush-era clean air programs in line with the Clean Air Act statute. On July 6, 2010, the EPA proposed a Clean Air Act rule to address the *North Carolina v. EPA* case that invalidated the Bush EPA's approach to regulating sulfur dioxide and nitrogen oxides from power plants (CAIR). The modified program would utilize a "hybrid" cap and trade program that limits interstate trading in order to address the court's objections to the Bush administration's strictly regional cap and trade program.[60] In December 2010, the administration delayed implementation of the rule, asking for extensions to the court order. Industry applauded the delay and environmentalists criticized it.[61] The court rejected the extension, and in late February 2011, the EPA proposed a new regulation that is expected to be less costly to industry.[62] As this book goes to press, the Office of Management and Budget is reviewing the new rule.

The Democrats and Global Warming Policy: A Foil to the Clear Skies "Scenarios"

The debate over how to address global warming is far more significant for the purpose of analyzing the politics of policymaking because it is far more visible to the general public and it will likely be a greater determinant of President Obama's legacy on environmental issues than the resolution of the Bush administration's policies on the other pollutants. On global warming policy, owing to the nature of clean air politics and policymaking, the relationship between the Democratic administration and the Republican opposition has reversed in comparison with the Clear Skies story. In addressing global warming, the Democrats' ideal policy is passing expansionary legislation, which is a foil to the Clear Skies Scenario I. Clear Skies legislation would have reduced the pace of air pollution reduction and did not include carbon dioxide caps. The Obama administration's Scenario I would expand environmental regulation to include carbon dioxide. Obama administration–favored Scenario I legislation of this sort did pass the House in June 2009. The American Clean Energy and Security (ACES) Act of 2009, H.R. 2454, passed by a vote of 219-212. If enacted, it would have created an economy-wide cap and trade program for carbon dioxide and other greenhouse gases that contribute to global warming. Eight Republicans joined 211 Democrats to form a majority in support of the legislation.[63]

The bill did not become law because the Senate did not pass legislation on global warming. Senator Lindsey Graham (R-SC) spent months negotiating with Senators John Kerry (D-MA) and Joseph Lieberman (I-CT) over what was expected to be the Senate's blueprint for action on the issue.[64] The Republican opposition articulated an alternative framing of the issue: this legislation will raise energy prices and amounts to a tax.

Republicans ridiculed the very notion of cap and trade in developing the moniker "cap and tax." A free-market think tank, the Competitive Enterprise Institute, claims credit for coining the pejorative term. Myron Ebell of the Competitive Enterprise Institute explains, "We turned it into 'cap and tax,' and we turned that into an epithet."[65] Ironically, it was a Republican administration—President George H. W. Bush's—that first implemented cap and trade on a national scale to address sulfur dioxide pollution that caused acid rain. Cap and trade was intended to be a more flexible environmental reduction mechanism than direct pollution controls on industry.

Twenty years later, however, congressional Republicans drew attention to the fact that the program had the potential to raise energy prices. Responding to criticism of cap and trade, Senator John Kerry made the remark, "I don't know what 'cap and trade' means," a tongue-in-cheek comment about how the issue should be framed as a pollution reduction bill. The proposals that were under discussion did include elements of cap and trade programs though.[66] The removal of the "cap and trade" term did not solve the underlying difficulty of articulating a message on the issue. West Virginia senator Jay Rockefeller explained, "Most of the members of Congress don't know how to explain it, much less the American people."[67] Meanwhile, Senator Graham failed to attract any GOP support for the proposal. In April 2010, he backed away from the efforts over what he saw as a "cynical" ploy by Majority Leader Harry Reid to place immigration—an issue of significant importance to the majority leader's reelection campaign—on the agenda ahead of global warming legislation.

Yet, once again, the politics and policy of the Clean Air Act do not permit this strand of the story to end so neatly. President Obama stated that "cap-and-trade was just one way of skinning the cat; it was not the only way." He continued, "I'm going to be looking for other means to address this problem."[68] One of the mechanisms for "skinning the cat" is to regulate carbon dioxide and other pollutants that contribute to global warming under the Clean Air Act. This is the Obama administration's foil for the Clear Skies Scenario II (the regulatory route). The Obama administration's Scenario II is still expansionary environmental action, but it is within the more limited confines of the Clean Air Act.

On December 23, 2010, in the same month that the EPA delayed air pollution regulations for sulfur dioxide and nitrogen oxides, the EPA announced its intention to propose rules for carbon dioxide and other greenhouse gases as part of the NSR program. Under the new rules, power plants and refineries will be required to meet yet-to-be-defined standards when making changes to their facilities. Before this announcement in June 2010, Senator Lisa Murkowski of Alaska tried to deny EPA the authority to take this action under a disapproval resolution.[69] Her proposal was rejected by a 53–47 vote.[70] Six Democrats and all forty-one Republicans supported the proposal.[71] Despite the close roll call, the president's veto threat of the legislation placed an additional obstacle to blocking EPA action.[72]

After winning control of the House in the 2010 elections, GOP representative Fred Upton, House chairman of the Energy and Commerce Committee, said that the House won't "let this administration regulate what they've been unable to legislate."[73] The chairwoman of the EPW Committee, Senator Barbara Boxer (D-CA), responded directly to Chairman Upton and said, "So when the new chairman of the Energy and Commerce Committee says E.P.A. cannot pass by regulation what Congress failed to pass by law, let me correct him—Congress passed our Clean Air laws, Republican Presidents signed them, and those are the laws the E.P.A. is following."[74] Once again, the Democrats are using the Clean Air Act as an important benchmark in this debate.

However, the Obama administration has generally not responded to Republican attacks on the EPA with as much force, although the administration's actions will be the more important thing to observe. In December 2010, a senior administration official who asked not to be identified told the *New York Times,* "If the administration gets it wrong, we're looking at years of litigation, legislation and public and business outcry." The official continued, "If we get it right, we're facing the same thing." "Can we get it right?" this official continued. "Or is this just too big a challenge, too complex a legal, scientific, political and regulatory puzzle?"[75]

As this book goes to press, the puzzle is far from being solved. It appears that the Republicans have been successful in articulating an "alternative framing" of the issue to make some voters believe that, just as Clear Skies was not what it appeared to be, cap and trade is also not what it appears to be because it could lead to higher energy prices. With Republicans in control of the House, it is unlikely that the Obama administration can achieve its Scenario I, expansionary legislation, in the near future. The battle has now moved to Scenario II, the regulatory route, where the Obama administration plans to implement carbon dioxide regulation under the Clean Air Act. What role the courts will play and whether Republicans will be able to block these regulations through congressional action remain open questions.

NOTES

1. Samuel Goldreich, "Hill Weighs Competing Plans for New Air Pollution Limits," *CQ Weekly,* February 22, 2003.

2. Robert Meltz and James McCarthy, "The Supreme Court Upholds EPA Standard-Setting under the Clean Air Act: Whitman v. American Trucking Ass'ns," *Congressional Research Service*, March 28, 2001.

3. Bruce Hassler and William T. Ackerman, *Clean Coal/Dirty Air; or, How the Clean Air Act Became a Multibillion-Dollar Bail-Out for High-Sulfur Coal Producers* (New Haven, CT: Yale University Press, 1981), 104.

4. Committee on Changes in New Source Review Programs for Stationary Sources of Air Pollution, *New Source Review for Stationary Sources of Air Pollution* (Washington, DC: National Academies Press, 2006), citing (CAA § 165(a), 42 USC § 7465(a)).

5. Committee on Changes in New Source Review Programs for Stationary Sources of Air Pollution, *New Source Review for Stationary Sources of Air Pollution* (Washington, DC: National Academies Press, 2006), citing (CAA § 172(b)(5), 42 USC § 7502 (b)(5)).

6. Barry Rabe, "Environmental Policy and the Bush Era: The Collision between the Administrative Presidency and State Experimentation," *Journal of Federalism* 37 (2007): 413–31, citing Dallas Burtraw and Karen Palmer, "SO2 Cap-and-Trade Program in the United States," in *Choosing Environmental Policy*, ed. Winston Harrington et al. (Washington, DC: Resources for the Future, 2004), 41–66.

7. *Air Quality Management in the United States* (Washington, DC: National Academies Press, 2004), 201.

8. Jeffrey Holmstead, interview by author, February 24, 2009.

9. Elizabeth Shogren, "Bush Drops Pledge to Curb Emissions," *Los Angeles Times*, March 14, 2001, http://articles.latimes.com/2001/mar/14/news/mn-37556.

10. Douglas Jehl and Andrew Revkin, "Bush, in Reversal, Won't Seek Cut in Emissions of Carbon Dioxide," *New York Times*, March 14, 2001.

11. James Ridgeway, "Behind Jr.'s 'Energy Crisis,'" *Village Voice*, March 27, 2001, 1.

12. Hearings on S. 385, "Clear Skies Act of 2003," U.S. Senate Committee on Environment & Public Works, Subcommittee on Clean Air, Climate Change, and Nuclear Safety Cong. (2003) (testimony of Christine Todd Whitman).

13. www.epa.gov/air/clearskies/.

14. Committee on Changes in New Source Review Programs for Stationary Sources of Air Pollution, *New Source Review for Stationary Sources of Air Pollution* (Washington, DC: National Academies Press, 2006). The report did include the caveat that it was not "expressing any judgment about the overall environmental effects of Clear Skies." Clear Skies weakened other air pollution reduction programs as well.

15. The two air quality standards are the eight-hour ozone and the fine particulate quality standards. Larry Parker and James E. McCarthy, "Clear Skies and the Clean Air Act: What's the Difference?" *Congressional Research Service*, February 25, 2005.

16. Christopher Drew and Richard Oppel Jr., "AIR WAR—Remaking Energy Policy; How Power Lobby Won Battle of Pollution Control at E.P.A.," *New York Times*, January 20, 2009.

17. Michael Bradley, interview by author, February 9, 2009.

18. Rebecca Adams, "Hill Demands Clean Air Act Rewrite Data," *CQ Weekly*, May 4, 2002.

19. Rebecca Adams, "Democrats Decry Bush's Clean Air Plan as Favoring Industry over Environment," *CQ Weekly*, August 3, 2002.

20. Hearings on S. 385, "Clear Skies Act of 2003," U.S. Senate Committee on Environment & Public Works (testimony of David Hawkins).

21. Jeffrey Holmstead, interview by author, February 24, 2009.

22. Hassler and Ackerman, *Clean Coal/Dirty Air*.

23. R. Shep Melnick, *Regulation and the Courts: The Case of the Clean Air Act* (Washington, DC: Brookings Institution Press, 1983), 45.

24. Ibid.

25. David Whitman, "Partly Sunny: Why Enviros Can't Admit That Bush's Clear Skies Initiative Isn't Half Bad," *Washington Monthly*, December 2004.

26. John D. Graham, "Saving Lives through Administrative Law and Economics," *University of Pennsylvania Law Review* 157 U. PA. L. REV. 395 (2008).

27. David Hawkins, citing George W. Bush's 2003 State of the Union; Hearings on S. 385, "Clear Skies Act of 2003," U.S. Senate Committee on Environment & Public Works (testimony of David Hawkins).

28. S. 131, "The Clear Skies Act of 2005," Committee on Environment and Public Works Cong., 70 (2005) (testimony of John Walke).

29. Shi-Ling Hsu, "What's Old Is New: The Problem with New Source Review," *Regulation*, Spring 2006, 42.

30. John D. Graham, interview by author, e-mail, March 4, 2009.

31. North Carolina v. EPA, 531 F. 3d 896.

32. Rebecca Adams, "Senate Panel OKs Clean Air Fix Adding Carbon Dioxide Limits," *CQ Weekly*, June 29, 2002.

33. Frank O'Donnell, interview by author, February 17, 2009.

34. Mary Clare Jalonick, "'Clear Skies' a Bit Cloudier after Alexander Defection," *CQ Weekly Online*, July 19, 2003, 1802, http://library.cqpress.com/cqweekly/weeklyreport108-000000770191.

35. Jennifer Lee, "Critics Say E.P.A. Won't Analyze Clean Air Proposals Conflicting with President's Policies," *New York Times*, July 14, 2003, A9.

36. John D. Graham, interview by author, e-mail, March 4, 2009.

37. Mary Clare Jalonick, "Clear Skies' Plan Stalls in Senate Panel," *CQ Weekly*, March 14, 2005, 657.

38. Christine Todd Whitman, *It's My Party Too: The Battle for the Heart of the GOP and the Future of America* (New York: Penguin, 2005), 187.

39. John D. Graham, interview by author, e-mail, March 4, 2009.

40. Andrew Wheeler, interview by author, February 24, 2009.

41. Jalonick, "Clear Skies' Plan."

42. C. Whitman, *It's My Party Too*, 185.

43. Jeffrey Holmstead, interview by author, February 24, 2009.

44. Drew and Oppel, "AIR WAR—Remaking Energy Policy."

45. Bruce Barcott, "Changing All the Rules," *New York Times Magazine*, April 4, 2004, www.nytimes.com/2004/04/04/magazine/04BUSH.html?pagewanted=1.

46. Ibid.

47. Ann Berwick, "EPA's NSR Enforcement Initiative Targeting Electric Power Plants," *Environmental Energy Insights (MJ Bradley and Associates)*, May 2000.

48. Larry Parker, "Clean Air: New Source Review Policies and Proposals," *Congressional Research Service* 28.

49. R. Daniel Kelemen, "Environmental Policy in the US and EU," in *Transatlantic Policymaking in an Age of Austerity: Diversity and Drift*, ed. Martin A. Levin and Martin Shapiro (Washington, DC: Georgetown University Press), 212.

50. Barcott, "Changing All the Rules."

51. Shi-Ling Hsu, "What's Old Is New," 38.

52. Jo Becker and Barton Gellman, "Leaving No Tracks," *Washington Post*, June 27, 2007, http://blog.washingtonpost.com/cheney/chapters/leaving_no_tracks/.

53. *New York v. EPA*, 443 F. 3d 880 (2006).

54. *North Carolina v. EPA*, 531 F. 3d 896 (2008).

55. Ibid.

56. John Walke, "EPA's 'Clear Skies' Straitjacket," July 29, 2008, http://switchboard
.nrdc.org/blogs/jwalke/the_demise_of_the_clean_air_in_1.html.

57. *New Jersey v. EPA*, 517 F. 3d 574 (2008).

58. Marc K. Landy, Marc J. Roberts, and Stephen R. Thomas, *The Environmental Protection Agency: Asking the Wrong Questions: From Nixon to Clinton* (New York: Oxford University Press, 1994), 271.

59. Jacob S. Hacker, "Reform without Change, Change without Reform," in *The Politics of U.S. Health Policy Reform in Cross-National Perspective*, ed. Martin A. Levin and Martin Shapiro (Washington, DC: Georgetown University Press), 15.

60. John Walke, "EPA Proposes Rule to Cut Smog and Soot Pollution from Power Plants in the Eastern & Midwestern U.S.," Natural Resources Defense Council Switchboard Blog, http://switchboard.nrdc.org/blogs/jwalke/epa_proposes_rule_to_cut_smog
.html.

61. Matthew Daly, "EPA Delays Stricter Smog, Mercury Limits," *Associated Press*, December 8, 2010.

62. John Broder, "EPA Eases Pollution Rules for Industrial Boilers," *New York Times*, February 24, 2011.

63. http://clerk.house.gov/evs/2009/roll477.xml.

64. Adam Greenblatt, "How Cap and Trade Was 'Trashed,'" *National Public Radio*, April 26, 2010, www.npr.org/templates/story/story.php?storyId=126280761.

65. John Broder, "'Cap and Trade' Loses Its Standing as Energy Policy of Choice," *New York Times*, March 25, 2010, www.nytimes.com/2010/03/26/science/earth/26climate.html.

66. Ibid.

67. Darren Samuelsohn, "Climate Bill Blame Game Begins," *Politico*, July 22, 2010, www.politico.com/news/stories/0710/40132_Page3.html.

68. Merrill Hartson, "EPA Moving Unilaterally to Limit Greenhouse Gases," *Associated Press*, December 24, 2010.

69. If a disapproval resolution is enacted, a government agency's rule may not take effect and the agency may issue no substantially similar rule without subsequent statutory authorization. See Richard S. Beth, "Disapproval of Regulations by Congress: Procedure under the Congressional Review Act," *Congressional Research Service*, October 2001.

70. Hartson, "EPA Moving Unilaterally."

71. Erika Bolstad, "Senate Defeats Bid to Limit EPA Authority to Regulate Emissions," McClatchy Newspaper, June 10, 2010, www.mcclatchydc.com/2010/06/10/95709/senate
-defeats-bid-to-limit-epa.html.

72. Erika Bolstad, "Obama Will Veto Alaska Sen. Murkowski's EPA proposal," McClatchy Newspaper, June 9, 2010, www.mcclatchydc.com/2010/06/09/95555/obama
-will-veto-alaska-sen-murkowskis.html.

73. "GOP-Led House Plans to Fight Obama Pollution Plan," *Associated Press*, January 2, 2011.

74. John Broder, "E.P.A Faces First Volley from the House," *New York Times Green Blog*, January 6, 2011, http://green.blogs.nytimes.com/2011/01/06/e-p-a-faces-first-volley-from-the-house/?hp.

75. John Broder, "E.P.A. Limit on Gases to Pose Risk to Obama and Congress," *New York Times*, December 30, 2010, www.nytimes.com/2010/12/31/science/earth/31epa.html.

CHAPTER NINE

National Security, the Electoral Connection, and Policy Choice

James M. Lindsay

The members of the Republican National Committee who gathered in Austin in January 2002 looked forward to hearing Karl Rove's address. The head of George W. Bush's White House Office of Political Affairs did not disappoint. He bluntly laid out the president's intention to focus the strategy for the 2002 midterm elections on the "war on terror." "We can go to the country on this issue because they trust the Republican Party to do a better job protecting and strengthening America's military might and thereby protecting America," he boasted. "Americans trust the Republicans to do a better job of keeping our communities and our families safe."[1]

Rove's speech shattered the bipartisan unity that had gripped Washington for several months after September 11. Democrats denounced the speech. House Minority Leader Dick Gephardt (D-MO) called it "a shameful statement."[2] Terry McAuliffe, the chair of the Democratic National Committee, called it "despicable."[3] Representative John Dingell (D-MI) urged "the president and others not politicize" the war on terror. The dean of Michigan's congressional delegation went on: "Patriotic Americans have always taken the view that politics stops at the water's edge."[4]

Representative Dingell's last comment highlights an essential truth: the notion that "politics stops at the water's edge" holds a strong grip on the American political imagination. Democrats and Republicans, internationalists and isolationists, proponents of strong presidential authority, and critics of the imperial presidency all pay homage to the idea that America should speak with one voice to the world. National security scholars routinely invoke the concept of the national interest as an objective fact. Commentators and pundits champion bipartisanship as a foreign policy ideal. Veterans of executive branch policymaking recoil in horror at suggestions that foreign policy should be made with an eye toward the ballot box. The expectation is that foreign policy, unlike domestic policy, stands both above and beyond politics.

The truth, however, is that foreign policy can be, to paraphrase Clausewitz, the continuation of domestic politics by other means. There is nothing new about that. Whether it was the Jay Treaty of 1793, the Mexican-American War, the occupation of the Philippines after the Spanish-American War, or the isolationist surge of the 1930s, politics has both infused and been shaped by foreign policy choices. Presidents know that what they do in foreign policy has the potential to advance their party's political interests as well as their own.

None of this should be surprising. The national interest is not an objective fact—or at least not entirely objective. Once the discussion moves beyond obvious bromides about promoting peace and prosperity, Americans disagree over what they want Washington to do overseas, as well as over which specific strategies will work. Moreover, while foreign policy issues generally do not drive how most Americans cast their votes in presidential or congressional elections, presidents and aspiring presidents know that the positions they stake out on foreign policy—even as much as what they do—can shape how the public perceives their patriotism, their judgment, and ultimately their ability to lead and their fitness for office. Just as important, as George W. Bush's presidency shows, foreign policy can be a powerful weapon to undermine the popular appeal of the opposition party.

The first section of this chapter explores the calculations that influence presidents as they consider whether to use foreign policy issues to advance their electoral interests. The second through fourth sections examine how Bush approached foreign policy from his first presidential campaign through the launching of the war on terror. The fifth section reviews a clear example of where Bush's foreign policy choices ran contrary to his electoral interests and those of the Republican Party, namely, his 2007 decision to "surge" more than twenty thousand additional U.S. troops to Iraq. The penultimate section returns to the broader question of when and why presidents use foreign policy for political gain. The final section looks at Barack Obama's experiences.

The Electoral Temptation

The temptation for presidents to use national security to advance their electoral interests can be strong because the United States in many ways has "two presidencies."[5] By virtue of constitutional design, the inherent advantages of the presidency, two hundred years of precedents and Supreme Court rulings, and deeply rooted public expectations about the necessity of strong presidential leadership overseas, presidents enjoy greater latitude—assuming they know how to seize it—in foreign policy than in domestic affairs. Unlike Medicare, tax cuts, welfare reform, and other domestic issues discussed in this volume, in foreign affairs the president often can act without having to undertake lengthy and tiring efforts to persuade Congress first. Congressional opponents might try to reverse a president's foreign policy choice through legislation, but their chances of success are slim. Congress last overrode a presidential veto of a foreign affairs bill in 1986.

By the same token, however, foreign policy—and especially national security policy—may be less fertile ground to exploit for electoral purposes than domestic policy. One reason is that presidents may have less control over their foreign policy agenda than their domestic one. Overseas crises can scramble the plans of even the most far-thinking presidents, either upending their plans or diverting them from favored foreign policy initiatives. At the same time, success in foreign policy usually requires the cooperation of other governments. But even close allies, let alone foes, can be more difficult to persuade than opposition committee chairs on Capitol Hill.

Foreign policy is less enticing politically for another, more important reason: voters generally care less about what presidents do overseas than what they do at home. The elder President Bush liberated Kuwait, managed the collapse of the Soviet Union, and brought about Germany's reunification. By virtually every measure, he had a splendidly successful foreign policy presidency. Yet the American electorate voted him out office. His main sin? He was seen as having neglected things at home while working on things overseas. In a similar fashion, Jimmy Carter's success in securing the Panama Canal Treaty, establishing diplomatic relations with China, and negotiating the Camp David

Accords—some of the most important foreign policy actions of the last fifty years—did not help him in his reelection race against Ronald Reagan.

The fact that foreign policy success does not necessarily translate into electoral success forces any president to answer a first-order question: How much weight should he (and someday she) place on national security issues versus domestic issues in the first place? The answer to that question is driven by numerous factors, with the president's own level of interest in foreign affairs and the events of the day being the two most obvious. Some presidents care deeply about foreign policy, while others want to make their mark on domestic policy. There are also the potential political costs to be weighed of not giving foreign policy enough consideration. Bill Clinton defeated George H. W. Bush on the campaign slogan of "It's the economy, stupid!" He made foreign policy a secondary priority during his first year in office, delegating much of the work to his secretaries of defense and state. The result was a series of missteps, culminating in the Black Hawk Down and Harlan County incidents, that helped Republicans win stunning victories in the 1994 midterm elections. And all other things being equal, a president's interest and ability to seize the lead in foreign affairs varies directly with the perceived level of threat facing the countries. Simply put, in times of peril, Americans expect presidents to lead.

Party affiliation matters as well in the emphasis that presidents place on foreign affairs. Democratic presidents have a political constituency that on average, and aside from trade policy, cares less about foreign policy than about domestic policy. At the same time, from the days of Vietnam until very recently, Republicans held a decided advantage over Democrats on the question of which party the public trusted more to handle foreign policy issues. Given these realities, it is not surprising that Democratic presidential candidates typically stress their domestic credentials and gloss over their foreign policy bona fides. They find it hard to make the case that national security is their strength, and it generally does not resonate with their key supporters.

The president's temptation to use foreign policy issues to advance his or her electoral chances also depends on whether an issue has intense supporters and weak opposition. Just as in domestic policy, squeaky wheels on foreign policy tend to get the grease. Because much of the public is indifferent to most foreign policy matters, presidents have an incentive to court the approval of single-issue foreign policy groups with intense preferences and can run few risks. Ethnic lobbies are an obvious case in point. Americans of Cuban, Greek,

Armenian, and Polish descent often have intense preferences about U.S. policy toward their ancestral homeland, while most other Americans are indifferent or even ignorant about the issues at stake.[6] Bill Clinton writes in his memoirs that he took up the cause of brokering a lasting peace in Northern Ireland during the 1992 campaign even though "I knew it would infuriate the British and strain our most important transatlantic alliance . . . because of the politics of New York" city, where Irish Americans were influential.[7] The same dynamic holds, however, with groups concerned about human rights, fearful of the rise of China, or worried about trade, to name a few.

As the example of Clinton and Northern Ireland suggests, the decisions presidents make about the electoral utility of their foreign policy choices begins even before they take office. Most presidential candidates hit the campaign trail with well-developed views on only a few foreign policy issues. Over the course of the campaign, they are asked to define their positions on countries, conflicts, and issues they have given no thought to before. Interest groups pore over their remarks and allocate their financial contributions and political support accordingly. Candidates are understandably tempted to tailor their remarks to please their audiences. It is no accident, for example, that presidential candidates in both parties routinely decline to challenge U.S. policy toward Cuba even though most foreign policy professionals question its wisdom. The cost of alienating Cuban American voters in the key state of Florida is simply perceived as too high to be worth challenging the status quo.

In many instances no doubt, candidates cultivate these groups for *defensive* reasons. They are less interested in expanding their electoral base than in keeping it together. But where an opposing candidate's grip on a key group appears shaky, efforts to reach out to single-issue groups can become a useful *offensive* strategy. For example, during the 2008 campaign John McCain sought to make inroads into the normally Democratic-leaning Jewish American vote by exploiting doubts about Barack Obama's commitment to Israel.

Presidential candidates similarly have a temptation to position themselves on foreign policy issues in ways that send desired signals about their image and leadership qualities. Because Democratic candidates have longer suffered from the perception that they are "soft" on foreign policy, and with the memory still strong of how John F. Kennedy used the so-called missile gap to his advantage in 1960, they often look for issues where they can demonstrate their "toughness." During the 1992 campaign, Bill Clinton found two such issues in U.S. policy toward China and the Balkans. On China, he denounced the

"Butchers of Beijing" for ordering the Tiananmen Square massacre and insisted he would deny China most-favored-nation trading status until it improved its human rights record. On the Balkans, he pledged to be more aggressive in helping civilians under siege in Bosnia and Herzegovina.[8] Whatever the substantive merits of the positions Clinton took, politically they put him to the "right" of George H. W. Bush on foreign policy and helped portray him as a more stalwart defender of the democratic values that Americans cherish. (Clinton's opposition to granting China most-favored-nation trading status also endeared him to the labor wing of the Democratic Party.)

This is not to say that candidates are always adjusting their personal policy preferences to build favor with key constituencies. Candidates may share the preferences of the groups they target on the campaign trail, as Senator McCain undoubtedly did in 2008. What is more relevant is that the statements presidential candidates make on the campaign trail can narrow their range of foreign policy choice and may even determine it long before they have decided who will be their national security adviser or secretary of state. Of course, presidents have long practiced the art of edging away from their campaign promises once in office, but doing so can be politically painful, as Bill Clinton discovered when he decided in 1994 to reverse his campaign promise to deny China most-favored-nation status. YouTube and the 24/7 news cycle may be making it more difficult than ever to escape the long reach of campaign rhetoric.

How much the electoral connection shapes specific foreign choices once presidents are in office varies across issues. The desire to score political points or to expand the existing political base probably is not an important driver of decisions to send troops into combat. There are extremely strong norms against doing so, and the electoral cost to be paid if caught sending troops into harm's way for political gain is high. Some Republican lawmakers accused Bill Clinton of engaging in such so-called wag-the-dog tactics when he ordered the missile attacks against suspected terrorist targets in Afghanistan and Sudan as Monica Lewinsky was testifying before a grand jury and then again when he ordered four days of air strikes against Iraq as the House debated his impeachment. Administration officials heatedly denied the charges, noting that both attacks came in the wake of legitimate provocations.[9]

On the other hand, fears of alienating voters often constrain presidential decisions on the use of military force. President Clinton insisted publicly in 1995 that the Dayton Accords would require U.S. troops to be deployed for only a year even though administration officials acknowledged privately that the U.S. military would be in Bosnia in a peacekeeping role for far longer than that. (U.S. troops were still based in the Balkans in 2011.) Likewise, when the United States went to war against Serbia over its treatment of Kosovo in 1999, Clinton explicitly ruled out sending U.S. ground troops. Most foreign policy professionals criticized the move for needlessly taking a crucial coercive threat off the table, thereby raising doubts about Clinton's willingness to prevail in the conflict and emboldening Serbia. The decision not to put boots on the ground was, as many administration officials said privately and Gen. Wesley Clark, the commander of NATO and the man responsible for running the war, later said publicly, "purely politics. . . . Clinton wanted to avoid a huge political problem."[10] The president believed that the American people would not accept losing troops in a conflict that did not directly affect the security of the United States, and he did not want to pay the political price that this would entail.

The norms against using foreign policy to advance the president's political interests no doubt erode as one moves away from war and peace issues because the costs of being caught acting politically go down. Even if presidents do not make their choices for political reasons, they (and their staff) know that how they present their national security choices can affect their electoral chances. That puts a tremendous premium on framing policy choices, however they are arrived at, in ways that make the best case for the administration's choice. How to frame decisions varies between the two parties because of the public's differing perceptions of their strengths and weaknesses. Democrats tend to try to paint Republicans as "reckless," while Republicans usually seek to paint Democrats as "soft" if not outright "unpatriotic."

The 2000 Campaign

When George W. Bush declared his candidacy for the presidency in 1999, he knew he could not credibly claim to be a foreign policy expert. He had spent his career as an oilman and the owner of a Major League Baseball team. Other than trips to Mexico, he had seldom traveled abroad. During his two terms as Texas governor, he had worked on some foreign policy issues. However, these typically involved matters such as managing water resources in the Rio Grande basin—concerns at the fringes of any president's policy agenda.

Bush's inexperience was hardly unusual in a major party presidential candidate, even a victorious one. Jimmy Carter, Ronald Reagan, and Bill Clinton all arrived at the White House with little firsthand foreign policy knowledge as well. Bush's effort to overcome his foreign policy shortcomings was helped by the fact that foreign policy was on the minds of few voters. Throughout the 1990s pollsters found that less than 10 percent of Americans—and often less than 5 percent—named any defense or national security issue as the most important problem facing the United States. Even when people were pressed to name a foreign policy problem, the most common response polls turned up was "Don't Know."[11]

Bush sought to turn his weakness into an advantage. He freely admitted that foreign policy was not his strength. "This is a big world," he said, "and I've got a lot to learn."[12] He reassured voters that he would compensate for the gaps in his own knowledge by surrounding himself with seasoned advisers. Photo opportunities showing him flanked by senior members of his father's foreign policy team undoubtedly helped reinforce that claim.

Nonetheless, Bush still had to develop a coherent foreign policy message. One possibility was to follow the lead of congressional Republicans. During the 1990s, they had driven the country's foreign policy agenda by pushing a mix of isolationist and protectionist policies—policies that in many instances ran against broader public opinion.[13] They sponsored legislation to bar presidents from putting U.S. combat troops under the command of a foreign officer, voted against sending peacekeeping troops to the Balkans, sought to prevent the World Trade Organization from being able to compel changes in American consumer and environmental laws, opposed efforts to pay U.S. back dues to the United Nations, and denounced the war in Kosovo.

Bush opted instead for a more mainstream message, one that could have been delivered by any American president since World War II. In his first major foreign policy address, delivered at the Ronald Reagan presidential library, he criticized those who argued that the wisest course for the United States at the start of the twenty-first century was to withdraw to its own borders. Implicitly rebuking congressional Republicans, he warned that giving into the temptation "to build a proud tower of protectionism and isolation" would be a "shortcut to chaos," "invite challenges to our power," and result in "a stagnant America and a savage world." He insisted that "American foreign policy cannot be founded on fear. Fear that American workers can't compete. Fear that America will corrupt the world—or be corrupted by it." A Bush administration, he pledged, would "not shrink from leadership."[14]

Bush's foreign policy aspirations mirrored those of every president for a half century in another way—he accepted Woodrow Wilson's view that the United States foreign policy should seek to promote its values abroad, as well as its interests. "Some have tried to pose a choice between American ideals and American interests—between who we are and how we act," Bush declared. "But the choice is false. America, by decision and destiny, promotes political freedom—and gains the most when democracy advances." The United States, he argued, had a "great and guiding goal: to turn this time of American influence into generations of democratic peace."[15]

Bush married his embrace of internationalism to an indictment of Bill Clinton's foreign policy. In Bush's judgment, Clinton had committed the cardinal sin of leadership—he had failed to set priorities. Bush clearly had Clinton in mind when he declared that presidents should not let the nation "move from crisis to crisis like a cork in a current." The result was "action without vision, activity without priority, and missions without end—an approach that squanders American will and drains American energy."[16] Clinton's failure to set priorities, Bush argued, was most visible in the way his administration had promiscuously dispatched U.S. military forces on peacekeeping missions around the globe. "Rarely has our military been so freely used—an average of one deployment every nine weeks in the last few years," he argued in one speech.[17]

Bush also criticized Clinton for appeasing a rising China and indulging a corrupt Russia. First Clinton called Chinese leaders "butchers," and then he aspired to make them America's "strategic partner." In the case of Russia, Bush criticized Clinton for "focusing our aid and attention on a corrupt and favored elite" and for excusing "Russian brutality" in Chechnya and elsewhere. What was needed was "nothing short of a new strategic relationship to protect the peace of the world."[18]

Although Bush made the need for clear foreign policy priorities a theme of his campaign, he did not make foreign policy a priority. Unlike Ronald Reagan, who spoke incessantly and unapologetically about the need to confront Soviet power in his run for the presidency in 1980, Bush did not put any foreign policy initiative at center stage. His top two priorities were instead domestic initiatives—a $1.6 trillion tax cut and education reform. While Bush provided detailed plans on how he intended to achieve these two objectives, his discussion of foreign policy initiatives—whether military readiness, missile defense, or better relations with Mexico—never went beyond listing aspirations.

When Bush did delve into the details of policy, his proposals often looked like Clinton's. Despite his criticisms about Clinton's promiscuous use of U.S. military forces, he agreed with every one of Clinton's decisions to intervene militarily except for Haiti. He supported Clinton on the Kosovo War; however, like many inside and outside the administration, he criticized Clinton for ruling out the possibility of sending ground forces. Bush did relabel Beijing a strategic "competitor," but he defended Clinton's policy of improving trade relations with China because "economic freedom creates habits of liberty. And habits of liberty create expectations of democracy." Bush likewise endorsed Clinton's efforts "to increase substantially our assistance to dismantle as many of Russia's weapons as possible as quickly as possible."[19]

What the campaign suggested, then, was that for Bush, as for Bill Clinton in 1992, foreign policy was a not matter of passion. He had to speak about world affairs to demonstrate his political credibility. He attempted to do so in ways that maximized his appeal to voters, or at least limited the chances that he would offend. On a few issues, most notably better relations with Mexico, he showed genuine enthusiasm and comfort, though obviously domestic political considerations played a part, given America's rapidly growing Latino population. But the main message he sent to the American electorate was that, unlike his father's administration, his would not be a foreign policy presidency.

The First Eight Months

George Bush's supporters expected he would move boldly on foreign policy upon taking office in January 2001. Hawks assumed he would boost defense spending and confront Saddam Hussein. Missile defense enthusiasts predicted a new Manhattan Project to shield the country against missile attack. Critics of Beijing anticipated a push to redirect the U.S. military to counter a rising China, a blunt declaration of the administration's intent to defend Taiwan, and massive arms sales to Taipei. Neo-isolationists on the Hill looked forward to the rapid withdrawal of U.S. troops from Bosnia and Kosovo. Latino activists expected an overhaul of U.S.-Mexico migration policy. Free traders looked forward to a revival of talks on a free trade agreement for the Americas and a new round of world trade talks.

None of these things happened. A case in point was defense spending. Throughout the campaign, Bush had argued that American military capability had eroded because the Clinton administration had failed to address growing problems of "poor pay, shortages of spare parts and equipment, and rapidly declining readiness."[20] Dick Cheney used his speech accepting the Republican vice presidential nomination to reassure the men and women in the military that "help is on the way."[21] In early February, however, Bush told members of Congress that "there will be no new money for defense this year."[22] Instead, he decided to proceed with the Clinton administration's proposed 2002 defense budget request. He also declined to seek a supplemental appropriation to increase the 2001 budget. The thrust of these decisions was that the Pentagon would have to close the gap between what it hoped to buy and what it got to spend by killing outdated weapons systems and rethinking how it did business. This philosophy of "starving the beast" to force internal reform was in keeping with Bush's campaign pledge to "skip a generation of technology" and create "a new architecture of American defense for decades to come."[23]

Bush took a similarly deliberate approach to other defense and foreign policy issues he had emphasized during the campaign. He declined to push for regime change in Iraq. He ignored calls to order an immediate withdrawal from the ABM Treaty and the rapid construction of a system capable of defending America from ballistic missiles. He was similarly reluctant to scale back U.S. peacekeeping deployments, despite having criticized Clinton for committing American forces to nation-building activities in the Balkans and elsewhere when their true mission was "to fight and win war."[24] Secretary of State Colin Powell announced in February that the United States would not remove its troops from Bosnia or Kosovo without the agreement of the NATO allies, saying, "The simple proposition is: We went in together, we will come out together."[25] Despite embracing free trade on the campaign trail, Bush declined to launch a trade initiative.

Rather than unveiling new initiatives, Bush spent his first eight months in office focused on extracting the United States from commitments the Clinton administration had made. In March, he abandoned his campaign pledge to curtail emissions of carbon dioxide from power plants. Rice subsequently told European Union ambassadors at a private lunch that the Kyoto Treaty on global warming was "dead."[26] Bush's decision did not derail the Kyoto process—it went into effect in mid-2002—but it did kill the hopes that Kyoto might provide the basis for an effective international response to climate change. Bush followed up on his opposition to Kyoto by directing his administration to oppose a string of international agreements, among them a pact to control the trafficking in small arms, a new protocol to the Biological Weapons convention, the Comprehensive Test Ban Treaty, and the International Criminal Court (ICC). Washington's opposition to these agreements was determined and often heavy-handed.

Bush's "Just Say No" foreign policy was not limited to international agreements. In the first months of his administration, he also reined in numerous U.S. diplomatic efforts around the world. He put U.S. engagement in the Middle East peace process on hold, declining to send an envoy to the last-ditch Israeli-Palestinian peace talks at Taba, Egypt, in late January 2001 and eliminating the post of special Middle East envoy. When South Korean president Kim Dae Jung traveled to Washington in March, Bush used the visit to publicly quash the idea that he would continue Clinton's efforts to reach out to North Korea, stating that he did not support President Kim's "sunshine policy" toward Pyongyang. U.S. efforts to mediate a peace agreement in Northern Ireland came to a similar halt.

In proceeding more deliberately on foreign policy than many had expected, Bush did not entirely disappoint his supporters. On his third day in office, he reinstated the "Mexico City Policy." This was an executive order that Ronald Reagan had imposed and Clinton had repealed mandating that private groups receiving federal funds agree to neither perform nor promote abortion as a method of family planning in other nations. The practical importance of the decision was questionable, but the symbolic importance was not—pro-life groups had demanded the reinstatement of the policy. With the stroke of a pen Bush shored up his support with the Republican base, many of whose members had previously doubted his conservative credentials. Likewise, the decision to withdraw from the Kyoto Protocol was aimed in part in reassuring Bush's supporters in the business community, especially those in the oil and gas industry. Indeed, Bush publicly defended his decision to withdraw from Kyoto solely on domestic considerations, arguing that the "idea of placing caps on CO_2 does not make economic sense for America."[27]

The decisions to reinstitute the Mexico City Policy and to walk away from Kyoto did not, however, stave off growing discontent among Republican defense and foreign policy intellectuals. By summer 2001 conservative activists were openly complaining. By refusing to increase defense spending, the administration "had turned its back" on the pressing problems facing the U.S. military.[28] On Iraq, Bush looked "content to continue walking down dangerous paths in foreign and defense policy laid out over the past eight years by Bill Clinton."[29]

Moreover, in the one major crisis of his first eight months in office—the collision of a U.S. spy plane with a Chinese jet fighter off the Chinese coast—conservatives saw weakness. Bush resolved the crisis by issuing a letter saying the U.S. government was "very sorry" for the loss of the Chinese pilot and for the U.S. plane making an emergency landing on China's Hainan Island. The *Weekly Standard* called the apology a "national humiliation" that revealed Bush's "weakness" and "fear: fear of the political, strategic, and economic consequences of meeting a Chinese challenge."[30] Gary Bauer, one of the men Bush defeated in winning the Republican presidential nomination, argued that if Al Gore had said he was sorry to the Chinese, "there would be nothing less than dozens of Republicans at the microphone yelling, 'Sellout!'"[31]

Conservative anger with Bush was especially high among defense hawks on Capitol Hill. They criticized his decision to stick with Clinton's FY 2002 defense budget and pressed to add funds to the FY 2001 budget. Rather than risk being trumped by Congress, the White House changed its tune. In August Bush submitted a 2001 defense appropriation supplemental request and raised the 2002 defense budget by $33 billion.

The defense spending reversal did not quiet Bush's conservative critics. They continued to wonder why he had not gone further in remaking the national security agenda. But in not launching bold new foreign policy initiatives during his first months in office, Bush was delivering precisely the presidency he had promised on the campaign. He had focused on a few key priorities and worked them hard. Those priorities just happened to involve domestic policy—especially tax cuts and an education bill—not foreign policy.

The War on Terror

The September 11 attacks changed American foreign policy—and American politics. In a replay of a phenomenon that has occurred repeatedly over the course of U.S. history when national security threats have dominated the political agenda, the pendulum of power shifted away from Capitol Hill and toward the White House. On September 14, after little debate about the consequences of what they were about to do, all but one member of Congress voted to authorize President Bush to "use all necessary and appropriate force against those nations, organizations, or persons he determines planned, authorized, committed, or aided the terrorist attacks that occurred on September 11, 2001, or harbored such organizations or persons."[32] In effect, Congress declared war and left it up to the White House to decide who the enemy was.

Capitol Hill's newfound deference manifested itself on an array of other foreign policy issues. Congress said nothing in late September when Bush waived sanctions that had been imposed on Pakistan after its May 1998 nuclear tests. Congress was similarly silent as Bush lifted restrictions on the CIA's ability to operate covertly, permitted government prosecutors to eavesdrop on conversations between people charged with terrorism and their lawyers, approved the roundup of thousands of young Arabs and Muslims, and made it more difficult to get some presidential papers made public. When the White House issued the Military Order of November 13 declaring that the foreign citizens the United States detained overseas while waging its war on terrorism could be tried before military commissions, Congress neither blocked the president's order nor acted to reinforce its legal basis. Senate Democrats dropped their plans to slash spending on missile defense, and they said little when Bush announced in December 2001 that the United States was withdrawing from the ABM Treaty. When Congress did act, it usually did so to ratify Bush's initiative. Just seven weeks after the attacks, Congress passed essentially intact the administration's proposed USA Patriot Act, which greatly expanded federal law enforcement and surveillance powers.

Congress's deference to Bush partly reflected the enormity of the attacks and a principled belief that lawmakers should defer to strong presidential leadership during a crisis. But it also reflected a healthy dose of politics. Rather than blaming Bush for failing to anticipate the attacks, Americans rallied around him. His public approval ratings soared to 90 percent—a figure seen only once before, when his father waged the Gulf War. Whereas the elder Bush's approval ratings quickly fell, the younger Bush's remained high for months. On the first anniversary of the terrorist attacks, 70 percent approved of the job he was doing as president, and more than 60 percent still did so in the summer of 2003. Bush's newfound popularity translated into political power. Lawmakers generally heed the demands of a popular president.

President Bush and his advisers—all of whom already had expansive views of presidential authority—happily seized on the opportunity to act without having to secure the agreement of 535 secretaries of state.[33] They did so largely to enact policies that they believed would make the country more secure. Yet, if political calculations did not drive most of the decisions the administration made in the war on terror, Bush and his advisers quickly grasped that the war could be used to his and the GOP's electoral advantage. For years Americans had told pollsters they had far more confidence in Republicans than Democrats when it came to handling national security issues. September 11 only reinforced this perception. Polls showed that Americans gave the nod to Republicans over Democrats when it came to dealing with terrorism by margins as large as 20 percentage points.[34] Confidence in Bush personally was even higher, with polls showing that the public had more confidence in him than in congressional Democrats by margins as high as three to one.[35]

The temptation to use the war on terror for political gain was especially strong because the Republicans had lost their majority status in the Senate in June 2001 when Senator Jim Jeffords of Vermont became an Independent. Shifting just one seat into the GOP column would give the Republicans control of both houses of Congress. But Bush and his advisers also knew that in midterm elections the president's party usually lost seats rather than gained them.

Karl Rove knew this when he told the Republican National Committee in January 2002 that Republicans should make the case that they would do a better job of keeping America safe. Democratic complaints that the White House had unwisely and inappropriately chosen to politicize the war did not deter the administration. In June 2002, a diskette containing a PowerPoint presentation that Rove gave to a gathering of Republicans on the midterm elections was found in Lafayette Park across from the White House. Slide number 20 was headlined "Republican Strategy." The first bullet point read "Focus on War and the Economy."[36]

Congressional Republicans were happy to help the White House use the war on terrorism against the Democrats. In February 2002, Senate Majority Leader Tom Daschle (D-SD) told reporters that Bush's efforts to expand the war on terrorism lacked "a clear direction" and that U.S. troops had to find Osama bin Laden and other top Al Qaeda leaders "or we will have failed."[37] Daschle's comments, and especially his insistence on the need to capture bin Laden, hardly seemed inflammatory. When asked a week after September 11 whether he wanted Osama bin Laden dead, Bush had replied, "I want justice. There's an old poster out West, as I recall, that said, 'Wanted Dead or Alive.' "[38]

Republican reactions to Daschle's remarks, however, were vitriolic. "How dare Senator Daschle criticize President Bush while we are fighting our war on terrorism, especially when we have troops in the field?" complained Senate Minority Leader Trent Lott. "He should not be trying to divide our country while we are united." House Majority Whip Tom Delay issued a one-word press release calling Daschle's comments "disgusting." Representative Tom Davis of Virginia, chairman of the National Republican Congressional Campaign Committee, accused Daschle of "giving aid and comfort to our enemies," the legal definition of treason.[39] These accusations did not persuade Daschle to retract or modify his comments. But few Democratic senators came to his defense even though many of them agreed with what he had said.

By mid-2002 it was clear that the war on terror would expand to include Saddam Hussein's ouster. Democrats initially reacted by arguing that the country could not go to war with Iraq without congressional approval. The White House countered by insisting that the 1991 Gulf War resolution, the September 11 resolution, and the president's inherent powers as commander in chief made another congressional vote unnecessary. In early September, however, Bush changed his mind and called for a congressional vote. The request put Democrats in a bind: they could oppose a popular president and appear weak, or they could support him and give a blank check to the White House to wage war. Daschle personally asked Bush to drop his insistence that Congress vote on the war authorization bill before the midterm elections, noting that his father had waited until a new Congress had been seated before requesting a vote on the 1991 Persian Gulf War. Bush refused.[40] With the elections just weeks away and hoping to salvage their electoral prospects by putting the issue behind them and moving on to economic matters, many Democrats voted to give Bush what he asked for. The Iraq War resolution passed in both houses in October by wide margins.

Republicans gained two seats in the Senate and four seats in the House in the 2002 elections, making Bush the first president since FDR to see his party pick up seats in both houses of Congress during his first congressional midterm election. This electoral success fueled the momentum to remove Saddam Hussein. In March 2003, U.S. troops invaded Iraq. In less than a month, they had captured Baghdad and forced Hussein to flee into hiding.

Bush played up the military success in Iraq and the broader war on terrorism to his political advantage. In May 2003, he flew to the aircraft carrier USS *Abraham Lincoln*, which was just off the coast of San Diego—not by helicopter, but by jet and wearing a fighter pilot's fatigues rather than a business suit—to announce the end of major fighting in Iraq. Bush's campaign featured the war on terrorism in his fundraising letters for the 2004 election. "I'll be depending on friends and supporters like you to get my campaign organized and operating across our country," he wrote in May 2003. "We have no more urgent and important duty than to wage and win the War on Terrorism."[41] To make sure that the war on terrorism stayed center stage in the 2004 elections, the White House arranged for the Republican Party to delay the start of its presidential nominating convention in New York City until the end of August 2004. The timing shift ensured that Bush's acceptance speech would flow seamlessly into the commemorations honoring the third anniversary of the September 11 attacks.

Although most of Bush's foreign policy decisions after September 11 reflected, for better or worse, his calculations about what constituted the best policy, some decisions were clearly made with the electoral connection in mind. One example was the proposal to create a new department of homeland security. Democrats had pushed the idea after the September 11 attacks, in good part because they saw an opportunity to outflank the White House and accuse it of failing to keep the country safe. Bush initially resisted the idea, insisting that his decision to create an Office of Homeland Security in the White House headed by Pennsylvania governor Tom Ridge was sufficient. "Creating a cabinet post," argued White House spokesman Ari Fleisher in March 2002, "doesn't solve anything."[42]

Throughout the spring of 2002, however, public support for a major reorganization grew, and congressional Republicans began to announce their support for the Democratic proposal. Meanwhile, a string of stories about how the CIA and FBI had bungled leads that might have uncovered the September 11 plot dominated the headlines. In June, Bush suddenly reversed course. On the same day that an FBI agent testified before Congress on the FBI's missteps, Bush went on national television to unveil a homeland security reorganization proposal that dwarfed anything being considered on Capitol Hill. The proposed department would merge twenty-two agencies, employ nearly 170,000 workers, spend more than $35 billion annually, and become the federal government's third largest bureaucracy.

After demanding the creation of a homeland security department for months, Democrats could only applaud Bush's proposal. However, his change of heart did more than just nullify the potential edge they had developed on homeland security. The boldness of Bush's plan and his insistence that Congress enact it by year's end pushed almost every other issue to the political sidelines. That was a blessing for a White House worried about the electoral consequences of a sluggish economy and a growing budget deficit. Some in Bush's circle crowed about their political jujitsu. The Department of Homeland Security is "the right thing to do for the right reasons," argued Mark McKinnon, Bush's chief media consultant during the campaign. "It also throws a huge blanket over the entire domestic agenda. The domestic agenda right now is security. It's covering up everything else."[43]

Besides entirely reshaping the domestic political agenda, Bush's proposal contained what was for Democrats a poison pill—a provision to strip workers in the new department of the civil service protections they had previously enjoyed. The Democrats faced a dilemma. They could endorse the president's proposal and alienate one of their key constituencies, organized labor, or oppose it and risk being accused of putting their party's interests ahead of the country's. The Democrats chose the latter. Republicans skillfully exploited the decision, with Bush at one point charging Senate Democrats with being "more interested in special interests in Washington and not interested in the security of the American people."[44] The charges stuck, at least with some voters. Although a Gallup poll taken in August 2002 showed voters preferring Democratic House candidates by 50 to 42 percent, Republicans triumphed in November.[45] A lame-duck Congress created a new homeland security department largely along the lines Bush had proposed.

Political calculations also figured prominently in Bush's decision in March 2002 to impose special tariffs on imported steel. U.S. steel manufacturers had argued that foreign producers were dumping steel on the American market. They wanted the administration to impose antidumping duties of up to 30 percent on imports. Bush's chief economic advisers, Secretary of Treasury Paul O'Neill and director of the National Economic Council Lawrence Lindsey, as well as chairman of the Federal Reserve Alan Greenspan, opposed the idea. They argued that the tariffs were not needed, contradicted the administration's commitment to free trade, and almost certainly violated international trade rules.[46]

Bush's political advisers, however, favored imposing the antidumping duties. During the 2000 campaign, Vice President Dick Cheney had promised steelworkers in West Virginia, a major steel-producing state that Bush had won narrowly, that the Bush administration would protect their jobs. Rove argued that the duties would win Republicans votes not only in West Virginia but also in the swing states of Michigan and Pennsylvania. The White House legislative staff believed that imposing the tariffs would secure Senate votes for passage of Trade Promotion Authority, which would give Bush enhanced authority to negotiate trade agreements.[47]

Bush sided with his political advisers. How much political benefit he derived from the decision is unclear. The tariffs drove up steel prices, angering U.S. industries that used steel in their products. The World Trade Organization ruled that the tariffs violated international trade law and authorized the European Union and other steel-producing countries to impose counter-tariffs on U.S. exports of their choosing. This alarmed many American manufacturers. They feared they would pay the price for protecting the steel industry. As a result, in December 2003 Bush gave ground and lifted the steel tariffs.[48]

The decisions to create the Department of Homeland Security and impose antidumping duties on steel imports were both instances in which politics persuaded the Bush administration to push initiatives. In the case of the travel ban to Cuba, however, politics persuaded the administration to block an initiative. In 2002, farm-state Republicans sought to ease restrictions on travel to Cuba. Their effort was motivated in good part by their own political needs. Farmers were looking for new export markets, and farm-state lawmakers hoped that repealing the travel ban would set the stage for a later repeal of the long-standing U.S. economic embargo on Cuba. By contrast, Cuban Americans were a key Bush constituency in Florida, the state he won by the narrowest of margins in 2000. Moreover, his brother Jeb was locked in a close race for Florida's governor. During his presidential campaign, as well as during his first year in office, President Bush had taken care not to alienate Cuban American hardliners. Two months before the bill on travel restrictions came to a vote, he affirmed that he would not lift sanctions on Cuba until Havana adopted sweeping democratic reforms.[49] Anti-Castro groups applauded the decision.

On the eve of the House vote on repealing the travel ban, Rove met privately with four Republican legislators. A leader of the Cuban exile lobby who attended the meeting said he read the "riot act" to the Republican lawmakers and they "went out with their tails between their legs." Representative George Nethercutt (R-WA), who attended the meeting, said of the administration's opposition to easing the travel restrictions, "I personally think there is a political component to it."[50] In the end, however, farm-state politics trumped White House politics as the House voted to relax the travel ban. Nonetheless, the White House's hardball politics succeeded in blunting the effort to pass broader legislation relaxing the economic embargo on Cuba.

The attacks on the Twin Towers and the Pentagon changed the direction of Bush's presidency. On September 10, he had been focused on domestic policy. After September 11, he was a wartime president. His public opinion approval ratings soared to unprecedented heights. Rather than persuading Bush and his advisers that he could rise above the fray of domestic politics, the sky-high approval ratings encouraged them to believe that they could use the public's insecurity to lock the Democratic Party into a minority status. For a time, the strategy worked.

The Surge

The banner that President Bush stood in front of on the deck of the USS *Abraham Lincoln* declared "Mission Accomplished." That optimism about what U.S. troops had accomplished in Iraq proved premature. By July 2003, some Iraqis were, in the words of General John Abizaid, the U.S. commander in the region, "conducting what I would describe as a classic guerrilla-type campaign against us. It's low-intensity conflict, in our doctrinal terms, but it's war, however you describe it."[51] By the end of 2003, more American soldiers had died occupying Iraq than in liberating it.

The rising death toll soured many Americans on the war. Senator John Kerry tried and failed to make Iraq the defining issue of the 2004 election. Although Bush turned back the Democrat's challenge, the security situation continued to deteriorate. At the start of 2006, Karl Rove signaled that the White House once again intended to encourage congressional Republicans to run on the war on terror in the upcoming congressional midterm elections. In another speech to the Republican National Committee, he criticized Democrats for opposing renewal of the USA Patriot Act and for what he saw as their "cut and run" policy on Iraq. "The United States faces a ruthless enemy," he said, and "we need a commander in chief and a Congress who [sic] understand the nature of threat and the gravity of the moment America finds itself in. President Bush and the Republican Party do. Unfortunately, the same cannot be said for many Democrats."[52] Despite this hot rhetoric, unease about the course of the war was growing among members of Congress on both sides of the aisle. In early 2006, Representative Frank Wolf (R-VA), chair of the Foreign Operations Subcommittee of the House Appropriations Committee, inserted an earmark into a supplemental spending bill on the war to create an independent, bipartisan panel to review the administration's Iraq policy.[53]

The Iraq Study Group, or the Baker-Hamilton group as it was more commonly called in recognition of its two chairs, former secretary of state James Baker and former House Foreign Affairs Committee chair Lee Hamilton, began operations in March 2006. The White House had originally been cool to the idea of a bipartisan commission but reversed course in the face of support for the idea both inside the administration and from Republicans on Capitol Hill.[54] Many observers initially wondered whether Bush would listen to the bipartisan commission's recommendations. Many of the commission's ten members shared the concern. "I wouldn't be doing this," Baker told them, "unless I thought he would be willing to listen and do it."[55]

The Democrats' impressive victory in the 2006 midterm elections, which gave them control of both the House and Senate, fueled expectations that Bush would heed the Iraq Study Group's recommendations. Most observers took Bush's decision the day after the election to replace Rumsfeld as secretary of defense as confirmation that the White House would soon be unveiling a new Iraq strategy. The timing of Rumsfeld's firing angered many congressional Republicans. They wondered why it had not happened months earlier. "I wanted to throw the breakfast dishes through the TV" after learning the news, said Representative Peter Hoekstra (R-MI), the outgoing chair of the House Intelligence Committee.[56] Like many Republicans, he believed that firing Rumsfeld before the election would have helped Republicans running in close races.

The Iraq Study Group released its final report in December.[57] Its ninety-six pages offered a stinging critique of virtually every facet of U.S. policy in Iraq. It faulted the Department of Defense for significantly underreporting the level of violence in Iraq, for failing to develop accurate intelligence on the insurgency, and for its failure to coordinate U.S. economic assistance to Iraq. The report's seventy-nine recommendations called for a major shift in U.S. strategy. Most significantly, the report recommended withdrawing all U.S. combat troops not necessary to protect the troops that were training Iraqi soldiers and opening up high-level dialogues with Iran and Syria. The White House had vigorously resisted both steps.

Bush praised the Iraq Study Group report as "an opportunity to find common ground."[58] In fact, although he had already concluded that U.S. policy in Iraq had to change, the change he envisioned was quite different from those the Iraq Study Group recommended. In January 2007 he used a nationally televised address to announce that he intended to send 21,500 additional troops to Iraq. Rather than decreasing the U.S. stakes in Iraq, he intended to raise them.

Democrats denounced the so-called surge. They pointed out that polls showed that most Americans wanted to withdraw troops from Iraq.[59] More troubling for Bush, some Republicans joined the Democrats in demanding that he reverse course. Senator George Voinovich (R-OH) said, "I've gone along with the president on this, and I bought into his dream. And at this stage of the game, I just don't think it's going to happen."[60] Senator Chuck Hagel (R-NE) called the surge "the most dangerous foreign policy blunder in this country since Vietnam, if it is carried out."[61]

Congressional Democrats tried to use the power of the purse to halt the surge. In late April, the House voted 218–208 to pass a defense spending bill that required U.S. troops to be withdrawn from Iraq by October 1. The next day the Senate followed suit. Bush vetoed the bill, however, and the effort to halt the surge collapsed. The additional troop deployments went ahead, and violence in Iraq fell. Experts disagreed, though, over whether the surge was responsible for the relative calm in Iraq or whether it came about for other, unrelated reasons.[62]

Regardless of the surge's merits, political calculations did not drive Bush's decision to send five additional brigades to Iraq. His choice came at considerable cost to his own political capital and to his party's. Whether he would have made the same choice if he were facing reelection is another question. By virtue of the Twenty-Second Amendment, however, he was not.

Beyond the Water's Edge

American political mythology holds that politics stops at the water's edge. In practice, it often doesn't. Foreign policy issues, like domestic ones, are sources of partisan division. Voters disagree on what they want the country to do overseas. Presidents can use these divisions to advance their own political interests and damage those of their opponents.

The incentives to use foreign policy to score political points, though, are not the same as in domestic policy. Domestic issues typically matter more to voters than defense or foreign issues do. It was hardly surprising, for instance, that George Bush focused on domestic issues during the 2000 presidential campaign and his first eight months in office. Foreign policy barely registered with the average voter. Embarking on a rapid defense buildup or launching a Manhattan project for missile defense would have diverted attention from more pressing domestic priorities without offering significant opportunities for political gain.

September 11 changed those calculations. Suddenly, the ability to keep the country safe became enormously relevant to the average voter. Bush's decisions to oust the Taliban in Afghanistan and to invade Iraq were not made for political gain. How he and fellow Republicans talked about the war on terror, however, was. Bush and Rove recognized that the long-standing public perception of Democrats as "weak" and "soft" on national security made them vulnerable to rhetoric and issue framing that implied, if not stated outright, that Democrats could not be trusted to keep Americans safe. So they took off the political gloves. But they were not alone in looking at the issue through a political lens. Senate Democrats gave in to the White House's request for a vote on the Iraq war resolution in good part because many of them wanted to put the Iraq issue "behind them" and turn to the economy in the weeks leading up to the midterm elections.

But if the Bush presidency demonstrates how presidents can use foreign policy to advance their own political interests and those of their party, it also demonstrates how presidents can find themselves forced to choose between what they think makes for good policy and what they know makes for good politics. In deciding to send twenty-thousand-plus additional troops to Iraq in early 2007, Bush knew he was running against public sentiment. It is a dilemma that many of his predecessors in the White House have known. Jimmy Carter spent considerable political capital in 1977 persuading the Senate to pass the unpopular Panama Canal Treaty. Bill Clinton likewise angered many of his fellow Democrats by pushing to grant China most-favored-nation status. Foreign policy can be a source of considerable electoral gain for presidents. But it may be more often a source of political pain.

The Early Obama Years

Barack Obama's successful run for the presidency and his first two years in office differ in one way from the story told in this chapter but on the whole confirm it. Unlike any other presidential candidate over the past half century, foreign policy helped catapult Obama to his party's nomination. But like most other presidential candidates and most presidents once in office, foreign policy did little to boost his electoral chances during the general election campaign or to persuade voters once he was in office that he was discharging his duties wisely.

Obama's chances of capturing the Democratic Party's presidential nomination looked slim when he announced his candidacy in front of the Old State Capitol in Springfield, Illinois, on a frigid day in February 2007. His campaign adviser later wrote that if a computer had simulated the forthcoming campaign, Senator Hillary Clinton (D-NY) would have won ninety-five times out of a hundred and Senator John Edwards (D-NC) would have won the other five times.[63] Obama's credentials for office were slight. His main claim to fame was a rousing address at the 2004 Democratic National Convention. He had no executive experience inside government or out, his legislative record during his two years in the Senate was sparse, and his positions on domestic issues of interest to voters mirrored those of his rivals. By contrast, Senator Clinton had lived in the White House for eight years, was a household name, had built a reputation in the Senate as a workhorse who could work across party lines, and had amassed an unrivalled campaign war chest that made her seemingly a shoo-in for the presidential nomination.

Obama had one thing going for him, though, besides impressive oratorical skills and an underrated fundraising operation—his opposition to the Iraq War. Clinton, Edwards, and several other Democratic candidates had all voted in October 2002 to authorize George W. Bush to go to war to unseat Saddam Hussein. A vote that had looked to be politically astute when cast had become a liability by 2007 as the United States was mired in a bloody insurgency in Iraq. The war weighed heavily on voters' minds. More than one in three Americans identified Iraq as the most important issue facing the country.[64] The war was so politically toxic among Democrats that Edwards publicly repudiated his vote and apologized to voters. The primary calendar further accentuated Iraq's importance as a campaign issue. The first official nominating event was Iowa, where Democrats were rabidly antiwar.

While Clinton, Edwards, and the rest of the Democratic field sought to explain their pro-war votes, Obama had a far simpler and more appealing message: He had opposed the war from the start. As Congress debated whether to authorize Bush to invade Iraq, Obama spoke at an antiwar rally in Grant Park in Chicago and denounced the march toward a "dumb war."[65] Five years later his primary opponents questioned the speech's significance, implying that he would have taken a different position had he been in the U.S. Senate at the time and forced to vote on the record and not just speak to antiwar crowds. These complaints failed to damage Obama's appeal to the antiwar spirit that animated Democratic Party activists during 2007 and into the spring of 2008. Similar criticisms on what his rivals presumed would be Obama's Achilles' heel, his relative foreign policy inexperience, largely backfired. Each time the inexperience charge was leveled, Obama countered that experience could not substitute for judgment, implicitly reminding voters that he had always opposed the Iraq War.

Even Obama's supposed gaffes worked in his favor. At a CNN-YouTube debate in South Carolina in July 2007, he answered "yes" when asked whether he would "be willing to meet separately, without precondition . . . with the leaders of Iran, Syria, Venezuela, Cuba, and North Korea, in order to bridge the gap that divides our countries."[66] The Clinton campaign immediately derided Obama's answer as "irresponsible and frankly naïve."[67] Even Obama supporters labeled the answer as at best a "flub" and urged him to walk it back.[68] Rather than reversing course, though, Obama reaffirmed his answer and implied that his rivals were echoing the Bush-Cheney approach to diplomacy. The decision to stand firm gave life to Obama's call for a strategy of engagement with other countries.[69] It also further distinguished him from his rivals, a distinction that many Democratic voters found significant.[70]

To be sure, not all of Obama's forays into foreign policy during the campaign succeeded. In February 2008 he emphasized trade as an issue for the first time, criticizing NAFTA in his television, radio, and print advertising in Ohio. His campaign adviser, David Plouffe, later acknowledged, "The campaign's message on trade at this point was admittedly simplistic; a witness to the Ohio campaign might have been left with the impression that our position was no different than that of Dennis Kucinich, an ardent anti-trader. Our message lacked nuance; our TV ads and mail pieces were stridently critical of NAFTA and offered little evidence of Obama's more complex take on trade."[71] Obama's "simplistic" trade message was no accident. Free trade agreements were deeply unpopular among rank-and-file Democrats. This was especially true in Ohio, a blue collar, heavily unionized state that had fallen on hard economic times, in good part because its industries were not internationally competitive. Obama's team hoped to use NAFTA as a wedge issue to pry labor support away from Clinton, whose husband had persuaded Congress to approve the much-hated trade deal.

Obama's tactic backfired. His sudden embrace of anti-trade rhetoric struck many pundits and many voters as inauthentic. Matters were made worse when the media reported that one of his economic advisers had told officials at the Canadian consulate in Chicago that his anti-NAFTA stance was rhetoric designed to win votes and not a guide to future policy. The official disputed the story's details, but it nonetheless damaged Obama. It ran contrary to the image he had carefully cultivated during the campaign of being a different kind of political leader who would not tailor his message to what voters wanted to hear. Obama lost Ohio decisively.

Obama overcame his stumble and eventually captured the Democratic nomination. But while Hillary Clinton and other Democrats had failed to exploit Obama's inexperience on foreign affairs, his Republican opponent, Senator John McCain (R-AZ), looked up to the challenge. McCain's well-documented prisoner-of-war experience in Vietnam and more than three decades of legislative service gave him what looked to be an inherent advantage on foreign policy. Polls conducted in the late summer of 2008 showed that more Americans placed confidence in John McCain's ability to deal with national security and foreign policy issues and that many voters worried that Obama would be too eager to pursue diplomatic solutions.[72]

It was Obama's good fortune, however, that by late summer 2008 Iraq and foreign policy more generally had all but disappeared as issues of voter concern. Turmoil in the housing and financial markets, which culminated in the collapse of Lehman Brothers in September, threw the economy in a tailspin. Economic issues suddenly dominated the public debate—nearly six in ten voters named the economy the single most important issue facing the country.[73] Here Obama held a significant advantage over McCain, an advantage that McCain reinforced with his deprecating comments about his own economic expertise and his tone-deaf insistence during the midst of the crisis that "the fundamentals of our economy are strong."[74] What looked to be a tight election race turned into a relative rout.

Obama took the oath of office in January 2009 with considerable freedom to act on foreign policy. No one could complain that his foreign policy plans were a mystery. He had put his intention to leave Iraq, devote more attention to Afghanistan, and revamp the tone of American diplomacy front and center in his campaign. Just as important, Obama came into office riding a wave of goodwill. As he started his presidency, roughly seven out of ten American's approved of the job he was doing.[75]

Obama largely followed through on his foreign policy campaign promises.[76] On his third day in office, he ordered that the U.S. detention facility at Guantanamo Bay, Cuba, be closed within a year and halted the coercive interrogation techniques that the Bush administration had authorized for use on terrorist suspects. On his fourth day in office he overturned the Mexico City Policy that George W. Bush had imposed barring government funds from going to private groups that performed or promoted abortion as a family planning technique. In mid-February he ordered seventeen thousand additional U.S. troops sent to Afghanistan. At the end of February he ordered the withdrawal of all U.S. combat troops from Iraq by August 2010. He appointed special envoys to tackle a range of tough diplomatic problems, including the Israeli-Palestinian conflict and Iran. And he traveled widely, more in fact than any previous president did during his first year in office, visiting twenty-one countries and delivering major speeches in Prague on nuclear weapons and in Cairo on U.S. relations with the Islamic world.[77]

Obama's foreign policy initiatives and diplomatic outreach made him widely popular abroad, and they eventually resulted in his being awarded the 2009 Nobel Peace Prize.[78] Foreign policy did little to help him at home, however, and in some cases it hurt him. His decision to close Guantanamo Bay quickly came under fire from Republicans. When the White House failed to override their objections, liberal Democrats accused Obama of backtracking on a signature policy promise. His decision to press Israel to impose a moratorium on all settlement construction in the West Bank failed to work and triggered a backlash among both Democrats and Republicans on Capitol Hill. In the fall of 2010, the White House finally abandoned the policy as unworkable.[79] Obama's withdrawal plan from Iraq proceeded apace, and in August 2010 the last U.S. combat troops departed from the country.[80] This achievement, however, did little to move Obama's approval ratings. And his Nobel Peace Prize became the object of jokes on late-night talk shows.

Obama's decisions on a few foreign policy issues put him at odds with his core constituencies. One such issue was Afghanistan. In August 2009 the commanding U.S. general in Afghanistan, Stanley McChrystal, wrote a dire assessment of the state of affairs in the country, warning of "mission failure" if more troops were not sent and the strategy changed.[81] The report quickly leaked, creating an uproar. Obama responded by launching a second strategic review of Afghanistan policy, a review that consumed most of the fall.[82] In December, he announced in a nationwide address that he was ordering an additional thirty thousand U.S. troops to Afghanistan, with the aim of beginning to withdraw by July 2011.

The Afghan troop surge was Obama's effort to be all things to all people. He admitted that domestic politics drove the July 2011 withdrawal date. "I can't let this be a war without end," he told Senator Lindsey Graham (R-SC), "and I can't lose the whole Democratic Party."[83] But the attempt to please everyone didn't work. Republicans complained that a withdrawal date encouraged Taliban forces to hold out, thereby defeating the point of the surge. Democrats complained that the surge was a policy whose costs far exceeded its benefits. Speaker of the House Nancy Pelosi (D-CA) told Obama she would not make the case to House Democrats to support the surge; he would have to do that on his own.[84] Obama maintained the necessary congressional support, but in doing so he had to rely more on Republican than Democratic votes.

Obama found normal political alliances similarly reversed on trade. He had largely avoided trade issues in 2009, with the exception of occasionally imposing punitive tariffs on China for violating international trading rules.[85] In his 2010 State of the Union address, however, he highlighted trade as a way to rejuvenate the American economy and pledged to double American exports by 2010.[86] Reaching that goal required, among other things, securing congressional approval of free trade pacts with South Korea, Colombia, and Panama that George W. Bush had signed in 2007 but that had languished ever since. Obama's problem was that most Democrats doubted that the agreements served America's economic interests. His natural support for enacting these free trade agreements was making common cause with Republicans, thereby further straining his relations with fellow Democrats.

As Obama began his third year in office, then, he found himself in an odd political position. The Democrats had taken a "shellacking" in the 2010 congressional midterm elections.[87] With political momentum on the GOP's side, Republicans were looking to damage Obama's reelection chances by dealing him additional defeats on both domestic and foreign policy. They came close to doing just that on the New START Treaty that the lame-duck session of the Senate eventually approved. But for Obama, success on two of his signature foreign policy issues for 2011—Afghanistan and trade—required working closely with Republicans and potentially alienating his Democratic base. Obama had discovered, like many of his predecessors in the White House, that foreign policy can at times be a source of political advantage, but it more often is a source of political pain.

NOTES

1. Quoted in Thomas B. Edsall, "GOP Tout War as Campaign Issue," *Washington Post*, January 19, 2002, A2.

2. Quoted in Alison Mitchell, "Democrats Say Bush Aide Uses War for Political Gain," *New York Times*, January 20, 2002, A1, http://query.nytimes.com/gst/fullpage .html?res=9402E5DB143BF933A15752C0A9649C8B63.

3. Quoted in Russ Smith, "Find Cheney, and Muzzle Rove; More Times Deception; Too Much Talk about Talk," January 29, 2002, www.nypress.com/print-article-5383 -print.html.

4. Quoted in "Should National Security Be a National Issue?" *Human Events*, January 28, 2002, http://findarticles.com/p/articles/mi_qa3827/is_200201/ai_n9052971.

5. The term *two presidencies* was coined in Aaron Wildavsky, "The Two Presidencies," *Transaction* 4 (December 1966): 7–14. Wildavsky's article spawned a long line of research that has variously confirmed, modified, and challenged his original findings. Many of these studies are reprinted in Steven A. Shull, ed., *The Two Presidencies: A Quarter Century Assessment* (Chicago: Nelson-Hall, 1991). The relevance of these subsequent studies to the question of how presidential power varies across policy domains is limited, however, because of methodological problems. See James M. Lindsay and Wayne P. Steger, "The 'Two Presidencies' in Future Research: Moving Beyond Roll-Call Analysis," *Congress and the Presidency* 20 (Autumn 1993): 103–17.

6. The literature on ethnic lobbies and their influence on American foreign policy is large. Among others, see Mitchell Bard, *The Water's Edge and Beyond: Defining the Limits to Domestic Influence on United States Middle East Policy* (New Brunswick, NJ: Transaction, 1991); Rodolfo O. de la Garza and Harry P. Pachon, eds., *Latinos and U.S. Foreign Policy: Representing the "Homeland"?* (Lanham, MD: Rowman & Littlefield, 2000); David Howard Goldberg, *Foreign Policy and Ethnic Interest Groups* (Westport, CT: Greenwood, 1990); John J. Mearsheimer and Stephen M. Walt, *The Israel Lobby and U.S. Foreign Policy* (New York: Farrar, Straus & Giroux, 2007); Tony Smith, *Foreign Attachments: The Power of Ethnic Groups in the Making of American Foreign Policy* (Cambridge, MA: Harvard University Press, 2000); and Paul Y. Watanabe, *Ethnic Groups, Congress, and American Foreign Policy* (Westport, CT: Greenwood, 1984).

7. Bill Clinton, *My Life* (New York: Knopf, 2004), 401.

8. See Thomas L. Friedman, "The 1992 Campaign: The Democrats; Clinton Asserts Bush Is Too Eager to Befriend the World's Dictators," *New York Times*, October 2, 1992.

9. See, e.g., "Cohen Criticizes 'Wag the Dog' Characterization," CNN.com, March 23, 2004, www.cnn.com/2004/ALLPOLITICS/03/23/wag.dog/.

10. Quoted in Derek Chollet and James Goldgeier, *America between the Wars: From 11/9 to 9/11—The Misunderstood Years between the Fall of the Berlin Wall and the Start of the War on Terror* (New York: Public Affairs, 2008), 224.

11. See James M. Lindsay, "The New Apathy," *Foreign Affairs* 79 (September/October 2000): 2–8.

12. Quoted in Dan Balz, "Bush Takes Soft Line on Abortion Stance of Running Mate," *Washington Post*, June 24, 1999, A7.

13. See I. M. Destler and Steven Kull, *Misreading the Public: The Myth of the New Isolationism* (Washington, DC: Brookings Institution, 1999).

14. Governor George W. Bush, "A Distinctly American Internationalism," Ronald Reagan Library, Simi Valley, California, November 19, 1999, www.mtholyoke.edu/acad /intrel/bush/wspeech.htm.

15. Ibid.

16. Ibid.

17. Governor George W. Bush, "A Period of Consequences," The Citadel, South Carolina, September 23, 1999, www.citadel.edu/pao/addresses/pres_bush.html.

18. Bush, "Distinctly American Internationalism."

19. Ibid.

20. Bush, "Period of Consequences."

21. Dick Cheney, "Dick Cheney's Acceptance Speech," Republican National Convention, Philadelphia, Pennsylvania, August 2, 2000, www.2000gop.com/convention /speech/speechcheney.html.

22. Quoted in Paul Krugman, "Guns and Bitterness," *New York Times*, February 4, 2001, 4.17.

23. Bush, "Period of Consequences."

24. "The Second 2000 Gore-Bush Presidential Debate: October 11, 2000," www .debates.org/index.php?page=october-11-2000-debate-transcript.

25. Quoted in Alan Sipress, "Powell Vows to Consult Allies on Key Issues," *Washington Post*, February 28, 2001, A22.

26. Quoted in Jeffrey Kluger, "A Climate of Despair," *Time*, April 9, 2001, 30.

27. "Remarks by the President and German Chancellor Schroeder in Photo Opportunity," March 29, 2001, www.whitehouse.gov/news/releases/2001/03/20010329-2 .html.

28. Tom Donnelly, "Cheap Hawks," *Weekly Standard*, June 11, 2001, 14.

29. Robert Kagan and William Kristol, "Clinton's Foreign Policy (cont.)," *Weekly Standard*, March 12, 2001, 11.

30. Robert Kagan and William Kristol, "A National Humiliation," *Weekly Standard*, April 16/23, 2001, 12–14.

31. Quoted in Evan Thomas and John Barry, "The Conflict to Come," *Newsweek*, April 23, 2001, 24.

32. S.J. Res 23, "Authorization for Use of Military Force," September 14, 2001.

33. See, e.g., Dick Cheney, "Congressional Overreaching in Foreign Policy," in *Foreign Policy and the Constitution*, ed. Robert A. Goldwin and Robert A. Licht (Washington, DC: American Enterprise Institute, 1990).

34. See, e.g., the survey by Gallup/CNN/*USA Today* conducted November 8–10, 2002.

35. See, e.g., the survey by Gallup/CNN/*USA Today* conducted January 25–27, 2002.

36. James Moore and Wayne Slater, *Bush's Brain: How Karl Rove Made George W. Bush Presidential* (New York: Wiley, 2003), 291.

37. Quoted in Todd Purdum, "Democrats Starting to Fault President on the War's Future," *New York Times*, March 1, 2002, A1.

38. George W. Bush, "Guard and Reserves 'Define Spirit of America,'" The Pentagon, September 17, 2001, www.whitehouse.gov/news/releases/2001/09/20010917-3 .html.

39. Quoted in Purdum, "Democrats Starting to Fault President."

40. Ronald Brownstein and Emma Vaughn, "Timing Entwined War Vote, Election," *Los Angeles Times*, November 28, 2005, A1, http://articles.latimes.com/2005/nov/28/nation/na-warvote28.

41. Quoted in Anne E. Kornbluth, "Bush '04 Fund-Raising Cites War on Terrorism," *Boston Globe*, May 25, 2003, A1.

42. "Press Briefing by Ari Fleisher," Washington, D.C., March 19, 2002, www.whitehouse.gov/news/releases/2002/03/20020319-7.html.

43. Quoted in Elisabeth Bumiller and Alison Mitchell, "Bush Aides See Political Pluses in Security Plans," *New York Times*, June 15, 2002, A1.

44. George W. Bush, "Remarks by the President at Anne Northup for Congress Luncheon," Louisville, Kentucky, September 5, 2002, www.whitehouse.gov/news/releases/2002/09/20020905-5.html.

45. John Judis, "Turd Blossom: Karl Rove's Dreams Go Down the Toilet," *New Republic*, August 20, 2007, www.carnegieendowment.org/publications/index.cfm?fa=view&id=19536&prog=zgp&proj=zusr.

46. See Ron Suskind, *The Price of Loyalty* (New York: Simon & Schuster, 2004), 216–21.

47. Ibid.

48. Richard W. Stevenson and Elizabeth Becker, "After 21 Months, Bush Lifts Tariffs on Steel Imports," *New York Times*, December 5, 2003, A1.

49. Elisabeth Bumiller, "Embargo Remains until Cuba Alters Policy, Bush Says," *New York Times*, May 21, 2002, A11, www.nytimes.com/2002/05/21/world/embargo-remains-until-cuba-alters-policy-bush-says.html?scp=1&sq=bush%20cuba%20democratic%20may%202002&st=cse.

50. Quoted in Christopher Marquis, "It's Republican vs. Republican on Cuba," *New York Times*, July 28, 2002, http://query.nytimes.com/gst/fullpage.html?res=9806EED8163BF93BA15754C0A9649C8B63&sec=&spon=&pagewanted=all.

51. "DOD News Briefing—Mr. Di Rita and Gen. Abizaid," Department of Defense News Transcript, July 16, 2003, www.defense.gov/transcripts/transcript.aspx?transcriptid=2845.

52. Quoted in Adam Nagourney, "Rove Lays Out Road Map for Republicans in Fall Elections," *New York Times*, January 21, 2006, A1, www.nytimes.com/2006/01/21/national/21rove.html?_r=2&oref=slogin.

53. David D. Kirkpatrick, "An Earmark with Impact," *New York Times*, December 5, 2006.

54. Lyndsey Layton, "The Story behind the Iraq Study Group," *Washington Post*, November 21, 2006.

55. Quoted in Bob Woodward, *The War Within: A Secret White House History, 2006–2008* (New York: Simon & Schuster, 2008), 123.

56. Quoted in ibid., 206.

57. *The Iraq Study Group: The Way Forward—A New Approach*, http://media.usip.org/reports/iraq_study_group_report.pdf.

58. Michael Abramowitz and Robin Wright, "Iran Panel Proposes Major Policy Shift," *Washington Post*, December 7, 2006, A1, www.washingtonpost.com/wp-dyn/content/article/2006/12/06/AR2006120600419.html.

59. Among others, see the *Washington Post*/ABC News Poll reported in Michael Abramowitz and Jonathan Weisman, "Bush's Iraq Plan Meets Skepticism on Capitol

Hill," *Washington Post*, January 12, 2009, A1, www.washingtonpost.com/wp-dyn/con tent/article/2007/01/11/AR2007011100437.html.

60. Quoted in ibid.

61. Quoted in Connie Bruck, "Odd Man Out," *New Yorker*, November 3, 2008, 53, www.newyorker.com/reporting/2008/11/03/081103fa_fact_bruck.

62. See, e.g., Stephen Biddle, Michael E. O'Hanlon, and Kenneth M. Pollack, "How to Leave a Stable Iraq," *Foreign Affairs* 87 (September/October 2008): 40–58.

63. David Plouffe, *The Audacity to Win: The Inside Story and Lessons of Barack Obama's Historic Victory* (New York: Viking, 2009), 17.

64. *The Gallup Poll: Public Opinion 2007* (Lanham, MD: Rowman & Littlefield, 2008), 315.

65. Quoted in Greg Bryane and Jane B. Vaughn, "300 Attend Rally against Iraq War," *Chicago Daily Herald*, October 3, 2002, 8.

66. Among others, see John Heilemann and Mark Halperin, *Game Change: Obama and the Clintons, McCain and Palin, and the Race of a Lifetime* (New York: Harper, 2010), 111; Plouffe, *Audacity to Win*, 84–86; and Matthew Yglesias, "The Accidental Foreign Policy," *Atlantic*, June 2008, 28–30.

67. Quoted in Yglesias, "Accidental Foreign Policy," 28.

68. David Corn, "An Obama Flub at the YouTube Debate?" *Capital Games: 2002–2007*, posted July 24, 2007, www.thenation.com/blog/156342/obama-flub-youtube-debate.

69. Barack Obama outlined his engagement strategy in "Renewing American Leadership," *Foreign Affairs*, July/August 2007, 2–16.

70. Plouffe, *Audacity to Win*, 85–86.

71. Ibid., 194.

72. E.g., a September 2008 *New York Times*/CBS News poll gave McCain an eight-point lead over Obama (49% vs. 41%) on their relative ability to handle national security and foreign policy issues. Dalia Sussman, "Poll Finds McCain Edge on Security," *New York Times*, September 25, 2008.

73. See, e.g., NBC News/*Wall Street Journal* Survey, Study #6087, September 19–22, 2008, 12.

74. Quoted in Heilemann and Halperin, *Game Change*, 379.

75. Obama's public approval ratings can be seen at www.pollingreport.com.

76. A convenient summary of Obama's major foreign policy decisions during his first months in office can be found in Jonathan Alter, *The Promise: President Obama, Year One* (Simon & Schuster, 2010), chap. 14.

77. Alter, *Promise*, 14.

78. "Confidence in Obama Lifts U.S. Image around the World; Most Muslim Publics Not So Easily Moved," Pew Research Center: Pew Global Attitudes Project, July 23, 2009, http://pewglobal.org/2009/07/23/confidence-in-obama-lifts-us-image-around-the-world/.

79. Mark Landler, "Clinton Says U.S. Is Committed to Mideast Peace but Reverting to Old Strategy," *New York Times*, December 10, 2010.

80. Ernesto Londoño, "'A Truly Historic End to 7 Years of War': As Last Combat Brigade Leaves Iraq, Soldiers Carry Hidden Costs of Conflict with Memories of Fallen Comrades," *Washington Post*, August 19, 2010.

81. Stanley A. McChrystal, "Commander's Initial Assessment," August 30, 2009, http://media.washingtonpost.com/wp-srv/politics/documents/Assessment_Redacted _092109.pdf.

82. The particulars of the Afghan strategy review are extensively documented in Bob Woodward, *Obama's Wars* (New York: Simon & Schuster, 2010).

83. Quoted in Woodward, *Obama's Wars*, 336.

84. Thomas Ferraro, "Pelosi: Obama Must Make Case for War Buildup," Reuters, December 16, 2009, www.reuters.com/article/idUSN16105303.

85. See, e.g., Peter Whoriskey and Anne Kornblut, "U.S. to Impose Tariff on Tires from China," *Washington Post*, September 12, 2009.

86. Barack Obama, "Remarks by the President in State of the Union Address," The White House, January 27, 2010, www.whitehouse.gov/the-press-office/remarks-presi dent-state-union-address.

87. Ibid.

CHAPTER TEN

The Dynamics of Presidential Policy Choice and Promotion

Daniel J. Galvin

When and why do presidents choose to tackle different types of policies? What explains the variation in the policy choices they make and the political strategies they use to promote them? As the previous chapters have illustrated, the dynamics of presidential policy choice and promotion are anything but straightforward. Not only do presidents have multiple motives and goals, as well as different ones at different times, but every policy presents its own peculiar challenges that may encourage or deter presidents from hazarding the attempt. In each instance, it seems, presidential behavior is driven by a myriad of factors. The task of this chapter, therefore, is to do some preliminary sorting and sifting. It offers some theoretical suggestions and develops some provisional claims, drawing upon the rich detail provided in the previous chapters.

First, I argue for a slight shift in the approach most commonly used to study presidential behavior so that we might gain more analytical leverage on the questions at hand. Then, I suggest certain conditions under which we might expect to observe specific patterns in presidential policy choice and promotion. Several hypotheses are subsequently tested, drawing upon the material presented in the previous chapters. In conclusion, I offer some further observations and suggest how the mid-range propositions offered here speak to several other questions of long-standing interest.

The Personal Presidency

American presidents are notorious for their oversized ambitions. Not content to simply preside over government, they strive to "secure a place in history" for themselves on their own terms (Skowronek 1997, 18). Rather than view the political landscape as fixed or unchangeable, they are driven to reshape their environment and create durable change (Moe 1985; Ginsberg and Shefter 1988; Skowronek 1997; Sheingate 2003; Galvin 2010). With an expansive administrative apparatus at their fingertips, presidents have the tools and resources they need to develop and promote comprehensive policy agendas. Consequently, the public has come to expect nothing less than transformative leadership from its incumbents (Lowi 1985).

Our typical approach to studying the presidency has been strongly shaped by these observations: we routinely evaluate presidents by their ability to accomplish their grand ambitions. Their policy choices, the timing of those choices, and the skills they display in following through on their choices, we think, have something rather essential to do with their success in office. Indeed, following Richard Neustadt, a long tradition of scholarship has viewed the incumbent's "personal capacity to influence the conduct of the men who make up government" as the primary measure of his success (Neustadt 1960, 4). We want to know how the president prioritized his initiatives, how he organized his administration, how he shepherded his agenda through Congress. Since we seek to understand and evaluate his decisions, our attention naturally turns to the "make" of the man, to his political instincts, to his governing style. When the president fails to accomplish the policy changes he seeks, we dwell on the deficiencies of his leadership; when he succeeds, we applaud his political savvy. In either case, we tend to focus on the individual president and his unique capabilities.

This tendency to personalize the study of the presidency has clearly yielded important insights. But it is also an approach that runs up against certain conceptual limitations. Specifically, while every presidential action might be explained with reference to the president's personal characteristics and pro-clivities (think LBJ's neurosis or Nixon's paranoia as explanations for their actions), many presidential actions are clearly strategic responses to the political environment, and thus not necessarily specific to, or dependent on, the president as an individual. That is, much of what presidents do is rational, and similarly situated presidents are likely to do the same sorts of things, irrespective of their distinctive personalities, skills, and styles (Moe 1993). When faced with the same basic incentives and constraints, very different presidents will often make the same sorts of calculations and move in the same basic directions. The task at hand is to specify which conditions tend to motivate similar behaviors and to offer some suggestions as to why.

In our examination of presidential policy choices, then, it is helpful to begin with the assumption that presidential choices are made with an eye toward maximizing the president's benefit, given certain constraints. Every president will understand the "benefit" he derives differently, of course, and every president will bring his own unique skills (or lack thereof) to bear in his actions: no two presidents should be expected to execute the choices they make equally well. But whatever his personal purposes or level of political skill, every president should be expected to take stock of his circumstances, weigh competing alternatives, and make his decisions *in light of those circumstances*. In the aggregate and over time, then, similarities in political context should tend to generate similar patterns of presidential behavior. Uncovering the dynamics of presidential behavior, therefore, would seem to require more investigation into the *context* in which decisions are made than the psychology of the decision makers.

Electoral Dynamics and Presidential Goals

While any number of contextual factors may shape presidential behavior, I propose that we zero in on the ways in which electoral dynamics—arguably the most consistent and consistently powerful contextual factor—motivate presidential action.

Electoral competition is a powerful motivator of political behavior: this much we know to be true (Downs 1957; Mayhew 1974). Indeed, we also know that different electoral circumstances tend to motivate different types of political behaviors. A long tradition of scholarship has shown, for example, that minority parties—that is, those parties currently out of power seeking to get back in—tend to act differently from majority, or "in," parties. These political "losers" are understood to be "the desperate ones; they are the ones whose survival is at stake; they are the ones driven by their despair to seek ways to triumph; they are, therefore, the inventors. Defeat is the mother of invention" (Shepsle 2003, 310). Prominent scholars from Anthony Downs to Robert Dahl to William Riker to Theodore Lowi have observed that in the wake of defeat, losing parties are driven to act in an innovative fashion: they attempt to co-opt the opposition, appropriate their ideas, recombine old policy proposals into new creative alternatives, and reach out to new groups in order to expand their coalition and increase their probabilities of winning in the next election (Downs 1957; Riker 1962; Lowi 1963; Dahl 1966). Winning parties, in contrast, tend to act in a consolidative fashion: they seek to solidify their base of support, distribute the fruits of victory to key coalition members, and deliver on the promises made in the course of the campaign.

What does this electoral-behavioral dynamic have to do with presidential policy choice? Clearly, presidents are not parties and cannot be assumed to act in a strictly Downsian fashion. But they are not immune to these electoral pressures, either—indeed, they may be more susceptible to them than we commonly realize. One of the greatest peculiarities of the American political system is that presidents can, and often do, get elected while their party remains in the minority by other measures. These presidents may share their party's incentive to regroup, rebuild, and expand their reach: not because they are altruistically driven to help their party collectivity, but because the state of their party factors into their calculations of their own probabilities of success (Galvin 2010). Of course, no president *needs* his party in order to vent his ambitions and pursue his agenda. Minority-party presidents, in particular, might be tempted to abandon their party, draw upon their expansive White House resources, adopt a strictly plebiscitary style of leadership, concentrate on their own reelections, and govern without concern for their party's future.

But to the extent that presidents affiliated with a minority party seek more than momentary success, they have a strong incentive to help rebuild their party, expand its reach, and add to its electoral coalition. John Aldrich has argued that the political party offers durable "institutionalized solutions" to many of the most common political problems actors face, and this may be an especially important consideration for presidents (though presidents do not factor into Aldrich's analysis) (Aldrich 1995, 26). For one thing, to the extent that reelection is more difficult for these presidents (given their party's lack of a "natural" majority), a stronger, broader party promises to help them achieve this central goal. But presidents also have ambitions that go beyond reelection—as noted, they also want to secure a historical legacy for themselves on their own terms. On this score, a rebuilt party promises to serve as a durable vehicle for perpetuating the president's policy commitments after he leaves the White House. It offers a solution to the president's "time" problem: it promises durability under conditions of impermanence. What's more, if he is successful in his party-building efforts, he might secure a place for himself in history as the one who led the party out of the wilderness—as the founder of a new majority in American politics. For minority-party presidents, in other words, party building is tantamount to legacy building (Galvin 2010).

Put in the language of expectations, we would therefore expect minority-party presidents to have the strongest incentive to expand their party. They are more likely to design policies that expand their party's appeal, invest in new organizational capacities, emphasize candidate recruitment, issue inclusive ideological rhetoric to expand the party's appeal, and so on. The long-term benefits of party building—for their historical reputation and for their party's future competitiveness—should seep into most of the calculations they make.

Majority-party presidents simply do not share the same party-building incentive. With their party in a strong competitive position, they need not be concerned with expanding its base, retooling its organizational structure, or reformulating its policy proposals for the sake of its long-term competitiveness. Their priority is to govern, first and foremost, and thus to "deliver the goods" to the party faithful. Their task is to exploit their party's electoral advantages and translate its basic commitments into public policies. Their aim is to put their party's majorities to work now, not to build a new majority for later. They seek to harness their party's strength, tap into it, and leverage it for collective gain.

Theoretically, then, depending on the competitive standing of the president's party, different incentives and goals will be at play. It may be useful to view these dynamics along a continuum ranging from one hypothetical extreme to the other (fig. 10.1).

Depending on which side of the spectrum the president falls in any given instance, we should expect certain behavioral tendencies. The weaker the

Figure 10.1. Competitive standing of the president's party.

party's competitive standing, the more the president will want to *expand* his party coalition; the stronger the party's competitive standing, the more he will want to *exploit* his party's strength. That is, presidents who feel more vulnerable—whose parties' future seems less certain—should be expected to adopt strategies to attract new groups, cut into the opposition party's electoral coalition, and expand the party's appeal to new and emerging demographics. Presidents who feel more politically secure—whose parties' future seems more certain—should be expected to seize the moment and "feed the base," deliver on shared ideological purposes within the party, and reward stalwart supporters.

Of course, in reality, it is often difficult to determine where along the spectrum a given incumbent president should be placed. Bill Clinton, for example, would seem to have been a "majority-party president" during 1993–94 but a "minority-party president" after the dramatic Republican gains in the 1994 elections. During George W. Bush's two terms, the Democratic Party remained the "majority party" in terms of partisan identification in the electorate, but the Republican Party was the "majority party" for six years in Congress and the two parties were close to parity in state-level elections: by these measures, the competitive standing of the Republican Party was decidedly mixed.

At issue, therefore, is not how we evaluate the president's competitive environment from afar, but how the president perceives his competitive environment. In any given moment, how does he evaluate his party's trajectory? When he considers recent events, evaluates the current state of politics, and estimates the possibilities for the future, how strong does he perceive his party's competitive standing to be? In some cases, it is clear what the president's perceptions are: presidential diaries, White House documents, tape recordings, and other primary sources provide invaluable information. For example, we know that Kennedy, Johnson, and Carter inherited a party with deep and durable majorities, and while they experienced difficulty managing their heterogeneous and internally divided coalition, they always expected their party's majorities to last. Eisenhower, Nixon, and Ford, in contrast, perceived their party's electoral standing and its "brand" to be weak, even a liability in their own reelection campaigns. Reagan and George H. W. Bush consistently referred to the GOP as the "minority party," even though Republican presidents occupied the White House for twenty out of the twenty-four years between 1968 and 1992 (Galvin 2010).

Yet even when we do not have access to such primary sources—as is the case for the Clinton, George W. Bush, and Obama presidencies—the basic dynamics described above should still be expected to hold. Using available evidence, we can make our best appraisal of how the president perceives his competitive environment, state our expectations, and then use observations of his behavior as a provisional test of those expectations. Though our conclusions will necessarily be tentative, we can use the exercise as a preliminary test of our general propositions.

Presidential Goals and Policy Approaches

Having posited that presidents pursue different goals depending on the shape of their competitive political environment, we can now move to a consideration of the kinds of strategies they may adopt in pursuit of those goals. A wide range of potential approaches are available to them. For example, as I have discussed elsewhere, presidents who belong to weaker parties tend to undertake efforts to rebuild their parties' organizational capacities as a means of recapturing the majority; those with stronger parties tend to neglect those party structures and operations and allow them to languish (Galvin 2010). But making changes to the party organization is only one way presidents can respond to their party's competitive standing. Policy promotion, for example, is a particularly attractive way for presidents to redress their party's competitive problems or exploit its strength. Choosing which policies to promote and how to promote them are some of the most important political decisions presidents make. The task before us, then, is to unpack the relationship between the contextual factors described above and the approach presidents are likely to choose in promoting their policy initiatives.

The approach presidents take in promoting their policies should be expected to follow, in large measure, from their larger political goals. Presidents who feel more vulnerable—whose parties' future seems less certain—should be expected to choose policies that have a higher probability of attracting new groups, that cut into the opposition party's electoral coalition, and that expand the party's appeal to new and emerging demographics. Their policy goals should be more open to adjustment in the course of debate than predefined and fixed. Rather than remain doggedly committed to the party orthodoxy, their policy proposals will be more innovative and aimed at moving the party onto new ground and attracting new constituents. Their approach will tend to be more *accommodative* and flexible.

Presidents who feel more politically secure—whose parties' future seems more certain—should be expected to seize the moment and promote policies that "feed the base." Their policy initiatives will aim to deliver on their party's basic ideological commitments and will be more closely associated with the party's "brand." Since these policies are more likely to be "off-center," presidents will be drawn to strong-arm tactics to accomplish their objectives (Hacker and Pierson 2005). They will set clear goals and be relatively unwilling to compromise on their fundamental objectives. Rather than work to accommodate the opposition and appease entrenched interests, they will tend to be more *combative* in their approach.

The conditions under which we would expect presidents to be more accommodative or more combative in their approach are illustrated in figure 10.2. Depending on the shape of the president's competitive environment and the nature of the political goals he derives from that environment, his approach should be expected to lean toward one pole or the other—to be relatively more accommodative or relatively more combative. Of course, every policy will be accommodative in some ways and combative in others, and the perception of the president's approach will differ depending on who is doing the evaluating; policy change invariably creates winners and losers, and both sides should be expected to weigh in on the debate. But by positing that presidential behavior will *tend* toward one end of the spectrum or the

Figure 10.2. President's policy approach, given party's competitive standing.

other depending on the political context, we can develop some hypotheses to test against the rich insights provided in the chapters of this volume.

Hypothesis 1: Driven to improve their party's competitive standing, less secure presidents will seek to expand their party coalition. They will design and promote policies that are likely to appeal to new groups and interests, cut into the opposition's base, and capitalize on new demographic trends. Their proposals will be designed to appeal to the "median voter" more than to their base and will be tailored to generate bipartisan support within the Beltway; thus, they will tend to be more pragmatic and less ideological. Their political approach will be characterized by accommodation more than conflict. They will seek to win allies, not create enemies. To put it more succinctly, the weaker the party's competitive position, the more the president will want to expand its reach, and the more flexible and accommodating he will be on policy matters.

Hypothesis 2: Presidents whose parties are perceived to be in a stronger competitive position will be less interested in building for the future than in capitalizing on current strength. Because they seek to leverage their party's strong standing to "deliver the goods" to the base, they will choose policies that follow through on the promise of power. Seizing the moment of opportunity, they will promote policies that embody their party's core commitments. Their proposals will adhere to fixed ideological goals, and they will be loath to compromise. Their approach, consequently, will be more combative than accommodating. Thus, the stronger the party's competitive position, the more the president will want to seize the opportunity to deliver on deeply rooted commitments, and the more inflexible and combative he will be on policy matters.

Organizing the Cases

The studies contained within this volume afford an opportunity to test these propositions—not in a comprehensive manner, but provisionally, as a down payment on further research. They enable us to translate our hypotheses into mid-range claims and make some theoretical suggestions to be tested on other cases.

The emphasis of this volume, of course, is on the presidency of George W. Bush, with Clinton, Obama, and a few other presidents making appearances as well. Yet even within the Bush presidency alone, we have a nice range of policies to consider: some more deeply rooted than others, some more innovative than others, some more ideological than others. What's more, throughout his presidency, Bush faced a variety of different competitive situations. As electoral conditions changed, his behavior should be expected to have changed as well.

For example, in the 109th Congress (particularly in 2005), Bush and the Republican Party reached perhaps their strongest point. Having secured re-election and swelled their numbers in Congress, at the state level, and in the electorate, Bush was confident enough to declare, "I earned capital in this campaign, political capital, and now I intend to spend it" (Bush 2004). In contrast, during the next congress, Bush and his party were perhaps at their weakest point, following the Democratic takeover of Congress in the 2006 elections and corresponding with Bush's "lame-duck" period. This contrast is evident in figure 10.3.

Somewhere in between these periods of relative strength and weakness lies Bush's first term. Throughout his first four years, the president and his team perceived the GOP to be "on the move" but not yet dominant. By repeatedly emphasizing their desire to build a "permanent Republican majority," they indicated clearly that they did not believe that that majority had yet materialized (Green 2007). Numerical majorities in Congress were not sufficient. As a result of 9/11 and other intervening events, it is difficult to make meaningful distinctions between the party's competitive standing during the 107th Congress (2001–2) and the 108th Congress (2003–4), but both clearly fall on the left ("weaker") side of the spectrum.[1] These rough orderings are necessarily subjective, oversimplified, and admittedly quite crude; nevertheless, they must be sketched out for analytical purposes.

The Clinton and Obama presidencies are not the primary subject of interest here, but for illustrative purposes, the expected variation in their competitive

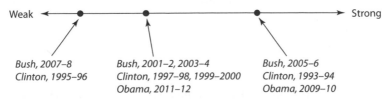

Figure 10.3. Variation in competitive environments.

political environments is arrayed along the same scale. The Democratic Party's strongest position during Clinton's presidency would seem to have been in his first two years, when Clinton enjoyed unified Democratic government and when he had every reason to expect his party's majorities to last. During Obama's presidency, these same conditions were evident during his first two years (2009–10). The Democratic Party's weakest point during Clinton's presidency would seem to be following the "Republican Revolution" in 1994, when the Newt Gingrich–led House sought to set the national policy agenda. Clinton's second term falls somewhere in between these points—as do Obama's second two years, which have yet to commence at the time of this writing—with meaningful distinctions between Clinton's final two congresses rather difficult to draw.[2]

With these rough rankings and hypotheses in hand, we can now turn to an examination of the data. Each hypothesis is first tested on case studies contained within this volume and is followed by a discussion of some "misfits."

Testing Hypothesis 1

The weaker the party's competitive position, the more the president will want to expand its reach, and the more flexible and accommodating he will be on policy matters.

To the extent that this hypothesis captures a portion of truth, we should expect to see Bush promoting policies and adopting strategies that adhere to these assumptions most strongly during the 110th Congress. His behavior would be expected to remain consistent with our expectations in the 107th and 108th Congresses as well, though to a lesser degree. Four episodes discussed in the previous chapters fall in these periods: Bush's attempt to reform national immigration policy (110th), his education reform proposal (107th), his effort to reform Medicare (108th), and his first round of tax cuts (107th).[3] For illustrative purposes, let us reconsider Bush's efforts to promote immigration and education reform.

Immigration Reform

Various attempts at immigration reform, in the Bush administration as well as in earlier administrations, illustrate quite nicely the hypotheses tested here. Stronger competitive conditions prompted the development of more ideological policy proposals that were advocated in a more combative, inflexible way. Weaker competitive conditions prompted more pragmatic, consensus-building policy proposals meant to accommodate the diversity of interests and compromise with opponents.

As Daniel Tichenor explains, Bush had both personal and political reasons for pursuing comprehensive immigration reform over the course of his presidency. Yet the striking thing about his approach was that he was willing to significantly alter his strategies as political conditions changed. Bush came into office with high hopes of producing comprehensive immigration reform, but after an early attempt was deemed politically infeasible in the wake of 9/11, the president removed the issue from his agenda. It reappeared in the run-up to the 2004 elections as Bush became "focused on adding more Latinos, the fastest-growing sector of the electorate and a crucial swing constituency in battleground states, to the GOP base." His guest worker proposal was designed to "help with Latino voters without sacrificing support from his conservative base" (chap. 3).

After securing reelection, Bush continued to push for reform, focusing again on his controversial guest worker proposal. In fact, early in his second term, when his competitive political environment reached its strongest point, Bush's efforts illustrate precisely what we would expect from a president seeking to "deliver the goods" to his party's base (hypothesis 2). Tichenor describes his 2005 proposal as a "polarizing initiative" that served the interests of the "business base" of the GOP (a "zealous and unwavering supporter of the president's guest worker plans") while simultaneously catering to "cultural protectionists" who sought more punitive measures emphasizing border enforcement. The administration announced its "strong" support for the "punitive bill" that dealt primarily with border enforcement even though Bush seemed personally committed to going much further. The bill passed the House but not the Senate, and when the Democrats took control of Congress in 2007, Bush shifted gears again.

His earlier efforts to reward the party faithful now gave way to pragmatism as he eagerly sought to forge a new "bipartisan effort."[4] Tichenor quotes Bush as saying, "There is a rational middle ground between granting an automatic path to citizenship for every illegal immigrant and a program of mass deportation, and I look forward to working with Congress to find that middle ground." As 2007 got under way, Bush began to seek out new ways of accommodating and persuading the multitude of conflicting interests. In May, with the competitive standing of the GOP reaching a new low point, Bush endorsed the bipartisan "grand bargain" proposal (called the Border Security and Immigration Act of 2007) constructed by a coalition of legislators led by Senator Ted Kennedy (D-MA). While this final attempt at reform was unsuccessful, it is hard to argue that its ultimate fate was due to Bush's unwillingness to be accommodating.

Interestingly, what we observe in this policy arena is that Bush's chosen approach—accommodating or combative, depending on the circumstances—was unrelated to the "stickiness" of the policy regime. Tichenor describes immigration policy as an unusually sticky area, characterized by four deep and "durable ideological traditions" (chap. 3). A political and policy minefield, immigration reform has always required "difficult negotiations" and "unpalatable compromise packages." The forces of inertia driving policy in this area are thus multiple and varied: interest groups are strong, mobilized, and passionate; legislators are deeply divided even within their own parties; and thanks to a legacy of policy failure, public opinion is characterized by "widespread cynicism and mistrust" regarding the ability of lawmakers to solve the problem.

Yet irrespective of these formidable obstacles, Bush pursued a political approach that varied with his competitive circumstances. When his party seemed stronger, his approach was more combative and aimed at pleasing his base; when his party seemed weaker, he pursued an approach that was more accommodating, flexible, and aimed at expanding his party's coalition. In other words, the "stickiness" of the policy offers little insight into how the president acted in any given moment—the intractability of immigration policy did not change, but Bush's approach did.

Tichenor's older historical cases lend additional support to our hypotheses. Jimmy Carter—whose party enjoyed deep and durable majorities in Congress, at the state level, and in the electorate in 1977–78—proposed a comprehensive plan that aimed to resolve all major sticking points in one fell swoop. It failed, but not for lack of boldness on Carter's part. In Bill Clinton's presidency, the opposite impulse is on full display. When Republicans took control of both houses of Congress for the first time in forty years in the 1994 elections, Clinton's party's competitive standing was uncertain at best, and Clinton's own reelection chances were up in the air. Forced to take a stand on immigration reform and welfare reform during the 104th Congress, Clinton adopted an unabashedly accommodative approach. Decrying the bills' more punitive measures even as he signed them into law, Clinton's "cautious opportunism" embodied what we would expect from a president who feels electorally insecure. His efforts on immigration were marked by their slow speed, political expediency, policy ambivalence, and modest reach.

Education Reform

The story of education reform in the Bush administration offers a good case of policy accommodation aimed at expanding the party coalition. Frederick Hess notes that Bush's stance on education reform was designed to "reassure moderates . . . woo key liberal constituencies like Latinos and African-Americans, and fracture the Democratic coalition by weakening the teachers' unions" (chap. 2). No Child Left Behind (NCLB), perhaps more than any other policy initiative of the Bush administration, was a coalition-building policy—one that would soften the "durable Republican image of heartlessness" and redound to the party's long-term benefit. In the words of a former official in Bush's education department, the initiative was an attempt to "improve America's schools—and to ensure that his Republican Party got credit for it" (chap. 2).

The GOP's competitive standing, as well as Bush's own legitimacy as president, was rather precarious during the first eight months of 2001. The two parties were evenly divided in the Senate, and Bush seemed committed to governing as a "compassionate conservative." Education represented a major policy area where Bush felt strongly about the issue of reform and where there seemed to be room to innovate and update the party's orthodoxy to new conditions (Skowronek 2005). In his first week as president, Bush announced four broad, general principles to guide the policymaking process: "increase accountability for student performance," "focus on what works," "reduce bureaucracy and increase flexibility," and "empower parents." Rather than insist on policy specificity and adherence to party orthodoxy, these ambitious yet ambiguous goals left much room for compromise and accommodation in the policy design process.

Seeking to "accommodate Democratic concerns and forge a bipartisan bill" (chap. 2), Hess writes, the administration reached out to "more liberal members of Congress" and centrist New Democrats who had proposed similar reform packages in the past. Most notably, Bush "actively courted two key liberals," Kennedy and Representative George Miller, and gave them an "outsized role in shaping final legislation." Throughout negotiations, the White House sought to walk a fine line of "appeasing Republican backbenchers without alienating its Democratic allies." To accomplish the president's political and policy goals—expanding the coalition and passing education reform with "substantial bipartisan support"—the Bush administration was flexible, accommodating, and willing to compromise on policy details.

As a result, Hess observes a conspicuous lack of policy specificity in the final legislation. NCLB lacked "careful attention to metrics, incentives, and targets" and remained "vague about costs and consequences." Even though the bill became law at the "high-water mark of post-9/11 bipartisan comity" (chap. 2)—a time when Bush might have been expected to leverage his high popularity to push for more radical change—its final wording represented "a radical overhaul of the original White House proposal." Hess describes NCLB as an "elephantine compromise" containing a "tangled assemblage of White House proposals, New Democratic ideas, and provisions championed by Kennedy and Miller" (chap. 2). Its testing and accountability mandates were "draped in ambiguity," and the new federal oversight authority was granted without clear specification of "particular standards, tests, targets, or definitions of 'adequate yearly progress.'" In short, the final bill epitomized the inclusive, offend-none approach the Bush administration took in order to expand the party's reach during a period of competitive uncertainty.

Earlier education reform attempts followed the same pattern, thus lending further support to our hypothesis. The landmark Elementary and Secondary Education Act, for example, passed in 1965, at a time of overwhelming Democratic electoral strength, and was promoted by a president (Lyndon Johnson) determined to leverage his party's majorities to deliver on core liberal commitments (hypothesis 2). Ronald Reagan, similarly, launched a "fierce attack" (albeit mostly rhetorical) on the federal government's role in education policy during a period of renewed Republican confidence. Reagan managed to cut funding for education, but because of the party's continued minority status in Congress, fundamental change proved elusive. During the competitive uncertainty of the Clinton years, we observe another period of pragmatism and compromise, as Clinton endorsed innovative New Democratic proposals and sought to preempt Republican calls for greater efficiency and accountability in public education (hypothesis 1).

Testing Hypothesis 2

The stronger the party's competitive position, the more the president will want to seize the opportunity to deliver on deeply rooted commitments, and the more inflexible and combative he will be on policy matters.

As discussed, this hypothesis holds up rather well in several minor episodes discussed above: Bush's ill-fated guest worker proposal in 2005, Carter's attempt at comprehensive immigration reform in 1977, Lyndon Johnson's major education initiative in 1965, and Reagan's education reform plans. In the Bush presidency, we would expect to see more ideological, combative strategies undertaken principally during the 109th Congress, and particularly during the first eight months of 2005 before Hurricane Katrina eroded his support. Bush's attempt to reform Social Security, pursued during this period, fits the bill quite nicely.

Social Security Reform

Social Security, the proverbial "third rail" of American politics, is a policy arena in which Bush knew that the "potential political risks were clear" and policy change would be an uphill battle. Yet as Kent Weaver argues, presidents "believe they can affect important aspects of their political environment in ways that will improve their prospects for achieving their preferred policy objectives, their objectives in building winning electoral coalitions, or both" (chap. 4). This is especially true, hypothesis 2 would suggest, under conditions of competitive strength, when the president believes that the moment is ripe to spend his political capital and service the party faithful.

As noted above, Bush was riding high after his reelection in November 2004; Karl Rove argued that the president had received a mandate, and Bush declared that he intended to "spend" the capital he had earned in the election to promote his policy agenda. Republican leaders were pleased with their party's enhanced competitive standing, and they began to argue that conservatism had now proven itself to be "the dominant political creed in America." Bush's main policy objective was to allow workers to put a portion of their Social Security payroll taxes into individual accounts. Political conditions through his first term, however, made the prospects for such a proposal dubious at best. During his first year, Bush put the proposal on the back burner, appointing a commission to study how to tailor his "opt-out" plan. Nevertheless, he charged the commission with achieving a rather rigid and specific set of policy goals—a much more orthodox set of goals than those laid out for education reform. Among other requirements, the commission was barred from increasing the Social Security payroll tax or changing the benefits for current retirees, and Bush insisted that "individually controlled, voluntary personal retirement accounts must be included." By setting clear, fixed priorities up front, Bush asserted his "control over the policy formulation process." This relatively more doctrinaire approach was, not unexpectedly, met with hostility from supporters of the existing policy regime. With political conditions increasingly perceived to be unfavorable for a major push (following 9/11, stock market declines, and the Enron scandal), Bush decided to wait.

But after his reelection victory in 2004, Bush decided to take a more aggressive and combative approach. He made the creation of private accounts the "centerpiece" of his 2005 State of the Union address and launched a major public relations campaign. Seeking to shape public opinion rather than cater to it, Bush adopted a risky "going public" strategy (reminiscent of Andrew Johnson's ill-fated "swing around the circle" campaign) to convince the public of the "compelling need" for reform, visiting "Sixty Stops in 60 Days." Making "full use of his agenda-setting powers," Bush sought to portray Social Security as broken and in need of urgent reform. Although his rhetoric was seen as "scaremongering" by opponents, Bush did not let up. He adopted the same approach to dealing with interest groups; to combat the many strong and well-endowed organizations mobilized in opposition to the "privatization" components of his plan, he mobilized his own supportive network of interest groups (albeit with less success). Taken all together, Bush's approach was characterized more by confrontation than accommodation, more by a determination to realize ideological goals than by pragmatism.

Indeed, the entire policy formulation process and political campaign effort stand in stark contrast to the "cautious and defensive" approach taken by Bill Clinton on the same issue (supporting the expectations of hypothesis 1). After the 1994 elections, Clinton found himself in a "very weak bargaining position," which Weaver argues had a clear impact on his administration's "goals and strategy." In the context of ongoing scandal and impeachment, and facing an "extremely hostile" Republican-led Congress, Clinton adopted a flexible, accommodating approach. His most ambitious reform proposal, announced in January 1999, was "carefully tailored to appeal to median voters." He dropped one of the main pillars of his proposal (investing budget surpluses in Social Security) when it met with opposition, and he abandoned the entire pursuit of legislative change when it became clear that he could use the debate to score rhetorical points and enhance the Democrats' "favorable images." The thrust of Clinton's policy choice and promotional strategy, in other words, could not have been more different from Bush's. Whereas Clinton was wholly pragmatic, Bush remained "focused on the values of the party's base." Whereas Clinton sought to rebuild and expand the Democratic Party's appeal through rhetorical frames, Bush sought to market his party's core values to growing constituencies without altering those principles in any significant way.

Obama's Health Care Reform

Hypothesis 2 would also seem to get provisional support from Barack Obama's campaign to reform health care in 2009 and 2010. Despite Obama's oft-stated desire to bring "post-partisanship" to the presidency and to engage in "inter-party coalition building" (see introduction), these efforts were abandoned when it became clear that Republican support would not be forthcoming. Under these conditions, Obama and the Democratic congressional leaders decided to exploit their party's numerical strength in Congress to get the measure passed in the spring of 2010—using the reconciliation process and strong-arm tactics in the House—irrespective of downstream political consequences. While their approach on health care thus involved accommodation during the early stages of the *policy creation* process, the realities of the competitive political environment made any hope of "post-partisanship" seem entirely quixotic. Obama was compelled to adopt a more combative approach in order to pass the bill and publicize its merits to a skeptical public. Health care reform thus became a "partisan project" through and through (see introduction and chap. 13).

Considering the "Misfits"

An important lesson emerges from Bush's policy initiatives described above: rather than take a cookie-cutter approach to his policy choices and political strategies, his behavior varied with political conditions. Though he was, of course, the same man throughout his eight years in office—presumably driven by a relatively stable set of ideological commitments and supported by a relatively stable "base"—he adopted a wide variety of approaches. My argument is simply that changes in the party's competitive standing can help to explain a good deal of this variation. The mechanism linking competitive standing to presidential behavior, I suggest, is the relative degree of confidence the president derives from that competitive political environment.

As we have seen, our two hypotheses—posited in their most extreme form—have held up rather well thus far. Hypothesis 1 receives support from Bush's immigration reform effort in the 110th Congress, education reform in the 107th, Medicare reform in the 108th, and tax reform in the 106th, as well as from Clinton's immigration, welfare, education, and Social Security initiatives over his final six years in office. Hypothesis 2 receives support from Bush's Social Security reform initiative in 2005, his guest worker proposal in 2005, Carter's comprehensive immigration proposal in 1977, Johnson's education initiative in 1965, and Obama's health care reform initiative in 2009–10. Yet not all of the cases taken up in this volume fit so neatly into our framework.

The Burke and Scherer chapter on judicial politics, in particular, offers a very different angle of vision on the question at hand. Over Bush's eight years in office, his approach to judicial politics remained relatively constant, seemingly immune to the ebb and flow of electoral conditions. As Burke and Scherer describe it, Bush consistently sought to use "controversies over the law and the legal system" to reward the party base and to deliver on the promise of power without alienating moderates and hurting his party's chances of expanding its reach (chap. 7). Whether by supporting "tort reform," asbestos litigation reform, medical malpractice reform, or by "reframing" cultural issues as "judicial overreaching" and appointing Federalist Society–affiliated judges, Bush found judicial politics to be a relatively easy way to appease his core business-conservative and cultural-conservative base without losing support among independents. Thus, in the arena of judicial politics, Bush's goals and strategies remained relatively constant: placate the base without alienating independents. Since we expect presidential strategies to change as competitive conditions change, these findings would seem to be disconfirming evidence.

But it is important to consider the nature of these judicial politics efforts. Unlike Social Security reform, education reform, and the like, judicial politics are generally of much lower salience, and the public tends to operate with much lower information. "It is hard to get the public much aroused about tort reform," Burke and Scherer write. Compared with Bush's ambitious policy strategies, "judicial politics strategies . . . proved relatively costless, both fiscally and politically." What's more, many of Bush's efforts simply flew under the radar. For example, by using "coded appeals . . . wrapped in an innocuous rhetorical package," Bush signaled his solidarity with anti-*Roe* forces and evangelical Christians on a range of issues without elevating the salience of polarizing issues like abortion (chap. 7). Whereas formal legislative initiatives of higher salience have the potential to undermine the support of the groups the president is hoping to attract, judicial politics strategies sent powerful political signals to the party's base without risking the president's outreach efforts in other areas.

Formal legislative initiatives, in other words, may be more responsive to electoral dynamics than symbolic and more subterranean initiatives. Put differently, when policy initiatives have the potential to exact higher political costs, the president is more likely to be attuned to changing competitive conditions, and his behavior may adhere more closely to our model. When initiatives can be pursued at a relatively low cost, the president need not be so sensitive to changes in the political environment. Judicial politics, in short, may be the exception that proves the more general rule.

Conclusion

By considering the influence of electoral dynamics on presidential behavior, we have begun to sketch out an explanation for why presidents tend to act similarly under similar conditions, despite significant differences in their personalities, ideologies, and policy commitments. Of course, it remains to be seen how well these mid-range propositions travel. Brief examples from other presidencies offer provisional support for the basic model, but the assumptions and expectations posited here await testing on other presidencies in other periods of American history (and the more diverse the cases, the better).

Before concluding, I wish to raise two additional points. First, in the cases discussed above, we have observed a somewhat ironic twist to the classic "responsible party government" model. According to this model, greater productivity and harmony between the branches is predicted during periods of unified, majority-party government. As the famous 1950 American Political Science Association report on responsible parties imagined, "with greater party responsibility, the president's position as party leader would correspond in strength to the greater strength of his party" (American Political Science Association 1950, 13). Yet for Bush and Clinton, the weaker their party's competitive standing, the more productive they seemed to become in the legislative arena. Indeed, they became more successful in advancing "programs to which they commit[ed] themselves" when they faced divided government, or something approximating it (17–18). In other words, presidents may choose more "appropriate" strategies (in these cases, the accommodative approach) and may appear more adept at shepherding "significant" legislation into law when their political environment reflects precisely the opposite of "responsible party government." These conditions—divided government, uncertain public support, a lack of consensus among power brokers—may not have resulted in policies that fostered a strong sense of accountability (i.e., NCLB) or offered clear, user-friendly rules (i.e., Medicare), but at least they did not end in a devastating collapse of the president's leadership authority, as was the case with Bush and Social Security reform or Clinton and health care reform. Thus, contrary to deeply rooted and long-held expectations, we have reason to think that presidents will display greater strategic acumen—and perhaps greater legislative success—under conditions of greater competitive uncertainty.

The second concluding point I wish to make is more academic. Recent political science scholarship has begun to reveal important distinctions between different *modes* of policy change, and these analytical distinctions have greatly enhanced our knowledge of how policies change in different and sometimes rather subtle ways. The main variants of policy change typically include *replacement, layering, drift,* and *conversion.* Respectively, these terms suggest that existing policies can be revised or entirely displaced, that new rules can be layered "on top of or alongside" existing rules, that environmental shifts can alter existing rules, and that existing policies can be strategically redeployed and converted to serve different functions (Hacker 2004; Pierson 2004; Mahoney and Thelen 2010).

While these conceptual frames offer useful insights into how retrenchment occurs and how institutions change over time, the preceding pages suggest that they are orthogonal to the dynamics of presidential policy choice and promotion. Bush's Medicare reform would seem to be a case of "layering," education reform a case of "replacement," immigration reform and Social Security reform cases of "conversion," and so on. But at any given moment, Bush was just as likely to promote one mode of policy change as any other. It is possible, of course, that one or more of these different modes will tend to correspond, over time, with more or less *successful* policy changes, and that the range of cases before us is simply too limited to discern this relationship; further research is needed to clarify the relationship between these dynamics. But the cases before us suggest no obvious relationship between the president's chosen mode of policy change and his strategic imperatives in any given instance.

In sum, when we treat the presidency as a political institution that exhibits similar activities under similar conditions, we may better understand why presidents sometimes choose strategies that might otherwise seem "inappropriate." Rather than view these choices as mistakes or miscalculations, we might consider the possibility that presidents are responding to more fundamental impulses derived from the peculiar nature of our competitive two-party system.

NOTES

1. The party's competitive standing during the 108th Congress (2003–4) might be seen as "weaker" than during the 107th Congress (2001–2), owing to escalating concerns about the Iraq War throughout 2003–4. In contrast, Bush and the GOP benefited from the "rally around the flag" effect after the 9/11 terrorist attacks. But matters are not so simple: before September 10, 2001, the GOP's competitive standing was arguably weaker than at any point during the entire 107th Congress. Not only did Bush lose the popular vote in 2000, but the Senate was evenly divided between the parties until May 24, 2001, when Senator James Jeffords (R-VT) switched parties and handed control of the chamber to the Democratic Party (for the first time since 1994) for the duration of the 107th Congress.

2. The Democratic Party's competitive standing was arguably somewhat stronger during the 106th Congress (1999–2000) than during the scandal-dominated 105th Congress (1997–98). The 106th followed upon the Democrats' surprisingly strong showing in the 1998 midterm elections, and it began with the conclusion of the impeachment hearings and Clinton's acquittal in the Senate. Yet the 105th followed upon Clinton's successful reelection campaign. However one chooses to rank them, the point is that both congresses should be viewed as falling somewhere in between the 104th and 103rd.

3. Note that our goal is not to offer an explanation for why a given policy proposal failed or succeeded in making its way into law, or why a given policy was implemented well or poorly: our concern here is strictly with the dynamics of presidential policy choice and promotion.

4. In Tichenor's account, Bush's final, more accommodating approach on immigration reform was more consistent with his more moderate personal commitments on the issue.

WORKS CITED

Aldrich, John. 1995. *Why Parties? The Origin and Transformation of Political Parties in America*. Chicago: University of Chicago Press.

American Political Science Association, A Report of the Committee on Political Parties. 1950. "Toward a More Responsible Two-Party System." *American Political Science Review* 44(3).

Bush, George W. 2004. "President Holds Press Conference." White House Press Release. www.whitehouse.gov/news/releases/2004/11/20041104-5.html.

Dahl, Robert Alan, ed. 1966. *Political Oppositions in Western Democracies*. New Haven, CT: Yale University Press.

Downs, Anthony. 1957. *An Economic Theory of Democracy*. New York: Harper.

Galvin, Daniel J. 2010. *Presidential Party Building: Dwight D. Eisenhower to George W. Bush*. Princeton, NJ: Princeton University Press.

Ginsberg, Benjamin, and Martin Shefter. 1988. "The Presidency and the Organization of Interests." In *The Presidency and the Political System*, Volume 2, ed. M. Nelson. Washington, DC: Congressional Quarterly Press.

Green, Joshua. 2007. "The Rove Presidency." *Atlantic*, September.

Hacker, Jacob S. 2004. "Privatizing Risk without Privatizing the Welfare State: The Hidden Politics of Social Policy Retrenchment in the United States." *American Political Science Review* 98(2).

Hacker, Jacob S., and Paul Pierson. 2005. *Off Center: The Republican Revolution and the Erosion of American Democracy*. New Haven, CT: Yale University Press.

Lowi, Theodore. 1963. "Toward Functionalism in Political Science: The Case of Innovation in Party Systems." *American Political Science Review* 57(3):570–83.

————. 1985. *The Personal President*. Ithaca, NY: Cornell University Press.

Mahoney, James, and Kathleen Thelen. 2010. "A Theory of Gradual Institutional Change." In *Explaining Institutional Change: Ambiguity, Agency, and Power in Historical Institutionalism*, ed. J. Mahoney and K. Thelen. Cambridge: Cambridge University Press.

Mayhew, David R. 1974. *Congress: The Electoral Connection*. New Haven, CT: Yale University Press.

Moe, Terry. 1985. "The Politicized Presidency." In *The New Direction in American Politics*, ed. J. E. Chub and P. E. Peterson. Washington, DC: Brookings Institution.

————. 1993. "Presidents, Institutions, and Theory." In *Researching the Presidency*, ed. G. C. Edwards III, John H. Kessel, and Bert A. Rockman. Pittsburgh: University of Pittsburgh Press.

Neustadt, Richard. 1960. *Presidential Power*. 1990 ed. New York: Wiley.

Pierson, Paul. 2004. *Politics in Time: History, Institutions, and Social Analysis*. Princeton, NJ: Princeton University Press.

Riker, William H. 1962. *The Theory of Political Coalitions*. New Haven, CT: Yale University Press.

Sheingate, Adam D. 2003. "Political Entrepreneurship, Institutional Change, and American Political Development." *Studies in American Political Development* 17(2):185–203.

Shepsle, Kenneth A. 2003. "Losers in Politics (and How They Sometimes Become Winners): William Riker's Heresthetic." *Perspectives on Politics* 1(2):307–15.

Skowronek, Stephen. 1997. *The Politics Presidents Make.* Cambridge, MA: Harvard University Press.

———. 2005. "Leadership by Definition: First Term Reflections on George W. Bush's Political Stance." *Perspectives on Politics* 3(4):817–31.

CHAPTER ELEVEN

Touching the Bases

Parties and Policymaking in the Twenty-First Century

Daniel DiSalvo

The most unexpected development in American politics has been the revival of political parties. In the 1970s, parties were said to be on the road to extinction. A variety of ailments afflicted them. Economic growth and the administrative state reduced the number and appeal of patronage jobs, cutting off the lifeblood of local party organizations. The states' adoption of primaries and reformed caucuses to nominate candidates for office handed control of nominations to voters. Consequent campaigns were conducted by ad hoc organizations created by individual candidates. To top it off, voter loyalty declined. By 1979, over a third of the electorate did not identify with either Democrats or Republicans in opinion polls. Abandoned by voters, deprived of control over nominations, ousted from the delivery of goods and services to constituents by a professionalized bureaucracy, and displaced by campaign management firms during election season, parties appeared to have lost their raison d'être.

Scholars thus dismissed parties as mechanisms to coordinate the national government and engage citizens in politics.[1] Nevertheless, the parties have re-emerged as channels of public sentiment, components of citizen identity, and instruments of institutional coordination. What America's fragmented institutions separate the parties once again try to yoke together. Today, the parties are more national, more programmatic, and more closely divided than at any time in the modern period. Intense party competition for control of government has produced a new set of incentives and constraints that powerfully shape government policymaking. Despite many obstacles, parties have made governance and electoral strategy once again a collective affair.

This chapter explores how recent party development has shaped the policymaking context of the new century in order to shed light on the relationship between party change and policy outputs. Party strategists, the congressional leadership, and the president have been forced to confront the "party maintenance dilemma." This dilemma is the result of parties' conflicting efforts to retain their existing support, while simultaneously taking steps to expand it. It has become commonplace in American punditry to refer to the former as the "base"—the set of voters, organized groups, activists, and intellectuals that are deeply attached to a party's core ideas and interests—and the latter as the "independents," "moderates," or "swing voters." The difficulty is that policies designed to appeal to the political center can leave the base flat, while appeals to the base can alienate the center. In a nearly evenly divided electorate, however, both groups are essential for success.

A theoretical motivation for this chapter is to examine the long-held proposition that America's two-party system drives the parties to the political center.[2] The center-seeking property of the system is held to apply to the party's campaign strategies and policy priorities and to determine the character of the congressional leadership. Yet, contrary to the Downsian view of parties as center-seeking organizations, powerful incentives today push national party leaders both toward and away from the political center. These competing incentives are a consequence of the parties' electoral bases of support, their institutional structures, ideological commitments, and modes of operation in Congress.

In addition, as political scientists have shown, the electorate is far from highly informed about politics and public policy, which relaxes the center-seeking incentives.[3] As Larry M. Bartels concludes a recent study, "Whatever elections may be doing, they are *not* forcing elected officials to cater to the policy preferences of the 'median voter.' "[4] Therefore, political elites have a good deal of room to maneuver in order to shape their party's brand and convert their views into public policy. Ultimately, how the balance is struck between the center and the base determines the public agenda and policy outcomes.

The analysis here concentrates on four elements of party change. First, intraparty factions transformed the parties by providing them with loyalists and making them more programmatic and nationally oriented. Second, intense competition for command of national institutions has sparked innovation in party organizing and institution building. Third, the congressional party leadership has been empowered and party discipline enhanced owing to the regional realignments of the Northeast and South combined with new procedural tools and fundraising techniques. Fourth, presidents have begun to involve themselves extensively in party affairs, raising large sums of money and campaigning widely for party candidates. The result over the last decade has been near parity in party strength and intense polarization.[5]

The focus of this chapter is on the Republican Party and its efforts to manage its coalition while it controlled the presidency and both houses of Congress for all but ninety-six days from 2000 to 2006. Yet, the experience of the Republican coalition in this period has important continuities with the Democratic majorities ushered in 2006 and 2008. As the new majority, Democrats struggled mightily to hold their base and satisfy independents in the face of the worst economic conditions since the Great Depression. While their policy program, especially the economic stimulus package and the health care overhaul, did much to satisfy the party's base, they had trouble retaining the support of independents. In 2010, as economic problems persisted in the fall campaign season, independent voters moved to the right and Republicans surged back to power, winning sixty-four seats in the House and control of the chamber and six seats in the Senate.

The Factional Origins of Polarized Parties

James Q. Wilson has argued that many important shifts in public policy in the last forty years are traceable to changes in elite opinion rather than to voter preferences.[6] According to Wilson, many policies prevailed and endured because "strategically placed elites favored them." Elite opinion has become more salient because today's elites are more programmatic than their predecessors: they want to see their ideals enacted into public policy.

Putting ideas into practice requires winning power. Political parties are the organizations designed for that purpose. Therefore, idea-driven elites ultimately helped revive the parties. They channeled their energies into intraparty factions with the objective of taking over the parties. The concept of faction is a useful way to see how elements within the parties interact and mobilize.[7] A faction is a party subunit that has enough ideological consistency, organizational capacity, and temporal durability to sustain intraparty conflict with implications for the party's self-conception and policymaking. These factions acquire names, create organizations, provide links to outside groups, and articulate different ideational positions from the mainstream of their party. They try to change the party's identity by challenging the ideas and interests that define the mainstream of their party. Ultimately, they seek to put their stamp on their party and the nation.

Two factions—the New Politics Democrats and New Right Republicans—emerged just as the parties were being read their last rights and supplied their respective parties with élan. Both demanded movement away from the political center. Rather than forge pragmatic compromises, they aimed to realize the ideals of the new elites. Looking at party change through the lens of faction shows how both parties moved almost simultaneously away from the political center. This corrects the assumption that one party moved away from the center first or has moved further from the center.[8] Factions' takeover of parties contributed mightily to today's "new" party system characterized by national organization and programmatic objectives.

In the 1970s, New Politics Democrats transformed the reputation, image, and policy priorities of the Democratic Party. Arising out of the middle-class suburbs, they brought a host of new ideas, issues, values, and lifestyles to national attention. Raised in the political caldron of the 1960s, they cut their teeth in opposition to the Vietnam War and imbibed a deep-seated skepticism about American beneficence abroad. On the domestic front, they were concerned about the behavior of office holders and advanced a number of policy goals of concern to suburban voters, most notably environmentalism and consumer protection. New Politics Democrats ardently believed that government should remedy the dishonor done to African Americans, women, the poor, Hispanics, homosexuals, and the disabled. In cultural matters, they emphasized individual rights and choice over duties and responsibilities, defending "alternative lifestyles" and "minority rights" against traditional social norms. Their effect was to shift liberalism's emphasis on bread-and-butter economic issues to "post-materialist" concerns.[9] Democrats' ideological emphasis has consequently underplayed the themes of majoritarianism and redistribution in favor of minority rights, toleration, and inclusion.[10]

While harboring deep suspicion of the "establishment" in government and business, New Politics Democrats sought to use the state, retooled for greater popular participation, to intervene in the economy and society. They wanted to make government more professional and responsive, especially to certain victimized constituencies. They envisioned a powerful bureaucracy run by experts that was also highly democratic and open to citizen input—especially the input of environmentalists, consumers, the poor, minorities, gays and lesbians, women, and the disabled. Therefore, they created new legal provisions that mandated citizen involvement, created new procedural rights, and funded "public interest" organizations.

To take over the Democratic Party, New Politics affiliates radically changed its procedures and modes of operation. They nationalized their party by disconnecting it from local organizations and outsourcing campaigns to a galaxy of issue and cause groups. Within the party organization, New Politics Democrats changed institutional structures to place identity politics at the heart of the Democratic Party by mandating that specific groups—African Americans, women, and youth—be represented in accordance with their proportions in the population in the national convention delegations and on the Democratic National Committee (DNC). In 1982, the DNC created official caucuses of women, blacks, Hispanics, Asians, gays, liberals, and business professionals. The idea behind these arrangements was that each group had a set of grievances, issues, and priorities to which the party and its presidential nominees should attend.[11]

New Politics Democrats also changed the party's presidential nominating procedures and redistributed power in Congress. Instituting a primary system for presidential selection enabled them to capture the nomination for one of their own. In 1972, Democrats nominated one of the most left-wing candidates in their history, Senator George McGovern.[12] In Congress, New Politics Democrats brought conservative committee barons to heel, expanded the power of subcommittees, and "opened up" the legislature to journalistic scrutiny. Working through a variety of "public interest" groups, bureaucrats, congressional subcommittees, and the federal courts, New Politics Democrats promoted, coordinated, and rationalized the new party agenda.

New Politics Democrats' takeover of the Democratic Party introduced a new cleavage between the parties by injecting a strong dose of secularism into the Democratic Party.[13] Secularists were the strongest supporters of progressive planks in the 1972 platform relating to women's rights, abortion, alternative lifestyles, and the family. "The partisan differences that emerged in 1972," Geoffrey Layman has written, "were not caused by any sudden increase in the religious and cultural traditionalism of the Republican activists but instead by the pervasive secularism and cultural liberalism of the Democratic supporters of George McGovern."[14]

The faction thus pushed the party's "brand" toward being one of accommodation in foreign affairs, experimentalism in cultural matters, moralism on issues of race and gender, and relative indifference to the white working class. In the mid-1980s, another faction, the so-called "New Democrats," emerged to combat these tendencies and had some success at domesticating them. But New Democrats' ideas have not deeply penetrated the party's rank and file. Today, according to Thomas Edsall, "the party's most influential wing . . . is elitist—affluent, well-educated, urban, indifferent (or hostile) to organized religion, and, on the controversial social issues of abortion and gay marriage, well to the left of the general public."[15]

The contemporary Republican Party has its roots in the insurgent "New Right" faction—often called the "conservative movement"—that burst unexpectedly onto the national stage with Arizona senator Barry Goldwater's nomination for president in 1964. Over the next thirty years, New Right activists honed their program until two "revolutions" (Reagan in 1980 and Gingrich in 1994) brought it to power.[16] As a faction within the minority party, the New Right initially found it difficult to get its policies a hearing in the public square. Out of power, it became a remarkably self-conscious ideological faction bent on transforming the GOP into a vehicle that could win a national majority. The New Right challenged the ideals of both Taftite conservatism and liberal Republicanism. Led by William F. Buckley Jr., it created a vast national network of conservative political associations whose principal elements were technical ability in electoral organizing and an intellectual counterestablishment that launched an assault on liberalism.[17] The suburban middle class, especially in the South and Southwest, proved open to New Right campaign appeals.[18]

In the late 1970s, the New Right helped draw neoconservatives and the Christian Right into the GOP. The former were a cadre of urban intellectuals who had been affiliated with the Democratic Party until they soured on the Great Society and Carter's foreign policy.[19] Writing in influential magazines, they criticized affirmative action, détente with the Soviet Union, and the gay and feminist movements. The latter were a number of fundamentalist Christian sects drawn to Republican concern with restoring moral order. Outraged by Democrats' acceptance of divorce, abortion, premarital sex, homosexuality, feminism, and Carter's leadership (whom they had supported in 1976), Evangelical ministers such as Jerry Falwell, Pat Robertson, and Jim Bakker embraced the Republican Party.[20]

The New Right refined different (and at times conflicting) defenses of three core propositions for which the GOP should stand. The first was anti-statism. Traditionalists held that government planning disturbed a fragile culture, the religious right that it imparted secular values, libertarians that it introduced gross inefficiencies, and neoconservatives that it produced unintended policy consequences. Second, the GOP should become the defender of the bourgeois family and traditional morality, since America was undergoing a period of moral decline. Third, Republicans needed to restore strength and resolve in the nation's foreign policy. By the 1990s, the New Right had succeeded in transforming the reputation and identity of the Republican Party.

Driven by ideas, factions made the parties more programmatic. They have become the party "bases," requiring attention and recognition but willing to stick with their party through feast or famine.

Party Competition and Organization

Unified government in the twenty-first century has made it easier for politicians to claim credit and for voters to place blame for government performance. American elections remain candidate centered, but the party label and the party organizations have taken on new importance.[21] The decline of state and local parties in the 1970s left candidates, especially challengers for House seats, without the savoir faire required to run a modern campaign. The parties responded, providing candidates with advice about fundraising, media relations, polling, and campaign management, as well as money. In the 1990s, the parties also began conducting "parallel" and "independent" campaigns in competitive states and districts. They now spend millions of dollars on television, radio, direct mail, mass telephone calls, websites, and other voter identification and mobilization efforts.[22] Close partisan competition has led the

Table 11.1   Change in party strength, 1994–2010 (Republican-Democrat-Independent)

Year	Senate	House	Governors
1994	52 R–48 D	230 R–204 D–1 I	30 R–19 D–1 I
1996	55 R–45 D	228 R–206 D–1 I	32 R–17 D–1 I
1998	55 R–45 D	223 R–211 D–1 I	31 R–17 D–2 I
2000	50 R–50 D	221 R–212 D–2 I	27 R–21 D–2 I
2002	51 R–48 D–1 I	229 R–204 D–1 I[a]	26 R–24 D
2004	55 R–44 D–1 I	232 R–201 D–1 I[a]	28 R–22 D
2006	50 D–49 R–1 I	198 R–234 D	22 R–28 D
2008	60 D–40 R	178 R–257 D	23 R–27 D
2010	53 D–47 R	242 R–193 D	29 R–20 D–1 I

Source: U.S. Census Bureau, *Statistical Abstract of the United States.*
[a]One vacant seat.

parties to raise vast sums of money, breaking their own record in each election cycle.

Passionate partisanship and razor-thin electoral margins (see table 11.1) have sparked increased party organization. Competition is a powerful motive because better organization can make the difference in tight races. Yet the ways and the extent to which Republicans and Democrats have undertaken this task vary considerably.[23]

Republicans have created a large national organization that closely links the national committee to state parties and county and precinct committees. They have been assisted by the increased sophistication of polling and voter-targeting techniques. The GOP now commands a massive database on the American electorate called "Voter Vault"—based on voting, attitudinal, and consumer data—and is able to target voters in specific media markets, states, and neighborhoods. The Republican National Committee (RNC) now coordinates with the Hill committees to recruit, train, and fund candidates, creating tighter links to state and local party operations. Fundraising operations have created networks of small contributors to cultivate a vast array of donors. The GOP has been less dependent than Democrats on large donors and relied to a greater extent on a mass of smaller contributions. Republicans also command an army of volunteers that can be sent into competitive states and districts to mobilize voters.

President George W. Bush's chief political advisor, Karl Rove, claimed that the administration's aim was to build a "national party machine" based on the model of Mark Hanna and William McKinley in 1896 and 1900. Bush's commitment to party affairs was on display in 2002, when the president engaged in candidate recruitment and fundraising and stumped for party candidates.[24] Two years later, Bush and Rove mobilized core Republican voters and fundraisers.[25] In 2004, some analysts contended that they had succeeded in creating the first national party machine in American history: an elaborate network of a million and a half volunteers in the competitive states.[26] Republican Party leaders were likened to "Boss Tweed armed with a Blackberry."[27]

The development of the Democratic Party apparatus has taken a much different course.[28] Over the course of the twentieth century reformers greatly weakened the party's local organizations. As early as the 1950s, it began to outsource campaigns to organized labor. Recently, the party has relied on public interest groups, unions, and 527 organizations to provide campaign foot soldiers. In 2004, America Coming Together, the Media Fund, America Votes, and other 527 groups outside the formal party structure handled the party's mobilization effort.[29] Democrats initially lagged behind Republicans in developing sophisticated voter targeting techniques and database building (their computer system is called "Datamart").[30] There was intense debate within the party over whether it should continue to outsource campaigns or rebuild its state and local organizations.[31] Barack Obama's 2008 presidential campaign was a highly efficient and well-run operation that was competitive in hitherto Republican-dominated states. Whether it will translate into sustained party development remains to be seen.

The "new" parties are empowered to make strategic choices that have flummoxed analysts of party competition. In the traditional view, a two-party system forced the parties to appeal to the center in pursuit of the elusive "median voter." Yet rather than appeal to the center, the parties in the new century have frequently appealed to their "bases." For instance, Rove received the credit, if it can be called that, for turning out Evangelical voters and other activist Republican supporters in 2004 to secure Bush's reelection. While appeals were made to the center, most notably in the selection of speakers at the Republican National Convention, the overall strategy was to appeal to the base rather than the middle. The Kerry campaign strategy was nearly identical: appeal to the center at the party convention but allow the 527 groups to take a partisan line at the grassroots level. In 2008, the calculations remained similar. As James W. Ceaser pointed out, "Neither party [selected] a candidate who campaigned on the basis of a call to alter or reconfigure their party's ideological position."[32] John McCain, the Republican nominee, was popular among independents and centrists. To shore up his support with the GOP base, he nominated Alaska governor Sarah Palin. Barack Obama's temperament and demeanor sent a message of moderation, while his policy proposals generally fit into traditional liberal positions. The parties now play on at least two registers.

The notion that the two parties can be well served by appealing to their bases rather than the center is a distinctive feature of recent American politics. Today, strategists argue that blurring differences between the parties is a recipe for electoral disaster.[33] The parties must show that they offer a "choice, not an echo." Over the last decade, returns from party investments in the center of the electorate diminished. A riskier but more profitable strategy was to invest in one's own side. Parties consequently diversified their portfolios.

In the situation of roughly equal party strength, two strategies tempt party tacticians. One is to play to the party base, hoping to turn out more committed voters than one's opponent. The other is to appeal to "swing" voters in the center, because the bases of each party are of roughly equal size, each making up about a third of the electorate, meaning that neither party can win with its base alone. Rather than fully embracing either one of these strategies, the parties have oscillated between them.

The Congressional Parties

American parties in Congress were traditionally seen as weak: they lacked discipline, strong organizations, effective leaders, and consistent policy positions. Power was decentralized in the committees, the minority party made significant contributions to legislation, and social life on Capitol Hill blurred party lines. In the new century, the traditional view has been stood on its head. Congressional party leaders control the agenda and outcomes to an exceptional degree. The parties display much more discipline on roll call votes, they tend ideologically to their respective poles, the minority party is usually excluded from legislative deliberations, and few members of opposing parties socialize together.[34]

Analysts have pointed to four factors to explain these changes. First, the regional realignments of the South and the Northeast have deprived the parties of wings that overlap the center (table 11.2). Liberal Republicans and conservative Democrats have become a thing of the past. The Republican Party's fortunes have fallen in New England, once a source of strength, but risen in

Table 11.2   Regional party strength, 1978 and 2004

Region	President	House	Senate	Governors	State legislatures
1978					
New England	D 53.0	D 18	D 7	D 5	D 7
	R 47.0	R 7	R 5	R 1	R 4
					Tie 1
South	D 54.8	D 77	D 15	D 8	D 22
	R 45.2	R 31	R 6	R 3	R 0
			I 1		
2004					
New England	D 58.6	D 16	D 6	D 2	D 10
	R 41.4	R 5	R 5	R 4	R 2
		I 1	I 1		
South	D 42.8	D 49	D 4	D 3	D 11
	R 57.2	R 82	R 18	R 8	R 11

Sources: James W. Ceaser and Daniel DiSalvo, "A New GOP?" *Public Interest* (Fall 2004); James W. Ceaser and Andrew Busch, *Red over Blue: The 2004 Elections and American Politics* (Lanham: Rowman & Littlefield, 2005).

Note: Percentage of two-party presidential vote and number of elected officials. New England: Connecticut, Maine, Massachusetts, New Hampshire, Rhode Island, and Vermont. South: Alabama, Arkansas, Florida, Georgia, Louisiana, Mississippi, North Carolina, South Carolina, Tennessee, Texas, and Virginia.

the South and Southwest. Republicans have also disappeared from many American cities and old-line suburbs. Today's GOP originates from states and districts that represent exurban, rural, and small-town America.[35] The Democratic Party's dominance in the North has been consolidated, but it has lost control of the South. Congressional Democrats today hail primarily from the coasts, big cities, and college towns. In sum, regional realignment has reshuffled the parties, making Democrats more liberal and Republicans more conservative.

Second, analysts have argued that the redrawing of congressional district boundaries after the 1990 and 2000 censuses hardened interparty divisions by increasing incumbent advantage in congressional elections. The effect of redistricting has been to tilt many districts heavily in favor of one party or the other. Because districts do not often switch parties, the increased number of "safe" seats in Congress magnifies the importance of low-turnout primary elections, which favor the more ideological and activist candidates. The result, many analysts argue, is that candidates position themselves further to the right or left in order to avoid primary challenges.[36]

Until 2006, Republicans' slight majority made the issue of whether redistricting privileged them the subject of contentious debate. Those who believe it did stressed (1) that the reallocation of House seats that rewarded the South and West was favorable to the GOP and (2) that the creation of "majority-minority" districts crowded African American voters into a few districts (especially in the South), making the surrounding districts more Republican.[37] Other analysts, however, have contested the majority-minority thesis.[38] Critics point out that there was only a small gap between the number of seats and votes for the House, which should be large if redistricting explained the Republican advance.[39] The Republican "advantage" seemed to stem from the natural distribution of voters across the country. The county-level purple electoral maps showing gradations of voter concentration revealed that Republicans were spread more evenly across the country, while Democrats are highly concentrated in certain areas.[40]

Third, the congressional party leadership has gained new powers to set the agenda and enforce party discipline. Many congressional scholars argue that the increased ideological homogeneity of each party caucus has empowered the leadership with new procedural prerogatives.[41] Leadership control of the Rules Committee has been essential in this process. In the 1980s, Democrats gave the Speaker of the House the power to name all the majority-party members of the committee. That practice has continued, allowing the leadership to use Rules as the instrument to limit the number of alternatives that members have to vote on, which privileges bills leaders favor. Consequently, more bills come to the floor under restrictive rules, which restricts or eliminates the possibility of amendments. Such tough procedural policy produces polarized votes.[42]

Control over two increasingly important sources of campaign funds—partly a result of the 2002 Bipartisan Campaign Finance Reform Act—also provides the leadership with new techniques of party discipline.[43] One is derived from members of the House and Senate themselves. Contrary to the view that a member's only goal is their own reelection, today they are increasingly concerned with the fate of their comrades. During the 2002 elections, congressional leaders of both parties established quotas for incumbent contributions to the party campaign effort. Incumbents from safe seats were asked to give large sums to the House and Senate campaign committees. In

2002, House Speaker Dennis Hastert (R-IL), Majority Leader DeLay, and NRCC chair Tom Davis (R-VA) all contributed $700,000, and the chairs of the powerful Ways and Means, Commerce, and Budget Committees were asked to provide $500,000.[44] In 2006, Charles B. Rangel (D-NY) contributed twice as much as his $300,000 assessment and John P. Murtha (D-PA) has nearly doubled his $250,000 requirement. Both men had their eyes on leadership positions. Willingness to contribute has become a criterion for future committee assignments. The power to deliver major campaign monies has handed the leadership a powerful control instrument.[45]

The other is the rise of "leadership" political action committees (PACs). In 1994, there were thirty-eight of these PACs. Today, there are nearly two hundred. These are PACs created by current and former members of Congress and do not represent an organized interest, such as a corporation, labor union, or association. These PACs are not technically party organizations, but the members who make these contributions usually share the party campaign committees' objectives. In 2002, for example, leadership PACs contributed $32 million to 692 primary and general election candidates. The biggest contributors were the House whips, DeLay and Pelosi, who led their parties in leadership PAC donations, each contributing more than $1 million to congressional candidates. The results for the 2006 elections were similar. The extensive involvement of party leaders in funding the election of new members allows party leaders to amass chits they can later call in.

The above factors have contributed to a change in the ideological profile of the congressional party leadership. It was long held that the party caucuses elected moderate leaders—those closest to their medians.[46] Since 1995, however, the leadership has steadily moved away from the center and toward the ideological poles. In the 1990s, Richard Armey (R-TX) and Richard Gephardt (D-MO) became the majority- and minority-party leaders. Both were from the ideological third quadrant from the center of their respective parties. The trend was completed in the 108th Congress. Republicans elected one of their most conservative members, Tom DeLay (R-TX), as majority leader, while Democrats chose Nancy Pelosi (D-CA), one of their most liberal members, as minority leader. When scandal forced DeLay to resign in 2005, House Republicans replaced him with John Boehner (R-OH), a "revolutionary" from the class of 1994. After the 2006 elections, Pelosi became the first female Speaker of the House. Scholars argue that the rise of ideologically "extreme" leaders in the House is partly a consequence of their ability to raise campaign funds for the party caucus. Because they are closer to the party base, they are better able to tap the financial resources of individual donors and interest groups. Raising money has taken on special importance in an age of near party parity and rising campaign costs. The need for money to maintain or win majority control has made fundraising ability an essential attribute of the new congressional leaders.[47]

Fourth, change in the culture of Capitol Hill has abetted partisan divisions. Since Watergate, scandals and personal attacks have exploded. There is now a preoccupation with ethics issues and "corruption." Scandal politics became an anvil on which Newt Gingrich (R-GA) forged a Republican majority in the House. In 2006, Democrats turned the tables, campaigning on the Republican "culture of corruption." Trafficking in Washington's dirty laundry is now a commonplace in partisan warfare. Veteran observers, however, report that there was little evidence that real corruption is on the rise.[48]

Change of the congressional schedule has also altered the atmosphere of Capitol Hill. After winning control of the House in 1994, Speaker Gingrich advised Republicans to spend more time in their districts and less in Washington. Gingrich and Senate Majority Leader Trent Lott (R-MS) decreased the length of the congressional workweek. Members subsequently spent more time at home in their states and districts and less time with their colleagues.[49] In addition, their spouses did not often live in Washington, which hindered the development of friendships across party lines. As part of a larger effort to capture the good-government banner, House Majority Leader Steny Hoyer (D-MD) announced in December 2006 that Congress would return to a five-day-a-week work schedule.[50]

These factors have produced a "new" Congress. The "old" Congress was a decentralized, committee- and subcommittee-based institution. Today, it is increasingly a centralized one where party trumps committee.[51] Institutional change and governing context have encouraged the parties to enact policies closer to the preferences of the median of their congressional caucuses, which is to the right or the left of the chamber median or the median voter in the electorate. As David Mayhew puts it, "Both parties occasionally fall victim to the temptation to try to 'enact their medians.' That is, to enact policies . . . favored by their own median members rather than favored by the median member of the American public."[52] Under contemporary conditions, this temptation has grown stronger. The Bush tax cuts and Obama's health care reform are evidence of policies that satisfy the party median while leaving the national median cold. In sum, there are new incentives for the congressional parties to satisfy their bases to the neglect of the center. Pleasing the base is imperative to secure the monies required to win the few races needed to maintain majority control. These are powerful incentives to move away from the political center.

The President and His Party

The Bush presidency was the lightening rod of the new century. Bush entered office having lost the popular vote but secured a victory in the Electoral College with the help of the Supreme Court. Bush arrived in the White House with the expectation of an administration focused on domestic issues. Early in his presidency, however, the terrorist attacks of September 11, 2001, dramatically reoriented the nation's focus from domestic to foreign affairs. Bush led the nation into wars in Afghanistan and Iraq as part of a broader strategy to transform the Middle East to reduce the threat of Islamic terrorism. These bold engagements, especially the war in Iraq, provoked massive public outcry.

Nonetheless, Bush's aim during the 2000 campaign and his first year in office was to move the Republican Party away from the shrill tone of the Gingrich years. The president's campaign theme of "compassionate conservatism" was a centrist doctrine, defined by "its willingness to expand as well as contract government."[53] His aim was to create a lean government that gave individuals choices in health care, education, and retirement. The "ownership society" would make individuals more self-reliant, responsible, and free from dependence on government.[54] Bush also took solidly conservative stances on social issues, such as abortion, stem cell research, and gay rights. While conservatives were hardly thrilled about some parts of Bush's program, they could still find things to support.[55]

Bush's domestic policy priorities alternated between seeking the center and satisfying the base, although this pleased almost no one. Infuriated by the president's willingness to pursue his agenda after the Florida debacle, Democrats remained intensely opposed to Bush and his program. His appeals to moderates and new constituencies fell on deaf ears, while his moves to satisfy the GOP base were amplified in the press. Nonetheless, No Child Left Behind (NCLB), the Medicare prescription drug benefit, and the president's immigration proposals were aimed at voters outside the GOP's traditional constituencies. NCLB was a policy the administration conceived as a strategy to weaken Democrats' grip on the issue of education. Medicare Part D was designed to neutralize attacks on Republicans' willingness to dismantle the welfare state and shore up GOP support among seniors. Immigration reform was meant to lure in Hispanics, a growing segment of the electorate. On the other hand, the tax cuts, the energy program, the bankruptcy legislation, and federal judicial appointments were meant to shore up the base, rewarding significant elements of the business community, social conservatives, or both.

The first two items on the administration's agenda were tax cuts and education reform. The passage of the first tax cut and NCLB shows how the administration's legislative strategy differed depending on whether the measure was aimed at the party base or the center. To secure policies congenial to the base, unified congressional majorities, especially the House, were essential. A firm alliance with the House leadership is a major asset to a president of the same party with only a slim majority in the Senate because the House can be used to leverage the Senate. With the House Republican leadership in his corner, Bush quickly got a tax bill passed that was very close to his initial proposal. Going first to the House allowed the president to set the terms of the debate and then slowly cede ground in the more individualistic Senate. This strategy meant staking out a clear position on the right and then giving ground to the middle.[56] It also requires that the president only pressure senators.

To pass centrist legislation on issues where the GOP is divided, building a legislative coalition in the Senate was essential. The president's strategy was to stake out a position on the center-right, negotiate with key senators, and work outward from there. For centrist legislation such as NCLB and Medicare Part D, the administration's bargaining technique was to include a few controversial measures within its proposals that could be dropped to lure in moderates. The president's education reform proposal included a controversial vouchers program, which was then given away as a bargaining chip to bring Democrats on board. To expand Medicare, the president cast overboard a provision stipulating that the prescription drug benefit only be given to those who agreed to join private insurance plans. Because GOP congressional leadership was only able to exercise limited party discipline on policies that appealed to the center, which resulted in more defections from the right, the president had to personally twist the arms of members of the House and Senate. This was especially evident in the passage of NCLB and Medicare Part D.[57]

After the 2002 and 2004 elections, the White House continued to occasionally employ a House-centered legislative strategy to pass controversial social legislation appealing to the base, such as the Partial-Birth Abortion Ban Act (October 2003) and the Unborn Victims of Violence Act (March 2004).[58] But with larger Republican majorities in the Senate, the president no longer needed to leverage the Senate with the House. Bush could confidently take his legislation directly to the Senate, where only a few Democrats' votes would be required to invoke cloture. He was reasonably sure that the House would go along in outline with the results of Senate negotiations. The president therefore relied on Senate Majority Leader Bill Frist (R-TN) to move legislation appealing to elements of the base—such as a new bankruptcy law and limitations on class action lawsuits—through the Senate.[59] In both cases, Frist reached a deal with House leaders in which the Senate would block any significant changes to the measures in exchange for a commitment from the House that it would adopt unaltered what the Senate approved. Frist unified Republicans to block Democrats' efforts to amend or delay the measures. This paved the way for the enactment of the Class Action Fairness Act and the Bankruptcy Abuse Prevention and Consumer Protection Act in April of 2005. Both measures appealed to core supporters of the GOP.

Bush's efforts to craft policies that, broadly speaking, appealed to the center—on issues of free trade, the environment, immigration, and Social Security—did not fare well. The president had to expend valuable political capital to secure the passage of the Central American Free Trade Agreement (CAFTA), despite centrist Democrat and much Republican support for such measures throughout the 1990s. The "Clear Skies" environmental proposal was badly managed in Congress and came to be seen as a measure designed to reward industry rather than reduce emissions.[60] It did not make it out of Senate committee. Although not exactly an appeal to the center, Bush's proposal to reform Social Security failed to gain traction. House Republican leaders were reluctant to force members to vote on a reform package unless it was clear the Senate would approve it.[61] But the votes to break a filibuster were just not there.

The president's immigration proposals also hewed to the center but divided the GOP. Bush outlined a reform package that combined tougher border enforcement, checks on businesses that employ illegal immigrants, a path to citizenship for those in the country illegally, and a guest worker program for businesses that rely on seasonal labor. Yet just as the president began to campaign in earnest for this package, public support for it dropped. In 2005, a bipartisan bill that reflected the president's proposals passed in the Senate. But the measure was opposed by conservative House Republicans, who derided it as "amnesty." The confrontation in Congress led to the passage of the Secure Borders Act just before the 2006 elections.[62] But this was not comprehensive reform. After Democrats won control of both chambers of Congress, a bipartisan coalition in support of reform seemed to be in the offing. But after much maneuvering, the leading bill was pronounced dead in the Senate in late June 2007. Not only did many conservative Republicans not support the president's proposals, but they became his most ardent opponents on the issue.

Not all of the administration's agenda was pursued through Congress. When the legislative route was blocked, President Bush, like other modern presidents, resorted to using executive orders, bureaucratic discretion, and executive appointments. Most notably, he created the Faith-Based Initiative, limited government funding for stem cell research, and increased spending on AIDS, all by executive order. The Environmental Protection Agency (EPA) partly enacted the president's Clear Skies program through the Clean Air Interstate Rule. The Department of the Interior changed forest management rules to expand logging in national forests. And the Department of Education allowed school districts more latitude in creating same-sex classrooms and schools—a policy popular with social conservatives.[63] A host of agencies also took steps to reduce the number of tort lawsuits.[64] Finally, Bush called for the appointment of judges to the federal courts who were not "activists." The campaign against judicial activism served as a means to obliquely address contentious social policies, because many have concluded that courts should handle issues such as abortion, gay rights, and affirmative action.

While conservatives claimed that Bush was "too liberal," giving up on limited government in favor of "big government conservatism," liberals suggested that Republicans did not make many overt moves to the center because the nation was at war. Whatever "positive" electoral effect Republicans garnered after September 11, however, quickly ran its course. The Iraq War became a major drag for Republican candidates in the 2006 and 2008 elections. Despite Republicans' attempt to merge the Iraq War with the war on terrorism, the issue plagued candidates in many states and districts. Many candidates distanced themselves from the president on the war, asserting their independence.[65] The war became a proxy to punish the majority party on a host of issues from corruption to economic management. In a striking reversal of fortune, Democrats captured both the House and the Senate in 2006 and then elected the first African American to the presidency in 2008.

Illinois senator Barack Obama capitalized on disenchantment with President Bush, concern about the economy, and seismic demographic shifts away from the Republican Party among young people, Hispanics, and college-educated voters.

Intense party competition and near parity in party strength in the twenty-first century have not produced gridlock. The Bush administration and more recently the Obama administration used party mechanisms to push through significant legislation. However, neither party's policy record solidified a durable national majority. No grand Republican coalition in support of "compassionate conservatism" or the "ownership society" emerged, and any hopes for one were beaten back during the 2006 elections and crushed in 2008. Domestically, Republicans have only been able to claim limited credit for the legislation aimed at the center, which has simultaneously angered conservatives. NCLB and Medicare Part D have come under sustained fire from Democrats and conservatives alike. Nor have other "liberal" aspects of Bush's tenure—such as the largest rise in discretionary domestic spending since the Great Society, liberal immigration proposals, and the signing of a campaign finance reform bill supported mostly by Democrats—allowed Republicans to score points with centrists and Democrats. The Obama administration successfully passed a major economic stimulus package to aid the economy, a massive reform of health care, and new regulations for the financial industry. But the Democrats lost independents and a huge number of seats in Congress (and their majority in the House) in 2010.

Conclusion

The American constitutional system was created to constrain policymakers. In the wooden language of political science, our institutional arrangements create "multiple veto points." The design was supposed to make policymaking incremental and occasionally inconsistent. But while the Constitution separated the government and the people, the creation of political parties brought them closer together. What the Constitution separated the parties partially united. However, the advent of the modern administrative state weakened parties, creating a new sort of divide between policymakers and the public. Today, parties have made a comeback.

The question is whether top-heavy, nationalized parties with programmatic objectives operating within a large administrative state can still connect with voters and reduce the distance between the nation's representatives and the represented. Intense party competition has mobilized new voters, and voter turnout has increased over the past few election cycles. However, intense party competition has yet to produce a winner. Neither party has been able to leverage their position into a durable majority. Events beyond the control of politicians continue to partially determine their fate. The GOP and President Bush were aided by the salience of terrorism and national security issues in 2002 and 2004. The Democratic Party and Barack Obama were given a major boost by the Iraq War in 2006 and an economic downturn and a financial crisis on Wall Street in 2008. And in another twist of fate, the Republicans benefited handsomely at Democrats' expense from a stalled economy and high unemployment in 2010.

Nonetheless, the great chess match between the parties will continue to be a powerful determinant of the policy product of American government. Parity in party competition does not necessarily produce deadlock. The last six years have shown that it can produce significant policies that capture the nation's attention. Constitutional government appears able to survive the rise of the administrative state and a revival of political parties.

The Early Obama Years

As we have seen, in America's two-party system both political parties need to secure the support of "independents" or "swing voters" in the political center. In November 2008, the Democratic presidential candidate, Barack Obama, successfully captured such voters. According to exit polls, he defeated his Republican opponent, John McCain, 52 percent to 44 percent among independent voters.[66] But in addition to voters in the center of the electorate, party leaders must also energize constituencies with deep partisan commitments for electoral mobilization and campaign contributions. Obama and his campaign outfit, Organizing for America, were very successful at enlisting the base of the Democratic Party, including labor unions, blacks, youth, and liberals. Candidate Obama's appeal to both moderate voters and deeply loyal Democratic groups created a winning formula. Since then, how has President Obama fared in holding together the coalition that elected him?

Obama entered the White House in January 2009 after an impressive electoral victory. The Democratic Party had a seventy-eight-seat majority in the

House of Representatives and, after Arlen Specter (PA) switched parties, a filibuster-proof majority in the Senate, which meant that technically it did not need a single Republican vote to pass laws in Congress. Congressional Democrats were also more united than ever before. The Democratic Caucus in the House of Representatives voted as a block 92 percent of the time in 2007–8, and Senate Democrats voted together 87 percent of the time.[67] In addition, Speaker of the House Nancy Pelosi and the Democratic leadership were armed with new rules and procedures that facilitated their control of the legislative process to the exclusion of Republicans.[68]

Maintaining a broad coalition has proved to be a major challenge for President Obama and his congressional allies. This is due to the political law that as time passes exercising power means accumulating grievances more than scoring points. This law is underpinned by the fact that the ideological preferences and political understandings of centrist voters and party activists often diverge substantially. Satisfying them both is extremely difficult. By the 2010 midterm elections, the Democratic Party had lost the support of independents, who swung massively in favor of Republicans, which helped them win control of the House of Representatives and chip away at the Democrats' majority in the Senate.

As the Democratic Party's congressional ranks expanded in the 2006 and 2008 elections, it brought in more centrist and moderate legislators. In the House, forty-eight Democrats were from districts where majorities voted for both Bush and McCain. The congressional Democratic Party was therefore divided between liberals (in the Progressive Caucus) and centrists (in the Blue Dog and New Democrat Coalitions) that hailed from more conservative areas. These centrists were skeptical of a leftist agenda and are often unwilling to risk their political careers by supporting liberal policies that are unpopular with their constituents. Similar divisions exist among Democrats in the Senate. As much as or more than Republicans, these centrist Democrats put the brakes on Obama's domestic legislative agenda.[69]

In addition to large legislative majorities, the Obama administration initially saw the financial crisis of 2008 as an opportunity to push through its program. As time passed, however, the crisis made enacting the president's domestic program more difficult. Rather than proceed directly to the issues he campaigned on, Obama was forced to confront the meltdown on Wall Street. He took five steps. First, Obama continued the Temporary Asset Relief Program

(TARP) begun under President Bush that funneled monies to large banks to ensure their solvency. Second, he ordered the bailout of the troubled automakers General Motors and Chrysler, which gave the government an ownership stake in these companies. Third, Obama proposed and Congress quickly passed a $787 billion dollar "stimulus" package to jump-start the economy or at least cushion the slide into a recession. Fourth, the administration developed a program to help distressed homeowners refinance their homes so that banks do not foreclose on them. Fifth, Obama brought the entire financial system under stricter federal supervision with a major regulatory overhaul. These bold moves ignited concern among many Americans about the growth of government power and gave birth to a vociferous grassroots social movement in opposition to the administration calling itself the Tea Party.

The stimulus package was Obama's signature law to address the economic crisis. The president's political strategy for advancing this complex piece of legislation had the advantages of passing a bill swiftly, allowing the president to claim credit for a rapid response to the emergency, and winning liberal support. Even though liberals wanted an even more generous measure, the stimulus law rewarded key Democratic supporters in the public sector. Yet many centrists expressed concern that it did too little in terms of short-term job creation.

While the stimulus package gave Obama political cover throughout the spring of 2009, when unemployment reached 9.4 percent nationally over the summer, there was public outcry. In July, nearly half of Americans said the stimulus plan had no effect on the economy, while 28 percent said it made the economy better and 21 percent said it made the economy worse.[70] Liberals responded by calling for more government spending, while moderates expressed concern about the ballooning size of the federal budget deficit. Roughly 60 percent of independents said that his proposals involved too much spending and too much government expansion.[71] As the economy's problems persisted, the president's job approval rating among independent voters, according to a *Wall Street Journal*/NBC News survey, fell from 60 percent in April to 45 percent in June.

In the midst of heightened concern over government spending and the economy among independents, Obama and the Democratic Congress turned their attention to their number one domestic priority: reform of the health care system. The objectives of reform were to extend insurance coverage to the roughly 46 million uninsured people in the United States and reduce the rising costs of health care.[72] These goals, however, work at cross-purposes because extending health care coverage inevitably costs more money. President Obama struggled to explain how the government could provide more health care with less money.

Divisions over the objectives of reform quickly made themselves evident in Congress. Liberals were more concerned about extending coverage, while centrists were more concerned about controlling costs. Liberals (and the president) favored a "public option," which would be a new government-run insurance program that would compete with private insurance plans, combined with either an "individual" or "employer" mandate. The mandates would either require that all citizens purchase health insurance or stipulate that businesses buy it for their workers or pay hefty fines. In mid-August, sixty liberal Democrats in the House drew a line in the sand, saying that they could not vote for a bill without a government insurance plan.

Centrists, on the other hand, were skeptical about the costs of such a plan—especially after the Congressional Budget Office said the current bills would cost over \$1 trillion over ten years—and whether it would create incentives for companies that purchase private insurance to push their employees into the government plan. Instead, moderates favored taxing expensive private health care plans, making cuts in the Medicare program for the elderly, and using the new revenue to pay for extending coverage. Because roughly 85 percent of Americans with health insurance (provided through their employers or the government programs Medicare and Medicaid) report that they are satisfied with the care they receive, any plan that threatens to change matters significantly was politically dangerous.

But liberals, labor unions, and the president strongly opposed the idea of taxing expensive plans, and senior citizens, a powerful constituency, oppose cuts in Medicare.[73] When the powerful Senate Finance Committee chairman, centrist Max Baucus (D-MT), produced his bill in September, liberals on the committee, such as Jay Rockefeller (D-WV), quickly criticized it. Approval of Obama's handling of health care declined from 57 percent in April to 49 percent in late July 2009, while disapproval rose from 29 percent to 44 percent. By late August disapproval had reached nearly 50 percent. More importantly, most independents began to disapprove of Obama's health care strategy. In March, only 32 percent of Americans thought Obama was a tax-and-spend liberal; in late July, 43 percent did.[74] The more Obama worked exclusively with a far less popular Democratic Congress, the faster his own standing fell. With no Republican support forthcoming, Democrats were forced to resort to unconventional legislative procedures to pass the measure on strictly partisan lines in March of 2010. The result was to make the bill even more unpopular with the public.

Another major initiative on Obama's domestic agenda is reform in the energy and environmental sector. Known as "cap and trade," it was a market-based technique for reducing carbon emissions by setting an overall ceiling for emissions and issuing companies tradable permits, which would give companies incentives to lower emissions so they can sell the permits. In the summer of 2009, the House of Representatives passed, by the slim margin of 219–212, a bill that was welcomed by many liberals and environmentalists for setting a cap despite the fact that it provided few incentives to reduce carbon emissions. Centrists, however, worried that the plan would increase energy costs for American consumers while not providing sufficient revenue to the federal government because 85 percent of the permits would be given away to industry rather than sold.[75] The bill was not considered in the Senate.

While the administration managed to pass a financial services reform bill, the measure did not go as far in penalizing Wall Street as some liberals would have liked. The other major items on Obama's domestic agenda were education and immigration reform; the former was pursued through the Department of Education with a legislative initiative promised for the future. Immigration reform was much discussed, especially after the state of Arizona passed a controversial law. But only one legislative attempt to address the issue was made, shortly after the Democrats' devastating losses in the 2010 elections. The measure did not pass.

Ultimately, the difficulty for President Obama was that by at least partially satisfying liberal Democrats with a major increase in the size of government through expanded health care benefits, greater public sector spending, and more financial regulation during an economic contraction, he led his party to a day of political reckoning with centrist voters, who delivered him a striking rebuke at the polls in November 2010. As of this writing, Obama has sought to move back to the center by signing an extension of the Bush tax cuts passed by the lame-duck Congress, deeply offending liberals. The process of balancing the base and the center continues unabated.

NOTES

1. A vast literature tried to show that the parties were "declining." David S. Broder, *The Party's Over: The Failure of Politics in America* (New York: Harper & Row, 1971); Gerald Pomper, ed., *Party Renewal in America: Theory and Practice* (New York: Praeger, 1980); Joel L. Fleishman, ed., *The Future of American Political Parties: The Challenge of Governance* (Englewood: Prentice-Hall, 1982); Walter Dean Burnham, *The Current Crisis in American Politics* (New York: Oxford University Press, 1982); William Crotty, *American Parties in Decline* (Boston: Little, Brown, 1984); Martin P. Wattenberg, *The Decline of American Political Parties, 1952–1980* (Cambridge, MA: Harvard University Press, 1984); David E. Price, *Bringing Back the Parties* (Washington, DC: CQ Press, 1984); Xandra Kayden and Eddie Mahe Jr., *The Party Goes On: The Persistence of the Two-Party System in the United States* (New York: Basic Books, 1985); John J. Coleman, *Party Decline in America* (Princeton, NJ: Princeton University Press, 1996); Martin Wattenberg, *The Decline of American Political Parties, 1952–1994* (Cambridge, MA: Harvard University Press, reprint ed., 1996).

2. Anthony Downs, *An Economic Theory of Democracy* (New York: Harper & Row, 1957). For a review of the literature on Downs's median voter theory, see Bernard Grofman, "Downs and Two-Party Convergence," *Annual Review of Political Science* 7 (2004): 25–46.

3. Philip Converse, "The Nature of Belief Systems in Mass Publics," in *Ideology and Discontent*, ed. David Apter (New York: Free Press, 1964); Michael Lewis-Beck et al., *The American Voter Revisited* (Ann Arbor: University of Michigan Press, 2008); John Zaller, *The Nature and Origins of Mass Opinion* (New York: Cambridge University Press, 1992).

4. Larry M. Bartels, *Unequal Democracy: The Political Economy of the New Gilded Age* (Princeton, NJ: Princeton University Press and Russell Sage Foundation, 2008), 287.

5. For a review of the literature on polarization, see Geoffrey C. Layman, Thomas M. Carsey, and Juliana Menasce Horowitz, "Party Polarization in American Politics: Characteristics, Causes, and Consequences," *Annual Review of Political Science* 9 (June 2006): 83–110. See also David W. Brady and Pietro S. Nivola, eds., *Red and Blue Nation? Characteristics and Causes of America's Polarized Politics* (Washington, DC: Brookings Institution Press and Hoover Institution, 2006); Morris Fiorina, *Culture War? The Myth of Polarized America* (New York: Longman, 2003); James Q. Wilson, "How Divided Are We?," *Commentary* (February 2005); Nolan McCarty, Keith T. Poole, and Howard Rosenthal, *Polarized America: The Dance of Ideology and Unequal Riches* (Cambridge, MA: MIT Press, 2006); Alan Abramowitz and Kyle Sanders, "Why Can't We All Just Get Along? The Reality of a Polarized America," *Forum* 3, no. 2 (2005); Phillip A. Klinkner and Ann Hapanowicz, "Red and Blue Déjà Vu: Measuring Political Polarization in the 2004 Election," *Forum* 3, no. 2 (2005); Keith T. Poole, "The Decline and Rise of Party Polarization in Congress in the Twentieth Century," *Extensions* (Fall 2005).

6. James Q. Wilson, "New Politics, New Elites, Old Publics," in *The New Politics of Public Policy*, ed. Marc K. Landy and Martin A. Levin (Baltimore: Johns Hopkins University Press, 1995), 255–60, 263–64.

7. Daniel DiSalvo, "Party Factions in Congress," *Presidency and Congress: A Journal of Capital Studies* (Spring 2009).

8. Jacob Hacker and Paul Pierson, *Off Center: The Republican Revolution and the Erosion of American Democracy* (New Haven, CT: Yale University Press, 2005).

9. Byron Shafer, *The Two Majorities and the Puzzle of Modern American Politics* (Lawrence: Kansas University Press, 2004), 156–69; Richard A. Harris and Sidney M. Milkis, *The Politics of Regulatory Change: A Tale of Two Agencies*, 2nd ed. (New York: Oxford University Press, 1996), 3–22, 53–97; Allen Matusow, *The Unraveling of America: A History of Liberalism in the 1960s* (New York: Harper & Row, 1984), 395–439; Terry H. Anderson, *The Movement and the Sixties* (New York: Oxford University Press, 1996); Alonzo L. Hamby, *Liberalism and Its Challengers: From FDR to Reagan* (New York: Oxford University Press, 1985), 277; Frederick G. Dutton, *Changing Sources of Power: American Politics in the 1970s* (New York: McGraw-Hill, 1972), 27–56; Jeffrey M. Berry, *The New Liberalism: The Rising Power of Citizen Groups* (Washington, DC: Brookings Institution, 1999).

10. John Gerring, *Party Ideologies in America, 1828–1996* (New York: Cambridge University Press, 1998), 238–50.

11. Jo Freeman, "The Political Culture of the Democratic and Republican Parties," *Political Science Quarterly* 101 (Fall 1988), 327–56; John F. Hale, "New Politics Liberals and DLC Centrists: Factionalism in the Democratic Party, 1968–1992" (paper delivered at the annual American Political Science Association Conference, Chicago, IL, 1992).

12. Bruce Miroff, *The Liberals Moment: The McGovern Insurgency and the Identity Crisis of the Democratic Party* (Lawrence: Kansas University Press, 2007).

13. Louis Bolce and Gerald De Maio, "Our Secularist Democratic Party," *Public Interest*, no. 149 (Fall 2002); James Davison Hunter, *Culture Wars: The Struggle to Define America* (New York: Basic Books, 1991).

14. Geoffrey Layman, *The Great Divide: Religious and Cultural Conflict in American Party Politics* (New York: Columbia University Press, 2001).

15. Thomas B. Edsall, "Party Hardy," *New Republic*, September 25, 2006.

16. Jerome L. Himmelstein, *To the Right: The Transformation of American Conservatism* (Berkeley: University of California Press, 1990), 63–65, 84–94; John Micklethwait and Adrian Wooldridge, *The Right Nation: Conservative Power in America* (New York: Penguin Press, 2004), 27–40, 63–93; Donald Critchlow, *The Conservative Ascendancy: How the GOP Right Made Political History* (Cambridge, MA: Harvard University Press, 2007); Sean Wiltenz, *The Age of Reagan: A History, 1974–2008* (New York: Harper-Collins, 2008); Bruce Schulman and Julian Zelizer, eds., *Rightward Bound: Making America Conservative in the 1970s* (Cambridge, MA: Harvard University Press, 2008).

17. George H. Nash, *The Conservative Intellectual Movement* (New York: Basic Books, 1976), 123–27; James Allen Smith, *The Idea Brokers: Think Tanks and the Rise of the New Policy Elite* (New York: Free Press, 1991); David M. Ricci, *The Transformation of American Politics: The New Washington and the Rise of Think Tanks* (New Haven, CT: Yale University Press, 1993).

18. Matthew D. Lassiter, "Suburban Strategies: The Volatile Center in Postwar American Politics," in *The Democratic Experiment*, ed. Meg Jacobs, William J. Novak, and Julian E. Zelizer (Princeton, NJ: Princeton University Press, 2003), 327–49; Lisa McGirr, *Suburban Warriors: The Origins of the New American Right* (Princeton, NJ: Princeton University Press, 2001); John A. Andrew III, *The Other Side of the Sixties: Young Americans for Freedom and the Rise of Conservative Politics* (New Brunswick, NJ: Rutgers University Press, 1997); Rick Perlstien, *Before the Storm: Barry Goldwater and the Unmaking of the American Consensus* (New York: Hill & Wang, 2001).

19. Justin Vaïsee, *Neoconservatism: The Biography of the Movement* (Cambridge, MA: Harvard University Press, 2010).

20. Shafer, *Two Majorities*, 169–82; Robert Freedman, "The Religious Right and the Carter Administration," *Historical Journal* (2005).

21. Donald Green, Bradley Palmquist, and Eric Shickler, *Partisan Hearts and Minds: The Social Identity of American Voters* (New Haven, CT: Yale University Press, 2002).

22. Paul S. Herrnson, *Congressional Elections: Campaigning at Home and in Washington*, 4th ed. (Washington, DC: CQ Press, 2004), 86–87, 90–94, 98–115. On the origins of these practices, see Herrnson, *Party Campaigning in the 1980s* (Cambridge, MA: Harvard University Press, 1988).

23. Daniel Galvin, *Presidential Party Building: Dwight D. Eisenhower to George W. Bush* (Princeton, NJ: Princeton University Press, 2009).

24. Michael Nelson, "George W. Bush and Congress: The Electoral Connection," in *Considering the Bush Presidency*, ed. Gary L. Gregg II and Mark J. Rozell (New York: Oxford University Press, 2003), 151; Lynton Weeks, "Red, White and Greenbacks at GOP Fundraiser," *Washington Post*, June 24, 2002; Mike Allen, "Bush Enlists Government in GOP Campaign," *Washington Post*, October 24, 2002; Brian Faler, "Bush Is Back on the Money Trail," *Washington Post*, November 24, 2002.

25. Elizabeth Drew, "Bush: The Dream Campaign," *New York Review of Books* 51, no. 10 (June 10, 2004); Kevin Price and John J. Coleman, "The Party Base of Presidential Leadership and Legitimacy," in *High Risk and Big Ambition: The Presidency of George W. Bush*, ed. Steven Schier (Pittsburgh: University of Pittsburgh Press, 2004).

26. Sidney M. Milkis and Jesse H. Rhodes, "George W. Bush, the Republican Party, and the 'New' Party System," *Perspectives on Politics* 5, no. 3 (2007): 461–88; Joe Hadfield, "The RNC Keeps on Rollin': The New Chairman's Plans to Grow the Vote for '08," *Campaigns and Elections* (April 2005).

27. James W. Ceaser and Andrew E. Busch, *Red over Blue: The 2004 Elections and American Politics* (Lantham: Rowman & Littlefield), 27.

28. Jo Freeman, "The Political Culture of the Democratic and Republican Parties," *Political Science Quarterly* 101 (Fall 1988): 327–56; Daniel Galvin, "Parties as Political Institutions in American Political Development" (paper presented at the Miller Center of Public Affairs, Charlottesville, VA, November 2007).

29. Richard M. Skinner, "Do 527s Add Up to a Party? Thinking about the 'Shadows' of Politics," *Forum* 3, no. 3 (2005); Byron York, *The Vast Left Wing Conspiracy* (New York: Crown Forum, 2006); Thomas B. Edsall, *Building Red America: The New Conservative Coalition and the Drive for Permanent Power* (New York: Basic Books), 227–30.

30. Leslie Wayne, "Democrats Take Page from Their Rival's Playbook," *New York Times*, November 1, 2008. To close the gap, longtime Democratic operative Harold M. Ickes created a for-profit company, Catalist, which is developing a massive databank, pieces of which can be sold to candidates for their get-out-the-vote efforts. Leslie Wayne, "Clinton Aide's Databank Venture Breaks Ground in Politicking," *New York Times*, April 12, 2008.

31. Matt Bai, "The Inside Agitator," *New York Times Magazine*, October 1, 2006; Thomas B. Edsall, "Democrats Fractured over Strategy, Funds," *Washington Post*, May 11, 2006; Adam Nagourney, "Dean and Party Leaders in a Money Dispute," *New York Times*, May 11, 2006; John Nichols, "Dean's Fifty-Fifty Strategy," *Nation*, January 24,

2006; Peter Savodnik, "Rahm Won't Echo Dean in Bold 2006 Forecasts," *Hill*, December 13, 2006; Steven Kornacki, "Emmanuel, Dean Still Sparring," *Roll Call*, July 3, 2006.

32. James W. Ceaser, "What a Long Strange Race It's Been," *Claremont Review of Books* (Spring 2008).

33. Dan Balz and Jim Vandehei, "GOP Aims to Scare Up Big Voter Turn Out," *Washington Post*, October 20, 2006.

34. Mark Kady, "Party Unity: Learning to Stick Together," *CQ Weekly*, January 9, 2006.

35. David W. Rohde, *Parties and Leaders in the Postreform House* (Chicago: University of Chicago Press, 1991); Earl Black and Merle Black, *The Rise of the Southern Republicans* (Cambridge, MA: Harvard University Press, 2002).

36. Barry Burden estimates that a credible primary challenge pulls a congressional candidate ten points toward the ideological poles on a scale of zero to one hundred. See Barry Burden, "Candidate Positions in U.S. Congressional Elections," *British Journal of Political Science* 34 (2004): 211–27; Alan I. Abramowitz, Brad Alexander, and Matthew Gunning, "Incumbency, Redistricting, and the Decline of Competition in U.S. House Elections," *Journal of Politics* 68 (2006); E. J. Dionne Jr., "Room Left to Govern?" *Washington Post*, July 2, 2004; Hacker and Pierson, *Off Center*, 124–25; Edsall, *Building Red America*, 68–69.

37. Bruce Reed, "Midterm Limits," *Slate*, October 10, 2006, www.slate.com/id/2151365/; Carol M. Swain, *Black Face, Black Interests: The Representation of African-Americans in Congress* (Cambridge, MA: Harvard University Press, 1993).

38. John R. Petrcik and Scott W. Desposato argue that the creation of majority-minority districts was not a fundamental reason for Republican advances. See "The Partisan Consequences of Majority-Minority Redistricting in the South, 1992 and 1994," *Journal of Politics* 60 (1998): 613–33; Kevin A. Hill, "Does the Creation of Majority Black Districts Aid Republicans? An Analysis of the 1992 Congressional Elections in Eight Southern States," *Journal of Politics* 57 (1995): 384–401.

39. On the gap between seats and votes, see John J. Pitney, "Off Base," *Forum* 3, no. 4 (2006); Hardy W. Stanley and Richard G. Niemi, *Vital Statistics on American Politics, 2005–6* (Washington, DC: CQ Press, 2006), 44–45. In addition, Democrats' loss of the House in 1994 enhanced the GOP's ability to secure PAC funding, prompting many senior party members to retire in 1996, which improved Republican opportunities to pick up seats. Gary C. Jacobsen, "Congress: Unprecedented and Unsurpassing," in *The Elections of 1996*, ed. Michael Nelson (Washington, DC: CQ Press, 1997), 143–67.

40. Peter E. Harrell, "House: Death of Close Races Makes Status Quo the Best Bet," *CQ Weekly Report*, October 23, 2004, 2506; Edsall, *Building Red America*, 224–27; Ceaser and Busch, *Red over Blue*, 148.

41. John Aldrich and David Rohde, "The Logic of Conditional Party Government: Revisiting the Electoral Connection," in *Congress Reconsidered*, 7th ed., ed. Lawrence C. Dodd and Bruce I. Oppenheimer (Washington, DC: CQ Press, 2001); Gary W. Cox and Matthew D. McCubbins, *Legislative Leviathan: Party Government in the House* (Berkeley: University of California Press, 1993). The power of congressional parties in general and the conditional party government model in particular have been the subject of

ongoing debate among congressional scholars. For a critique, see Keith Krehbiel, "Where Is the Party?" *British Journal of Political Science* 23 (1992): 235–66.

42. Thomas Mann and Norman J. Ornstein, *The Broken Branch: How Congress Is Failing America and How to Get It Back on Track* (New York: Oxford University Press, 2006), 72–75, 97–106; Eric Sandalow and Erin McCormick, "Pelosi's Goal," *San Francisco Chronicle*, April 2, 2006; Lois Romano, "The Woman Who Would Be Speaker," *Washington Post*, October 20, 2006.

43. Raymond La Raja, "From Bad to Worse: The Unraveling of the Campaign Finance System," *Forum* 6, no. 2 (Spring 2008).

44. Jeff Zeleny, "Of Dues and Deadbeats on Capitol Hill," *New York Times*, October 1, 2006.

45. Herrnson, *Congressional Elections*, 92–93.

46. Roderick Kiewiet and Matthew McCubbin, *The Logic of Delegation: Congressional Parties and the Appropriations Process* (Chicago: University of Chicago Press, 1991).

47. Eric Heberling, Marc Hetherington, and Bruce Larson, "Redistributing Campaign Money and the Polarization of Congressional Leadership," *Journal of Politics* 68 (November 2006). See also Hacker and Pierson, *Off Center*, 118–20, 131–33, 139, 142–49.

48. Mann and Ornstein, *Broken Branch*, 85, 75–80, 84. Nevertheless, they report that between 1975 and 1995 the number of prosecutions of federal public officials increased by 1,500%.

49. Norman J. Ornstein, "Our Do Nothing Congress," *Roll Call*, September 27, 2006.

50. Lyndsey Layton, "Culture Shock on Capitol Hill: House to Work Five Days a Week," *Washington Post*, December 6, 2006.

51. Mann and Ornstein, *Broken Branch*, 11–12, 122–40, 179–91.

52. David R. Mayhew, "Much Huffing and Puffing but Little Change," in *Seeking the Center: Politics and Policymaking at the New Century*, ed. Martin A. Levin, Marc K. Landy, and Martin Shapiro (Washington, DC: Georgetown University Press), 343.

53. Ceaser and Busch, *Red over Blue*, 35; Michael Gerson, *Heroic Conservatism* (New York: HarperCollins, 1997).

54. Fred Barnes, *Rebel-in-Chief: Inside the Bold and Controversial Presidency of George W. Bush* (New York: Crown Forum, 2006), 125–35.

55. Bill Keller, "Reagan's Son," *New York Times Magazine*, January 26, 2003, 26–31, 42–44, 62; see also James W. Ceaser and Andrew E. Busch, *The Perfect Tie: The True Story of the 2000 Presidential Election* (Lantham: Rowman & Littlefield, 2001), 35, 41–46, 57, 59.

56. Bertram Johnson, "A Stake in the Sand: George W. Bush and Congress," in *High Risk and Big Ambition: The Presidency of George W. Bush*, ed. Steven Schier (Pittsburgh: University of Pittsburgh Press, 2004).

57. Mann and Ornstein, *Broken Branch*, 137, 158, 160, 172–73, 217. On education reform, see 128–30.

58. The partial-birth abortion ban was overwhelmingly approved, first by the House on October 2 (281–142) and three weeks later by the Senate (64–34, with seventeen Democrats joining forty-seven Republicans). Sheryl Gay Stolberg, "Senate Approves Bill to Prohibit Type of Abortion," *New York Times*, October 22, 2003; Gay Stolberg, "Bill Barring Abortion Procedure Drew on Backing from Many Friends of Roe v. Wade," *New York*

Times, October 23, 2003. The House passed the Unborn Victims of Violence Act on February 26, 2004 (245–113), and the Senate a month later (61–38). Carl Hulse, "Senate Outlaws Injury to Fetus during a Crime," *New York Times*, March 26, 2004.

59. Editorial, "The Great Wall of Congress," *Washington Post*, March 13, 2005; David Broder, "A Bankrupt 'Reform,'" *Washington Post*, March 13, 2005; Kathleen Day, "Bankruptcy Bill Nears Final Senate Vote," *Washington Post*, March 9, 2005; William Tucker, "Bush versus the Trial Lawyers," *Weekly Standard*, January 17, 2005; Edsall, *Building Red America*, 118–27; Mann and Ornstein, *Broken Branch*, 141–46.

60. David Whitman, "Partly Sunny," *Washington Monthly* (December 2004).

61. David Broder, "Social Security's Capitol Divide," *Washington Post*, February 20, 2005.

62. Carl Hulse and Rachel L. Swarns, "Senate Passes Bill on Building Border Fence," *New York Times*, September 30, 2006; David Stout, "Bush, Signing Bill for Boarder Fence, Urges Wider Overhaul," *New York Times*, October 27, 2006.

63. Diana Jean Schemo, "Federal Rules Back Single-Sex Public Education," *New York Times*, October 25, 2006.

64. Cindy Skrycki, "Agencies Quietly Enable Tort Reform," *Washington Post*, September 27, 2005.

65. Peter Slevin and Michael Powell, "War Now Working against GOP," *Washington Post*, October 26, 2006.

66. www.cnn.com/ELECTION/2008/results/polls/#USP00p1.

67. Shawn Zellar, "2008 Vote Studies: Party Unity—Parties Dig in Deep on Fractured Hill," *CQ Weekly Report*, December 15, 2008. The House Democrats' party unity score was the highest since *CQ* began tracking this percentage in 1952.

68. Sarah A. Binder, Thomas E. Mann, Norman J. Ornstein, and Molly Reynolds, "Assessing the 110th Congress, Anticipating the 111th," *Mending the Broken Branch*, vol. 3 (Washington, DC: Brookings Institution, 2009).

69. John J. Pitney Jr., "Holding All the Cards and Still Losing: Republican Power Is Not Responsible for Democrats' Unpopularity," *National Review*, August 25, 2009, http://article.nationalreview.com/?q=OGQ3ZGRiZmJhZDZlZDY0ZjE3OG FmNDEyZmNjMTVlZDI.

70. Lymari Morales, "Americans Take Longer-Term View on Stimulus, Recovery," *Gallup*, July 23, 2009, www.gallup.com/poll/121832/Americans-Longer-Term-View -Stimulus-Recovery.aspx. In the same poll, 64% of Americans said that the economic stimulus plan has had no effect on their family's financial situation, while 14% said it has made their family's financial situation better and 22% said it has made their financial situation worse.

71. Frank Newport, "Americans Concerned about Government Spending, Expansion," *Gallup*, July 22, 2009, www.gallup.com/poll/121829/Americans-Concerned -Govt-Spending-Expansion.aspx.

72. Barack Obama, "Why We Need Health Care Reform," *New York Times*, August 15, 2009.

73. Jonathan Martin and Carrie Budoff Brown, "Liberals Revolt over Public Option," *Politico*, August 18, 2009; David Rogers, "Blue Dogs Pulled in Two Directions," *Politico*, July 31, 2009.

74. David Brooks, "Liberal Suicide March," *New York Times*, July 20, 2009; "Obama's Ratings Slide across the Board," *Pew Research Center for the People and the Press*, July 30,

2009, http://people-press.org/report/532/obamas-ratings-slide; "On Health Reform, Public Opinion Shifts," *Washington Post*, August 21, 2009. See also "Poll: More Wary of Obama on Health Care," *CBS News*, September 2, 2009, www.cbsnews.com/stories /2009/09/01/opinion/polls/main5280373.shtml?tag=stack.

75. "In Need of Clean," *Economist*, July 27, 2009.

CHAPTER TWELVE

Bush's "Our Crowd"

Martin M. Shapiro

"Let us suppose . . ." or "once upon a time. . . ." I begin my story with those words, and I call it a story to suggest that, although I believe it is nothing but the truth, it may not be the whole truth. It is, however, a simple truth, and, as one of President Bush's fellow Texans once insisted, simple has its virtues, among them making actions speak louder than words.

George Bush always wanted to be a member in good standing of "our crowd," of the rich and privileged, the oil barons, the corporate executives, the slightly older money, and the so moneyed that the age of the money doesn't matter. I will resist, pleading total lack of qualifications, the psychological delving and reference to the current academic fascination with "networks" that might explain this desire to belong. For Bush the route to belonging became service to the rich. As this volume emphasizes, however, democratic politicians can't provide public policies of service to anybody unless they get elected. Bush policies were designed to serve the rich with whatever covers and concession were necessary in order to stay elected. The best cover is prestidigitation, distracting the electorate's eye from what you are really doing. Sometimes you have to really give something in order to cool out the mark.

All the policy chapters in this book can be summarized in terms of two priorities in descending order of preference: (1) serve the rich; (2) when some policy of potential service to the general public pushes itself onto the agenda, seek to subvert it or at least use it as cover, even if a costly cover, for service to the rich.

Assisting in the pursuit of these preferences was a partly fortuitous, partly carefully crafted set of circumstances. The obvious electoral hindrance to service to our crowd by elected politicians is that working-class and lower-middle-class whites constitute a huge proportion of the electorate. Fortunately, however, a significant proportion of this category of voters, or potential voters, is fundamentalist, or something like fundamentalist, Christians. Service to them by way of antiabortion and other "lifestyle," "family values" stances would not much interfere with service to our crowd, would cost our crowd little or nothing, and would help win elections. An amalgam of fundamentalism, racism, general fear of "big government," a cold war inheritance of belief that somehow Republicans are stronger than Democrats on national security, and, in spite of overwhelming evidence to the contrary, a belief in trickle-down economics, plus the continued perception that the Democratic Party serves all kinds of Americans except the real American Americans, provides the Republican Party with a voter base that would seem to be the very antithesis of our crowd and yet will vote for politicians who reward it. Polling data repeatedly show that somewhat over 50 percent of voters favor various new or extended government programs while a far higher percentage want less government in general. This phenomenon is more than simply the age-old desire for more government services with lower taxes. Apparently something very close to a majority of Americans are prepared to vote for a Republican Party whose platform is simply "no" precisely because its platform is "no." Very few voters need be added by the offer of positive incentives to make a majority. What better situation for a crowd that wants to keep government as far away from its moneymaking as possible?

It would be tedious systematically to march through all the policy chapters of this volume demonstrating the our crowd point. At the risk of restating the obvious from those chapters, let me highlight some of my simplifications.

The high point of our crowd service obviously was the high end bracket income tax cuts covered by small concessions at the very low end and to the middle classes. As Conlan and Posner note, the initial 2001 Bush proposals would have yielded the rich nearly $1 trillion over ten years and everybody else about $300 billion, and Bush adamantly refused to separate proposals for the rich from the rest. Estate tax cuts, which looked beneficial to the middle class but yielded high benefits to the rich, and corporate tax "reforms" favored our crowd. All these cuts were covered by trickle-down, job creation talk and gave our crowd a particularly great bonanza at a time when corporate profits and executive compensation were rapidly advancing. The tax cuts provided an even thicker layer of gilt for the principal beneficiaries of the new gilded age.

The Bush administration employed a number of policy-by-prestidigitation strategies in aid of our crowd. Most noteworthy was the long-term, rearguard action against the recognition of global warming fought by the denial, distortion, and suppression of scientific information that delayed regulation contrary to the interests of the energy barons. Similarly, Bush proposed legislation purporting to reduce air pollution that actually granted the energy industry licenses to pollute and provided subsidies for energy industries. As is the custom in social science volumes such as this one, the word *lying* is avoided, but lying, either by commission or omission, frequently occurred. In their chapter Burke and Scherer point out the corporate interests served by tort and bankruptcy "reform." They also note that Bush's judicial appointments were as much about achieving a pro-business as pro–"family values" judiciary. Other policy moves were more openly for our crowd, such as the attempt to open the Arctic Wildlife Refuge to oil drilling.

Four episodes are of particular significance for my once-upon-a-time story. The first is Social Security. Here is a hated New Deal program with nothing for the rich. It is, however, electorally too entrenched to attack frontally. Instead, sabotage through privatization is the answer. It is even a better answer than pure destruction because it will yield a new source of high profits for our crowd in the financial industry.

Prescription drug benefits tell a parallel story. Doing something about medical benefits became, as Oberlander's chapter in this volume explains, an electoral necessity. Here the general population, not our crowd, is the beneficiary. Here again privatization is a promising mode of sabotage. Perhaps the non-rich could be lured away from the highly successful, "socialized medicine" Medicare into private insurance schemes. Here again the double benefit occurs. Subsidies to the private schemes were both essential to the luring away and a source of further profit for our crowd.

Because this volume proceeds policy area by policy area, it does not tell institutional as opposed to policy sabotage stories. Our crowd hates the Justice

Department for obvious reasons and with some justification given the entrenched Democratic inclinations of its career lawyer staff. What appeared to be a scandal damaging to Republicans generated by Bush administration attempts to Republicanize the U.S. Attorneys fortuitously produced just the destruction of morale in the Justice Department and losses in its career staff that were a desired Republican outcome. Republican appointments to key positions in the department were followed by a marked decline in antitrust prosecutions.

Perhaps the masterstroke of sabotage was at the Federal Reserve. The Fed functions as both a central bank and a regulator. President Bush appointed a chairman who had the desire, the moral authority, and the expertise to maintain the independence of the Fed as a central bank but also believed that any and all regulation of the financial industry was wrong. Strong independence, weak regulation—this was a perfect combination as far as the financial end of our crowd was concerned.

Immigration is our third policy episode. Perhaps it doesn't really fit our simple story at all or at least very well. To be sure, big agriculture, from the Bush Southwestern perspective a particularly in part of our crowd, badly wanted a migrant worker program, particularly after the farm worker union movement had faltered, leaving the continued prospect of very low field wages. Neither heightened border security nor eased routes to naturalization, however, were in the interests of the rich. Nevertheless, as David Tichenor notes in his chapter, the business community consistently supported Bush immigration initiatives through its many vicissitudes and permutations. A guest worker program was always a central feature of Bush proposals no matter how much else was added or dropped. Yet, as Mayhew notes, Bush never gave up on a "comprehensive" approach. Our crowd didn't mind a little something for someone else so long as they got what they wanted. It must be conceded, even at some cost to the simplicity of our story, that here, at least at times, Bush may have been motivated as much by the hope of attracting Hispanic voters as by his desire to serve our crowd and even by a desire to serve the public interest.

The fourth episode is the most problematic. "No Child Left Behind' is most certainly a massive assault on a central value of the Republican traditional canon, federalism. Nothing makes clearer that President Bush's mindset was some other than that of simple Republicanism. Does it overstretch my argument to point to the business community's increasingly vocal concerns about the need for an at least literate if not skilled workforce? There is also a distinct union-breaking aspect to Bush's education initiative. In education is Bush again simply trying to please our crowd? I think that it would be over-reaching to make that argument. There is, of course, the electoral connection. Every president now wants to be the education president for electoral reasons if no other. No Child Left Behind, however, goes so far beyond an electoral gesture. There is a genuinely egalitarian thrust that cannot be denied. No Child Left Behind began as a Texas success for Bush. His enthusiasm's origins may lie in Texas terrain that I know nothing of. Or the matter may be a very personal one of family relationships. Mrs. Bush has been a keen champion of elementary and secondary education. Clearly Bush was not motivated by traditional Republican principles. No Child Left Behind would elicit at the least indifference and at best a nod of approval from our crowd, who, after all, needed an effective workforce, but I cannot claim that it was that nod that President Bush was primarily seeking.

Our crowd, after all, is not composed simply of, or at least they do not like to think of themselves as, people without heart. R. Kent Weaver in his contribution to this volume supposes that President Bush personally was convinced that private investment accounts were genuinely a good policy solution to an undoubted long-run Social Security problem. I am perfectly happy to suppose that too. But Bush's good-hearted solution is very much an our crowd solution. Prescription drugs may be either good-hearted or an electoral necessity, but the Bush solution, like that in education, is one that would keep him in good standing in our crowd.

Bush's foreign policy and defense budget moves, as described in James Lindsay's contribution to this volume, also show the our crowd mentality pretty clearly. Rejection of the Kyoto Protocol quite obviously runs in favor of the most inner circle of the Bush-defined our crowd, the energy industry. Perhaps more telling, because they run against traditional Republican protectionist ideology as then strongly expressed by congressional Republicans, were Bush's free trade policies. American big business was benefiting from economic globalization. The Bush administration's push for fast-track authority was not only a strong presidency move but a pro-business move.

Of course, electoral pressures sometimes interfered with pleasing our crowd. The antidumping tariffs imposed on foreign steel in 2002 were opposed by Bush's pro-business economic advisors but needed to harvest votes in West Virginia. As Lindsay notes, however, when big business complained about the higher steel prices that resulted, the tariff was cancelled.

As I said at the start, all this is too simple and too crude and too much seat-of-the-pants. Core and median and coalition are much to the point and rightly central to this volume, but surely science, including social science, is not the enemy of simple truth. Indeed, contributors to this volume repeatedly acknowledge the personal element in all politics, but most particularly in presidential politics. In the midst of wholly proper social science attempts at precision, rigor, and political neutrality, it seems worthwhile near the end of this volume to emphasize that President Bush, like all the rest of us, in the words of comic George Carlin, was trying to slide home safely, and that home for President Bush is inhabited by our crowd.

CHAPTER THIRTEEN

Politics, Elections, and Policymaking

David Mayhew

How do presidents and congressional party leaders try to win elections by shaping policy choices? In particular, as this volume asks, what is the record in this regard during the presidencies of Bill Clinton and especially of George W. Bush? Also, what can be said about the early Obama years?

Anthony Downs's *Economic Theory of Democracy*, a half century after it was published, remains the leading theoretical guide on matters like these.[1] I will draw on it here as an analytic framework, as do Daniel DiSalvo (chap. 11) and Daniel Galvin (chap. 10), yet I will use the work by embroidering it. The history of these recent times, as well as the treatments of that history supplied in this volume, seems to invite the embroidering. I hope that both the resorting to and the embroidering of Downs are of use. I organize my discussion under a series of rubrics that for theoretical or practical reasons seem to merit distinct examination.

The Center versus the Base

In one respect, possibly no president in U.S. history has surpassed George W. Bush. Especially in his first term, Bush stood out as an eyes-open promoter of a policy menu targeting, on the one hand, "the party base" but also, on the other hand, "the center" or "the median voter" or voters who might "expand the party coalition." The "base" may be an ambiguous term, and the median voter may be empirically elusive, swervable to some degree by elite manipulation and responsive in different ways to different issues, but the common-sense frame entailing these terms seems useful enough. The early Bush menu was a judicious inside-outside mix. Bearing the prints of Karl Rove, it has drawn notice for both its astute calculation and the balance of appeal that resulted from that calculation (see chap. 11).

For the Republican base, the tax cuts of 2001 and 2003 crowned the agenda, although the White House in crafting these plans did take care to offer aid to the median voter, too. These tax proposals were a marvel of variegated calculation (see chap. 6). In addition, the White House offered to the cultural conservatives of the party base "faith-based" initiatives, which ran into trouble on Capitol Hill, and a ban on partial-birth abortion that won enactment in 2003 (see chaps. 7 and 11). To the Federalist Society, a key wing of the conservative intelligentsia, went a wealth of federal judicial appointments, including those of Supreme Court Justices John Roberts and, after the nomination of Harriet Miers foundered, Samuel Alito (see chap. 7). The White House's energy plans pleased the business community. After a warm-up during Bush's first term, bankruptcy reform and a curb on class action suits pleased business during his second term, although a curb on medical malpractice suits failed (see chaps. 7 and 11).

Yet the early Bush presidency gave the median voter aggressive attention, also.[2] This kind of thrust suited the leadership of a party struggling at that time for electoral parity, never mind electoral supremacy (see chap. 10). During 2001–4, there were two major drives. In a paradigm instance, the White House "aggressively courted the center" in advancing the No Child Left Behind Act (see chap. 2). This drive and enactment helped put the Bush administration on the boards as "compassionately conservative." No less venturesome was the Medicare Modernization Act of 2003, setting a new government role in making prescription drugs accessible (see chap. 5). In both of these cases, the Republicans sought to show they were not slouches in policy sectors such as education and health care ordinarily dominated by the Democrats. In the Medicare enactment, the Republicans did not ignore their conservative base: the measure, although expansionary, brought a welcome triumph for private market interests by way of its mechanisms (see chap. 5). Yet in the cases of both education and Medicare, the final enactments ended up rather too "center-seeking" for the tastes of many conservatives. In both of his terms, Bush also pursued a center-seeking strategy, at least in large part, in immigration policy. His program's ingredients of sternness toward illegal immigration sought to please the nativists, and a guest worker program sought to please the business community, two key elements of the party's base, but the Bush White House never gave up on framing a "comprehensive" settlement of immigration policy that would go over well with Hispanic voters (see chap. 3).

As a theoretical matter, how should we think about an inside-outside strategy like Bush's and Rove's? For one thing, it was true to the theory of Downs, who does *not* argue that parties dwell only on the median voter. Base voters have a place, too, even if Downs emphasizes the median. In his analysis, a major party in a two-party system always needs to pursue a complex, tension-ridden, inside-outside strategy that appeases the median voter but also, given the existence of a dominant ideological dimension, caters to the range of voters all the way to the left or right extreme on its own side of the median. If a party does not do the latter in both campaigning and governing, enthusiasm and participation may fall off among the base. Appeasing the base is a necessary *electoral* strategy, not just a "deliver the goods" policy payoff that can stem from successfully appeasing the median voter in the last election.[3] Certain authors of this volume touch on this argument. Bush's tax policies "served to satisfy and solidify" the Republican base (see chap. 6). The mix of verbs is apt. A base that is not solidified is not solid. In another reflection, both parties are said to depend heavily on "energizing a set of political base constituencies for political contributions, acting as 'foot soldiers' in retail politics, and producing a disproportionate turnout on Election Day" (see chap. 4). That solicitude is, among other things, for a ruling party, a campaign blueprint for next time.

All this is not to say that parties or presidents never make political mistakes. They can alienate their party bases and suffer accordingly. Such failures do not admit to easy measurement, but there are familiar instances. Carter antagonized his liberal base, and they rose up and damaged him in the midterm party conference of 1978, in the presidential renomination contest of

1980, and probably, although solid evidence is problematic, in a certain sitting on their hands in the November election of 1980.[4] It is conventional wisdom that George H. W. Bush violated his 1988 "read my lips" pledge of no new taxes by pressing his huge deficit reduction measure of 1990 and thus punctured the enthusiasm of his party base in the later presidential election of 1992 (see chap. 6).

Do we see this kind of mistake in the Clinton and George W. Bush presidencies? Probably not, or at least not to the same degree. Clinton, advised in the mid-1990s by Dick Morris, a predecessor to Karl Rove as White House strategist, risked tension with his party base by signing on to the Republican-inspired version of welfare reform in 1996, but Clinton had already paid his dues. He had pressed his liberal program hard in 1993–94 and had heroically staved off Newt Gingrich's drive to enact a comprehensive Republican-flavored budget in 1995. George W. Bush, perhaps heeding his father's difficulties, never positioned himself on the wrong side of his party base on tax policy. Neither of these recent presidents brought on the level of base tension that afflicted the Carter and George H. W. Bush presidencies.

Instrumental versus Intrinsic

Downs's theory of parties, elections, and policymaking has many complexities, but at the core of it is a simple premise that he insists be taken straight. He does not relax it. This premise jibes with a popular understanding of what goes on in the political world. First, last, and always, the political parties are interested in getting elected and staying elected. Everything else, including all policymaking, is a derivative concern. To win and rewin elections, parties will promise whatever they need to and execute in office whatever they need to. This simple premise, even if it shaves off some reality, has proven to have considerable analytic power.

Let me follow this statement with a presentation of certain historical material, much of it abstracted from the chapters of this volume, that is 100 percent true in its own way to the Downsian election-seeking premise. That is, everything in the presentation maps perfectly onto a premise that the parties as leadership teams (think of Karl Rove as the distillation of a leadership team), as well as the presidents and presidential candidates that lead the parties, are pure election seekers.

That is the premise. Again, in line with it in the real American world, parties trying their best to abide by it need, whatever else, to deliver the goods to at least their party bases. Otherwise, as was argued above, they may bring on big base trouble in the next election. Granted, it is not easy to cater to the center and the base simultaneously, but it is not impossible (see, e.g., chap. 7 on the George W. Bush administration's subtle management of judicial politics) and, anyway, the parties do not have a choice. They cannot ignore their bases. The interest groups and ideological activists in the party bases mobilize as well as participate. They purvey ideas, supply campaign money, and flex organizational muscle.

Yet in policy terms the party bases are very insistent folks. They really want policies. Consider the "idea-driven elites" that Daniel DiSalvo discusses as party "factions" (chap. 11)—for example, the New Politics Democrats tracing to the McGovern era and the Christian Right and the Federalist Society nestled in recent decades on the Republican side. There is an additional wrinkle. The ideologues and core interest groups in the party bases probably think more long-term than does the typical median voter.[5] The median voter, who as a practical matter in campaign strategies tends to morph into something of a floating, volatile, quirky, not very interested, not very ideological voter, does not seem to have much of a time horizon. A good economy right now, a government check in the mail, an agreeable stance on education, or an astute response to a hurricane might be enough to snare the median voter.

But the bases are more astute. They are in it for the long run. As designing intellectuals or as the officials of permanent organizations such as labor unions, the long run is what they are supposed to consider. Also, not only do the bases want policies that promise long-term payoff, but they are canny enough, knowing the vagaries of the American system of institutions, to insist on policies that try to *commit* the government, insofar as that is possible, to policies that promise a long run.

Here is the result. Even if presidents and party managers like Karl Rove are pure election seekers, they do not have any politically appealing escape (although a president like Carter might choose to escape anyway) from catering to policy activists in their base who aim to commit the government to major long-lasting policies. Those policies, at least in the short term, might be met by ignorance, indifference, bewilderment, or antagonism in the mind of the median voter. But for base-oriented political reasons, those policies need to be pressed.

This line of thinking jibes with a good deal of political and policy history during recent decades. Once a party wins a position of power, the activist juices run. Plans are hatched to enact major policies that, by virtue of the ways they are crafted and merchandised, may last forever—or at least for a long time. One effect is to incite immediate activist juices on the other side and thus in turn bring on intense controversy in which, to the cognoscenti of both sides, the stakes are manifest.

In this vein, the Reagan administration pressed its tax cuts in 1981. Those were wrapped in a "tax policy legacy—and fiscal public philosophy" that even today "remains remarkably resilient" (see chap. 6). The Clinton administration in its health care drive in 1993–94 promised health insurance "that can never be taken away."[6] It is not surprising that the Republicans went to the wall in opposition. The Republicans in 1996 aimed to kill the traditional Aid to Families with Dependent Children "welfare" program stone-cold dead; once the program was off the books completely, it could never be brought back. The same applied with repealing the estate tax in 2001.[7] In practical dollar terms, the parties might have seemed to differ little on the estate tax question at that time, but to the politically well tuned in, the complete abolition of the tax had a distinct commitment implication. Once gone, the tax might be gone forever. It had taken a huge emergency defense buildup to get it on the books in the first place in 1916.[8]

The stakes also soared high on Medicare and Social Security policy during the George W. Bush administration. To the median voter, the Medicare Modernization Act of 2003 might mean better access to prescription drugs. But to policy activists on both sides, at issue was a welcome, or ominous, drift toward privatizing the American welfare state (see chap. 5), hence the close contestation and the famous three-hour frozen roll call count on the measure in the House of Representatives that brought on great bitterness. Munificent though the new program might be, the ordinarily benefit-conscious Democrats would not buy it although the ordinarily cost-conscious Republicans would. Each side saw that voters might get hooked on a new kind of benefit structure that could infuse into social provision, generally. The stakes soared again in the White House's 2005 drive to privatize part of Social Security, although that plan's poor reception by the public warded off any showdown on Capitol Hill (see chap. 6).

The import of these observations is the following. Given the force of policy-directed activism in both parties' bases, there might be only a slight distance as an empirical matter between the parties appearing to be *instrumental* policy seekers and their appearing to be *intrinsic* policy seekers. Presidents and party leadership teams aiming solely toward the next election as generic Downsian instrumentalists will come to look like parties whose sole, or at least dominant, aim is lasting policy achievement for its own sake. That is, they will look like intrinsic policy seekers. In the frictionless case, the empirical difference will fall to zero, bringing an observational equivalence in which it is impossible to distinguish an instrumental animation from an intrinsic animation.

Relax an additional assumption and the frictionless case draws even nearer. That is, abandon the theoretical distinction between what animates the party base, on the one hand, and what animates the president and the party leadership team on the other. Allow the president and the party leadership team to become in principle *elements of* the party base rather than calculating politicians who in principle operate outside it and cater to it. Then where are we? This is not a fanciful speculation, given, say, Reagan's evidently sincere—indeed deeply embedded—attitude toward tax cuts or Clinton's toward health care reform. In the case of George W. Bush, Kent Weaver in chapter 4 points to that president's "personal policy conviction" or his "personal belief" as the chief factor in his campaign for Social Security privatization. By himself, Bush was operating as an off-median Republican base.

These are complicated matters. But it is interesting to glimpse a brand of theorizing rather divergent from the central thrust of Downs's. Tweak the facts and arguments a bit, and the basic question "How do presidents and party leaders seek to win elections through shaping policy choices?" can transmute into the alternative basic question "How do presidents and party leaders win elections in order to shape policy?" Note that in the latter formulation presidents and party leaders will still need to cater to the median voter in sufficient fashion to accomplish their ends.

Root Canal Politics

In a universe where parties seek to win elections through shaping policy choices, and that's all, there is no room for policies that alienate voters rather than gratify them. There is no room for root canal politics. The Downsian theory has no place for such policies. A qualification arises—indeed, one that is true to the root canal metaphor. A policy move might turn off voters right now but then promise to turn them back on again before the next election occurs. A canny presidential administration might choose to pay the upfront public opinion costs of a policy *position* that looks bad right now so as to profit from the distant felicitous *effects* of that policy once it is implemented before the next election takes place.[9] A flavor of that calculation is said to have figured, for example, in the promulgation of the omnibus Clinton budget of 1993. That plan's unpalatable tax hikes were supposed to help along an economy that would be in good shape by 1996.[10] This calculation was at least plausible.

But in the real world, some root canal policies do not promise any such favorable turnaround before the next election—or, at least, the risk is very great in any hope for such a turnaround. A dose of common sense is in order here. There is nothing foolish or mysterious in the idea of presidents or parties engaging in root canal policies that face bleak near-term horizons in the realm of public opinion. Consider the role of Gary Cooper as Sheriff Will Kane in *High Noon*. It is not all that difficult to conceive of policy moves that might be good medicine in some basic sense for the American public—or for the world, for that matter—but that the American public or the world might fall short of appreciating before the next election or possibly ever. At the least, we can envision policy moves that presidents or parties might themselves sincerely categorize that way (see chap. 9). In recent times, Jimmy Carter is probably the closest to a root canal president in this politically bleak sense. His ambitious energy plan of 1977 called for sacrifice—not an easy sell. His Panama Canal treaties pleased many Panamanians but not, on balance (especially if opinion intensities are reckoned with), Americans (see chap. 9). His bleaching of the economy courtesy of Paul Volcker promised better days *after* the 1980 election, not before it.

Did we witness root canal policymaking in this bleak sense during the presidencies of Clinton and George W. Bush? Through 2006, at least, there does not seem to have been much of it. Yet two major initiatives during Bush's last two years may fit the description. There was the White House's "surge" in Iraq in the winter of 2006–7—a direct and emphatic violation of an apparent mandate to do exactly the opposite registered by voters in the 2006 midterm (see chaps. 9 and 11). As James Lindsay reports, Bush's decision "to send five additional brigades to Iraq was not motivated by political calculations. Indeed, he made the decision at considerable cost to his own political capital and to his party's" (chap. 9). True, it is conceivable that a consequent improved U.S. political context in time for the 2008 election figured as a nontrivial theme in the administration's crystal ball as of late 2006, given a successful Iraq surge, but that seems a stretch. In the Downsian model, surges bearing the unpopularity and the engineering risk of the Iraq one would be rare at best. The second instance came in late 2008. Faced by the Wall Street crash, the Bush White House advanced its $700 billion bailout of the financial services industries. Getting this plan through Congress was pure root canal politics. Public opinion weighed in somewhere between skeptical and stonily hostile, but President Bush, the presidential candidates John McCain and Barack Obama, and three of the congressional parties (all but the House Republicans) signed on and the plan was enacted.

Position versus Valence Issues

Donald E. Stokes introduced a distinction between "position" issues, on which the parties stand for opposing goals, and "valence" issues, on which they stand for the same goal yet target each other on the question of whether the goal is being achieved right or who would be better at achieving it.[11] The Downsian model accommodates both position and valence issues, although their textures differ. In the case of valence issues, the distinction between the base and median voter seems to shed utility. The median voter remains prominently in the picture by way of performance ratings. Is the White House managing the war well? How about the economy? Would the other party be less corrupt?

Valence issues unquestionably played a role during George W. Bush's presidency. In the wake of the 9/11 attack, the White House's high ratings for management of national security keynoted the 2002 midterm and the 2004 presidential election and possibly tipped both contests to the Republicans. The GOP leadership team did not shrink from calling attention to that management (see chap. 9). During Bush's second term, however, the advantage in the valence sphere lurched to the Democrats. Position issues did not disappear, however: whether it was a good idea to have undertaken the Iraq War at all persisted as a position issue,[12] and the Republicans' stance on the Terri Schiavo matter (see chap. 7)[13] and their drive to partly privatize Social Security (see chap. 6)[14] brought them woeful results on the position front. Yet during Bush's second term a cascade of mishaps, missteps, and other surprises of near-biblical relentlessness came to mire the Republicans in a classic valence slump. Whether or not the Iraq War had been a good idea, it was going poorly—a profile and judgment that seems to have reached exceptional salience in October of 2006, just before the congressional midterm.[15] Hurricane Katrina brought on a huge management mess (see chap. 7).[16] Too many Republican members of Congress seemed to be headed to prison. The Mark Foley scandal centering on House pages struck just before the 2006 midterm.[17] Then the Wall Street crash struck just before the presidential election of 2008 and possibly tipped that contest to the Democrats. One cannot size up the electoral politics of the George W. Bush years without giving attention to valence issues.

Foreign Policy versus Domestic Policy

Analysis of parties and elections ordinarily hinges on domestic policy. But as James Lindsay argues, that is a mistake. It is also a misreading of Downsian theory in which *all* of a party's promises and performances of all kinds may have electoral relevance. At the least, foreign policy can bring on position and valence judgments by voters, as happened unquestionably albeit in roller-coaster fashion during the George W. Bush presidency.

As a matter of election-centered theory, what are presidents or parties doing as they craft foreign policies—most relevantly, in light of the Bush years, policies involving wars? Wag-the-dog scenarios posit the idea of war making as a scurrilous route to reelection. But logic and experience do not seem to bear out that hypothesis (see chap. 9). Wars are, and are ordinarily seen to be, inherently unpredictable. They can incur unpopular costs. In practice, wag-the-dog moves are quickly sniffed out. Every politician knows that governments can get bogged down in Korea- or Vietnam-type morasses that cost elections. Also, generally speaking, the American median voter does not seem to care much about the rest of the world.

So why would a president or a party undertake a war? This question is particularly apt in the case of discretionary wars, that is, ones where as a practical matter the American government's choice of whether to go to war or not is unusually open. It is not more or less dictated by the situation at hand. Consider again the distinction between instrumental and intrinsic animation. Presidents and base-led parties are, among other things, intrinsic policy seekers. As policy undertakings, wars can promise future end states just as pleasing as, say, the future end states offered by the enactment of Medicare in 1965 or the Reagan tax cuts in 1981. It is a matter of aspiration. During American history, many wars have been not only discretionary but, in a sense, party projects. By the latter term I mean a war that (1) a ruling party under-took animated by intrinsic policy aims and (2) the other party opposed in principle from the start or else backed lukewarmly or soon soured on and came to oppose.

Meeting this description are all major American wars before 1917—the War of 1812, the War with Mexico, the Civil War, and the Spanish-American War. A war against France in 1798, which almost came about, would have fit. For a variety of reasons involving their nondiscretionary origins or their compli-cated and evolving cross-party support bases, not meeting this description are the two world wars, the Cold War, and probably the Korean and Vietnam Wars. But a renewed experience of wars as party projects has come in recent times. Thus, against fierce Democratic opposition on Capitol Hill, the Reagan admin-istration backed the Central American Contras in a covert war in the 1980s. The George H. W. Bush administration undertook the Gulf War of 1991 on a party-versus-party congressional vote—a warning signal of all-out Democratic opposition if that enterprise had soured. The Iraq War of 2003 fits into this policy tradition. It joins the War of 1812, the Gulf War of 1991, and the rest as a party project. As for the intrinsic animation, an Iraq victory seemed to promise in the minds of the Bush Republicans a blend of geopolitical and neo-Wilsonian results worth fighting for.

All this having been said, it takes a bit of additional shoehorning to adapt war making to a generic view of parties, elections, and policymaking. For one thing, the median voter becomes an unusually multifaceted and volatile crea-ture. The median on what dimension? With abortion, gay rights, or taxing the rich, the answer is relatively easy. But wars bring on valence as well as position judgments, and they proceed unpredictably. On-the-ground volatility in a war zone can bring a matching volatility in voter views at home. And regarding wars, who, what, and where is the party base? On major domestic policy ques-tions, a party's base will more or less stay put before, during, and after any presidential administration. We know who and where the Republican base is on tax cuts or the Democratic base on health care. But wars can renovate, re-configure, or even create party bases. By 2006, the Republicans had a pro-Iraq-flavored base and the Democrats had an anti-Iraq-flavored base. Possibly no other issue defined or excited the bases as much by then. In both philosophical and empirical terms, it is an interesting question to what degree either party enjoyed *the same* base by 2006 that it had enjoyed in, say, 1999.

Presidential Parties and Congressional Parties

Parties are parties pure and simple in the Downsian model, but of course the American constitutional structure has brought us congressional as well as presidential parties. In theoretical and practical terms, wrinkles arise. A congressional party acting as a collectivity may angle for its own reputation with the public notwithstanding the policy wishes of a president bearing the same party label. The congressional parties acting this way, or else their individual members acting on their own hook, may advance their own intrinsic policy aspirations or else direct their own distinctive pitches to the median voter or the party base.[18] An un-Downsian mix of cacophony, complexity, and conflict can result.

This volume supplies ample evidence of these frictions. Alert to the oncoming median voter in the 2006 midterm, House Republicans undercut the White House's Iraq policy by signing on to creation of the bipartisan Iraq Study Group, which advised withdrawal (see chap. 9). That same oncoming median voter figured in the House GOP's abandonment of Bush's Social Security drive in 2005: "Most congressional Republicans did not share the president's enthusiasm for touching the third rail" (see chap. 4). Yet alternatively, a congressional party acting on its own may cater to the party base rather than to the median voter. That was the story on immigration in 2005–6. The Bush administration pressed a comprehensive plan agreeable to Senate Republicans and to Democrats in both chambers, yet the House GOP stuck with the party's restrictionist base, which was in an uproar at the time, and balked (see chap. 3). That was the end of comprehensive immigration reform, at least for a while.

These instances reflect White House setbacks, but a president can also win victories in the U.S. separation-of-powers context through being, in party terms, flexible. I offer in table 13.1 a list of instances during recent decades in which presidents have gotten their way on Capitol Hill, or at least agreed to overall deals that they found on the whole pleasing, thanks to coalitions that included majorities of the other party in both congressional chambers but that failed to attract a majority of their own party in at least one of the two chambers. This is versatility of a high order. Clinton joined with chiefly Republicans on welfare reform in 1996 and on trade agreements in 1993 and 2000. In something of a family tradition, both Bushes, father and son, joined with majorities of Senate Republicans, Senate Democrats, and House Democrats,

Table 13.1 Major White House legislative victories won since 1980 by working chiefly the other side of the street

Year	President	Measure	Story
1990	G. H. W. Bush	Omnibus deficit reduction act	The White House made a deal that accommodated House Democrats, Senate Democrats, and Senate Republicans, but most House Republicans would not buy.
1993	Clinton	North American Free Trade Agreement (NAFTA)	The White House won the support of majorities of Republicans in both chambers but lost most Democrats in both chambers.
1996	Clinton	Welfare reform	The White House made a deal that accommodated Republicans in both chambers and most Senate Democrats but lost exactly half of House Democrats.
2000	Clinton	Permanent Normal Trading Relations with China (PNTR)	The White House won the support of Republican majorities in both chambers and of Senate Democrats but lost a majority of House Democrats.
2008	G. W. Bush	$300 billion housing industry guarantees (July)	The White House bought into a deal that accommodated most Democrats in both chambers and most Senate Republicans but lost most House Republicans.
2008	G. W. Bush	Paulson's $700 billion financial industries bailout (October)	The White House agreed to a deal that accommodated most Democrats in both chambers and most Senate Republicans but lost most House Republicans.

Note: These are examples in which the White House joined with majorities of the opposition party in both chambers but lost at least half the members of its own party in at least one chamber.

leaving most House Republicans as outliers, to enact major root canal settlements involving vast money manipulations in the deficit reduction drive of 1990 and the housing and banking bailouts of 2008. Note the policy importance of all six measures listed in table 13.1.

Table 13.2 exhibits versatility of a different kind, although one legislative measure, NAFTA, makes an appearance in both tables. Presidents can be powerful advocates. They can go public. They can speak for national security. On occasion, they can penetrate and divide the congressional parties—even parties that formally control their chambers. In theory, the majority parties of especially the House are posited to be nearly immune to this sort of intrusion.[19] The party leaderships of the House, even if they may not be able to *enact* measures favored by their party caucuses yet not by the chamber's reluctant median member, are supposed to be able to *block* measures not favored by their typical party member even if the median House member favors enactment. A party leadership should be able to do this blocking, it is theorized, through at least agenda control.

Yet in practice presidents often pull off such intrusions. They "roll" the House majority party by assembling a winning floor coalition that includes the bulk of the House minority party plus a pivotal dissenting rump of the House majority party. Table 13.2 presents a list of seven White House victories

Table 13.2   Major White House legislative victories won since 1980 by "rolling" the majority party of the House

Year	President	Majority-party vote	Minority-party vote	Measure
1981	Reagan	48–194	190–1	Tax cuts (ERTA)
1981	Reagan	63–176	190–0	Expenditure cuts (OBRA)
1991	G. H. W. Bush	86–179	164–3	Gulf War resolution
1993	Clinton	102–156	132–43	North American Free Trade Agreement (NAFTA)
2007	G. W. Bush	86–140	194–2	Fund Iraq War
2008	G. W. Bush	80–151	188–4	Fund Iraq War
2008	G. W. Bush	105–128	188–1	Authorize domestic surveillance procedures (the FISA fix)

Note: These are examples in which the bulk of the House minority party combined with a dissenting rump of the House majority party to win a showdown roll call victory. In all cases, the Democrats were the House majority party.

of this sort racked up during recent decades. I selected them for their importance, and all of them are indeed significant. Included are the two major legislative instruments of the Reagan revolution, George H. W. Bush's Gulf War resolution, and Clinton's NAFTA. Most recently, it is not possible to understand the last phase of the George W. Bush presidency absent recognition of such majority-party "rolls" in the House of Representatives. At stake then were highly publicized showdown votes over the funding of the Iraq War (twice, in 2007 and 2008) and the authorization of domestic surveillance procedures (the FISA fix in 2008). A grudging yet compliant Nancy Pelosi commented in arranging the procedure that yielded the war funding in 2007, "I'm the Speaker of the House. . . . I have to take into consideration something broader than the majority of the majority in the Democratic Caucus."[20]

Is the System "Off-Center"?

Some political scientists suggest a wrinkle of a different kind. A Downsian universe is perfectly symmetrical. In theory, the parties in a two-party system compete and perform in equal terms. They contest elections and make policy without anybody's thumbs on the scale. But is that true of the United States these days? Jacob S. Hacker and Paul Pierson argued in 2005 that the American system has grown "off center" (see chaps. 4 and 6).[21] During the George W. Bush years, it is said, the Republicans managed to jam down a thumb on their side of the scales. Through an alarming capacity to firm up their base, mobilize voters, discipline their politicians, and "frame" issues in mind-clouding ways—not least by using "terrorism" as a trope—the Republicans crafted a procedural unfairness that swerved government policy their way unfairly. Larry M. Bartels, using data from 1952 through 2004, has introduced a similar argument. During these years, the Republicans are said to have excelled in presidential elections by revving up the economy in the fourth years of their presidencies—an achievement that the Democrats did not match.[22]

I do not see much in this volume's accounts, or in the full record of the Clinton and George W. Bush years through 2008, that bears out these ideas. In conducting their major policy drives, these presidents of both parties could run into a wall of public opinion. In the spring of 1994, it was apparently curtains for Clinton's health care drive when two-thirds of respondents in a national Gallup poll reckoned that "quality of care would decline and they would be worse off" if the Clinton plan passed.[23] An equal-opportunity killing occurred in 2005 when George W. Bush's plan to partly privatize Social Security faced public opinion (see chap. 4). In addition, both Clinton and George W. Bush could run into filibuster walls in the Senate—Clinton, for example, on an economic stimulus plan, campaign finance reform, and lobbying reform in 1993–94, Bush on repeal of the estate tax, oil drilling in Alaska, and curbing medical malpractice suits in 2005–6. On the whole, Clinton and Bush probably enjoyed roughly equal success in pressing their domestic policies. Also, during the full eight-year span of the George W. Bush administration, the capacities of the two parties to mobilize voters, raise campaign money, and frame issues seem to have equilibrated. In all these venues the Democrats were on top by 2008. Both Clinton and Bush entered office with their parties already controlling both houses of Congresses, yet both of them blew that advantage before exiting. Finally, in 2008 the Republican White House spectacularly failed to present a revved-up economy to presidential voters. So much for the Republican rev-up generalization. Paging Herbert Hoover as of 1932. The extraordinary Wall Street crash of election year 2008 took place on the GOP watch. In general, on the evidence of these recent times, the Downsian idea of competitive symmetry looks pretty good.

Building a Permanent Party Advantage?

If a specter haunts this volume, it is that of Karl Rove (see chaps. 2, 3, 5, 6, 9, 10, and 11). Rove, "the Architect" of George W. Bush's presidency, laid plans for not only the short run but, more ambitiously and interestingly, the long run. He was billed as a new Mark Hanna. In Rove's imagination, it is said, "the Bush administration could forge a political realignment that would ensure a 'permanent' Republican majority." This could be done by "transforming the political environment through policymaking" (see chap. 5), hence the "compassionate conservatism" and the calculated policy appeals on education, Medicare, immigration, and, following 9/11, terrorism and national security.

Where are we now on Rove and his plans? Well, the White House designs for domestic policy were probably a plus for the 2002 and 2004 election cycles. This case is at least plausible, although it is hard to peer beyond the intruding effects of the 9/11 attack. In general, tax cuts are popular with voters.[24] Education and Medicare reform gave the Bush administration something of a centrist profile and disarmed the Democrats of signature issues. Yet, in the longer term, these policies designed to build a permanent Republican majority have not been great popular hits (see chaps. 2, 4, 5, and 11),[25] and the permanent Republican majority was not built. In 2006 and 2008, the Democrats came back. Does this mean that Rove was a failure? It does not. He was a striking managerial success for a few years, and in American presidential politics that is probably the best anyone can reasonably aspire to. That realm is inherently too volatile to accommodate any building of permanent party coalitions. In the elections since World War II, for example, now including 2008, the party controlling the White House has kept it eight times but lost it eight times. You cannot get any more even than that. There is no reason to believe that anything Karl Rove could have done, or that anything anyone else could have done or could still do, might impair that fundamental volatility.[26]

Not the least of the reasons for that volatility is luck. The George W. Bush presidency described an arc of luck. Absent the supreme adventitious gift of the butterfly ballot in Palm Beach County in 2000, leaving aside everything else that happened in Florida that year, Bush would not have reached the White House.[27] Absent the grim events of 9/11, the Republicans might have fared worse in the elections of 2002 and 2004, which were dominated by national security concerns. In 2006, Iraq collapsed into apparently irreversible sectarian violence just before that year's U.S. midterm elections. Then during the election season of 2008 came the Wall Street crash. In the long term, beyond everything else, a major guarantee of the not-off-center symmetry of the U.S. system seems to be luck.

The Early Obama Years

During its first two years, did the experience of the Obama administration violate the analytic themes of this chapter? It did not. As in the Bush/Rove case, the idea of a new permanent majority party has proven, at least so far, to be groundless. The Democrats no less than the Republicans can fall victim to bad luck—in Obama's case an obdurately lame job market, an inherited war in Afghanistan, and the Gulf oil spill. Each side can experience a general valence-issues slump. Each side can suffer a homeostatic kickback in elections.[28] Now, as an instance of voter reaction, the midterm election of 2006 has acquired an opposite bookend in the midterm election of 2010. In voter kickback effects, the Republicans' off-median positioning under Bush on the

Iraq War, partly privatizing Social Security, and a stream of lesser domestic issues came to be matched by the Democrats' off-median positioning under Obama on vast stimulus spending, cap and trade energy reform, and health care reform. The voter verdict was deadly both times.[29] As for symmetry otherwise, I do not see any improvement these days for the idea of an ingrained systemic bias favoring either party in any major process or policy respect. For one thing, Bush won his tax cuts in 2001, Obama his health care reform in 2009–10.

The Obama health care drive offers rich fodder for analysis. In one aspect, this ambitious initiative seems to have been aimed at the median voter. Even if the reform appeared questionable while being enacted, its actual benefits, the hope was, would win friends by the time of the 2010 or at least the 2012 election. But that account of the enactment politics has limits. In fact, of core importance were "ideological conviction and commitment to the Democratic base" (chap. 5). The party's activist base was insistent: enact health care or else, at whatever cost; remember what Carter's sluggishness on this front had brought him. In animation terms for the ruling Democrats, the instrumental—the base needed to be satisfied—blended with the intrinsic in a quest for a long-term, irrevocable government policy commitment. The result was a strained and curious exercise in coalition building. Neither the base nor the center ended up pleased. For much of the party's liberal base, the reform as enacted fell considerably short. For the median voter of 2010, the measure seemed to approach root canal territory—a costly, invasive, and gratuitous liberal enterprise.

Against the background of the Clinton and George W. Bush presidencies, there is one clear dissimilarity. The transition from Clinton to Bush was not a time of crisis management. The transition from Bush to Obama was. Wars and an economic crash were on offer. On both these fronts, the policy continuity from 2008 through 2009 and 2010 has been striking. In the case of the economy, I would guess that future historians will point to, among other things, a sequence of responsive legislative moves that sprawled across the Bush and Obama administrations. This included a Bush $168 billion stimulus package in early 2008, a $300 billion housing market guarantee in mid-2008, the $700 billion TARP bailout of the financial sector in October 2008, the Democrats' $787 billion stimulus package of early 2009, and the Democrats' ambitious reform of the financial sector in mid-2010. The first three of these instruments bore the imprints of both parties. It goes without saying that the contents of the latter two instruments had a distinctive Democratic flavor, yet it is an excellent bet that a Republican Party in power would have devised its own kinds of enactments under similar labels.

Capping the reach of this volume is the explosive midterm election of November 2010. Two reflections seem in order. First, the era of Clinton, Bush, and Obama now seems all of a piece in its openness to a striking voter volatility that has levered, in turn, party alternation in power in both Congress and the White House. There has been no stability. One cause of this instability, dented though it sometimes might be by a dualistic center-cum-base strategy like that of Bush and Rove in 2001, has been the parties' apparent inability, or unwillingness, to contain their bases. Victorious in elections for whatever reasons, spurred by their activist bases that seem to have grown unusually crystallized and demanding in recent times, the parties have come storming into power bent on pleasing those bases. If such catering is done in defiance of the median voter,[30] homeostatic kickback in later elections is an unsurprising reaction. A further effect might be long-term policy instability. Here today, gone tomorrow is a plausible trajectory for policies enacted in such a whirl of volatility.

Second, the 2010 midterm election returned the country to a condition of divided party control. In statistical terms, for better or worse, this has become a normal condition. As of 2012, American government has seen divided party control 61 percent of the time since World War II. Every president since Carter, now including Obama, has faced it for at least a while. It is well to remember that a formally divided legislative context does not mean the end of lawmaking. Under divided control, key laws have passed addressing, for example, taxation under Truman, Nixon, and Reagan; infrastructure development under Eisenhower (the national highway system); the minimum wage under Eisenhower, George H. W. Bush, Clinton, and George W. Bush; education under Eisenhower and George W. Bush; the environment under Nixon and George H. W. Bush; campaign finance reform under Ford and George W. Bush; the financing of Social Security under Reagan; deficit reduction under Reagan, George H. W. Bush, and Clinton; immigration under Reagan, George H. W. Bush, and Clinton; welfare reform under Clinton; and trade under Eisenhower, Ford, Reagan, Clinton, and George W. Bush.[31] In recent years, the on-point legislative responses to the 9/11 crisis and the Wall Street crash occurred during divided control. There is also the realm of appointments. Since World War II, Justices John Marshall Harlan, William Brennan, Charles Whittaker,

Potter Stewart, Warren Burger, Harry Blackmun, Lewis Powell, William Rehnquist, John Paul Stevens, Anthony Kennedy, David Souter, and Clarence Thomas have joined the Supreme Court during times of divided control.[32] For presidents and members of Congress, the condition of divided control may call for a certain inventiveness in coalition making. Tables 13.1 and 13.2 offer exhibits of such inventiveness.

In the wake of the Democrats' midterm disaster, the congressional lame-duck session of December 2010 came to *feel* like an exercise, perhaps a rehearsal, of divided party control even if it was not exactly that. In the large area of economic policy, the Obama White House swiftly jettisoned its customary deference to House Democrats and the liberal party base. Promoted instead, thanks to a cross-partisan compromise, was that season's "surprisingly large $858 billion package that gave Republicans a temporary extension of all of the Bush-era tax cuts" in combination with various outlays agreeable to the Democrats (chap. 6). Here was an exercise of centrism. In opinion surveys, the median voter seemed to sign on. Was this agreement a clue to dealings between the parties during 2011–12? It was hard to say. Vistas of accord were available in the areas of education, trade, and deficit reduction. Tougher would be immigration, where neither party's base was showing much give (chap. 3), and energy. Health care reform promised a motif of continuing conflict. Programmed for 2012 was another joust on the Bush tax cuts.

NOTES

1. Anthony Downs, *An Economic Theory of Democracy* (New York: Harper & Row, 1957).

2. For a statement of this case regarding Bush and the median voter, see David W. Brady, John FereJohn, and Laurel Harbridge, "Polarization and Public Policy: A General Assessment," chap. 5 in *Red and Blue Nation*, vol. 2, *Consequences and Correction of America's Polarized Politics*, ed. Pietro S. Nivola and David W. Brady (Washington, DC: Brookings Institution Press, 2008), 191–95.

3. Ibid., 117–18, 131–35.

4. For one thing, there was a drain of votes to the independent candidate John Anderson.

5. For a discussion of the distinctive far-sightedness that well-organized sectoral interests such as business and labor can impart to the policy process, see Alan M. Jacobs, "The Politics of When: Redistribution, Investment and Policy Making for the Long Term," *British Journal of Political Science* 38 (2008): 193–220.

6. Haynes Johnson and David S. Broder, *The System: The American Way of Politics at the Breaking Point* (Boston: Little, Brown, 1996), 267.

7. Michael J. Graetz and Ian Shapiro, *Death by a Thousand Cuts: The Fight over Taxing Inherited Wealth* (Princeton, NJ: Princeton University Press, 2005).

8. W. Elliot Brownlee, "Woodrow Wilson and Financing the Modern State: The Revenue Act of 1916," *Proceedings of the American Philosophical Society* 129, no. 2 (1985): 173–210.

9. Note that aiming for an election four years away can play fast and loose with the electoral fortunes of congressional members of the president's party facing voters two years away.

10. For a sense of the discursive setting and the considerations relevant to this argument that entered into the Clinton budget plan in 1993, see Bob Woodward, *The Agenda: Inside the Clinton White House* (New York: Simon & Schuster, 1994), 69–70, 74, 83–84, 121, 246–47, 262–63. Also as of 1993, according to Woodward, the Clinton plan for comprehensive health care reform was seen to offer an electoral payoff in 1996. "'You don't understand,' Hillary [Clinton] replied. 'If we don't get this done this year, we are three years away from the benefits. And the only savings will be in the fourth year. So we've got to get it done right away, or we're going to be beaten in 1996'" (120).

11. Donald E. Stokes, "Spatial Models of Party Competition," chap. 9 in Angus Campbell et al., *Elections and the Political Order* (New York: Wiley, 1966).

12. Gary C. Jacobson, *A Divider Not a Uniter: George W. Bush and the American People* (New York: Pearson Longman, 2007).

13. Jacobson, *Divider Not a Uniter*, 219–21; Donald P. Haider-Markel and Carol K. Carr, "The Political Fallout of Taking a Stand: The President, Congress, and the Schiavo Case," *Presidential Studies Quarterly* 37, no. 3 (September 2007): 449–67.

14. Jacobson, *Divider Not a Uniter*, 206–17.

15. Ibid., 222–32.

16. Ibid., 253–58.

17. Michael D. Cobb, "Paging Congressional Democrats: It Was the Immorality, Stupid" (paper presented at the annual conference of the American Political Science Association, Chicago, 2007).

18. On the parties acting as collectivities, see Gary W. Cox and Mathew McCubbins, *Legislative Leviathan: Party Government in the House* (Berkeley: University of California Press, 1993). On the individual members acting alone, see David R. Mayhew, *Congress: The Electoral Connection* (New Haven, CT: Yale University Press, 1974).

19. Gary W. Cox and Mathew D. McCubbins, *Setting the Agenda: Responsible Party Government in the House of Representatives* (New York: Cambridge University Press, 2005).

20. Susan Davis, "Pelosi Brings End to 'Hastert Rule,'" *Roll Call*, May 29, 2007, 1.

21. Jacob S. Hacker and Paul Pierson, *Off Center: The Republican Revolution and the Erosion of American Democracy* (New Haven, CT: Yale University Press, 2005).

22. Larry M. Bartels, *Unequal Democracy: The Political Economy of the New Gilded Age* (Princeton, NJ: Princeton University Press, 2008), chap. 4.

23. Reported in Johnson and Broder, *System*, 371.

24. The Bush tax cuts of 2001 were. See Bartels, *Unequal Democracy*, chap. 6.

25. On the non-resonance of the Medicare reform, see also David Blumenthal and James A. Morone, *The Heart of Power: Health and Politics in the Oval Office* (Berkeley: University of California Press, 2010), 405.

26. For a full statement of this argument, see David R. Mayhew, *Electoral Realignments: A Critique of an American Genre* (New Haven, CT: Yale University Press, 2002).

27. Henry E. Brady et al., "'Law and Data': The Butterfly Ballot Episode," *PS: Political Science and Politics* 34 (2001): 59–69.

28. On the general pattern of homeostatic kickback, see Robert S. Erikson, Michael B. MacKuen, and James A. Stimson, *The Macro Polity* (New York: Cambridge University Press, 2002), chap. 9.

29. For an analysis of the nontrivial electoral costs incurred by individual House Democrats who voted for the economic stimulus, cap and trade, and health care reform in 2009–10 (as well as TARP earlier in October 2008), see "Did Controversial Roll Call Votes Doom the Democrats?" *The Monkey Cage*, November 5, 2010, www.The monkeycage.org/2010/11/did_controversial_roll_call_vo.html. For the particular electoral costs incurred by voting for health care reform, see David W. Brady, Morris P. Fiorina, and Arjun S. Wilkins, "The 2010 Elections: Why Did Political Science Forecasts Go Awry?," *PS: Political Science and Politics* 44, no. 2 (April 2011): 247–50.

30. Possibly aiding this vision of defiance is an idea of "distortion" recently proposed by HeeMin Kim, G. Bingham Powell Jr., and Richard C. Fording. "Distortion" is defined as "short-term representation failure—the distance [on a left-right dimension] between the median voter and the legislature or government immediately after the election." Thus defined, and with suitable measurement, distortion according to the authors tends to peak in single-member-district electoral systems. The United States has such a system, and the study's logic may thus apply, although the United States is not included in the twenty countries in the analysis. See "Electoral Systems, Party Systems, and Ideological Representation," *Comparative Politics* 43, no. 1 (January 2010): 167–85, quotation at 167. On this question, see also Joseph Bafumi and Michael C. Herron, "Leapfrog Representation and Extremism: A Study of American Voters and Their Members in Congress," *American Political Science Review* 104, no. 3 (August 2010): 519–42.

31. On trade, the Clinton reference is to the establishment of normal trade with China in 2000. NAFTA was ushered through by Clinton in 1993 at a time of unified party control, although the measure did depend on chiefly Republican congressional votes.

32. In this context, divided control refers to a party distinction between the presidency and the Senate. The justices appointed during times of unified party control correspondingly defined beginning with the Truman presidency have been Harold Burton, Fred Vinson, Tom Clark, Sherman Minton, Earl Warren, Byron White, Arthur Goldberg, Abe Fortas, Thurgood Marshall, Sandra Day O'Connor, Antonin Scalia, Ruth Bader Ginsburg, Stephen Breyer, John Roberts, Samuel Alito, Sonia Sotomayor, and Elena Kagan.

Contributors

Thomas F. Burke is professor of political science at Wellesley College. He has been a visiting professor at Harvard, the University of California–Berkeley, and the Judicial Studies Program at the University of Nevada–Reno and a research fellow at the Brookings Institution and in the Robert Wood Johnson Scholars in Health Policy Research Program. He is the coauthor, with Lief Carter, of the eighth edition of *Reason in Law* (2009) and the author of *Lawyers, Lawsuits and Legal Rights: The Struggle over Litigation in American Society* (2002).

Tim Conlan is University Professor of Government and Politics at George Mason University and a fellow of the National Academy of Public Administration. In 2002, he received the Daniel J. Elazar Distinguished Federalism Scholar Award from the American Political Science Association. His books include *Intergovernmental Management for the 21st Century* (2008) and *From New Federalism to Devolution: Twenty-Five Years of Intergovernmental Reform* (1998).

Daniel DiSalvo is an assistant professor of political science at the City College of New York (CUNY). He is the author of *Engines of Change: Party Factions in American Politics* (2012).

David Emer's scholarship focuses on health care and environmental policy. He has served as a top advisor for the Health Care Financing Committee of the Massachusetts House of Representatives and also served in the executive branch state agency with responsibility for conducting policy analysis for Massachusetts health reform. He is a law student at the University of Chicago.

Daniel J. Galvin is an assistant professor of political science and faculty fellow at the Institute for Policy Research at Northwestern University. His research and teaching focuses on political parties, the American presidency, and American political development. He is the author of *Presidential Party Building: Dwight D. Eisenhower to George W. Bush* (2009) and coeditor of *Rethinking Political Institutions: The Art of the State* (2006).

Frederick M. Hess is director of education policy studies at the American Enterprise Institute and author of influential books on education, including *The Same Thing Over and Over* (2010), *Education Unbound* (2010), *Common Sense School Reform* (2004), *Revolution at the Margins* (2002), and *Spinning Wheels* (1998). His work has appeared in scholarly and popular outlets. He serves as executive editor of *Education Next*.

Martin A. Levin teaches at Brandeis University and is the founding director of the Gordon Public Policy Center. He is the author of many books, including *Making Government Work* (1994) and *After the Cure: Managing AIDS and Other Public Health Crises* (2000). He served as president of the Association for Policy Analysis and Management.

James M. Lindsay is senior vice president at the Council on Foreign Relations, where he oversees the work of the more than seventy-five fellows in the David Rockefeller Studies Program. He has written extensively on various aspects of U.S. government, U.S. foreign policy, and international relations. His book with Ivo H. Daalder, *America Unbound: The Bush Revolution in Foreign Policy*, won the 2003 Lionel Gelber Prize.

David Mayhew is Sterling Professor of Political Science at Yale University. He specializes in U.S. politics and government and has authored works on the incentives and animations inhering in members of Congress, party organization, party control of the government, incumbency advantage, electoral realignments, and the political effects of wars. His most recent work is *Partisan Balance: Why Political Parties Don't Kill the U.S. Constitutional System* (2011).

Jonathan Oberlander is professor of social medicine and health policy and management at the University of North Carolina–Chapel Hill. He is the author of *The Political Life of Medicare* (2003) and numerous articles on the politics of health reform, Medicare, and health care cost control.

Paul Posner is the director of the Public Administration Program at George Mason University. He is immediate past president of the American Society for Public Administration and is a board member of the National Academy of Public Administration. He was formerly with the Government Accountability Office (GAO), leading their federal budget and intergovernmental work for fourteen years. He consults widely on budget and federalism issues for the Organisation for Economic Co-operation and Development (OECD), the Peterson-Pew Commission, and the Pew Foundation, among others.

Nancy Scherer is an associate professor of political science at Wellesley College. Her first book, *Scoring Points: Politicians, Activists and the Lower Court Appointment Process* (2005), addressed the growing politicization of the lower federal court appointment process in the modern political era. Currently, she is completing a book manuscript exploring the relationship between race, ethnic, and gender diversity on the U.S. courts and the public's trust in the U.S. justice system.

Martin M. Shapiro is the James W. and Isabel Coffroth Professor of Law at the University of California–Berkeley and teaches in the Jurisprudence and Social Policy Program. He is the author of 6 books and more than 150 scholarly articles dealing with law and public policy in the United States and abroad.

Daniel J. Tichenor is Philip H. Knight Professor of Political Science at the University of Oregon and senior faculty fellow at the Wayne Morse Center for Law and Politics. His publications include *Dividing Lines: The Politics of Immigration Control in America* (2002), which won the American Political Science Association's Gladys M. Kammerer Award for the best book in American national policy; *A History of the U.S. Political System* (2009), a three-volume set on American political development; and *The Oxford Handbook on International Migration* (2011), as well as forthcoming works on contemporary immigration reform and on wartime presidents and civil liberties. He also has written more than fifty scholarly articles and book chapters on the presidency, social movements, political parties, immigration, and public policy and has been a faculty scholar at the Center for the Study of Democratic Politics at Princeton University, research fellow in governmental studies at the Brookings Institution, Abba P. Schwartz Fellow in Immigration and Refugee Policy at the John F. Kennedy Presidential Library, and a research scholar at the Eagleton Institute of Politics.

R. Kent Weaver is a professor of public policy and government at Georgetown University and a senior fellow at the Brookings Institution. His current research focuses on the reform of public pension systems in OECD countries.

Index

Page numbers in italics refer to figures and tables.

AARP: Medicare and, 152; MMA and, 164–65; Social Security reform and, 130, 137, 139–40
Abizaid, John, 294
abortion issues: Bush administration and, 220–22; judicial nominations and, *233,* 233–35, *234;* Mexico City Policy, 286, 301. See also *Roe v. Wade* decision
Abraham, Spencer, 78, 92
Academic Achievement for All Act (Straight A's), 52, 58
accommodative approach, 314–15, *315*
Ackerman, Bruce, 248
Afghanistan policy, 301–2
AFL-CIO, 99, 103, 138–39
African Americans, policy targeting of, 32
agency-forcing statutes, 248, 255
agenda control: congressional party leadership and, 343–45; description of, 123; Social Security and, 129–30
air pollution. *See* Clean Air Act of 1970; Clear Skies proposal
Aldrich, John, 311–12
Alexander, Lamar, 68, 254, 259
Alito, Samuel, 227, 228, *229,* 232, 233, *234*
Alliance for Worker Retirement Security (AWRS), 138, 139
Alternative Minimum Tax (AMT), 189, 198–99, 207
Altmire, Jason, 107
American Clean Energy and Security Act of 2009, 268–69
American Recovery and Reinvestment Act (ARRA), 68–70, 206–7
Americans for Tax Reform (ATR), 100, 188, 192

amnesty or legalization programs, 86
AMT (Alternative Minimum Tax), 189, 198–99, 207
Angle, Sharron, 111
Antos, Joe, 167
Archer, Bill, 133
Arizona, immigration legislation in, 111
Armey, Richard (Dick), 56, 78, 90, 344
ARRA (American Recovery and Reinvestment Act), 68–70, 206–7
Asians, policy targeting of, 95–97, 109
ATR (Americans for Tax Reform), 100, 188, 192
AWRS (Alliance for Worker Retirement Security), 138, 139

Bachmann, Michelle, 236
backlash insurance, 120
Baker, James, 295
Bankruptcy Abuse Prevention and Consumer Protection Act of 2005, 348
Bartels, Larry M., 333, 383
Barton, Joe L., 253
bases of political parties: appeals to, 341, 345–46; competitive elections and, 11–12; definition of, 19; elites and, 39; as long-term thinkers, 373; party maintenance dilemma and, 333; policy-directed activism of, 372–75; Republican, 26, 364, 370. *See also* business base of Republican Party
Baucus, Max, 172, 192, 254, 259, 260, 261, 354
Bauer, Gary, 287
Bayh, Evan, 52
Beck, Roy, 110
Bennett, William, 47, 88, 93

Berman, Howard, 93–94
bin Laden, Osama, 289
Blunt, Roy, 58–59
Boehner, John, 51, 56, 57, 174, 344
border enforcement, 117n98
border hawks, 79, 82, 109, 111
Boxer, Barbara, 270
Bradley, Michael, 29, 252, 259
Breaux, John, 192, 195, 198
Brennan, William, 224
Brewer, Janet, 111
Breyer, 228, *229*
Brooks, David, 70
Brown, Janice Rogers, 230, 264–65
Brown, Scott, 9
Brownbeck, Sam, 93–94
Browner, Carol, 254
Buchanan, Patrick, 79, 95, 102
Buckley, William F., Jr., 337
budget reconciliation process and tax cuts, 31
Burke, Thomas F., 6, 37, 326, 365
Bush, George H. W., 47, 224, *226*, 277, 314, 372
Bush, George P., 97
Bush, George W.: abortion and, 220–22; arc of luck and, 385; as big government conservative, 216–17, 236, 349; career of, 281; on Clear Skies legislation, 251; competitive environment of, 313; credibility of administration of, 255–57; education and, 49–50, 321–22; fiscal permissiveness of, 163–64, 170; foreign policy of, 281–84; gay and lesbian rights and, 222–23; on government, 235–36; immigration reform and, 96–108, 318–20; judicial politics of, *226–27*, 326–27; on malpractice lawsuits, 219; media coverage of, 148n42; Medicare legacy of, 150–51; "our crowd" of, 363–68; personal beliefs of, 97–98, 134; policy approaches of, 325–26; policy choices of, 26–29; policy targeting by, 247, 370–72; presidential campaign of, 44; programmatic agenda of, 23–24; public opinion and, 288; Republican Party and, 346–50; "Sixty Stops in Sixty Days" campaign, 137, 324; Social Security reform and, 134–41, *138, 139,* 323–24; tort reform of, 217–20. *See also* compassionate

conservatism; No Child Left Behind (NCLB); tax policy of Bush
Bush, Jeb, 293
Bush, Laura, 230
business base of Republican Party: Bush administration and, 26–29, 365–68; Clear Skies and, 36, 248, 251–52; delay approach to environmental protection and, 265–66; immigration and, 33, 78–79, 92–93, 102; prescription drug benefit and, 34; Social Security privatization and, 35; tax cuts and, 30–31; tax policy and, 189, 194–95, 196–97; tort reform and, 217–20
Byrd, Robert, 106

CAIR (Clean Air Interstate Rule), 263–64, 267, 349
California, opposition to immigration in, 87, 88–89
Cannon, Christopher, 101
cap and trade programs, 249, 250, 256–57, 268–69, 355
carbon dioxide pollution: alternative proposals and, 257, *258*, 259; cap on, 250, 260–61, 285; global warming and, 268–69
Card, Andrew, Jr., 261
Carper, 257, *258*, 259–60
Carter, Jimmy: competitive environment of, 313–14; Department of Education and, 46; foreign policy of, 277–78, 282, 297; immigration and, 83, 320; judicial appointments of, 239; liberal base and, 371–72; as root canal president, 376
Castle, Michael, 11, 59
Cato Institute, 129
Ceaser, James W., 340
"center," political, 18–19
Chafee, Lincoln, 191, 195, 196, 254, 259, 260, 261
Cheney, Dick, 26, 191, 261, 285, 292
Christian Right, 337, 338
Chrysler, Dick, 93–94
Citizens United decision, 216, 236–37
Citrin, Jack, 88
civil rights and NCLB, 45
Clark, Wesley, 281

Class Action Fairness Act, 37, 219, 348

Clean Air Act of 1970: agency-forcing nature of, 255; delay strategy and, 252; 1977 amendments to, 248–49; Obama and, 267; overview of, 35, 248; rulemaking under, 251, 261–65, *264*. *See also* Environmental Protection Agency (EPA)

Clean Air Interstate Rule (CAIR), 263–64, 267, 349

Clean Air Mercury Rule, 264–65

Clear Skies proposal: alternatives to, 257, *258,* 259; business base and, 28–29; delay scenario, 252, 265–66; legislative scenario, 252, 253–57, *258,* 259–61; overview of, 247–48; political aims of, 35–36; political strategy for, 249–52; realpolitik explanatory framework for, 252–53, 266–67; regulatory scenario, 252, 261–65, *264*

Clement, Edith, 230

Clinton, Bill: competitive environment of, 313; education and, 47, 48, 322; ESEA reauthorization and, 45, 51–52; foreign policy of, 278, 279–81, 282, 283–84, 297; immigration reform and, 87–96, 108, 320–21; Medicare reform and, 153; programmatic agenda of, 23; Social Security reform and, 131–33, 324–25; State of the Union speech of, 133; tax cuts and, 209; "third way" approach of, 1; welfare reform of, 15, 94–95, 154, 372

Clinton, Hillary, 298, 300

Club for Growth, 138, 188, 192

coalition building: approaches to, 182; from Bush to Obama, 8–10; challenges of, 38–40, 144–45; from Clinton to Bush, 4–7; interparty, 3, 8, 10–11, 15, 24; intraparty, 10–11, 15, 24; legislative, 124; model of, 2; types of, 3

Coalition for Modernization and Protection of Americans' Social Security, 138

code words/coded appeals, 221, 222

combative approach, 315, *315*

compassionate conservatism: description of, 23–24, 346; "duty of hope" speech and, 49; education reform and, 44; faith-based initiatives, 235; immigration policy and, 97;

Medicare reform and, 151. *See also* No Child Left Behind (NCLB)

competitive environments of presidents: education reform case, 321–22; health care reform and, 325; immigration reform case, 318–21; modes of policy change, 328–29; policy goals and, 310–18, *313, 315, 317*; responsible party government model and, 327–28; Social Security reform and, 323–25

Comprehensive Retirement Security and Pension Reform Act, 190–91

Congress: 104th, 90, 93, 96, 321; 105th, 329n2; 106th, 188, 326, 329n2; 107th, 253, 317, 318, 326; 108th, 144, 253, *258,* 317, 318, 326; 109th, 253, *258,* 317, 323; culture of, 345; ideological profile of leadership, 344–45; lame-duck session of 2010, 14–15, 29, 388; midterm elections of 2010, 12–13, 387–88; political parties in, 341–46, *342,* 380, *381, 382,* 382–83; procedural tools and fundraising techniques of, 22–23; redrawing of district boundaries for, 342–43; Rules Committee, 343

Conlan, Tim, 6, 14, 29, 30, 364

Constitution, "original meaning" of, 225

Contract with America, 32, 48, 92, 131

co-opting interest groups, 171

Corker, Bob, 106–7

Cornyn, John, 103

crafted talk, 123, 221

Crist, Charlie, 11

Cuba, policy toward, 90, 293

cultural protectionists and immigration, 79

culture of Capitol Hill, 345

Dahl, Robert, 311

Daschle, Tom, 195, 289–90

Davis, Tom, 290, 344

Dean, Howard, 99, 100

Death Tax Elimination Act, 190

Defense of Marriage Act, 237, 238

defense spending, 285, 286–87

deficits, federal, and tax policy, 208–10

DeLay, Tom, 56, 190, 290, 344

DeMint, Jim, 58

Democratic Leadership Council, 47
Democratic National Committee, 336
Democratic Party: critique of NCLB by, 63;
    elections in 2006 and 2008, 169; factions
    within, 335–37; foreign policy and, 278;
    immigration and, 95–96; Medicare reform
    and, 157–58; national organization of, 340;
    New Politics Democrats, 335–37; Obama
    and, 351–55; senior citizens and, 155; Social
    Security reform and, 140; tax policy of,
    208–9. *See also* New Democrats
Dingell, John, 275
DiSalvo, Daniel, 6, 22–23, 25, 37–38, 247, 369
disapproval resolutions, 273n69
distortion, 390n30
divided party control of government, 387–88
Dobbs, Lou, 81, 102
Dole, Robert (Bob), 32, 48, 89, 95, 96
"Don't Ask Don't Tell," 237–38
Dorgan, Byron, 106
Douglass, Frederick, 78
Downs, Anthony, 19, 311, 369, 371, 383–84
Dred Scott v. Sanford case, 221–22
Duncan, Arne, 68, 69
Durbin, Richard, 224

Eastland, James, 83
Ebell, Myron, 268
economic protectionists and immigration,
    77–78, 81
Edsall, Thomas, 337
education reform. *See* Elementary and
    Secondary Education Act (ESEA) of 1965; No
    Child Left Behind (NCLB)
Education Trust, 62, 66
Edwards, George C., 23
Edwards, John, 298
electoral strategy and policy choice, 19–21,
    122–26, 310–14, *313. See also* competitive
    environments of presidents
Elementary and Secondary Education Act
    (ESEA) of 1965, 45, 46, 51–52, 322. *See also*
    No Child Left Behind (NCLB)
elites: median voters compared to, 39;
    programmatic orientation of, 334, 372–75
Emer, David, 28, 35, 36, 247

Emmanuel, Rahm, 9
empathy approach to judicial nominations,
    239–40
employer sanctions and immigration, 83, 85
endogenous uncertainty, 125
energy sector, 36, 251–52, 367
Enron Corporation, 135
environmental policy of Obama, 267–70
Environmental Protection Agency (EPA), 35,
    248, 249, 262, 263
environmental uncertainty, 125, 142
Environment and Public Works (EPW)
    Committee, 251
Essential Worker Immigration Coalition
    (EWIC), 102, 106
estate tax, 184, 187–88, 204–5, 207, 365
Estrada, Miguel, 241n7
EWIC (Essential Worker Immigration
    Coalition), 102, 106
expert pathway, 203

factions within political parties, 334–38. *See
    also* Tea Party faction
failure of presidential initiatives, 125–26, 144,
    215, 254–57
faith-based initiatives, 235, 349, 370
Federalist Society, 37, 224–25, *226–27,* 227–29,
    228
Federal Reserve, 366
Feinstein, Dianne, 53
filibuster process, 10
Finn, Chester, 55
Flake, Jeff, 101
Fleisher, Ari, 291
Ford, Gerald, 314
foreign policy: in campaign of 2000, 281–84;
    decision to undertake war, 378–79; electoral
    temptations of, 277–81; Iraq War and surge,
    294–96; Obama and, 297–302; overview of,
    296–97; politics and, 276; before September
    11, 284–87; war on terror, 25–26, 287–94
Fox, Vincente, 98, 99
Frist, Bill, 161, 348
funding: for congressional campaigns, 22–23,
    343–45; for education, 62; for Medicare, 127,
    159, 174

Gallegly, Edward, 89, 93, 94, 100
Galvin, Daniel, 38, 369
gay and lesbian rights, 222–23, 237–38
Gephardt, Richard (Dick), 99, 275, 344
Gerson, Michael, 44
Gilchrist, James, 102
Gingrich, Newt, 89, 90, 91, 93, 96, 318, 345
Ginsberg, Ruth, 228, *229*
global warming policy, 268–70, 365
Goldwater, Barry, 337
Goodridge v. Department of Public Health, 222, 223, 238
GOP. *See* Republican Party
Gordon, Robert, 55–56
Gore, Al: on "code words," 221; education and, 49–50; immigration reform and, 97; loss to Bush by, 26; prescription drug coverage and, 153; tax reduction plan of, 183–84, 185, 209
Graham, John, 256, 257, 260–61
Graham, Lindsey, 110, 268, 269, 302
Gramlich, Edward, 132
Grassley, Charles, 106, 192, 196
Greenspan, Alan, 133, 186, 189–90, 191, 292
guest worker programs: alternative proposals for, 105; border hawks and, 82; Bush administration and, 98, 99–100; business and, 102; economic protectionists and, 81; history of, 86
Gutierrez, Luis, 81, 105

Hacker, Jacob, 12, 41, 120, 185, 266, 383
Hagel, Chuck, 296
Hamilton, Lee, 295
Hanna, Mark, 339, 384
Hassler, William, 248
Hastert, Dennis, 161, 188, 190, 344
Hawkins, David, 254–55
health care reform of Obama: competitive environment and, 325; Democratic Party and, 353–55; overview of, 8–10; parallels to Medicare reform of Bush, 170–75; policy targeting and, 386; political consequences of, 13–14; Social Security reform and, 142
Health Savings Accounts, 162
Heritage Foundation, 129
Hess, Frederick, 5–6, 31, 32, 321–22

Hickock, Eugene, 56
Hoekstra, Peter, 58, 295
Holmstead, Jeffrey, 255, 260, 261
Holtz-Eakin, Douglas, 181
Homeland Security, Department of, 98, 291–92
House-centered legislative strategy, 347–48
Hoyer, Steny, 345
Hsu, Shi-Ling, 256, 263
Hussein, Saddam, 290, 298

ideological profile of congressional party leadership, 344–45
Illegal Immigration Reform and Immigrant Responsibility Act of 1996, 94
Immigrant Workers Freedom Ride, 99
Immigration Act of 1990, 79–80, 87–88
immigration reform: Bush and, 96–108, 371; business and, 366; Clinton and, 87–96, 108; competitive environments of presidents and, 318–21; grand bargain of, 105–7; Obama and, 108–12; overview of, 75–76; political aims of, 32–33, 347; political challenges of, 75, 80–86; Republican Party and, 348–49; rival ideas and interests, 76–80
Immigration Reform and Control Act (IRCA) of 1986, 84, 85–86, 106
Inhofe, James, 253, 254, 256, 261, *264*
inside-outside strategy of Bush, 370–71
interest groups: ethnic lobbies, 278–79; health care reform of Obama and, 171; immigration and, 77–80; Medicare reform and, 158, 164–65; role of, 20; Social Security and, 138–40; as "veto groups," 202. *See also specific groups*
interest mobilization, 123–24
interparty coalition building, 3, 8, 10–11, 15, 24
intraparty coalition building, 3, 10–11, 15, 24
Investing in Innovation (i3), 68–70
Iraq War: policy and surge, 294–96; resolution, 290, 298
IRCA (Immigration Reform and Control Act) of 1986, 84, 85–86, 106
issue framing: cap and trade, 268–69; Clear Skies, 254–55, 257; cultural issues, 220–23;

issue framing (*continued*)
    definition of, 123; of judiciary and litigation,
    216; Social Security and, 130, 136–38

Jackson, Jesse, 88
Jarvis, Charlie, 139
Jeffords, James: Clean Power Act, 257, *258*,
    259; as Independent, 289; party change by,
    5, 40, 156; tax cuts and, 192
Johnson, Lyndon Baines, 43, 46, 313–14, 322
Jordan, Barbara, 78, 88, 89–90, 93
Juddis, John, 91
judicial politics: competitive environment
    and, 326–27; critiques of, 236–37; cultural
    conservatives and, 224–25, *226–27*, 227–35,
    228, 229; Obama and, 237–40; overview of,
    37, 215–17

Kassebaum, Nancy, 92
Kelemen, R. Daniel, 262
Kemp, Jack, 88, 93
Kennedy, Anthony, 227
Kennedy, Edward (Ted): election to replace, 9;
    immigration reform and, 33, 83, 103, 105; as
    liberal cosmopolitan, 77; NCLB and, 32, 51,
    53–54, 57–58, 62, 63, 66
Kennedy, John F., 279, 313–14
Kennedy, Robert, 51
Keppel, Francis, 51
Kerry, John, 55, 139, 268, 269, 294, 340
Kildee, Dale, 56
King, Steve, 111
Koch, Ed, 204
Kohn, Alfie, 54
Kolbe, Jim, 101
Kress, Sandy, 56–57, 63
Kristol, William, 93
Kucinich, Dennis, 299
Kyl, Jon, 103
Kyoto Protocol, 285–86, 367

lame-duck session of 2010, 14–15, 29, 388
Landy, Marc K., 265
Latinos: Bush and, 104, 107; demonstrations
    by, 103; Obama and, 107–8, 109, 111; policy
    targeting of, 32, 33, 95–97, 100

Layman, Geoffrey, 337
legal immigration, 93
legislative coalition building, 124
Levendusky, Matthew, 22
liberal cosmopolitans and immigration, 77, 81
Lieberman, Joseph (Joe), 11, 52, 99, 268
Lindsay, James M., 7, 14, 26, 367, 376, 378
Lindsey, Lawrence, 250, 292
Long, Russell, 152
Lott, Trent, 290, 345
Lowell, A. Lawrence, 79
Lowi, Theodore, 311
Lubell, Samuel, 3

Mack, Connie, 198
majority-party presidents, 312
Mann, Thomas, 22
Marriage Penalty and Family Tax Relief Act,
    190
Mayhew, David: chapter by, 6, 38, 366; on
    coalition building by Obama, 8; *Congress:
    The Electoral Connection*, 2, 21; on lame-duck
    session, 14; on median voters, 345; on
    midterm election of 2010, 12–13; on party
    dilemmas, 9; on pleasing base, median, and
    target voters, 20; on policy targeting, 247;
    realignment and, 155
Mazzoli, Romano, 83–84
McAuliffe, Terry, 275
McCain, John: foreign policy of, 279, 300;
    immigration and, 33, 78, 101, 103, 109;
    NCLB and, 64; presidential campaign of,
    340–41, 351; primary challenges to, 11;
    senior voters and, 169; tax bill and, 196
McCaskill, Claire, 107
McChrystal, Stanley, 301
McClellan, Scott, 100, 101
McCluskey, Neal, 50
McCollum, Betty, 54–55
McGovern, George, 336
McInturff, Bill, 154–55, 157
McKinley, William, 339
McKinnon, Mark, 292
median voters: Bush and, 247, 370–71;
    "center" and, 18–19; characteristics of, 39; as
    multifaceted and volatile, 379; nominees to

Supreme Court and, 232–34; of political parties, 345–46; Social Security initiatives and, 119–20

Medicaid, 152

medical malpractice reform, 218–20

Medicare: Advantage plans, 167, 172; characteristics of, 151–52; funding for, 127, 159, 174; in health care reform, 172–73; political calculus on, 154–55; politics of reform of, 157–60, 173–75; realignment with conservative philosophy, 155–56; reform to, 152–53; Ryan reform plan, 173; in 2000 campaign, 153–54

Medicare Catastrophic Coverage Act of 1988, 153, 169

Medicare Modernization Act (MMA) of 2003: enactment of, 160–65; implementation and record of, 165–67; median voter and, 370–71; Republican base and, 34

Medicare Part D. *See* prescription drug coverage

Melnick, Shep, 255

mercury, cap and trade program for, 253, 259

Mexican immigrants, 98

Mexico City Policy, 286, 301

Meyer, Eugene, 225

midterm elections of 2010, 12–13, 387–88

Miers, Harriet, 228, *229*, 229–32

military force, decisions to use, 280–81, 378–79

Miller, Banks, 227–28

Miller, George, 54, 55, 57, 62, 63, 66

Miller, Zell, 196

minority-party presidents, 311–12

MMA. *See* Medicare Modernization Act (MMA) of 2003

modes of policy change, 328–29

Moe, Terry, 58

Moffitt, Robert, 150

Morris, Dick, 372

Murkowski, Lisa, 11, 269

Murtha, John P., 344

Nader, Ralph, 4

National Education Association, 65

national interest, views of, 276, 296–97

national security, electoral temptation of, 277–81

NCLB. *See* No Child Left Behind

Nelson, Alan, 85

Nelson, Ben, 172, 192

neoconservatism, 337–38

Nethercutt, George, 293

Neustadt, Richard, 309

Nevada, Senate campaign in, 111

New Democrats, 47, 52, 53–54, 57, 337

New Politics Democrats, 335–37

New Right Republicans, 335, 337–38

New Source Review by EPA, 249, 262, 263

Ngai, Mae, 84

9/11: bipartisan unity after, 275; Bush administration and, 7; commemorations for, 291; focus on national security issues after, 120, 346; immigration reform and, 98–99; tax legislation and, 194; war on terrorism and, 25–26, 287–94

Nixon, Richard, 224, 314

No Child Left Behind (NCLB): business and, 366–67; competitive environment and, 321–22; congressional support for, 54–56; conservative views of, 58–59, 63; federal role and, 43; flexibility and, 58; funding for education, 62; highly qualified teacher provision of, 57–58; implementation of, 59–64; media voter and, 370–71; overview of, 46, 64–65; passage of, 50–51; political aims of, 31–32, 346–47; political outcomes of, 65–67; proficiency goals of, 45; proposal for, 52–54; public attitudes toward, 64; reauthorization of, 63–64; school choice, vouchers, and, 56–57; states and, 61–62

Norquist, Grover, 94, 100, 188

Novak, Robert, 155

Obama, Barack: Carper bill and, 261; *Citizens United* decision and, 236–37; deficit and, 29; Democratic Party and, 351–55; education and, 67–70; environmental policy of, 267–70; foreign policy and, 297–302; gay and lesbian rights and, 237–38; immigration reform and, 108–12; judicial politics and, 237–40; midterm elections and, 12–13,

Obama, Barack (*continued*)
387–88; NCLB and, 64; political parties and, 385–86; presidential campaign of, 340, 341, 351; programmatic agenda of, 24; Republicans and, 10; Social Security reform and, 141–43; tax policy of, 205–8, 209; transition from Bush to, 386–87. *See also* health care reform of Obama
Oberlander, Jonathan, 6, 8, 27, 34, 365
O'Connor, Sandra Day, 227, 229, 230
O'Donnell, Frank, 259, 262–63
off-center, system as, 120, 383–84
Old Age and Survivors Insurance. *See* Social Security
Oliver, Tom, 161
O'Neill, Paul, 188, 191, 292
opinion polls: affirmative action, 241n8; attitudes toward candidates' views on education, *50*; most important problem, *48*; nominees to Supreme Court, 232–34; support for tax cuts, 184–85; war on terror, 289
"original meaning" of Constitution, 225
Ornstein, Norman, 22
Owen, Priscilla, 230

PACs (political action committees), 22–23, 344
Paige, Rod, 57
Palin, Sarah, 236, 341
partisan pathway, 202–3, 209–10
party maintenance dilemma, 333
path dependence, 20
Patient Protection and Affordable Care Act of 2010, 171. *See also* health care reform of Obama
pay-as-you-go (PAYGO): Democrats and, 171; Republicans and, 163; Social Security and, 126, 129
Payzant, Tom, 53
Pelosi, Nancy, 100, 107, 302, 344, 352
Perot, Ross, 4
Personal Responsibility and Work Opportunity Act of 1996, 94–95. *See also* welfare reform of Clinton
Petrilli, Michael, 66

Pfizer, 139
PhRMA, 171
Pierson, Paul, 12, 41, 120, 185, 383
Planned Parenthood v. Casey, 224
Plouffe, David, 299
pluralist policymaking, 194, 201–2
polarization of parties, 22
policy choice: of Bush administration, 26–29; electoral strategy and, 19–21; political context of, 37–38; programmatic parties and, 21–25. *See also* presidential initiatives
policy pathways, 200–205, *201, 205*
policy regime, "stickiness" of, 320
policy targeting: of Bush, 247–48, 370–72; challenges of, 144–45; of Clear Skies legislation, 248; definition of, 66; ethnic minorities, 32, 95–97, 109; health care reform, 386; Latinos, 32, 33, 100; limitations of, 170; senior citizens, 34, 151, 153, 154, 155; Social Security and, 120–21; younger voters, 27–28, 35, 121
political action committees (PACs), 22–23, 344
political parties: change in strength of, *339*; competition between, 40–41, 338–41; competitive standing of and presidential goals, 310–12, *313*; in Congress, 341–46, *342*, 380, *381, 382*, 382–83; as election seekers, 372–75; factions within, 334–38; midterm elections of 2010, 387–88; as nationalized and programmatic, 350–51; Obama and, 351–55, 385–86; permanent advantage for, 384–85; presidents and, 346–50, 380, *381, 382*, 382–83; as programmatic, 21–25; regional realignments of, 22, 341–42, *342*; revival of, 332–34; third parties, 3–4; types of coalition building, 3. *See also* bases of political parties; Democratic Party; Republican Party
position issues, 377–78
Posner, Paul, 6, 14, 29, 30, 364
Powell, Colin, 101, 285
prescription drug coverage: business base and, 27; "doughnut hole," 168, 173; enactment of legislation for, 160–65, 347; outside Medicare, 159–60; policy legacies of, 165–67; political

aims of, 34; political legacies of, 168–70; privatization of, 162–63

presidential candidates and foreign policy, 279–80

presidential election of 2000: cap on carbon dioxide in, 250; closeness of, 5, 26, 202; cultural issues in, 220, 221, 222; domestic issues in, 296–97; education in, 31, 44, 49–50, *50*; foreign policy in, 281–84; Medicare reform in, 153–54, 156; policy targeting in, 96–97; Social Security in, 134; tax cuts in, 30, 183–86, 209; tort reform in, 218. *See also* compassionate conservatism; Gore, Al

presidential initiatives: decisions to undertake or forego, 143–44; electoral dynamics and, 310–14, *313*; failure of, 125–26, 144, 215, 254–57; overview of, 308; personal presidency and, 309–10; policy approaches and, 314–16; political parties and, 346–50; programmatic, 23; root canal policies, 376–77. *See also* policy targeting

primary elections and party bases, 11–12

pro-immigration conservatives, 78–79, 81–82, 93

public opinion. *See* opinion polls

public policy, determinants of, 4–5

Putnam, Adam, 107

Race to the Top (RTT), 68–70

Rangel, Charles B., 344

Reading First initiative, 53

Reagan, Ronald: antigovernment conservatism and, 216, 235; competitive environment of, 314; Department of Education, 46–47; education policy and, 322; environmental policy of, 265; foreign policy of, 282; immigration and, 78, 84; judicial appointments of, 224; Medicare and, 152–53; Social Security and, 35, 131–32; tax policy of, 181, 186, 198, 208

redistricting, congressional, 342–43

regional realignments of parties, 22, 341–42, *342*

Rehnquist, William, 229

Reid, Harry, 111, 231, 269

Republican National Committee, 339

Republican Party: Bush and, 346–50; business base of, 26–29; Contract with America, 32, 48, 92, 131; factions within, 334, 337–38; fiscal permissiveness of, 163–64, 170; foreign policy and, 278, 289; Medicare reform and, 157–58, 161–63; national organization of, 339–40; nominating convention in 2004, 291; Obama and, 10, 24; platform of 1996, 43, 95; platform of 2000, 218; platform of 2008, 231; Social Security reform and, 140–41; tax cuts and, 181–82

responsible party government model, 327–28

rich, Bush policy as service to, 363–68

Ridge, Tom, 101, 291

Riker, William, 311

Roberts, John, 227, 228, *229,* 229–30, 232, *233*

Roberts, Marc J., 265

Rockefeller, Jay, 269, 354

Rodino, Peter, 83

Roe v. Wade decision: Bush and, 220; judicial nominations and, 221, 224, 230, 233; public opinion and, *233*

root canal politics, 13, 375–77, 382

Rosenblum, Marc, 81

Rosotti, Charles, 198

Rove, Karl: address to Republican National Committee, 275, 289; Cuba and, 293; on Federalist Society, 225; immigration reform and, 99, 100, 101; national party machine and, 339; political strategy of, 188, 370, 371; presidential campaign of 2004 and, 340; realignment vision of, 155, 156, 161, 169, 170, 384; steel tariffs and, 292–93; war on terror and, 294

RTT (Race to the Top), 68–70

Ruckelshaus, William D., 260

Rudalevige, Andrew, 59

Rules Committee, 343

Rumsfeld, Donald, 295

Ryan, Paul, 173

sabotage by Bush policy, 365–66

same-sex marriage, 223, 238

Santorum, Rick, 148n52

Scalia, Antonin, 221
Schaffer, Bob, 53, 54, 59
Schattschneider, E. E., 112, 200
Scherer, Nancy, 227–28, 326
Schiavo, Terri, controversy over, 223
school choice, 46, 47, 56–57
Scully, Tom, 156
secularism, 337
Secure Borders Act, 33, 349
Secure Fence Act of 2006, 104
Seeking the Center, 1–2, 4, 5, 200
senior citizens: Bush and, 168; McCain and,
    169; Medicare reform and, 34, 151, 153, 154,
    155; as percentage of electorate, 142; Social
    Security and, 121
September 11, 2001. *See* 9/11
Simcox, Chris, 102
Simon, Ray, 61
Simpson, Alan, 83–84, 85, 89, 90, 92, 94
Smith, Lamar, 89, 90, 91–92, 93–94, 111
Snowe, Olympia, 8, 141, 195, 196
Social Security: Bush and, 134–41; characteris-
    tics of, 126–28; Clinton and, 131–33,
    324–25; competitive environments of
    presidents and, 323–25; double payment
    problem, 130; gaps between discussion,
    initiatives, and policy change, 129–30;
    individual investment accounts, 128–29,
    134, 138, *138*; interest groups and, 130–31;
    media coverage of, 148n42; median voters
    and, 120; Obama and, 141–43; partial
    privatization proposals, 27–28, 35; Reagan
    and, 131–32; sabotage of, 365; strategic
    politicians and, 122–26; as third rail, 119
Social Security Act of 1935, 126
Sotomayor, Sonya, 239
Souter, David H., 227, 228, *229*, 231
Specter, Arlen, 103, 191–92, 352
Spellings, Margaret, 43, 45, 61
stealth candidates for Supreme Court, 231–32
steel tariffs, 292–93, 367
Stein, Dan, 101
Steurele, Eugene, 181
stimulus bills, 24, 68, 206–8, 353. *See also*
    American Recovery and Reinvestment Act
Stokes, Donald E., 377

Straight A's (Academic Achievement for All
    Act), 52, 58
strategic politicians, 122–26
sunsets of tax cuts, 193
surplus in federal budget: Medicare reform
    and, 153, 158, 163; projected, *187*; Social
    Security privatization and, 135; tax cuts
    and, 186
Swain, Carol, 81
Swartz, Rick, 91
Sweeney, John, 100
swing voters: appeals to, 341; importance of,
    17. *See also* median voters
symbolic pathway, 204–5

Tancredo, Tom, 79, 98, 100, 102, 110
targeting. *See* policy targeting
tariffs on imported steel, 292–93, 367
Tauzin, Billy, 159
taxation, trend in levels of, 185–87, *186*
tax cuts: base and, 370; Bush and, 182; in
    election of 2000, 30, 183–85, 209; extension
    of Bush-era, 15, 29, 207–8, 388; Obama and,
    205–8; political aims of, 30–31; public
    support for, 184–85; Republican Party and,
    181; as service to rich, 364–65; share received
    by various groups, *193*; sunsets of, 193, 200
tax policy: federal deficits and, 208; partisan
    pathway and, 209–10
tax policy of Bush: base and, 371, 372;
    pathways of, 200–205, *201*, *205*; political
    dynamics (2001) of, 187–93; political
    dynamics (2003) of, 194–97; reform of
    system, 197–200; stimulative rebate, 200
Tax Relief, Unemployment Insurance
    Reauthorization, and Job Creation Act of
    2010, 210
Tea Party Convention, 110
Tea Party faction, 4, 142–43, 170, 236, 353
tensions characteristic of coalition building, 3
terrorism: immigration and, 88–89; Obama
    and, 238; war on, 25–26, 287–94. *See also*
    9/11
Tester, Jon, 107
third parties, 3–4
Thomas, Bill, 161, 197

Thomas, Clarence, 221, 227, 228, *229*
Thomas, Stephen R., 265
Tichenor, Daniel J., 6, 7, 10, 319, 320, 366
tort reform, 36–37, 217–20
trade policy: of Bush, 285, 292–93, 348, 367; of
    Clinton, 284, *381, 382*; of Obama, 299–300,
    302
trust fund for Social Security, 126–27, 133
two-party system, Downsian quality of,
    38–39

unity scores of parties, 22
Upton, Fred, 270
USA Next, 139–40
USA Patriot Act, 288, 294
U.S. Chamber of Commerce: Class Action
    Fairness Act and, 219; immigration and,
    78–79, 92, 102; Institute for Legal Reform,
    218; NCLB and, 66–67
Utah, and NCLB, 61–62
Uzzell, Lawrence, 62

valence issues, 377–78
venue control: definition of, 124; Social
    Security and, 130, 140–41
Virginia, and NCLB, 61
Voinovich, George, 195, 196, 261, *264,* 296

Walke, John, 256, 257, 264
war: decision to undertake, 378–79; in Iraq,
    290, 294–96, 298; on terrorism, 25–26,
    287–94
Warren, Earl, 224
"water's edge," politics stopping at, 7, 296–97
Weaver, R. Kent, 7, 254, 257, 323, 324, 367,
    375
Webb, Jim, 107
Weiss, Joanne, 69
welfare reform of Clinton, 15, 94–95, 154,
    372
Wheeler, Andrew, 261
White, Joe, 163
Whitman, Christine, 251, 260, 261–62, 263
Williams, Joe, 69
Wilson, James Q., 334
Wilson, Joe, 110
Wilson, Pete, 88, 89, 95
Wilson, Woodrow, 283
Witte, John, 201
Wolf, Frank, 294–95
worksite enforcement campaigns, 104, 116n97
Wu, David, 56

younger voters, policy targeting of, 27–28, 35,
    121